Microsoft®
OFFICE 2010
Training Guide

Visual Approach to Learning Office 2010 Package

By

Satish Jain

B.S.c., B.E. (IISc), M.E. (IISc), M.Tech. (I.I.T. Kanpur)
Wing Commander (Retd.)
Professor of Information Technology,
Institute of Information Technology & Management,
GGS Indraprastha University, Delhi.

M. Geetha

B.Com., Diploma (IT)

Kratika

B.Com., Advanced Diploma (IT)

www.bpbonline.com

REPRINT 2026
FIRST EDITION 2011

ISBN: 978-81-8333-406-8

Distributors:

BPB PUBLICATIONS
20, Ansari Road, Darya Ganj
New Delhi-110002
Ph: 23254990 / 23254991

DECCAN AGENCIES
4-3-329, Bank Street,
Hyderabad-500195
Ph: 24756967 / 24756400

MICRO MEDIA
Shop No. 5, Mahendra Chambers,
150 DN Rd. Next to Capital Cinema,
V.T. (C.S.T.) Station, MUMBAI-400 001
Ph: 22078296 / 22078297

BPB BOOK CENTRE
376 Old Lajpat Rai Market,
Delhi-110006
Ph: 23861747

To View Complete BPB Publications Catalogue Scan the QR Code:

Published by Manish Jain for BPB Publications, 20 Ansari Road, Darya Ganj, New Delhi-110002 and Printed by him at Manipal Technologies, Manipal

www.bpbonline.com

Dedicated to

Sri Raja Rajeshwari and Sai Baba

Who bless Immense Power of Knowledge

OTHER TITLES OF INTEREST

Microsoft **Excel Professional 2021** Guide
ISBN: 9789355510457

Excel 2022 Pro 100+ PivotTables, Charts & Reports
ISBN: 9789355512475

Management Science using **Excel**
ISBN: 9789355518811

Mastering Advanced Excel
ISBN: 9789355518651

Data Analysis with **Excel**
ISBN: 9789388176675

Advance Excel 2016 IN **DEPTH**
ISBN: 9788183335980

Excel 2019 All-In-One
ISBN: 9789388511582

Advanced Analytics with **Excel 2019**
ISBN: 9789389845808

EXCEL FUNCTIONS & **FORMULAS**
ISBN: 9788183331821

200+ Excel Formulas & **Functions**
ISBN: 9789355513786

Advance EXCEL 2016 TRAINING GUIDE
ISBN: 9789386551825

Excel for **Finance** & **Accounting**
ISBN: 9789355517999

Fundamentals of **Software Engineering**
ISBN: 9789388511773

Computer Fundamentals 8th Edition
ISBN: 9788176567527

Office 365 with SharePoint Online Cookbook Solutions
ISBN: 9789355518392

Mastering SEQUENCE
ISBN: 9789355518545

Preface

The objective of this training guide is to meet the growing need of different types of users who wish to explore the full capability of MS Office 2010 in a simple manner. It is observed that most of the books available in the market are written by foreign authors and such books do not explain MS Office 2010 from the first time user's point of view.

MS Office 2010 is a set of packages such as ***Word, Excel, PowerPoint, Access,*** and ***Outlook*** that enable you to work on complex jobs using PC in a very easy way. Most of the capabilities of these packages are explained in this guide with many screens.

A very useful feature of this guide is its visual approach showing steps on the screen and printed in the book as seen on the PC monitor. Buttons, Ribbons, Commands etc. are also explained in text, so as to enable a reader to understand subject matter without any outside help.

This guide covers all important features of MS Office 2010 packages. It may also serve as a useful reference guide for experienced users of earlier versions of MS Office.

We have made this guide user friendly by adding a comprehensive index at the end of the book. The index is very handy for locating page number of major topics discussed in this book.

A special feature throughout this book is that the salient and crucial information has been encapsulated within parallel and horizontal lines with a (✍) mark to draw the attention of the reader.

We shall feel obliged to the readers if they e-mail us their critical opinion of presentation, readability and coverage in this book and give us suggestions if any, in improving the subject matter. Our e-mail address is *reviewsjain@gmail.com.*

15th January, 2011

Authors

OTHER TITLES OF INTEREST

Basics of
Python Programming
ISBN: 9789388511803

Python Training Guide
ISBN: 9788183335416

Selenium with **Python** -
A Beginners Guide
ISBN: 9788194401872

Programming In **Python**
ISBN: 9789386551276

Python Made Simple
ISBN: 9789388511025

Python for **Professionals**
ISBN: 9789389423754

Python for Developers
ISBN: 9788194401872

Python In - Depth
ISBN: 9789389328424

Test Your Skills in
Python - 2nd Edition
ISBN: 9789355511812

Basic **Core Python**
Programming
ISBN: 9789390684953

Advance
Core Python Programming
ISBN: 9789390684069

Python
Interview Questions
ISBN: 9789389898460

Data Analysis
with **Python**
ISBN: 9789355510655

Data Structures
with **Python**
ISBN: 9789355513304

Web Data Mining
with **Python**
ISBN: 9789355513632

Python
Quick Interview Guide
ISBN: 9789389423303

Contents

Computer Introduction

Computer Introduction

Computer is the most versatile electronic machine man has ever created. Computers have made a great impact on our everyday life. It is basically a programmable computing machine and its presence is felt in almost every walk of life be it home, school, college, office, industry, hospital, bank, retail store, railways, research and design organizations etc. A computer can not only store and process data but also retrieve data i.e. take out data from its memory or storage as and when desired. Thus, computer is a general term that refers to an electronic data processing machine used for a wide range of activities. The two basic types of computers are the following:

1. **Analog computers:** It handles or process information which is based on the measuring of analogues or equivalent physical value.
2. **Digital computers:** It process information which is essentially in a binary or two-state form, namely zero and one.

Notes:

*A **tablet** PC or simply **tablet**, is a medium-sized mobile computer integrated into a flat touch screen and primarily using stylus, digital pen or fingertip input along with a virtual onscreen keyboard in lieu of a physical keyboard*

In 2010 Apple launched the iPod tablet computer which is basically used for accessing the web, viewing photos and videos, gaming, or reading eBooks, newspapers and magazines

Tablet PC can be as large as laptops and as small as PDAs.

A Laptop PC

A Tablet PC

Tablet PC is a touch-pad device that combines the features and qualities of a smart phone and a laptop.

Elements of Computer System

A computer is made up of integrated components (input and output devices, storage, CPU) that work together to perform the required output. The input or output units cannot function until they receive signals from the CPU. Similarly, the storage unit or the CPU alone is of no use. So, the usefulness of each unit depends on other units and can be realized only when all units are put together (integrated) to form a system. Computer System has two major elements. These are:

1. Hardware
2. Software

Hardware

The physical components of a computer are called hardware. For example, microprocessors, hard disks, floppy disks, optical disks, monitors, keyboard, printer, plotter, CD-ROM, etc.

Software

The set of computer programs, procedures and associated documentation related to the effective operation of a computer system are termed as software.

Notes:

The term software includes both system software and user's programs.

The five major functional units of a digital computer are CPU, Input units, Output units, Storage devices and Communication Interface.

The software required to execute user's programs is known as *system software*. It includes operating system, assembler, compiler, interpreter, debugging programs, text editors, etc.

Hardware Components of PC

Various parts of a personal computer (PC) system are the following:

1. Front panel,
2. Rear panel, and
3. Inside the system unit.

Parts of the Front Panel

Various parts of the front panel of a PC are given in the following figure.

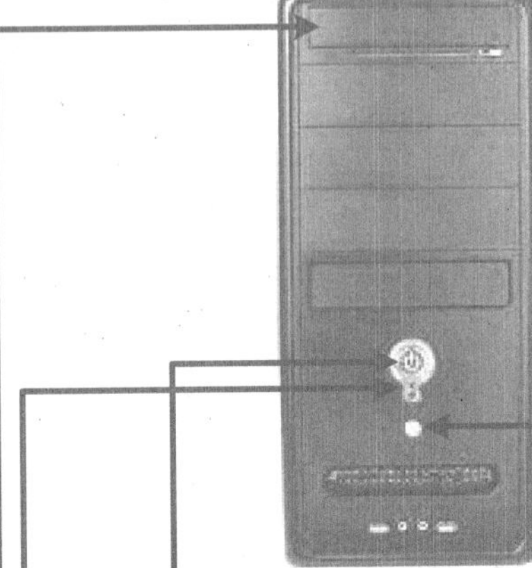

Power Switch: Depending on the model, this switch is located either in the front or at the side of the system unit and it is used to switch the system ON or OFF.

Reset Button: This is a switch which can be used to restart the PC without switching off the mains power supply.

Indicator Lights Computer unit may have colored lights to indicate the working of the PC. These lights also glow whenever data is recorded onto or read from CD, USB Drive or hard disk.

DVD Drive: It accepts CD and DVD and if the drive is capable of it, it might also write to writeable CDs & DVDs.

Use Reset switch as a last resort when the PC hangs and does not accept a command from the keyboard. When you restart the PC, it will lose all the information currently stored in its memory.

Parts of the Rear Panel

If you look at the rear panel of the system unit of your PC, you will see certain holes and slots with different cables. Details of such parts are explained below:

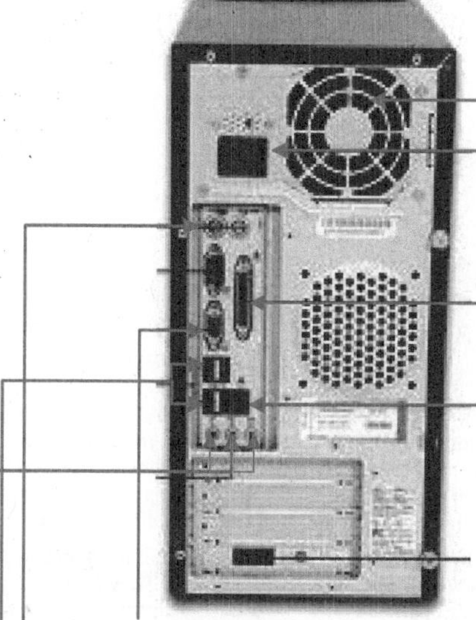

Video Port for Monitor: This is a 5 pin socket used to connect a monitor with the system unit.

PS/2 Port: This is used to connect the keyboard and mouse with the system.

Power Sockets: Cables plugged into these sockets carry electric power supply from the electrical outlet to your system unit and from the system unit to your monitor.

Parallel Port or Sockets: These ports or sockets are used for expanding the capability of your PC. For example, you can connect a printer, mouse, modem or some other peripheral to your system unit by using these ports.

Fan Housing: The power supply fitted inside the system unit has a small fan to take the heat out of the machine.

USB Port: These small rectangular slots accept Universal Serial Bus (USB) cables. Many types of devices use USB interfaces, including scanners, digital cameras, Mouse, Keyboard, Pen drive and printers.

Sound Connectors: Sound connectors are built-in but, in some systems they are on a separate in an expansion slot. There are three identical round rings i.e. output for speakers, input for microphone, and input for other devices.

Network Interface: It is a RJ-45 connector. It is used to connect the network wire in the system.

Inside the System Unit

Inside the system unit are the electronic components that run programs, handle typed instructions and determine the result. Some of common components are as follows:

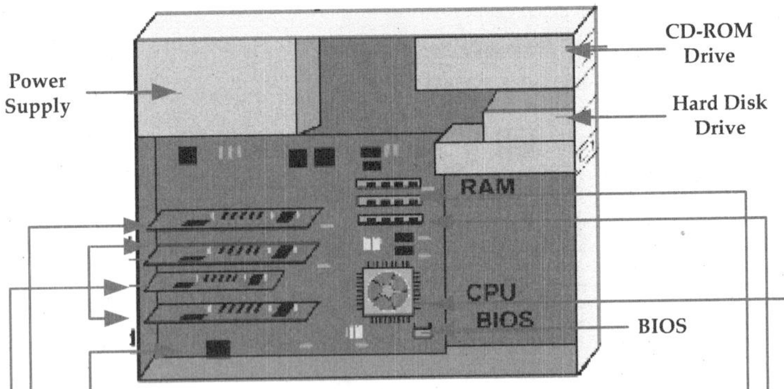

Motherboard: All the electronic components in a system are mounted on a piece of fiberglass called the motherboard. Fiberglass is used because it is a nonconductor of electricity . Thin metal lines on the fiberglass connect pins from one component to another, forming the computer's electrical circuits.

RAM (Random Access Memory) Chips: RAM chips consist of black plastic integrated circuit (IC) chips with a row of pins on each side. They may be inserted onto a printed circuit board.

ROM Chips: ROM chips such as BIOS contain data written on them during manufacture. It stores important instructions such as instructions that tell the CPU what to do immediately when you switch on your PC.

Display Adapter Card (Video Graphics Card): Display Adapter Card provides the link between the CPU and the Monitor. It converts binary form of information into human readable form.

Disk Interface Card: Disk Interface Card is necessary for communicating with a hard disk and other peripherals, such as floppy disk drives.

Input/Output Interface Card: Input/Output Interface Card is for input output devices such as printers or modems. It usually has one or two parallel ports, one or two serial ports and a joystick port.

Expansion Slots: Expansion Slots are long narrow connectors that allow you to plug in adapter cards, which offer extra options not available on a normal PC mother board. For example, one can plug sound card, network card etc. into these slots to enhance the capability of a PC.

Microprocessor: A microprocessor executes all the program instructions and is truly the heart of the personal computer. It consists of a silicon chip on which tiny circuits are engraved through a photochemical process.

CPU Support Chips: These chips help the CPU in managing different parts of the computer. Intel chip set is the one used on motherboard for supporting other devices.

Battery: Rechargeable, small capacity battery provides a small amount of constant power to the motherboard so that the items that always need to be on can stay even when the PC is unplugged from the main power supply.

Notes:

TFT-LCD is a variant of liquid crystal display (LCD) which uses thin film transistor (TFT) technology to improve image quality. It is used in televisions, flat panel displays, projectors, etc. Figure below shows TFT LCD monitor.

The CPU of a small computer has a single microprocessor. But, the CPU of a large computer may contain a number of microprocessors on one or more circuit boards. Each microprocessor in a large CPU performs a specific task.

Components of a Computer System

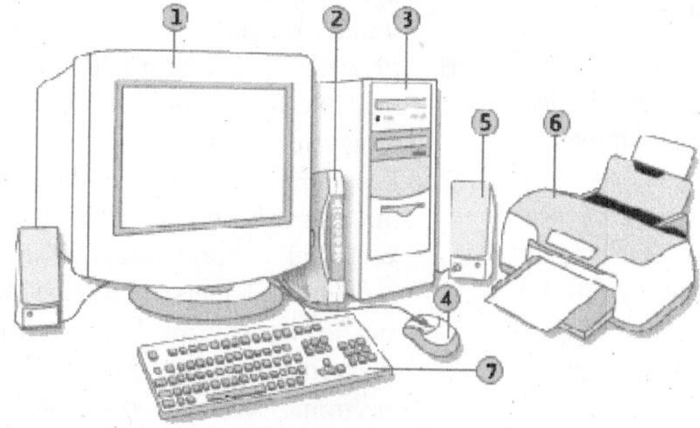

1. ***Monitors***: Monitors comes in two types:
   (a) *CRT (Cathode Ray Tube) Monitor:* A VDU or CRT monitor is very similar to a television. It shows text or picture. Whatever you type on the keyboard, you can see it on the monitor.
   (b) *TFT-LCD (Liquid Crystal Display):* LCD monitor is the flat panel type of monitor found on notebook PCs. TFT LCD has a sandwich-like structure with liquid crystal filled between two glass plates.
2. ***Modem:*** It is a communication device that acts as an interface between a computer or terminal and a communication channel. It enables computer to transmit information over a standard telephone line. Because a computer is digital and a telephone line is analog, therefore modems (modulator/ demodulator) are needed to convert digital to analog signal and vice versa.
3. ***System Unit:*** System unit or CPU is the brain of a computer. Its primary function is to execute programs and control all the components such as memory, input and output devices. Under its control, programs and data are stored in the memory and outputs are displayed on the monitor screen or printed on paper. (details are already described).
4. ***Mouse:*** A mouse is a pointing device. It is held in one hand and moved across a flat surface. The mouse can also be used to draw sketches, diagrams etc. on the monitor screen. One type of mouse uses a rolling ball; others use optical sensing techniques. They are linked to the PC by using a cable or by using infrared light.
5. ***Speaker:*** The computer speakers are similar to the ones that are connected to the stereo. In a computer a sound card is necessary for speakers. Speakers receive the sound in form

of electric current from the sound card and then covert it to sound format.

6. *Printers:* Printers provide information in a permanent readable form. They produce printed outputs of results, programs and data.
7. *Keyboard:* Programs and data are entered into a computer through a keyboard which is attached to a computer. A keyboard is similar to the keyboard of a typewriter. It contains alphabets, digits, special characters, function keys and some control keys. When a key is pressed, an electronic signal is produced which is detected by an electronic circuit called *keyboard encoder.*

Notes:

Impact printers *use an electro-mechanical mechanism that causes hammers or pins to strike against a ribbon and paper to print the text. For example, available: dot matrix printers.*

Non-impact printers *use thermal, chemical, electro-static, laser beam or inkjet technology for printing the text. Usually a non-impact type printer is faster than an impact type. For example, Laser Printer.*

Static RAMs *can retain stored information as long as the power supply is on. But a* ***dynamic RAM*** *loses its stored information in a very short time (a few milliseconds) even though the power supply is on.*

Main Storage

RAM (Random Access Memory): RAM is a read/write memory. Information can be written into and read from a RAM. It is a volatile memory. It retains the stored information as long as it is supplied with power supply. When power supply is switched off or interrupted, the stored information in the RAM is lost. RAMs of various capacities are available such as 512 MB, 1GB and so on.

ROM (Read Only Memory): ROM is a permanent type memory. Its contents are not lost when power supply is switched off. The user cannot write into a ROM. Its contents are written into at manufacturing time. ROMs store permanent programs and other types of data which are needed by the computer to execute user programs.

Secondary Storage Devices

Magnetic Disk (Hard Disk): Hard disk is a device used for mass storage of data. The data stored on a hard disk can be retrieved at a very fast speed. A hard disk is made up of a group of disks or disk platters, piled on top of one another in an airtight, dustproof case. Hard disks are available in the capacity of 80 GB or more. Figure below shows a hard disk and its inside contents.

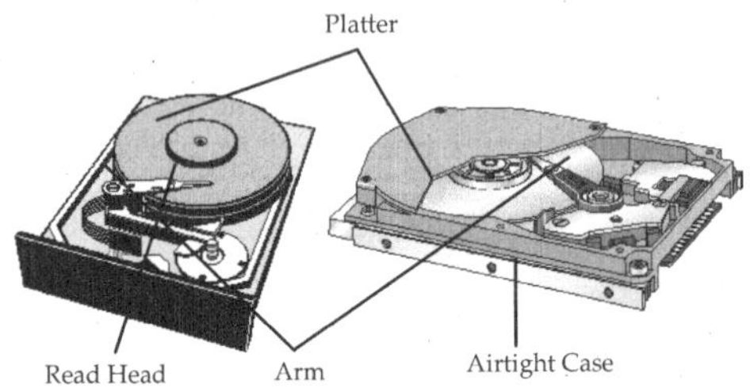

Notes

Pen drives are typically small, lightweight, removable and rewritable. It is also known as a flash drive, keychain drive, key drive, USB key and memory key.

A set of instructions given to a PC that perform a particular task is called the program. The instructions in the program direct the computer to perform different functions such as input operations, data processing and printing the results.

***Android** a new operating system or computing platform offered by Google. It is an open-source platform (can be modified under some conditions by other developers). It is becoming a hot platform for smart phones as it offers sturdiness at affordable prices.*

CD-ROM (Compact Disk Read Only Memory): It is an optical Read Only Memory (ROM). CD-ROM provides random access data retrieval and data indexing, and the disks have a shelf life of more than 40 years. CD-ROM can store about 700 MB of data, (about 800 floppies) making it an excellent medium for storing massive amount of data. Figure below shows a CD disk.

Digital Video Disk (DVD): It is an optical storage device that looks the same as a CD. A DVD has the same dimensions as a standard CD but cannot be read by a CD player, although a DVD player can read standard CDs. A DVD can store up to 4.7 gigabyte of data.

Pen Drive: USB flash drives or pen drives are NAND-type flash memory data storage devices integrated with a USB (universal serial bus) interface. It is a flash memory card that plugs into the computer's USB port. It allows data to be easily transferred from one machine to another. (See Figure below)

Software

The set of computer programs, procedures and associated documentation related to the effective operation of a computer system are termed software packages. The system software packages include operating system, assembler, compiler, interpreter, debugging programs and text editors, etc.

The software packages are classified into the following categories:

1. System software
2. Application software
3. Utilities

The classification of software packages are given below:

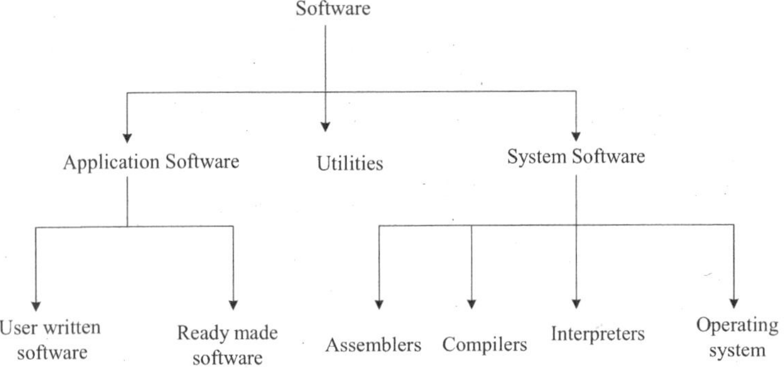

Notes:

System software *makes the operation of the computer system more effective and efficient.*

An assembler which runs on a computer for which it produces object codes (machine codes) is called a self assembler (or resident assembler). But an assembler that runs on a computer other than that for which it produces the machine codes is called cross assembler.

If a compiler runs on a computer other than that for which it produces object code, then it is called a ***cross-compiler****.*

System Software

System software packages are one or more programs that are basically designed to control the operations of a computer system. These are general programs written to assist users in using a computer system. In general, system software packages support the following :

1. Running of other application programs.
2. Communicating with peripheral devices such as printers, card readers, disk and tape devices, etc.
3. Development of other types of software packages.
4. Monitoring the use of various hardware resources such as memory, peripherals, CPU, etc.

System software packages are classified as follows:

1. *Operating systems:* An operating system is a master control program that runs a computer and acts as a scheduler. It controls the flow of signals from CPU to various parts of the computer. It is the first program loaded (copied) into the computer's memory after the computer is switched on. Popular operating systems includes Windows XP, Windows Vista, Windows 7, Unix, etc.
2. *Assemblers:* A program which translates an assembly language program into a machine language program is called an *assembler*.
3. *Compilers:* A program which translates a high-level language program into a machine language program is called a compiler.
4. *Interpreters:* An interpreter is a program which translates one statement of a high-level language program into machine codes and executes it and then translates and executes the next statement of the program.

Notes:

***Application software** differs from an operating system (which runs a computer), a utility (which performs maintenance or general-purpose chores) and a language (with which computer programs are created).*

*An **anti virus software** is critical for providing a precise identification of a virus in computer system. Without a precise identification, you cannot know the best course of action for removing it and you cannot be sure that you have removed it completely.*

Application Software

Application software is a computer program designed to help users to perform a specific type of work. Depending on the work for which it was designed, an application program can manipulate text, numbers, graphics, or a combination of these elements. Some application packages offer considerable computing power by focusing on each task. Others, called integrated software packages offer somewhat less power but include several types of applications, such as a word processor, a spreadsheet and a database program.

Utility Software

The *utility program* is a program designed to perform maintenance work on the system or on system components. For example, a storage backup program, a disk and file recovery program, or a resource editor are utility software packages.

Utility programs, also known as service programs are routines that perform services such as editing texts or debugging programs to correct logical mistakes, sorting records into a particular sequence for processing, or transferring data from one I/O device to another.

Examples of Utility Software are as under:

1. *Compression Tools:* Compression tools help to compress data storage in a computer. Compressed data saves the storage space and read/write as well as transmission time. Compressed data is stored in computer in an unusual manner.
2. *Anti Virus scanners and Virus Removers:* Anti Virus are the programs designed to identify viruses within files, boot sectors, master boot sectors, memory and other hiding places in computer.
3. *File Management Tools:* A file management tool is a program which permits programmers to create, copy, update or delete files on the storage devices.
4. *Disk Management tools:* Disk management tool mainly consists of disk defragmentation. Disk management tool or disk defragmentation rearranges the files and stores them in contiguous storage locations on the disk and thus speeds up the disk access

Fragmentation is a condition in which there are many scattered areas of storage that are too small to be used productively.

Setting up a New PC System

When you set up a new computer system, assembly of various components is required. If the new computer is a personal computer, then it consists of several pieces. These are as follows:

1. central processing unit (CPU), which is the box that contains the computer's processor,
2. memory chips
3. disk drives
4. ports (serial or parallel) for connecting external devices;
5. monitor
6. keyboard
7. mouse
8. speaker

For connecting electrical wire, turn the CPU around. The back of the CPU has a collection of ports and jacks which we have already described in Parts of real panel section. Although they might be arranged differently. To connect the computer hardware, follow these steps:

Keyboard and Mouse

If the connector on the wire cord that is attached to the keyboard or mouse is round then plug the cord into a PS/2 port on the back of the computer. If the connector on the cord is flat, plug it into any available USB port. Both types of connectors are designed so that you cannot plug them in the wrong way.

Monitor to the Display Adapter

Most monitors use a standard analog cable with a 5-pin connector that plugs into a matching port. Some specialized monitors use digital connectors, which require a matching digital display adapter and a custom cable. Plug in the monitor cord in the 5-pin port. Also power cord to the main supply.

Speakers to the Computer's Audio Output

The connector for stereo speakers is typically color-coded lime green. If the computer comes with different sound system, check the computer manual to find out where to plug in the center and back speakers. If the speaker cables have connectors that don't match the ports on the CPU, you might need to buy an adapter cable.

Connect the CPU to an AC Power Source

Look for the thick power cord that comes with your computer. Plug the female end into the power supply on the back of the

Notes:

Before buying a new computer from a computer manufacturer ensure that the computer has no physical damage by inspecting the ports as well as the inside and the outside of the case.

While purchasing a new mouse, purchase an optical mouse because it never needs cleaning. It can be used on almost any surface and the resolution and accuracy are much higher.

computer, and plug the male end into a wall socket. If there is an uninterruptible power supply (UPS) connected to the AC power source, plug the CPU power cord into that power source instead.

Connect the Monitor to an AC Power Socket

Now plug the power cord of the monitor into the power socket and switch the power supply ON. Press the power switch on the monitor to turn it on. Press the power switch on the front of the computer. Soon, a series of status messages appears on the monitor, the last of which is the Windows 7 desktop screen that will appear as under:

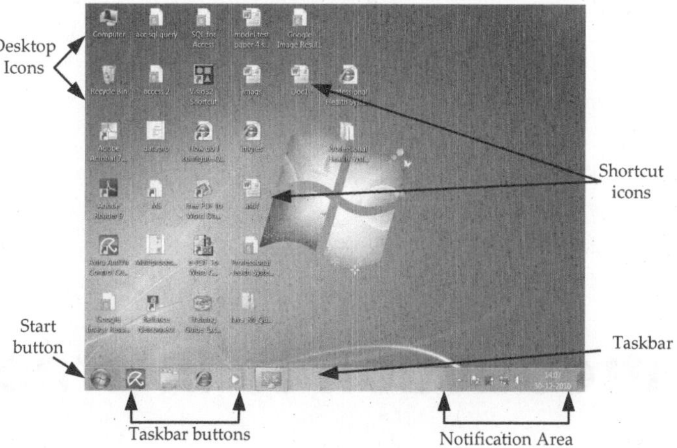

Starting MS Office 2010 Application Package

1. Click the **Start** Button on the Taskbar.
2. Highlight **All Programs**, Click **Microsoft Office**.
3. Click on any Microsoft Office Application Package which you want to open.

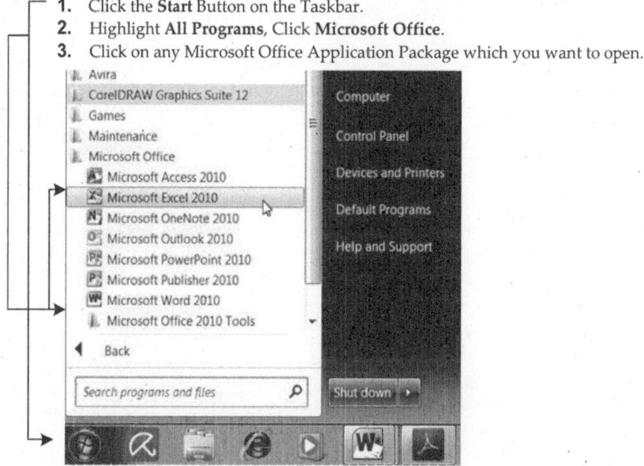

4. Go to the Chapter dealing with the selected package.

Introduction to Internet

Introduction to Internet

Internet is an interconnection between several computers of different types belonging to various networks all over the world. *It is a network of networks*. Millions of people throughout the world use Internet to share information and ideas, to search information on any topic, etc.

Internet is an immensely complex combination of thousands of technologies and dozens of services used by millions of people around the world each day. Internet is thus, a network of networks.

The Internet is a network of thousands of computer networks. Every network and every computer in these networks exchange information according to certain rules called protocols. These different computers and different networks are united with the common thread of two protocols, i.e. Internet Protocol (IP), and Transmission Control Protocol (TCP).

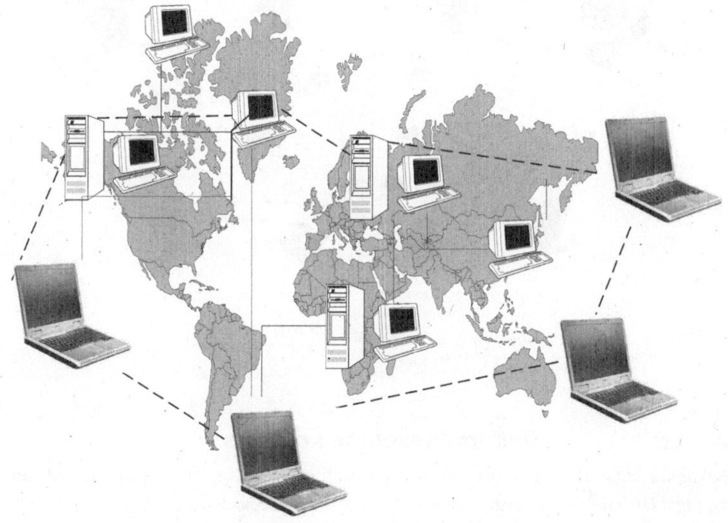

Notes:

Internet is a computer-based world wide information network.

Internet Services

The Internet is a combination of many of networks, and a large number of databases and other services. The major services offered on the Internet are given in following Figure.

Most of the services can be accessed by using a Web browser such as Netscape Navigator, Microsoft Internet Explorer or Mozilla. Web browsers also provide e-mail as well as access to mailing lists.

 ***The Internet brings the outside world to your desktop in your home or in your office.***

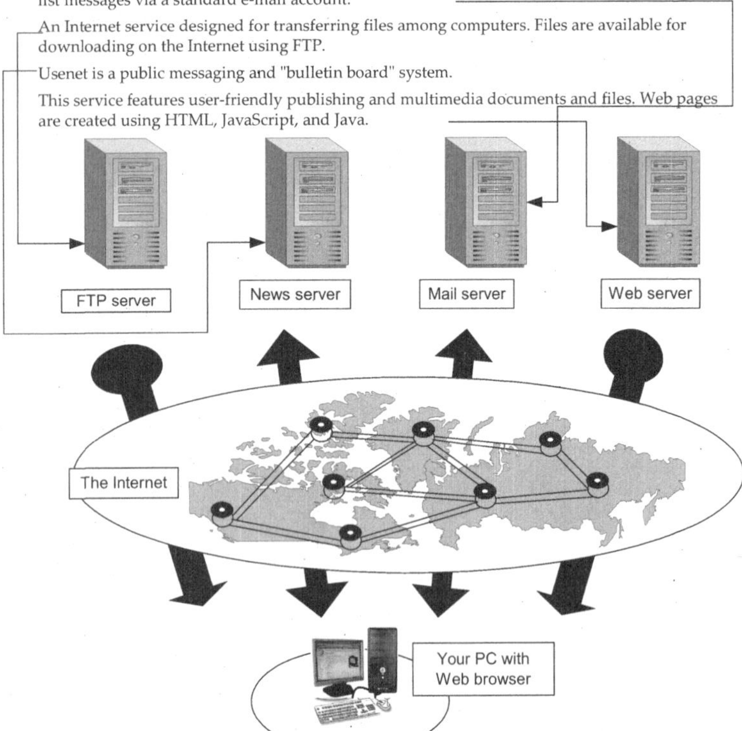

Uniform Resource Locators

Uniform Resource Locators, or URLs, are the unique addresses of Internet resources. A URL is divided into four.

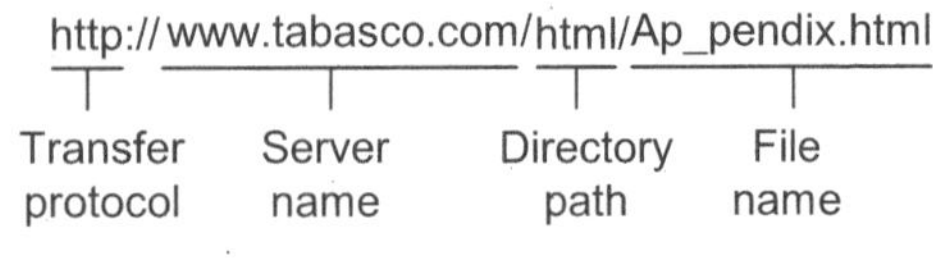

Notes:

Be careful while typing a URL into a Web browser; a single wrong character in the address will give an error message or download the wrong Web page.

A web client is the requesting program associated with the user. The web browser in your computer is a client that requests HTML files from the web server.

Elements of the Internet

A simplified hierarchical model of the Internet includes client PCs, server computers and networks (composed of both clients and servers).

Nodes: It (composed of clients and servers) is a generic term used to describe a client, server, or network (These are composed of one or more server computers and multiple client PCs).

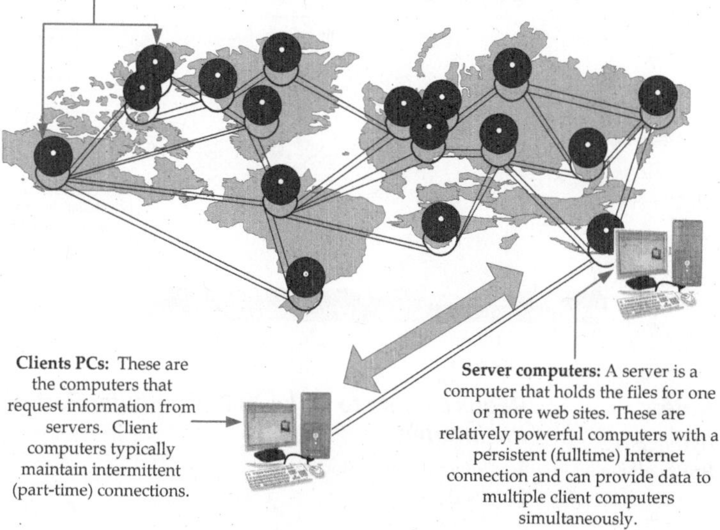

Elements of the Web

Web Browser

A *Web browser* is a software application program that resides on your PC and can display text, images, and multimedia data found on different Web pages. It allows you to specify a Web page, navigate using links, and "bookmark" your favourite Web pages. The commonly used web browsers are *Internet Explorer, Netscape Navigator* and *Mozilla Firefox*.

Web Sites vs.Web Pages

Web site is a place on internet where information about an organization has been stored. Information can be a single page or multiple pages. Pages are linked in such a way that by clicking you can move to another page.

A Web page is a part of a complete Web site. Web sites can consist of only a few Web pages or many hundreds of Web pages.

Notes:

A Web browser is a program that helps the user to navigate the World Wide Web.

Web site is a collection of information stored as web pages which may be on one or more computers. A Web page is an electronic document written in computer language called HTML (Hypertext Markup Language).

The relationship between Web server and Web browser is shown in following figure:

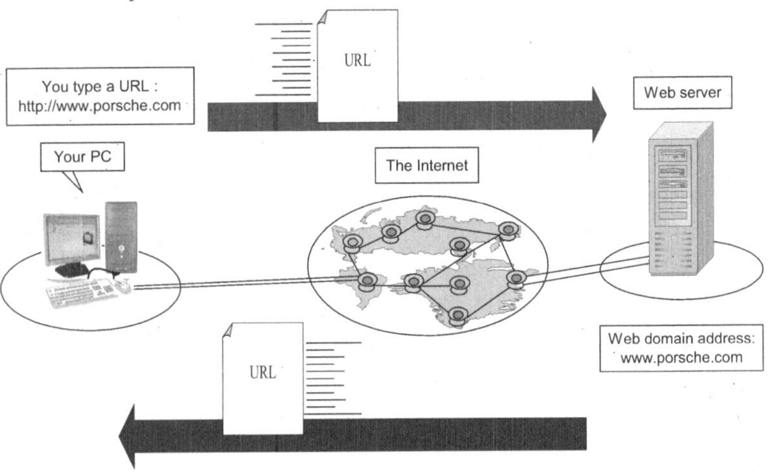

Requirements to Make Your Computer Part of the Internet

1. Internet connection
2. Modem
3. Telephone line
4. Program which controls the communication of data over the hardware component.

Internet Connection by ISP

Internet Service Provider (ISP) allows you to connect your computer to the internet.

Internet connections are provided by Internet Service Providers who install a main server and through the server they give connections to users. Server is a computer with high storage capacity and memory. It is in turn connected to other servers installed at different places in the world through satellites. Connections issued through the server are allotted private place on the servers in order to store the e-mails for the connected user. Some of the ISP's are:

1. Tata VSNL (Videsh Sanchar Nigam Limited)
2. MTNL (Mahanagar Telephone Nigam Limited)
3. Reliance
4. Mahendra Satyam
5. Airtel

Notes:

IP (Internet Protocol) *is a set of rules for exchanging information over the network. Each computer which is connected to the Internet has at least one IP address which uniquely identifies this computer from other computers.*

Internet service provider is a company that provides access to the internet. An Internet Service Provider, or ISP is one gateway to the Internet.

Types of Connectivity

There are several ways to connect to the Internet. The more expensive services provide more features, more flexibility, and greater data transfer capacity.

Telephone Line Options

If you are using the telephone system (old land-line) to get onto the internet your telecommunication connection follows either the normal phone system or an ISDN or ADSL, line until it reaches the telephone company's central office. The central office router calls to a long distance carrier's point of presence or POP. The POP is the point at which a local call is handed off to a long distance company. The call is then routed to the central office nearest your Internet Service provider (ISP).

Dial up Connections through the Telephone System

A *dial-up connection* is a temporary connection, setup between your computer and ISP server. A dial up connection is established using a modem, which uses the telephone line to dial up the number of ISP server. The modem converts electronic signals to analog signals and vice versa.

Dial-up connection is simple access to internet. It is less expensive as compared to leased line and makes the Internet available to you as long as you remain connected.

Dedicated Connections

The most popular Internet access for companies and institutions is a dedicated phone line connecting your LAN to the Internet 24 hours a day. However, a dedicated Internet access requires substantial initial investment in equipment. The main continuing cost is a flat monthly fee for the use of the line. It varies with line capacity, and line capacity determines how many users can connect to Internet simultaneously.

In dedicated connection, the speed of direct line is very high. It is very fast but expensive.

Leased Line

An inexpensive modem based connection, which is set up only when it is needed, is the ideal solution for occasional user on the Internet. Running a Web server, handling a large volume of mail, connecting an entire network of users or, offering other information services require a permanent connection to the Internet and higher bandwidth than a normal modem can deliver.

Notes:

With more than 500 million active mobile phone users, industry experts have estimated that the next generation of Internet users would be connecting via phone and not their desktop computers.

Dedicated connections are also called leased lines. Leased lines are direct cables laid to connect your computer to an Internet service provider's (ISP's) server.

Cloud-based computer services rely on shared resources such as servers (network computers) and software stored online for their operation. A company need not physically own infrastructure for the IT set-up. Instead, it "rents" storage, software or computing power from a cloud services company.

Notes:

In a dial-up connection to the Internet, you use a modem to connect your computer with the ISP's computers on your normal regular telephone line.

The solution is a leased line connection to the Internet which is fast and permanent. Depending on your bandwidth requirements. ISP's can provide leased line ranging from 10 Mbps to 100 Mbps or more.

Wi-Fi (Wireless Fidelity) Connection

Wi-Fi technology was used for both home computer networks and Internetworks because it eliminated the need to run wires between computers.

It requires computers equipped with Wi-Fi circuit cards or chips to connect to the Internet without visible communications links. Intel introduced Centrino microchips that provided laptops with built-in Wi-Fi capability.

Now wired telephone companies have an extra service as Wi-Fi to keep digital subscriber line (DSL) customers from defecting to cable modems, which operated over networks.

Getting Connected to Internet

The most common way to connect to the Internet is by way of an *Internet Service Provider* (ISP). ISPs are essentially a "passthrough" connection. Beside the basic technical support for the connection itself, an ISP just sets you up so that you can use Internet mail as well as the World Wide Web.

To setup an Internet connection using Windows:

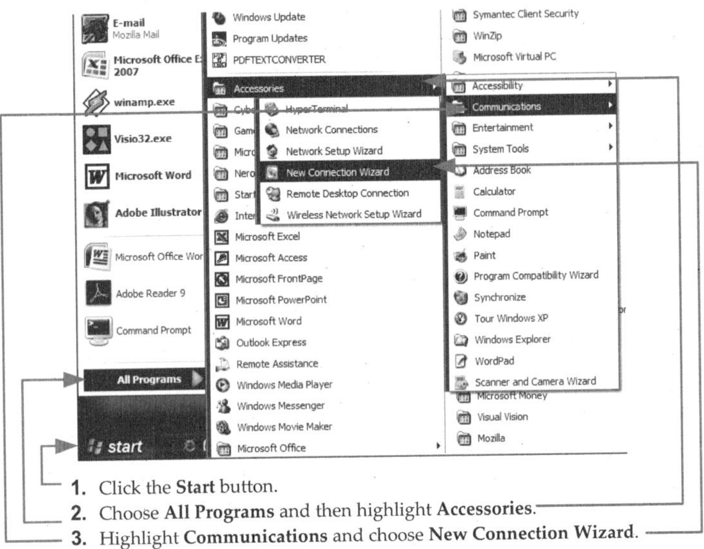

1. Click the **Start** button.
2. Choose **All Programs** and then highlight **Accessories**.
3. Highlight **Communications** and choose **New Connection Wizard**.

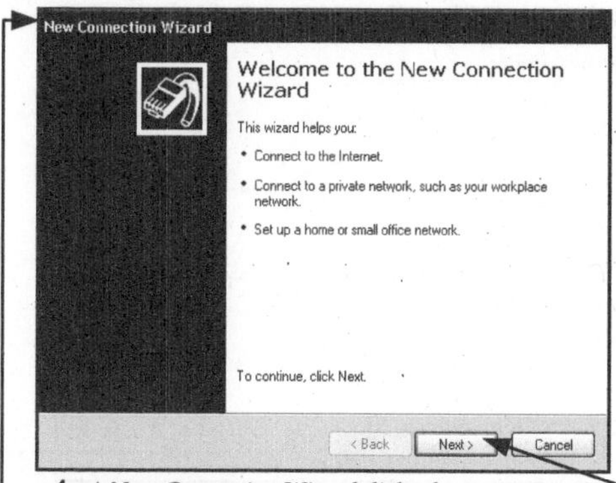

4. A New Connection Wizard dialog box appears.
5. In this dialog box click **Next**.

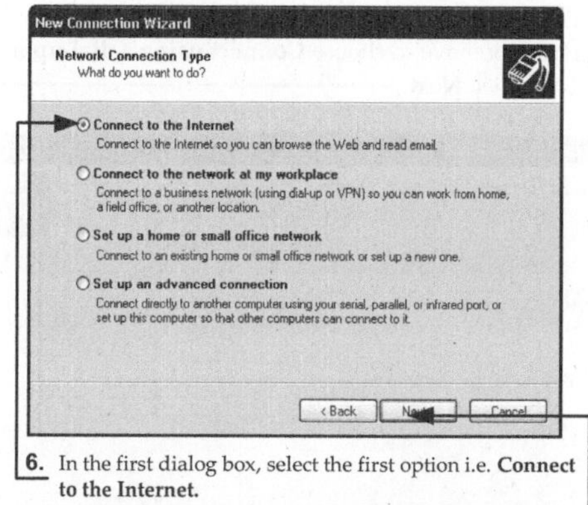

6. In the first dialog box, select the first option i.e. **Connect to the Internet.**
7. Then Click **Next.**

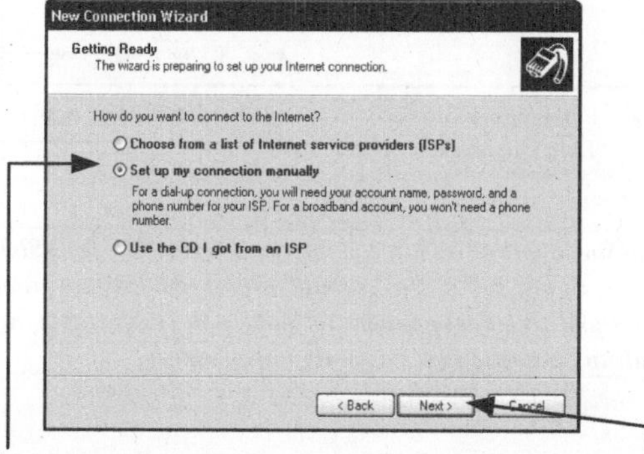

8. In next dialog box , choose **Set up my connection manually.**
9. Then Click **Next.**

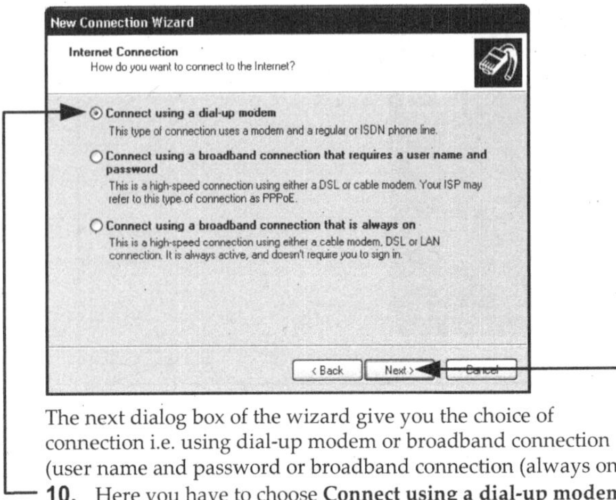

The next dialog box of the wizard give you the choice of connection i.e. using dial-up modem or broadband connection (user name and password or broadband connection (always on).

10. Here you have to choose **Connect using a dial-up modem**.
11. Then click **Next**.

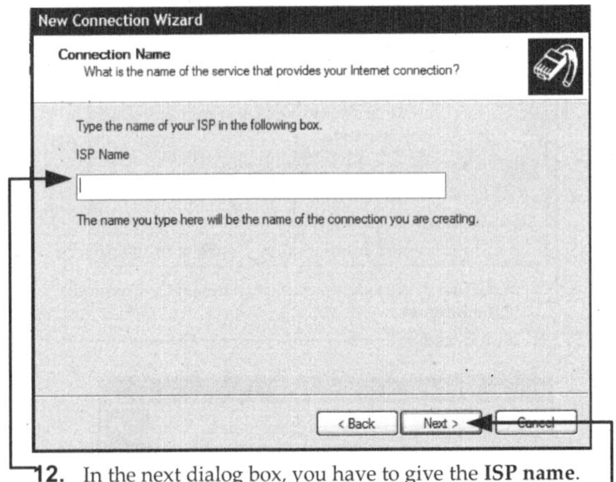

12. In the next dialog box, you have to give the **ISP name**.
13. Then click **Next**.

Most of the major cities have access to Internet via the VSNL and services of other private ISP's. You should expect an ISP to provide you with software and technical support to make you comfortable. Make sure that the dial-up connection uses a local phone number

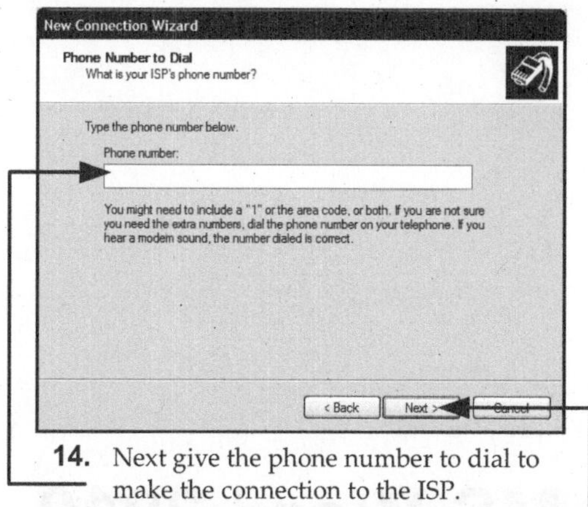

14. Next give the phone number to dial to make the connection to the ISP.
15. Click **Next**.

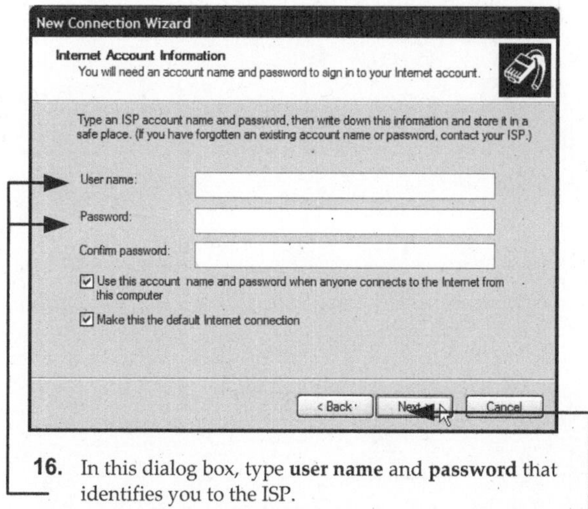

16. In this dialog box, type **user name** and **password** that identifies you to the ISP.
17. Then click **Next**.
18. And then click **Finish**.

The connection you have made for Internet accordingly to your need will be saved in Network Connection folder.

MS Word 2010

Starting MS Word 2010

Notes:

To open any MS Office Package you need to use the same method as explained in the following steps.

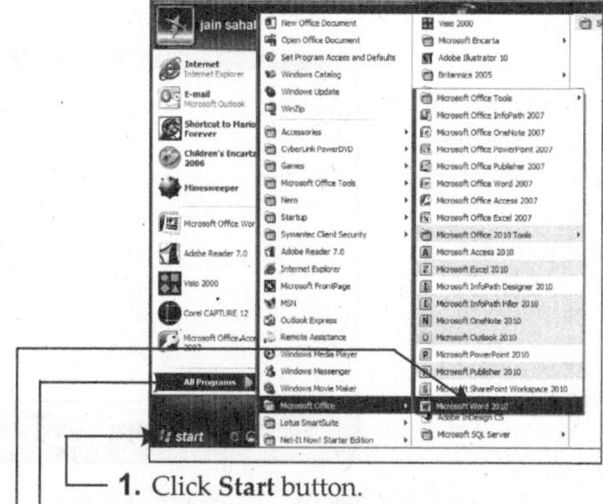

1. Click **Start** button.
2. Highlight **All Programs**. A sub menu appears, select **Microsoft Office**.
3. Select **MS Office Word 2010**.

When you open a file of another format, such as a file from a previous version of Word, it will automatically convert the file to current Word format.

Open a Document

Word 2010 opens files in any of the several formats such as (doc, docx, docm, html, etc.)

1. Click **File** menu, and then click **Open** command. The **Open** dialog box appears. Or you can click from **Quick Access Toolbar**.

Word 2010 needs ***Windows Vista*** *or* ***Windows 7*** *as operating system to run on an IBM PC. However, Word 2010 can also be used with* ***Windows XP*** *operating system, if* ***service pack 3*** *is installed on Windows XP.*

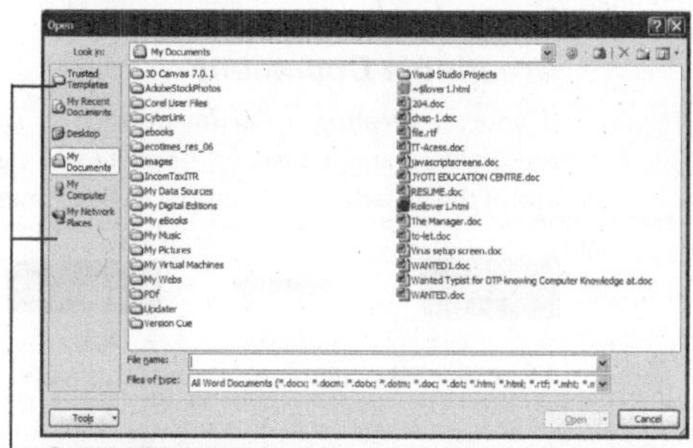

2. Click a folder button to change the file group displayed in the window.
3. Choose the desired folder:

Notes:

The Quick Access Toolbar is a customizable toolbar that contains a set of commands that are independent of the tab that is currently displayed. You can add buttons that represent commands to the Quick Access Toolbar. You can move the Quick Access Toolbar from one of the two possible locations.

Word gives you two methods to create new documents. The first is, to create a new document starting with a blank page. The second is, use a template to open a blank, preformatted document.

The keyboard shortcut to open a document is Ctrl + O.

a. Click the **Up One Level** button to display the folders that are stored along with the folder currently displayed in the Look **in:** text box.

b. Double click a folder icon in the list window to display the contents of that folder.

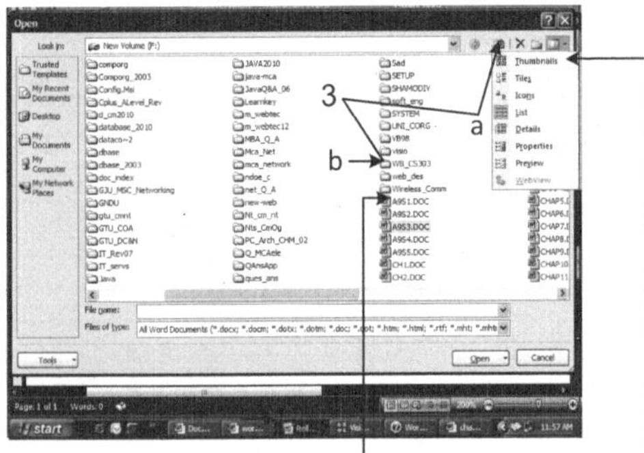

4. Click the name of the file you want to open.

5. Click the drop-down arrow next to the **Views** button to change the way the folder and file list is displayed.

a. **Thumbnails:** It displays icons as Thumbnails. When you click a folder name, a thick highlighted border appears.

b. **Tiles:** It displays icons in medium size.

c. **Icons:** It displays icons in smaller size.

d. **List:** Displays a list of commands.

e. **Details:** Displays the details of the size type, last modified, etc.

f. **Properties:** Displays the properties of the file.

g. **Preview:** Displays a preview of the file.

6. Click the **Open** button to open the file.

Creating a Document

If you are creating a document such as *memo, letter, report,* or *resume, Brochures, Calendars, Card* etc you can save time by using one of the wizards or the templates that come with Word 2010.

1. Click **File** menu and then select **New.**

Backstage view is where you manage your files and the data about them – creating, saving, inspecting for hidden metadata or personal information, and setting options.

Notes:

Opening a file automatically creates in the current directory a temporary file, the name of which begins with a tilde (~). When the document is correctly closed, the temporary file is deleted.

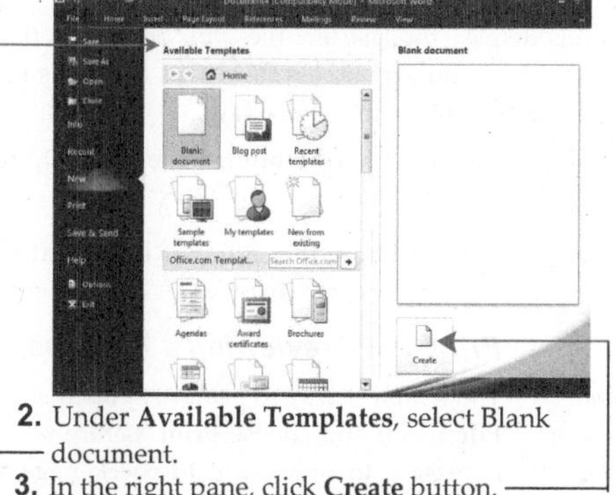

2. Under **Available Templates**, select Blank document.
3. In the right pane, click **Create** button.
4. A blank file appears ready to start storing data in it.

Saving a Document

The first time you save a file, you need to specify three items:

a. The drive and folder to store your file.

b. The name of your file.

c. The format to save your file.

*The shortcut key to save a document is **Ctrl + S**.*

*The **Save As** dialog box appears only when you are saving the document for the first time. Each additional save command will save the most recent changes to the file you have already named. The Save As dialog box will not reappear unless you choose **Save As**.*

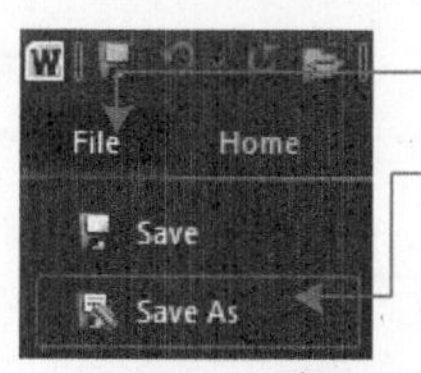

1. Click the **File** tab.
2. Then click **Save As**.

Or, Alternatively, choose the **Save** button on the **Quick Access** toolbar.

3. When you save a document for the first time, Word 2010 displays the **Save As** dialog box, so that, you can type a name for the document.

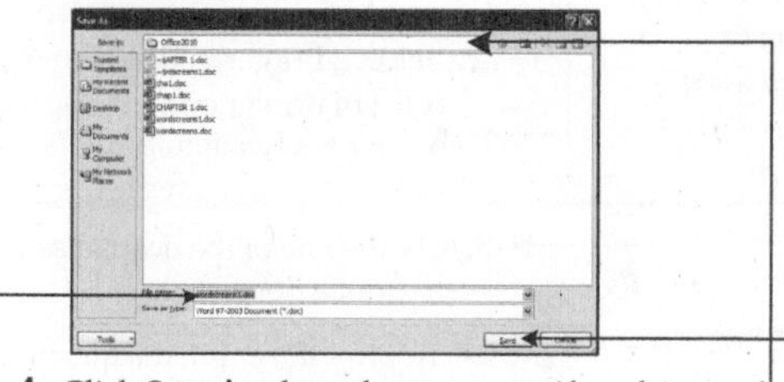

4. Click **Save in:** drop-down, to specify a drive and folder to save your file.
5. Click in the **File name:** text box and type a name for your file.
6. Click **Save** button.

Customize the list of Recently used files

Many programs display the last few files you opened in that program. You can use the links on this list to quickly access files. This feature is turned on by default. You can adjust the number of files that it displays.

7. Click the **File** menu and then **d Options.** The **Word Options** dialog box appears.
8. Click **Advanced.**
9. Under **Display**, in the **Show this number of Recent Documents** list, click the number of files that you want to display.

Notes:

The keyboard shortcut to open a Print dialog box is by pressing Ctrl+Shift+F12 keys together.

Print and Previewing a Document

The simplest way to print is to open a document and then click **File** menu and choose **Print**. Before you print a document, it is necessary to preview it to check page breaks and the overall appearance of the document. Previews include graphics, headers, and footers, but you cannot edit the document in Print Preview.

File → Print

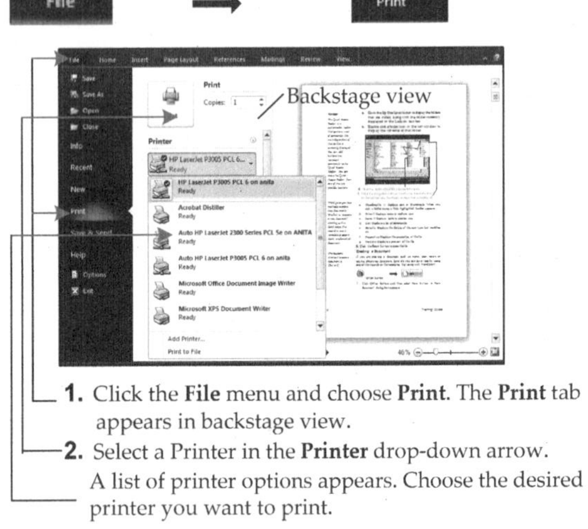

A document's temporary name (Document1, Document 2, etc.) can be changed when you save it.

1. Click the **File** menu and choose **Print**. The **Print** tab appears in backstage view.
2. Select a Printer in the **Printer** drop-down arrow. A list of printer options appears. Choose the desired printer you want to print.

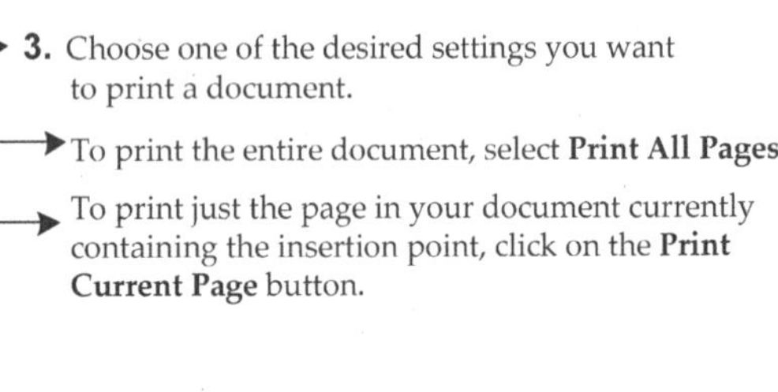

3. Choose one of the desired settings you want to print a document.

To print the entire document, select **Print All Pages.**

To print just the page in your document currently containing the insertion point, click on the **Print Current Page** button.

Notes:

To change the properties for your printer, under the printer name, click Printer Properties.

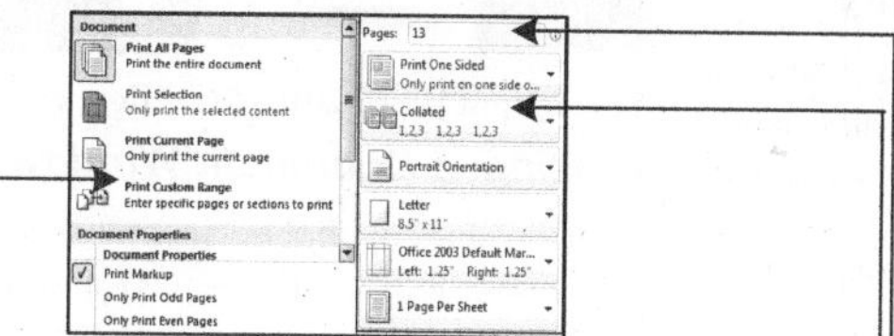

If you choose **Print Custom Range,** enter specific pages to print say, pages 6-10 in a document. Type the first page number and the last desired page number in the **Pages:** text box. Separate the numbers with hyphens like 6-10.

Collate: This option determines how multiple copies are printed. Say, you print five copies of a 10-page document without the Collate option, Word will first print all five copies of page 1 then all five copies of page 2 and so on.

*The new design in **Microsoft Office 2010** that includes the File tab replacing the **Microsoft Office Button** included in the 2010 Microsoft Office system release in the following programs: Word, Excel, PowerPoint, Access, and Outlook*

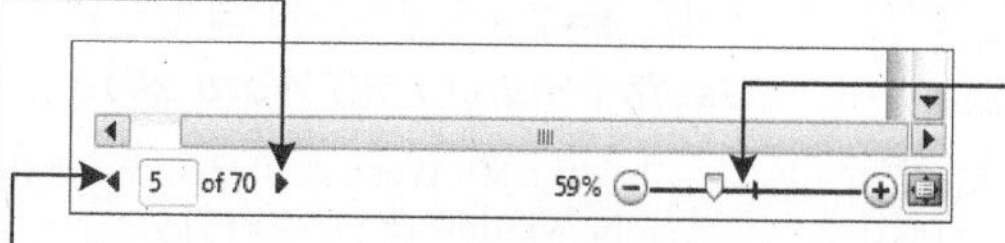

4. Click this triangle to go the previous page of the document. Or type the page number in the box.
5. Click this triangle to go to the next page of the document.
6. Drag this slide to zoom in and out of the document.
7. To close the **Print Preview** click the **Esc** key or click the **Home** tab.

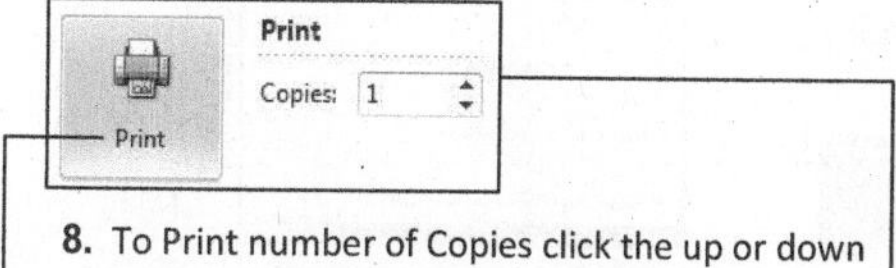

8. To Print number of Copies click the up or down spinner box. Or type the number in the Copies you want to print.
9. To print a document click the **Print** icon.

To close the active document window click the document Control menu icon on the left side of the document's title bar.

Closing and Quitting MS Word

1. If you want to close the open documents, choose **File** menu and then select **Close**.

Notes:

*The keyboard shortcut to open a Print dialog box and press **Ctrl+Shift+F12** keys together.*

1. To quit Word 2010 click **File** menu and choose **Exit** button.

Closing a Document Window

After finishing with a document, you should close the window to remove it from the screen and to free computer's main memory.

1. Click the **File** menu and choose Close.

   The window closes if no changes have been made to the document since the last save. However, if you made changes since the last time you saved the document, Word 2010 displays an **Alert** dialog box, asking whether you want to save your work before closing.

To resize the Help window, move the pointer over a corner of the Help window until you see the double-headed arrow and then drag the corner until the window is of the size that you want it to be.

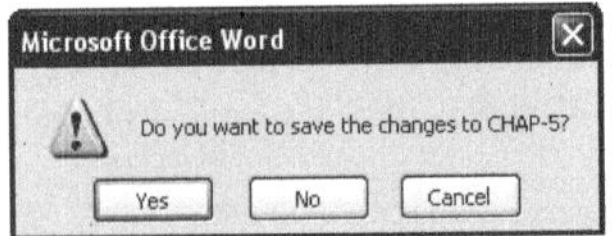

Getting Help in MS Word 2010

1. Click the MS Word 2010 Help button at the right corner of the window or press **F1** key.
2. Type the word such as Alignment text in the Type words to search for box and press Enter key.

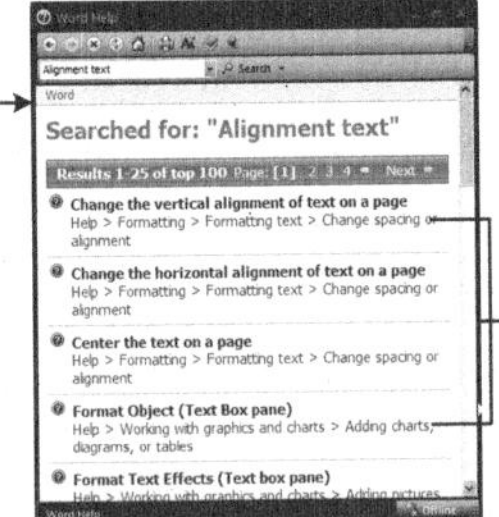

3. The help window displays a list of topics, i.e searched for related topics. Choose the selected list topic you want.
4. The help window displays step-by-step explanations.
5. Click the **Close** button to close the **Help** window.

*1. To **restore the Ribbon**, click **Expand the Ribbon** as shown below.*

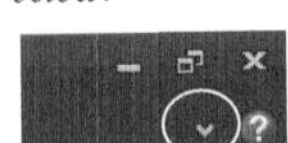

To keep the Ribbon Minimize

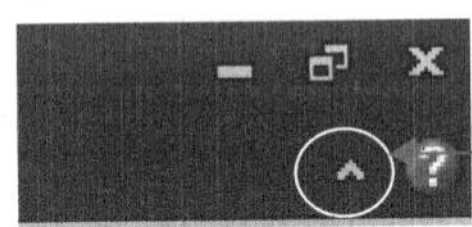

1. To minimize the Ribbon, click Minimize the Ribbon. The Minimize the Ribbon button is in the upper-right corner of the program window.

Notes:

ScreenTips are small windows that display descriptive text when you rest the pointer on a command or control.

Enhanced ScreenTips are larger windows that display more descriptive text than a ScreenTip and can have a link to a Help topic. Enhanced ScreenTips are available in the following 2010-Office system programs: Access, Excel, PowerPoint, and Word. (see below icon)

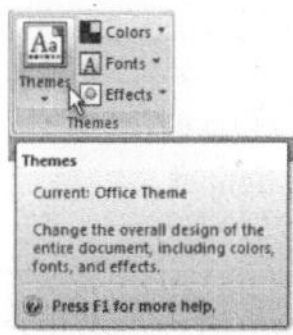

Show or Hide ScreenTips

1. Click **File** menu and choose **Options**.
2. The **Word Options** dialog box appears.

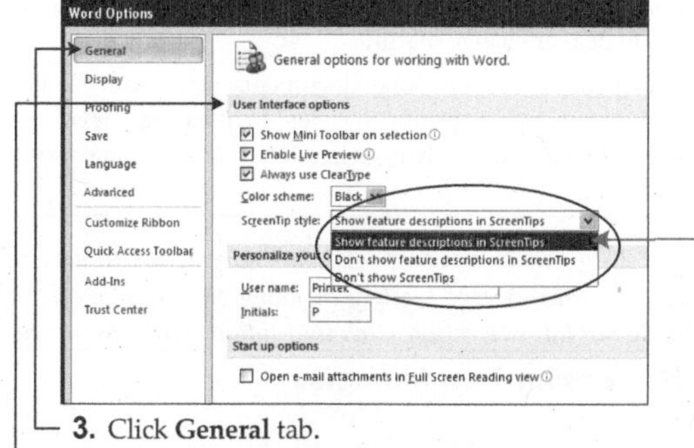

3. Click **General** tab.
4. Under **User Interface options.**
5. In the **ScreenTip Style:** list, select the options that you want.
   - **Show feature descriptions in ScreenTips** – This option turns on ScreenTips and Enhanced ScreenTips. This is the default setting.
   - **Don't show feature descriptions in ScreenTips** – This option turns off Enhanced ScreenTips. You still see ScreenTips.
   - **Don't show ScreenTips**—This option turns off ScreenTips and Enhanced ScreenTips.

What is Word Processing?

Word 2010 is a Word Processor that operates under Windows Operating System namely XP, Windows Vista and Windows 7. When you use a computer program to create, and edit text documents, you are using word processing power of this package. Word 2010 is one of the most sophisticated word processing program available to day. With Word 2010, it is easier than ever to efficiently create a wide range of business documents namely, a simple letter to a complex project report. Word 2010 includes many desktop features that you can use to enhance the appearance of documents so that they are easy to read.

You can emphasize the selected words by printing them in boldface, italics or in bold italics.

Why use MS Word 2010?

Use Word 2010 as word processor for printing letters, preparing mailing lists, creating documents and reports. The speed of these operations is much faster and easier than what is possible on any other word processing package. You can even check the spellings in documents. You can get help to select appropriate words in a sentence. Moreover, you can add page numbers or change margins.

Word 2010 can store very long documents in computer's hard disk. You can then modify such documents or print copies just by pressing a few keys from the keyboard. In case you have to make some changes in a letter, you can do so without retyping the whole letter.

 ***Word 2010 can be used to send the same letter to several different addressees using the Mail-Merge facility or using electronic mail facility on the Internet. You do not have to retype each individual letters for every person.***

Word Processing Terminologies

Word Wrap

A word processor automatically moves the text to the next line when you type beyond the right margin. This is known as word wrap.

Editing of Text

On a typewriter, when you miss a word or a line, you need to re-type the whole letter again. But using Word 2010, you can insert new words, new sentences or paragraphs anywhere in the text typed earlier. New text will get adjusted automatically.

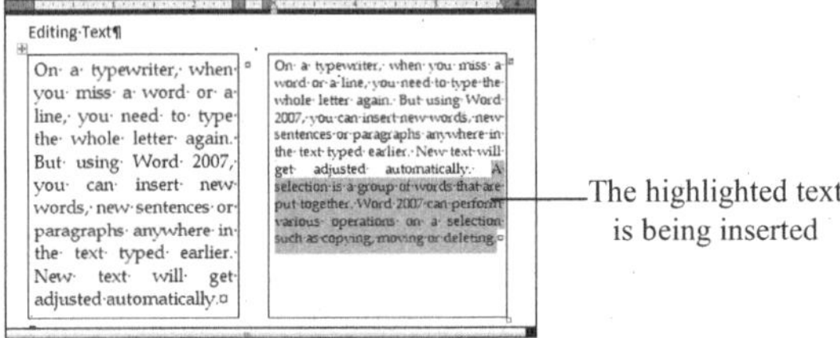

Selection

A selection is a group of words that are put together. Word 2010 can perform various operations on a selection such as copying, moving or deleting. The selection in Word 2010 gets highlighted. By giving the appropriate command, you can move or copy the selection to another place in the same document or to another document.

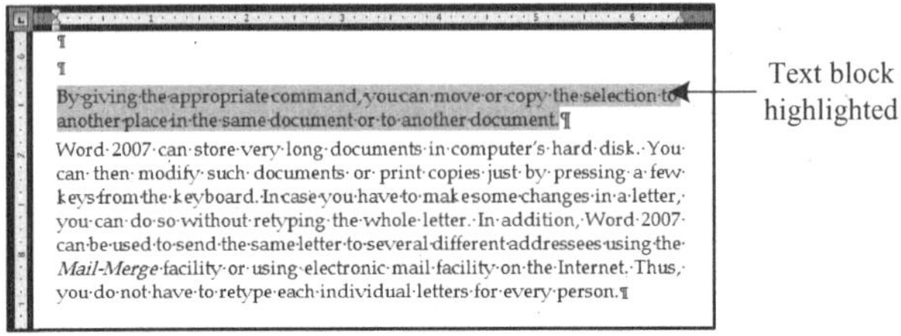

Moving/Copying Selected Block of Text

You can move a selected block of text to another location in the same document or copy the text at another location with the help of Word 2010. This saves the effort of retyping the text.

> Word 2007 can store very long documents in computer's hard disk. You can then modify such documents or print copies just by pressing a few keys from the keyboard. In case you have to make some changes in a letter, you can do so without retyping the whole letter. In addition, Word 2007 can be used to send the same letter to several different addressees using the *Mail-Merge* facility or using electronic mail facility on the Internet. Thus, you do not have to retype each individual letters for every person.¶
>
> By giving the appropriate command, you can move or copy the selection to another place in the same document or to another document.¶

To move in new location

Search and Replace

Word 2010 can conduct a search for any specified word or character in a document and replace it with another word as desired. For example, suppose you have written Pencile in a document and you wish to replace it with Pencil throughout the document, then you can use search and replace feature of Word 2010 to do the same.

Dictionary/Grammar Check

You can check spellings and locate errors in your document using Word 2010. To check spelling in every word of the text you can use the dictionary available in Word 2010.

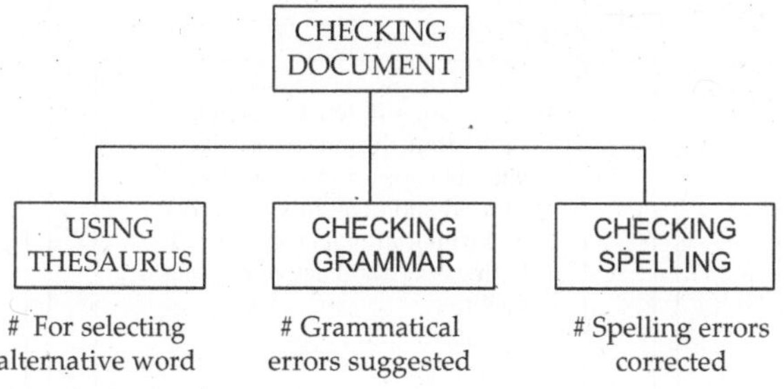

Character Styles and Sizes

You can change the type and the size of characters so that a printed document appears more attractive and professional. You can use bigger and bold letters for main headings. You can use italic characters to emphasize a word. Some examples of styles and sizes of characters are shown below:

Style	**Size**
Bold	12 Pt. Times New Roman
Italics	14 Pt. Arial
~~Strikeout~~	18 Pt. Arial Narrow
Underline	**20 Pt. Arial Bold**

Justification of the Text

Justification is the alignment of the text, typed within the given margins. The text can be *left, right, centre* or *even* justified. Various types of text justification are shown below:

In **left justification**, the text has a straight left edge and an uneven right edge.

In **right justification**, the text has a straight right edge and an uneven left edge.

In **center justification**, the text will be printed between the right and left edges of the paper.

In **even (full) justification**, the text is aligned on both the left and right margins of the page.

Header, Footer, Page Numbering and Margins

The document contains header, footer, page numbering and margins which, are shown below.

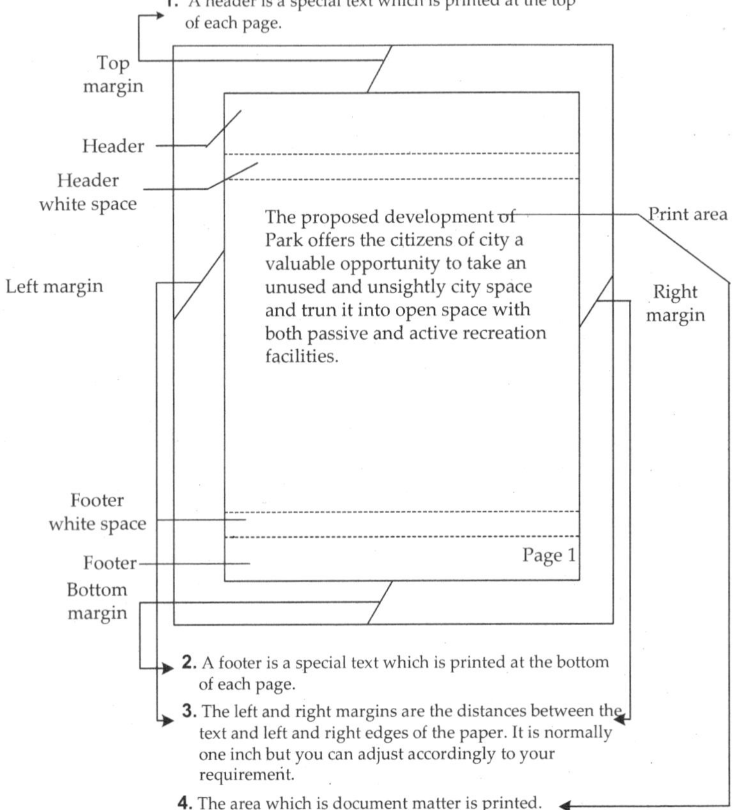

Line Spacing

In Word 2010, the spacing between the lines can be adjusted. You can leave one or more blank lines between every two typed lines but the default line spacing is single line spacing. When one line is left blank between two typed lines, then it is known as double line spacing. Double line spacing is normally used for draft letters. Below figure shows a paragraph first typed in single line spacing and then made in double line spacing.

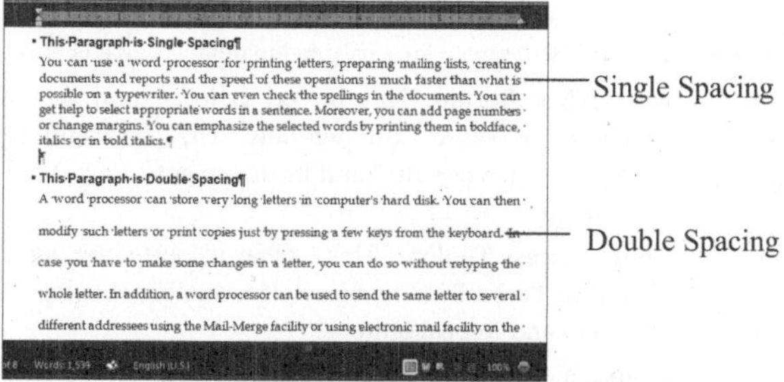

- **This Paragraph is Single Spacing**

You can use a word processor for printing letters, preparing mailing lists, creating documents and reports and the speed of these operations is much faster than what is possible on a typewriter. You can even check the spellings in the documents. You can get help to select appropriate words in a sentence. Moreover, you can add page numbers or change margins. You can emphasize the selected words by printing them in boldface, italics or in bold italics.

- **This Paragraph is Double Spacing**

A word processor can store very long letters in computer's hard disk. You can then modify such letters or print copies just by pressing a few keys from the keyboard. In case you have to make some changes in a letter, you can do so without retyping the whole letter. In addition, a word processor can be used to send the same letter to several different addressees using the Mail-Merge facility or using electronic mail facility on the

Tab Setting

You can set tabs in a Word 2010 for typing columns in a document as in the case of a typewriter. You may want to use the ruler to set Manual tab stops at the left side, middle and right side of your document as seen below:

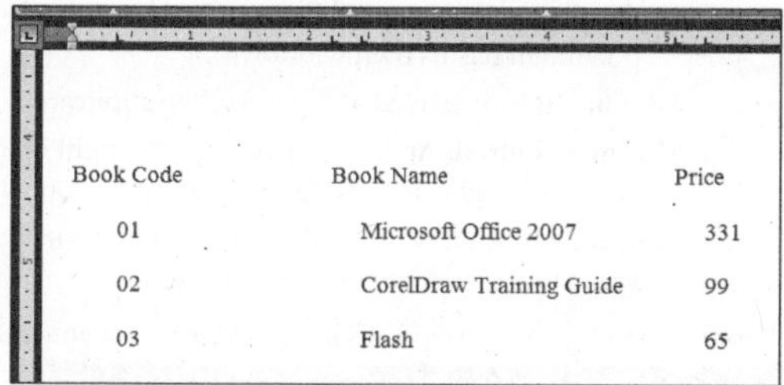

Book Code	Book Name	Price
01	Microsoft Office 2007	331
02	CorelDraw Training Guide	99
03	Flash	65

Table

A table is made up of rows and columns of cells that you can fill with text and graphics. You can use tables to align numbers in columns and then sort and perform calculations.

Hyphenating Documents

Hyphenation feature of Word 2010 can break or hyphenate words so that they may fit better on a line. It can hyphenate the words in a document automatically as you type a document or manually when you have finished typing.

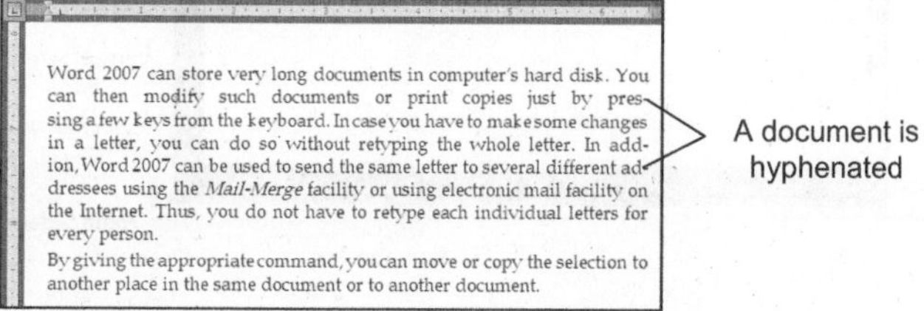

Word 2007 can store very long documents in computer's hard disk. You can then modify such documents or print copies just by pres-sing a few keys from the keyboard. In case you have to make some changes in a letter, you can do so without retyping the whole letter. In add-ion, Word 2007 can be used to send the same letter to several different ad-dressees using the *Mail-Merge* facility or using electronic mail facility on the Internet. Thus, you do not have to retype each individual letters for every person.

By giving the appropriate command, you can move or copy the selection to another place in the same document or to another document.

MS Word 2010 Interface

Notes:

*The **Quick Access Toolbar** is a customizable toolbar containing a set of commands that are independent of the tab that is currently displayed.*

There is a new look for Word 2010 and a new user interface that replaces menus, toolbars and most of the task panes from previous versions of Word. Moreover, it is very simple and easy to learn. The new interface is designed to help you to be more productive also. You can find the right features of various tasks more easily, discover new functionality and work more efficiently. The elements of Word 2010 screen are explained in detail as given below.

MS Office Button: This button is located in the upper-left corner of Word 2010 window. The command related to managing Word 2010 and its documents are put together on a menu.

Quick Access Toolbar: This toolbar is located by default at the top of Word 2010 window. This toolbar displays the Save, Undo and Repeat buttons.

Dialog box Launchers: The dialog box launchers are small icons that appear in some groups. Clicking a Dialog Box Launcher opens a related dialog box or task pane, providing more options related to that group.

__Home Tab:__ This button contains commands related to working with clipboard, font, paragraph, styles and editing.

Document window: You create a document in the document window. When more than one document is opened, each document has its own window.

Title bar: It is displayed at the top of the application window.

Minimize button: An underscore (_) at the right of a title bar which stores an application programme at the bottom of the screen

Maximize button: A box at the right of a title bar that fills available space with the document or application.

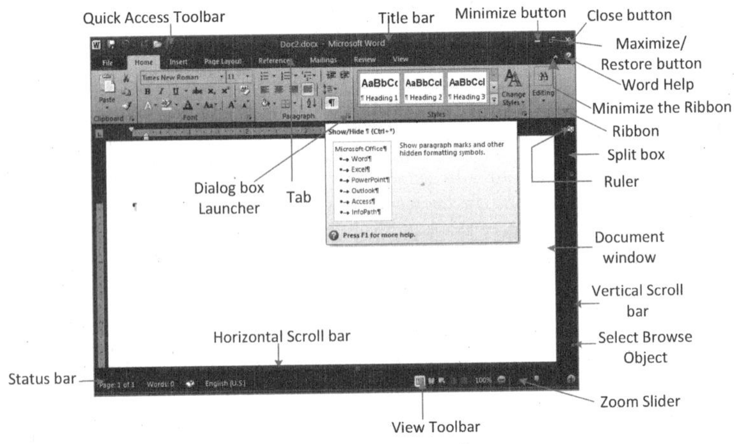

Notes:

Insert Tab: *This button contains commands for related items you can insert such as tables, header, footer and symbols.*

Page Layout Tab: *This button contains commands for items related to the appearance of your document such as Page Setup, Page Background, Paragraph, Theme and Arrangement of text.*

References Tab: *This button contains the commands that are related to items you can add to long documents, such as Tables of Contents, Footnotes, Bibliography, Index etc.*

Mailings Tab: *This button contains commands related to creating mass mailings.*

Close button: A box at the right of a title bar (X) that closes the window or dialog box.

Restore button: A double box at the right of a title bar that restores an application or document into a sizable window.

Help button: It appears at the right end of the Ribbon. When the mouse pointer is over any button for a few seconds (called hovering), it displays a ScreenTip with not only the button's name but also its function.

Status bar: At the bottom of the window, the status bar gives you information about the current document. You can turn off the display of an item of information by right-clicking the status bar and then clicking that item.

View toolbar: At the right end of the status bar is the view toolbar. It provides tools for adjusting the size of document.

Mouse pointer: On-screen arrow, I-beam, or drawing button indicates the current location affected by your mouse actions.

Select Browse Object: The toolbar that enables you to browse through an active document by field, endnote, footnote, etc. Go To command and Find functions are also part of this toolbar.

Ruler: A bar containing a scale that indicates tabs, paragraph indents, and margins in the paragraph where the insertion point (cursor) is located.

Split box: Light gray bar at the top of the vertical scroll bar that you can drag down to split a window into two different views of the same document.

ScreenTips: Screentips show the name of the command button displayed in ribbon. Screentips appear as soon as you position the mouse pointer on the toolbar button.

Ribbon: Ribbon is displayed just below the title bar. In Ribbon, the Commands are organized in logical groups, which are collected together under tabs. You can hide the Ribbon by double-clicking the active tab. Different types of Tabs are available in Word 2010.

Displaying or Hiding Rulers

Word 2010 gives you the flexibility to hide or display ruler according to your working needs.

Notes:

The Status bar, seen at the bottom of the Word 2010 window shows information about the active document or the work you are processing.

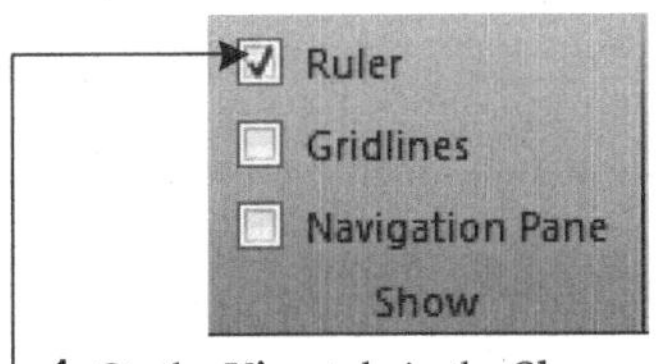

1. On the **View** tab, in the **Show** group, select the **Ruler** check box.

The Status Bar

The Status bar is seen at the bottom of the Word 2010 document.

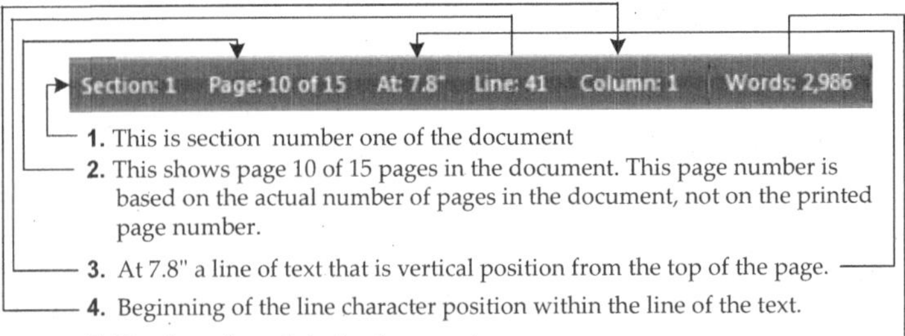

1. This is section number one of the document
2. This shows page 10 of 15 pages in the document. This page number is based on the actual number of pages in the document, not on the printed page number.
3. At 7.8" a line of text that is vertical position from the top of the page.
4. Beginning of the line character position within the line of the text.
5. Number of words in the document.

Notes:

Pointer Shapes

I *Type, select text, or reposition the insertion point.*

Choose commands, such as Ribbon tabs, scrollbar and ruler, etc.

Mouse Terminology

The mouse terminology used in Word 2010.

Point: Position the mouse pointer on an item.

Single Click: If you Single-click the mouse, Word 2010 moves the cursor wherever you click.

Double-click: If you Double-click the mouse, Word 2010 selects a word.

Drag: Point to an item (i.e. any word or paragraph). Press and hold the left mouse button as you move the mouse to a new location, and then release the mouse button.

Triple-click: If you Triple-click the mouse, Word 2010 selects the entire paragraph where you clicked the mouse.

Shapes of the Mouse Pointer

The mouse pointer changes shape, depending on what you are pointing to or the task you are performing. When you click the text, the pointer looks like an I-beam and if you point to a menu or toolbar, the pointer becomes a left pointing arrow.

Notes:

Select lines, paragraphs, or double click the entire paragraph.

Drag the selection to a new location where you "drop," or insert it by releasing the mouse button.

Drag to resize a window, frame, graphics, or embedded object or picture vertically or horizontally.

Using Undo and Redo command

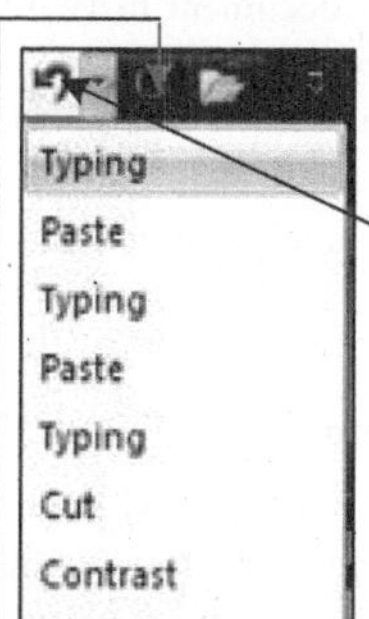

1. When you click the **Undo** button, the deleted sentence reappears. Clicking the Undo button reverses the last command or deletes the last entry you typed.

   Click the down-pointing arrow at the right side of the Undo button and a drop-down list displays containing changes made to the document.

2. Clicking the **Redo** button deletes the selected sentence. If you click the Undo button and then decide you do not want to reverse the original action, click the Redo button.

Moving around in a Document

Scroll through a document

You can scroll through a document by using the mouse or the keyboard. If you split the document window, you can display two different parts of a document.

To	Do this
Scroll up one line	Click the up scroll arrow
Scroll down one line	Click the down scroll arrow
Scroll up one screen	Click above the scroll box
Scroll down one screen	Click below the scroll box
Scroll to a specific page	Drag the scroll box
Scroll left	Click the left scroll arrow
Scroll right	Click the right scroll arrow
Scroll left, beyond the margin, in normal view	Hold down **Shift** key and click the left scroll arrow.

For a quick way to scroll up or down one page, click Select Browse Object on the vertical scroll bar and then click the desired option.

Notes:

In Word Options dialog box, click Display. ***Always show these formatting marks on the screen*** *options, you can display or hide all nonprinting characters such as paragraph marks, tab characters and spaces.*

To restore the deleted text, click ***Quick Access toolbar****, click the Undo button. Or press* ***Ctrl + Z*** *keys together.*

Typing Text

When you open a new document in Word 2010, the insertion point is at the top left corner of the screen. You can start typing in this document. You can make changes at any time by editing the document.

1. Position the insertion point where you want to begin typing.
2. Type the text.

Starting a New Line

Word 2010 automatically wraps text to the next line when the typed text reaches the end of the right margin.

1. Position the insertion point where you want to start the new line and then press **Shift + Enter** keys together.
2. Word inserts a line break character and moves the insertion point to the beginning of the next line.
3. To see the line breaks, click the **Show/Hide** command on the paragraph group of **Home** tab.

Applying Correction in the Typed Text

To correct simple typing mistakes, press Backspace or Del keys. To delete more characters, first select the text you want to delete and then press the **Backspace** or **Del** key. For deleting text and graphics do the following.

To select	Press
Selected text	Press **Backspace** or **Del** key.
Characters before the insertion point	Press **Backspace** key
Characters after the Insertion point	Press **Del** key
A word after the insertion point	**Ctrl + Del** key
A word before the insertion point	**Ctrl + Backspace**

Notes:

While you are in Extend Selection mode, the word appears on the status bar at the bottom of the screen.

Selecting Text

Word 2010 works on the principle select, then do. If you want to delete a word in the text or move a sentence, you must first select what you want to change and then change. You can also use a mouse or a keyboard to select the text.

Selecting Text with a Mouse

You can select a piece of text, or a single character or an entire document. You can also combine mouse and keyboard selection techniques.

If the pointer touches the edge of the window as you are dragging, the window scrolls in that direction if more text exists.

1. Click and hold the left mouse button at the beginning of the text you want to select.
2. Drag the pointer in any direction across the text you want to select.

Selecting text using mouse

Text to select	Mouse Action
A word	Double-click the word.
A line	Click selection bar (blank margin to left of a line of text).
Multiple lines	Click selection bar and drag up or down till the end of lines.
A paragraph	Double-click selection bar.
Document	Press **Ctrl** key and click in selection bar.
Rectangular block or column (not within a table)	Click the top left of the column to be selected and then hold **Alt** key while you drag to select the text.

Selecting Text with a Keyboard

The method for selecting text is to hold down the key as you move the insertion point. You can select text by using in combination with any move key. Some of these key combinations are listed below.

To select	Press
A word	**Shift + Ctrl** + ← or → arrow key
To the beginning of a line	**Shift + Home**
To the end of a line	**Shift + End**
To the end of a paragraph	**Ctrl + Shift** + ↓
To the beginning of a paragraph	**Ctrl + Shift** + ↑
One line at a time	**Shift** + ↑ or **Shift** + ↓
To the beginning of a document	**Shift + Ctrl + Home**
To the end of a document	**Shift + Ctrl + End**

Displaying Different Views of a Document

The type of work that you do will help you to determine the best screen view as per your needs. There are different views available in Word 2010.

Print Layout View

This is the default view. Print Layout view is used to see how text, graphics and other elements such as header, footer, etc. will look on the printed output. This view is useful for editing headers and footers, for adjusting margins and for working with columns and drawing objects.

Notes:

Full Screen Reading: *Full screen view displays as much of the typed area of the document as will fit on the screen at a size that is comfortable for reading. In this view, the Ribbon is replaced by a single toolbar at the top of the screen. You can print the document, highlight text and write comments.*

1. Click the **View** tab, in the Document views group and click **Print Layout** command. Alternatively, click on the status bar icon.

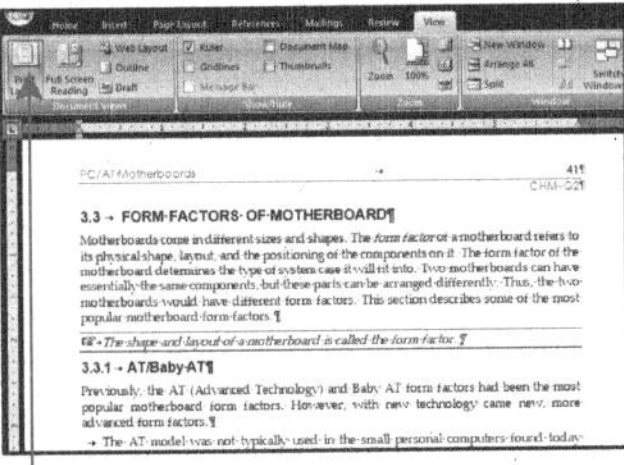

Print Layout view

Viewing Full Reading and Other Options

Highlight text in Full screen view

Previous screen

Jump to a page

View Options

Next Screen

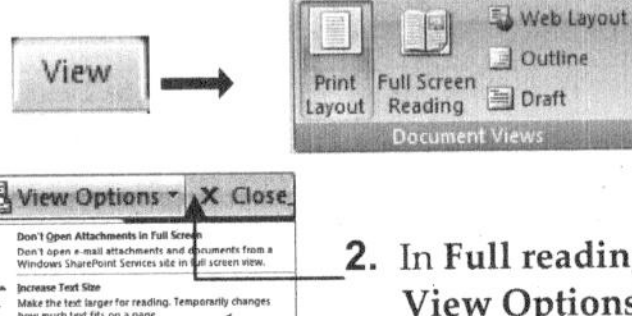

1. Click the **View** tab, in the **Document Views** group and click **Full Screen Reading** command.
2. In **Full reading** screen, click the **View Options**, a drop-down menu appears.
3. You can make the text larger or smaller for reading by clicking **Increase Text Size** or **Decrease Text Size**. This will temporarily change as to how text fits on a page. It does not affect the original document.
4. You can read one page at a time by clicking **Show one page**, or you can read two pages at a time by clicking **Show Two pages**.

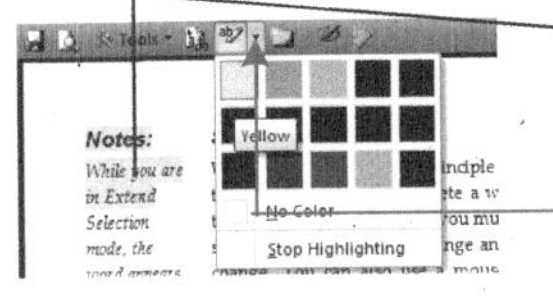

The selected text gets highlighted

5. You can highlight text in the **Print Preview**. Choose **Text highlight color** in the top of the Print Preview window.

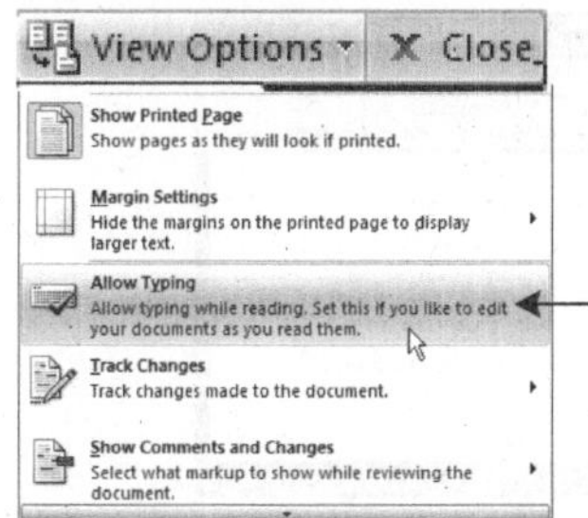

6. While reading in full screen view, you can edit document by clicking **Allow Typing**.
7. To go to the previous screen or to the next screen, click jump to a screen at the top of the title bar in the full screen view.
8. To exit Full Screen Reading view, click the **Close** command or **Esc** key.

Notes:

Web Layout View: *While creating a web page in Word 2010, you should work in Web Layout view. In Web Layout view, you can see that background text is wrapped to fit the window.*

Web Layout view

1. Click the **View** tab, in the **Document Views** group and click **Web Layout** view command. Alternatively click from the status bar icons.

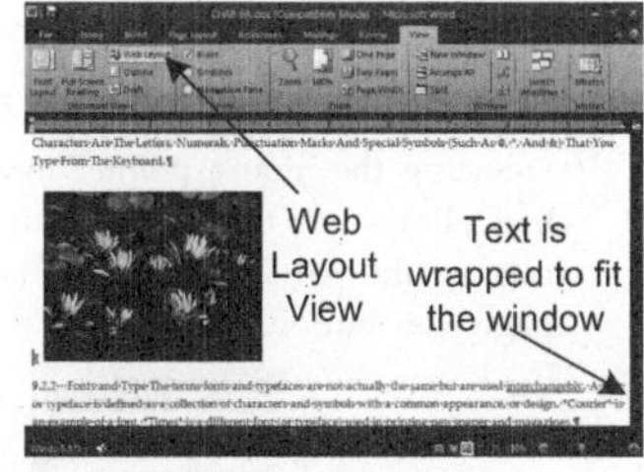

In the ***Outline View****, you can collapse a document to see only the main headings or expand it to see the entire document. In this view it is easy to scroll or move text to a longer distance or to change the hierarchy of topics.*

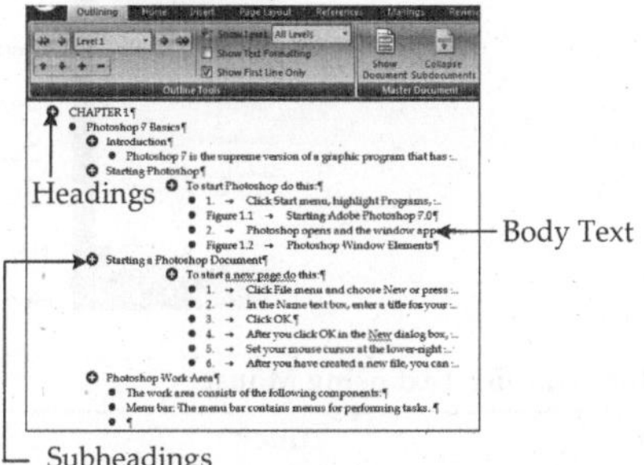

1. Click the **View** tab, in the **Document Views** group and click **Outline view** command. Alternatively click from the status bar icons.
2. In the outline view, the outlining tabs appear. Note that (+) or ( ) sign appears to the left of each heading.
3. A plus sign (+) indicates that subheading or paragraphs of the body text are associated with the heading.
4. A minus sign (–) indicates that no headings or paragraphs are beneath the heading.

Notes:

Document Map: *Displays a list of headings and helps you navigate through large documents.*

The location of the scroll box in the vertical scroll bar shows the screen's location relative to the entire document's length and width.

To move the insertion point using the mouse:

1. Using the scroll bars, scroll until you reach the location you want the text to be inserted.

2. Click the location where you want to position the insertion point.

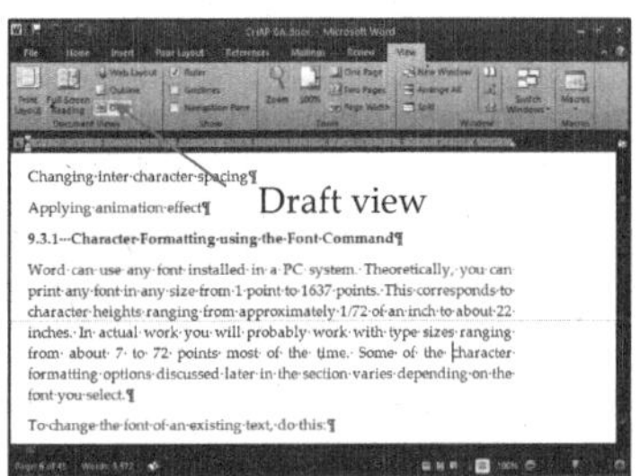

Draft View: It is the best view for most of your typing and editing. In this view, you can see character and paragraph formatting as the page will be printed. Line and page breaks, tab stops and alignments are accurate. The area outside the text body the area containing headers, footers, footnotes, page numbers, margin spacing, etc. do not appear. Images are also not shown in Draft view.

Moving or Scrolling with a Mouse

Directing the mouse pointer in the horizontal and vertical scroll bars allows you to scroll a document easily. Below the screen you can see the parts of the scroll bars, including the scroll box and page view buttons.

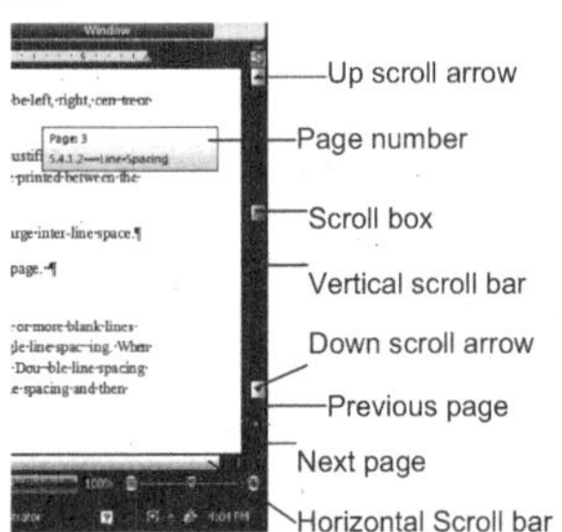

Methods for Scrolling Text using Mouse

To move	Click
One line up or down	Click once up or down scroll arrow for one line up or down.
One screen up or down	Click gray area above or below the scroll box in the vertical scroll bar.
One page up or down	Click next or previous page buttons.
Large vertical moves	Click drag vertical scroll box to a new location in the vertical scroll bar.
Horizontally	Click right or left scroll arrow and drag.

Moving or Scrolling with the keyboard

Using the keyboard you can also move or scroll in a document.

To move	Press
One character left	← arrow key
One character right	→ arrow key
One line up	↑ arrow key
One line down	↓ arrow key
One word to the left	**Ctrl** + ← keys
One word to the right	**Ctrl** + → keys
To the end of a line	**End**
To the beginning of a line	**Home**
One paragraph up	**Ctrl** + ↑
One paragraph down	**Ctrl** + ↓
Up one window	**Pgup** key
Down one window	**PgDn** key
To the top of the next page	**Ctrl + PgDn**
To the top of previous page	**Ctrl + PgUp**

Notes:

*You can press **Ctrl +G** or double-click Page on the status bar to display the **Go To tab** of the **Find and Replace** dialog box.*

Using Go To Command

You can move quickly to a location in a document using the Go To command.

1. Click the **Home** tab and choose **Editing** command. A drop-down menu appears. Click the **Find** drop-down and the select **Go To… .**

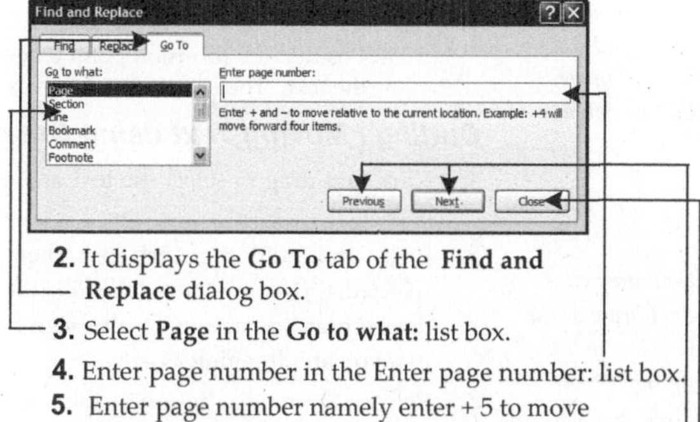

2. It displays the **Go To** tab of the **Find and Replace** dialog box.
3. Select **Page** in the **Go to what:** list box.
4. Enter page number in the Enter page number: list box.
5. Enter page number namely enter + 5 to move forward 5 pages and -5 to move back 5 pages.
6. Enter page number namely enter + 5 to move forward 5 pages and -5 to move back 5 pages.
7. Click **Previous** button to go to the previous of the document. Or click **Next** button to go the next of the document.
8. Click **Close** or press **Esc** key to close the Find and Replace dialog box.

The Go To features is especially helpful when working with long documents. It enables you to search quickly through a document and locates specific information.

Notes:

*The keyboard shortcut for cutting selected text is **Ctrl + X***

*Word 2010 Drag and Drop feature must be turned on in order to copy text using the drag and drop method. To turn it on, Click **File** menu, then click **Options**. In Word Options dialog box, click the Advanced options in the left pane. Click Allow text to be dragged and dropped under Editing options.*

You must click the I-beam at the new location for typing. If you scroll to a new location and leave the insertion point at the old location, your typing or editing appears at the old location.

Cutting / Moving Text

With the Cut, Copy and Paste buttons in the Clipboard group in the Home tab, you can move or copy many words, sentences, or entire sections of text or graphics to other locations in a document. You can cut and paste text or copy and paste text within the same document.

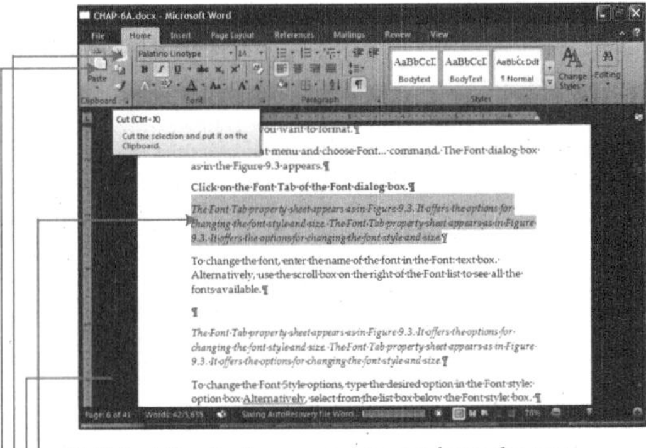

1. Select the text you want to cut from the text.
2. Click the **Cut** button in the **Clipboard** group in the **Home** tab.

   Clicking the **Cut** button places the text in a special location within Word called the clipboard.
3. Then, click the **Paste** button in the **Clipboard** group in the **Home** tab.
4. Position the insertion point where you want to paste the text. The selected text moves into new location.

Cutting / Moving Text using Drag and Drop

1. Click and drag to select the text and graphics you want to copy.
2. Press and hold the **Ctrl** key, then click and drag the selected text to the new location (the insertion point will have a gray square with a plus sign (+) inside it to indicate that you are dragging a copy.
3. Release the mouse button at the spot where you want the copied information to appear.

Cutting / Moving Text using Pop-up Menu

1. Click and drag to select the text and graphics you want to **Cut**.
2. Right-click and choose **Cut**. The selected portion gets removed. Select the new location where you want to paste.
3. Right click and choose **Paste** option.

Notes:

*The keyboard shortcut for copying selected text is **Ctrl** + C.*

Copying Text

Use the **Copy** command to copy text and graphics and place them elsewhere in the document, or in a different document. Because it is such a common word processing task, there are several ways to copy information.

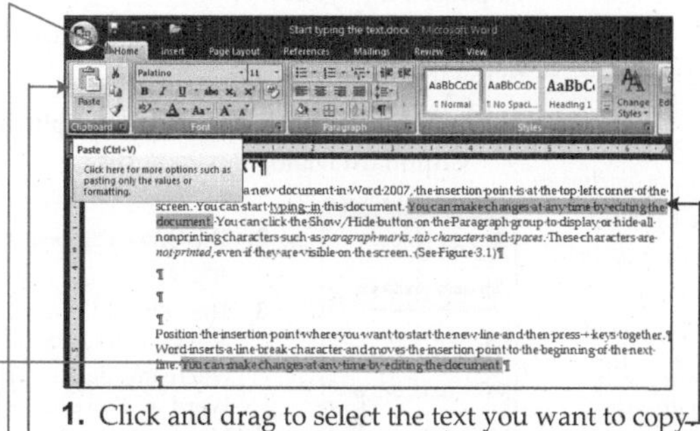

Copied information is placed on the Clipboard, where it remains until something new is copied or cut over it. (The Clipboard contents exist in main memory, and so it is not saved when the system is shut down)

1. Click and drag to select the text you want to copy.
2. Click the **Copy** button on the **Clipboard** group of **Home** tab.
3. Click the **Paste** button on the **Clipboard** group of **Home** tab.
4. From above selected portion gets copied, and then Paste it to the new location.

Copying Text using Drag and Drop

1. Select the text or the graphics you want to copy.
2. Press and hold down Ctrl key, point to the selected text or the graphics, and then press and hold down the left mouse button while you drag the dotted insertion point to the new location.

Copying Text using Pop-up menu

1. Click and drag to select the text and graphics you want to Copy.
2. Right-click and choose **Copy**. The selected portion gets copied. Select the new location where you want to **paste**.
3. Right click and choose **Paste** option.

Make sure you really want to delete an item from the Office Clipboard because after you delete it, you can not retrieve it.

Using the Clipboard Task pane

When you cut or copy data, Windows stores it in a special part of memory called the Clipboard. This Windows Clipboard can only hold one item at time, So Office 2010 comes with its own Clipboard called the Office Clipboard, which can store up to 24 items at one time.

Notes:

The Office Clipboard works only with Office 2010 programs (such as Word, Excel, PowerPoint, Access and Outlook). To store data on the Office Clipboard, you just need to use the Cut or Copy command, and Office 2010 automatically stores your data on the Office Clipboard.

Viewing and Pasting Items from the Office Clipboard

After you use the Cut or Coy command at least once, your data gets stored on the Office Clipboard. You can view the Clipboard and choose which data you want to paste from the Clipboard into your file.

To view the Office Clipboard and paste item from it do the following steps:

1. Click the **Home** tab in the **Clipboard** group, click the **Clipboard** Dialog Box Launcher.

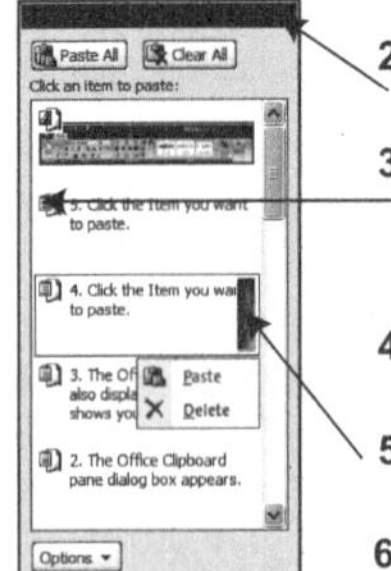

2. The Office Clipboard pane dialog box appears.
3. The Office Clipboard also displays an icon that shows you the program where the data came from, such as Word or PowerPoint.
4. Move the cursor to where you want to paste an item from the Office Clipboard.
5. Select the item, a drop-down list appears. Click the Paste.
6. It pasted your chosen item into the file.
7. Click the **Close** box of the Office Clipboard.

Deleting items from the MS Office Clipboard

You can add up to 24 items to the Office Clipboard. The moment you add a 25th item, Office 2010 deletes the oldest item from the Clipboard to make new cut or copied item.

If you click the Clear All button, you can delete every item currently stored on the Office Clipboard.

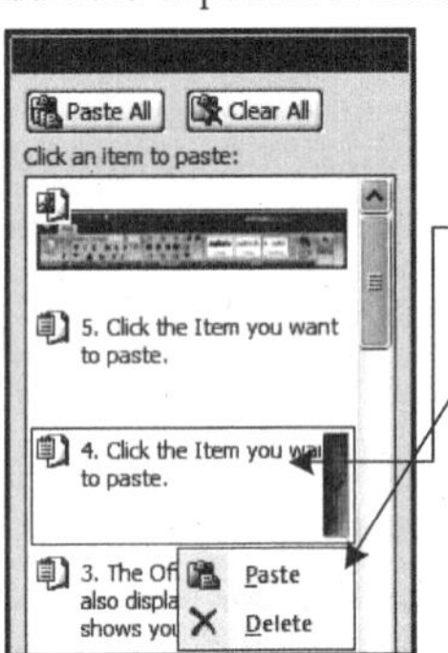

1. Move the mouse pointer over an item on the Office Clipboard. A downward pointing arrow appears to the right.
2. A pop-up menu appears.
3. Click Delete.
4. It deletes your chosen item.

Copied information is placed on the Clipboard, where it remains until something new is copied or cut over it. (The Clipboard contents exist in main memory, and so it is not saved when the system is shut down)

Keyboards Shortcuts for moving and Copying Text or Graphics

Action	Key combination
Copy the selected text or the graphics to the Clipboard	**Ctrl + C** keys pressed together.
Move the selected text or the graphics to the Clipboard	**Ctrl + X** or **Shift + Del** keys pressed together
Paste Clipboard contents into a document	**Ctrl + V**, or **Shift + Ins** keys pressed together.
Move a paragraph Up	**Alt + Shift + ↑** arrow keys pressed together

Notes:

*The keyboard shortcut for searching the word is **Ctrl +F** keys together.*

Using Find and Replace

Word 2010 has a very powerful, Find and Replace feature which greatly simplifies editing of text. The Editing command is in Home tab for Finding and Replacing text. You can use this command to search for text, footnotes, graphics, etc. To replace these items, you can then use the Replace command.

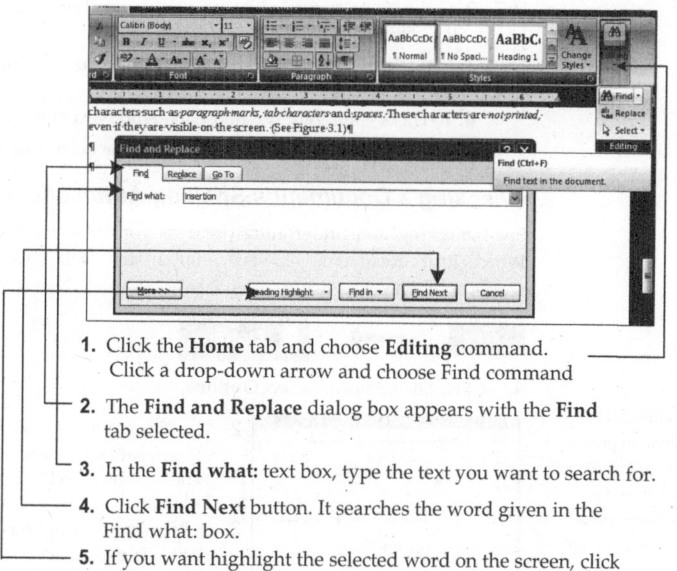

1. Click the **Home** tab and choose **Editing** command. Click a drop-down arrow and choose Find command
2. The **Find and Replace** dialog box appears with the **Find** tab selected.
3. In the **Find what:** text box, type the text you want to search for.
4. Click **Find Next** button. It searches the word given in the Find what: box.
5. If you want highlight the selected word on the screen, click **Reading highlight** down arrow and click Highlight All. The selected word gets highlighted in the document.
6. To remove the highlighted word, select **Clear** highlighting. It removes the selected word.

Replacing Text

Notes:

*If you want to confirm each change, click **Find Next**. When Word finds an occurrence of the text, click the **Replace** button to change the text.*

You can replace searched text automatically using replacing text facility in Word 2010. For example replacing incorrect word *dcument* by *document*.

1. Click the **Home** tab and choose **Editing** command. Click a drop-down arrow and choose **Replace** command or press **Ctrl + H** keys together. The **Find and Replace** dialog box appears with the **Replace** tab selected.

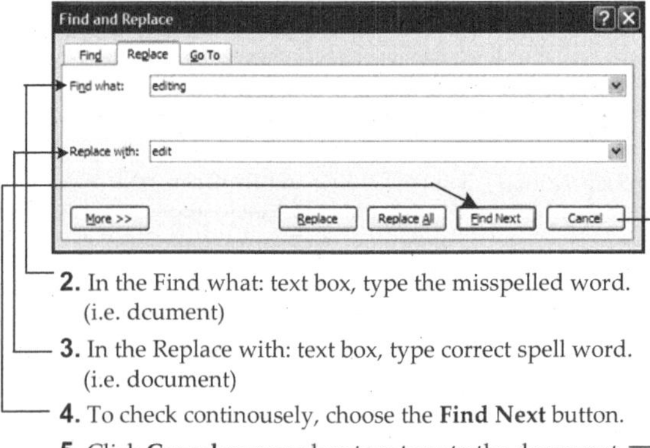

2. In the Find what: text box, type the misspelled word. (i.e. dcument)
3. In the Replace with: text box, type correct spell word. (i.e. document)
4. To check continousely, choose the **Find Next** button.
5. Click **Cancel** or press key to return to the document.

Checking a Document's Spelling Automatically

Spell checking and underlining occur as you type the text in Word 2010 document. However, automatic spell checking works only when this feature is enabled.

1. Click **File** menu and select **Options**.

If you want to search for or replace text in only a portion of a document, then select the portion of the text and then follow the general instructions for finding or replacing text.

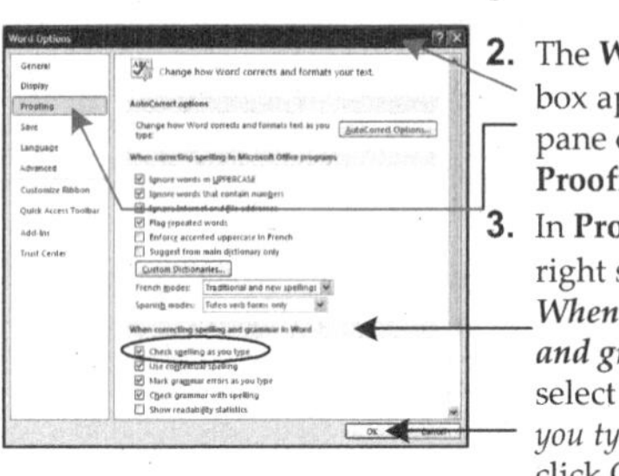

2. The **Word Options** dialog box appears. In the left side pane options, select **Proofing**.
3. In **Proofing** page options, right side pane, under ***When correcting spelling and grammar in Word,*** select *Check spelling as you type* check box. Then click OK.

Notes:

The shortcut key to start a Spelling & Grammar is F7.

Using Spelling Checker

Spelling checker is a flexible and powerful tool that will automatically check spellings in a paragraph or the entire document. When automatic spell checking is on, Word 2010 uses a red wavy line to underline words it thinks are not spelled correctly, so that you can spot them easily on the screen.

1. Select the word or select a document that you want to check for spelling. If you select nothing, Word 2010 checks the entire document.

The wavy red line under misspelled words does not print.

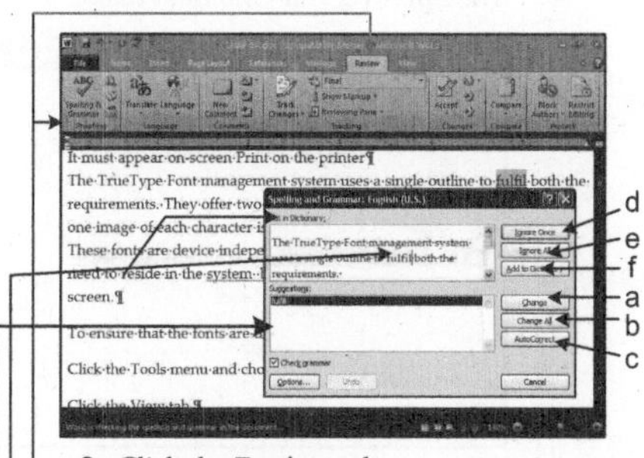

2. Click the **Review** tab.
3. In **Proofing** command group. Click the **Spelling & Grammar** icon.
4. Word 2010 scrolls through your document and selects the misspelled word is highlighted in the text and displayed in the **Not in Dictionary:** box
5. Select the correct word from the **Suggestions:** list and then choose any one from the following list:

When Word 2010 spelling checker detects double words, (say the the) then the Not in Dictionary: box changes to the Repeated Word: box, and the repeated word is highlighted in red. To delete the repeated word, click the Delete button.

   a. Click the Change button to change the word.
   b. Click Change All to change all occurrences of the misspelled words in the document.
   c. Click the correctly spelled word in the Suggestions: list and click the AutoCorrect button to automatically correct the identical misspelling when you type it in future.
   d. Click Ignore Once to leave the word as it is.
   e. Click Ignore All to ignore all occurrences of the word in the document.
   f. Click the Add to Dictionary button to add this word to the Word 2010 dictionary. The selected word will be added to the dictionary.

6. Word will now continue searching misspelled word. Click **Cancel** to stop the spell checking if so desired. Or
7. Click the **Close** button.

Notes:

*The Spelling and Grammar dialog box has the **O**ptions... button. Clicking this button opens up the Word Options with Proofing page options dialog box appears. In this page, you can select different options to customize the spell checking operations.*

Using Grammar Check

The grammar checker evaluates a document for grammatical errors. Word 2010 uses collections of rules while reading a document.

1. Word 2010 may underline one or more words with a green wavy line to highlight some possible grammar errors.
2. Click the **Review** tab and choose **Proofing** command. Or
3. Click the **Spelling & Grammar** icon or press **F7** key.
4. The **Spelling and Grammar** dialog box appears on the screen.

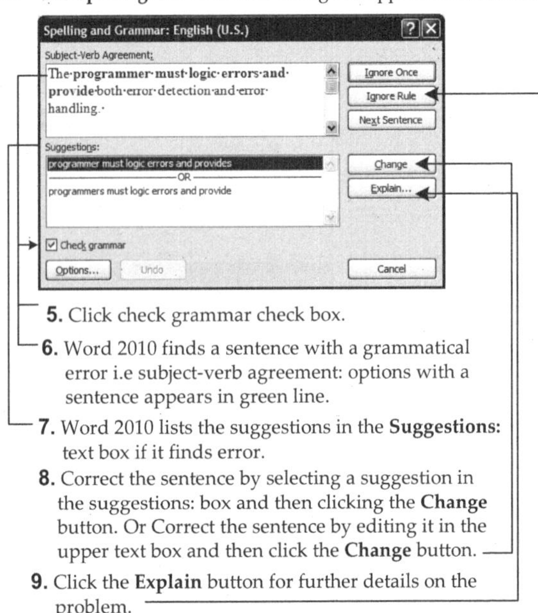

5. Click check grammar check box.
6. Word 2010 finds a sentence with a grammatical error i.e subject-verb agreement: options with a sentence appears in green line.
7. Word 2010 lists the suggestions in the **Suggestions:** text box if it finds error.
8. Correct the sentence by selecting a suggestion in the suggestions: box and then clicking the **Change** button. Or Correct the sentence by editing it in the upper text box and then click the **Change** button.
9. Click the **Explain** button for further details on the problem.
10. If Word 2010 finds a word that is not really misspelled, click the Ignore Once button. Word will ignore the word and continue checking the rest of the document.
11. If you want Word 2010 to ignore a grammatical problem it might find as it checks the rest of the document, click the **Ignore Rule** button.

*The Thesaurus task pane appears when you press **Shift + F7** keys together from keyboard.*

Setting Options for Checking Spelling

The Spelling and Grammar dialog box has the **O**ptions... button. Clicking this button opens up the Word Options with Proofing page options dialog box appears. In this page, you can select different options to customize the spell checking operations.

Notes:

If you want Word 2010 to check your document's spelling but not the grammar, click to uncheck the Spelling & Grammar dialog box's option check grammar.

1. In the Spelling and Grammar dialog box click **Options...** button. **Word Options** dialog box appears.
2. Various options available are as follows:

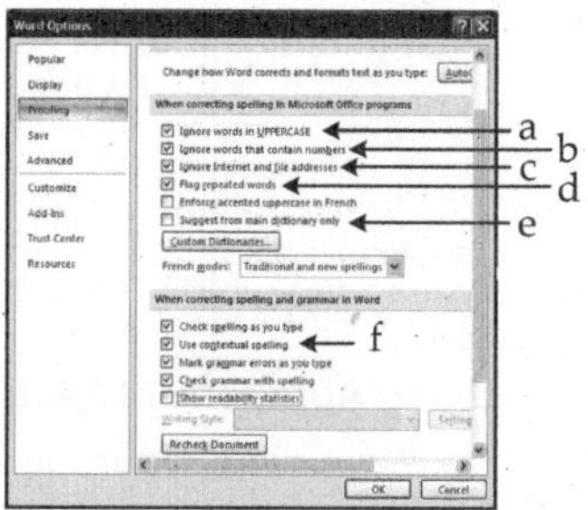

a. **Ignore words in UPPERCASE**– Ignores words in all upper case letters namely proper nouns.

b. **Ignore words that contain numbers**—Ignores words that include numbers.

c. **Ignore Internet and file addresses**—Ignores Internet addresses and file names.

d. **Flag repeated words**—Ignores the repeated words in the document.

e. **Suggest from main dictionary only**—Suggestions will come from the Main dictionary only, not from any open custom dictionaries.

f. **Use Contextual spelling**—It suggest related spelling.

You can turn off Word 2010 automatic spelling checker by changing your Word Options dialog box. When correcting spelling and grammar in Word to uncheck, Check spelling as you type and Mark grammar errors options.

Using Thesaurus

Thesaurus is a Word 2010 electronic database that contains English words with similar meaning. It defines selected words and offers alternative terms. Thesaurus is one of a set of Research services provided by Word 2010.

1. Select the word for which you want to locate a synonym (similar meaning word).
2. Click the **Review** tab and choose **Proofing** command. Click the **Thesaurus** button or press **Shift +F7** keys together.

✍ ***After you display the Grammar Settings dialog box and modify various settings, you may decide to restore the settings to their default states. To do this, click Reset All.***

Notes:

Look up words in the Thesaurus

1. Using the Research feature, you can look up synonyms (different words with the same meaning) and antonyms (words with the opposite meaning) in the thesaurus.

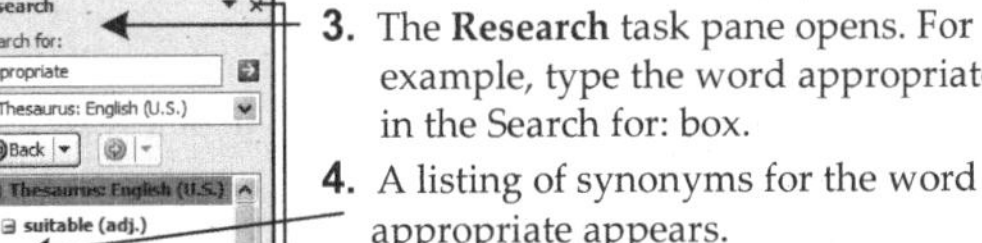

3. The **Research** task pane opens. For example, type the word appropriate in the Search for: box.
4. A listing of synonyms for the word appropriate appears.
5. For example, select the word suitable. Click the arrow next to suitable and then click **Insert**.
6. The word suitable replaces appropriate in the document.
7. Close the **Research** task pane.

Using Autocorrect Feature

The AutoCorrect feature in Word 2010 recognizes typing mistakes and automatically corrects them. AutoCorrect feature can also be used to type long words from an abbreviation automatically. For example, to automatically type the phrase *not applicable*, when you type the abbreviation *na*.

1. Click the **File** menu and then click **Options**.

Rename a text entry in the AutoCorrect list

*1. On the **AutoCorrect** tab, make sure the **Replace text as you type** check box is selected.*

*2. In the list under the **Replace** box, click the entry.*

*3. Click **Delete**.*

*4. Type a new name in the **Replace** box.*

*5. Click **Add**.*

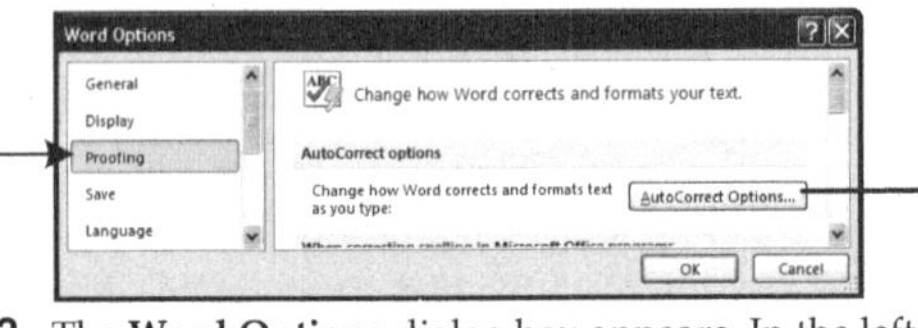

2. The **Word Options** dialog box appears. In the left side pane options, select Proofing.
3. In **Proofing** page options, right side pane, under AutoCorrect options, click **AutoCorrect Options...** .

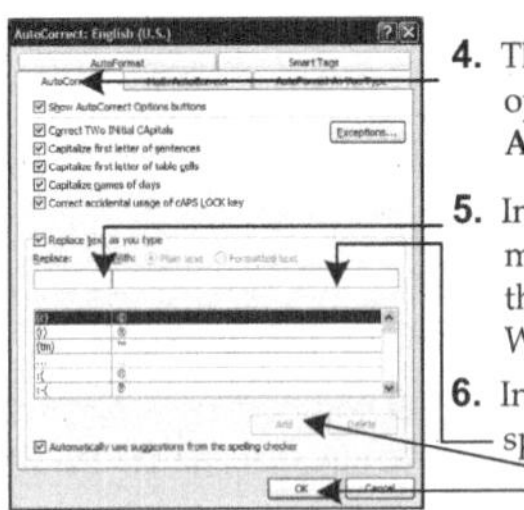

4. The **AutoCorrect** dialog box opens, displaying with **AutoCorrect** tab.
5. In the **Replace:** text box, type misspelled words or abbreviations that you wish to get corrected by Word 2010 automatically.
6. In the **With:** text box, type the correct spelling of the word or phrase.
7. Click **Add** to add these selected entries to the list of AutoCorrect list.
8. Click OK.

Word 2010 will insert the phrase and then return(s) into the **With:** text box.

Notes:

The Word Count feature is useful when creating reports that require a minimum or maximum number of words or lines.

Customize AutoCorrect

AutoCorrect feature works automatically as you type, but offers several options that you can change to suite your working style and preferences.

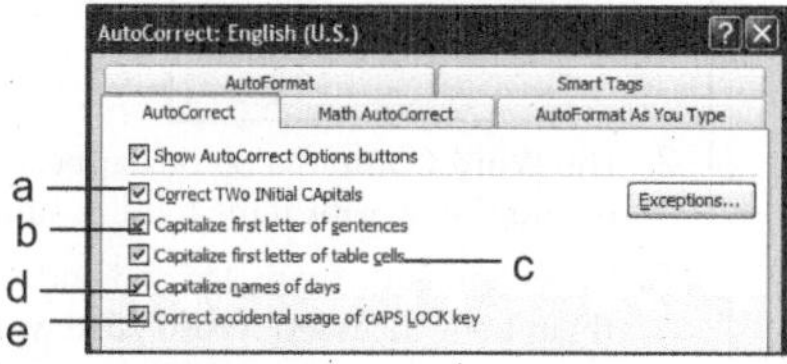

The AutoCorrect options are discussed:

Option	Result	Example
a. Correct TWo INitial CApitals	Changes the second of two capital letters at the beginning of a word to lowercase	"THe" becomes "The".
b. Capitalize first letter of sentences	Changes the first letter of a word beginning a sentence to uppercase	"now is the time…" becomes "Now is the time…".
c. Capitalize first letter of table cells	Changes the first letter of cells in a table to uppercase	Building blocks becomes "Building blocks".
d. Capitalize names of days	Capitalizes the first letter of names of days of the week	"Monday" becomes "Monday".
e. Correct accidental usage of cAPS LOCK key	Corrects the case of text accidentally typed while the Caps Lock key is on (automatically turns off the Caps Lock key after the first correction)	"wORD FOR wINDOWS" becomes "Word for Windows".
f. Replace text as you type	Replaces misspelled words with correct spellings, based on the list of entries maintained by AutoCorrect	"the" becomes "the".

Using Word Count Command

The Word Count command totals the number of *pages, words, characters paragraphs* and *lines* in a document. You can also find the word count in the status bar at the bottom of the window.

1. Click the **Review** tab and choose **Proofing** command. Click the **Word Count** button.

Notes:

***Serif fonts:** Serif fonts have fine lines that finish off the main strokes-for example, at the bottom of a capital T or at the end of the T's crossbar.*

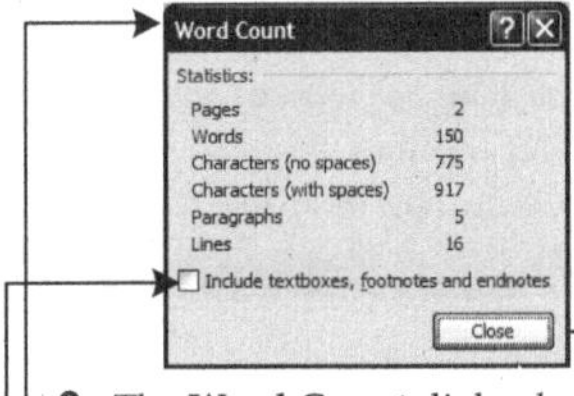

2. The **Word Count** dialog box appears. Word 2010 would then perform the totaling and show the results.
3. Choose Include footnotes and endnotes if you wish them to be included. Word 2010 would do the total again and show the result.
4. Click the **Close** button.

Text Formatting

Formatting is the process of specifying how a document should appear when printed. Formatting can be divided into two categories. These are Character formatting and Paragraph formatting.

***Sans Serif:** The "finishing strokes" called serifs are absent in sans serif fonts (T)*

Characters formatting

Word 2010 enables the under mentioned character formatting options:

a. Font, font style and font size changes
b. Underline options, and colour applications
c. Applying font effects namely italics, bold, etc.
d. Changing inter character spacing

Character formatting using Font Dialog box

By formatting the font, you can change the typeface, appearance (such as bold or italic), size, color and other aspects of the type in documents.

*The **shortcut** key to increase font size, press **Ctrl +Shift** + > keys together.*

*To decrease font size, press **Ctrl + Shift** + < keys together.*

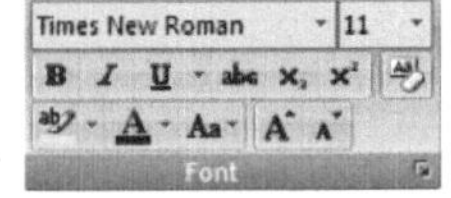

1. Select the text where you want to format.
2. Click the **Home** tab of **Font** group. Click **Font** launcher. The **Font** dialog box appears.

Fonts and Typefaces: A font or typeface is defined as a collection of characters and symbols with a common appearance or design. Courier is an example of a font. A time is a different font (or typeface) which is used in printing newspaper.

Notes:

Font Families

A collection of all of the variations of a font is called a font family. For example, the Arial font family. This family includes Arial, Arial Black and Arial Narrow characters.

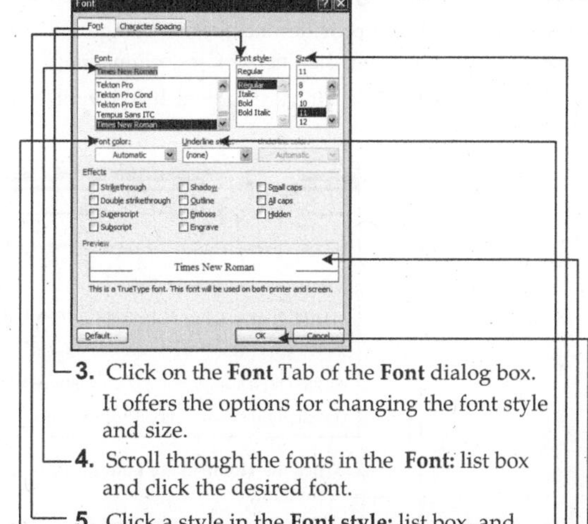

3. Click on the **Font** Tab of the **Font** dialog box. It offers the options for changing the font style and size.
4. Scroll through the fonts in the **Font:** list box and click the desired font.
5. Click a style in the **Font style:** list box, and choose desired style for the text.
6. Click a size in the **Size:** list box. Or type the desired point size in the **Size:** text box.
7. Click the **Font color:** drop-down arrow to choose the desired font color.
8. Click the **Underline style:** drop-down arrow to choose the desired underline color.
9. View a preview of the formatted font in the **Preview** box.
10. After choose the desired setting, click **OK** button.

Character formatting using the Ribbon

To modify character appearance, you can also use the Ribbon command.

Font Sizes

The size of the font is measured in points, and as the point size increases, the size of the letter also increases. One point equals 1/72th of an inch.

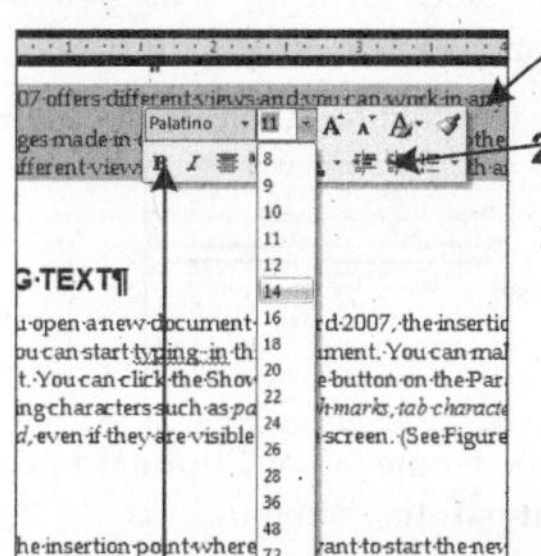

1. Select the text that you want to change the font.
2. After selecting text, a small mini toolbar appears.
3. The drop-down list shows all the available fonts. Use the scroll arrow on the right of the drop down list to scroll throught the list. When you move the cursor over the font you can see the changes in the appearance of text.
4. To make the character *Regular, Bold, Italic* click the corresponding button on the mini toolbar.

Notes:

The keyboard shortcut to Bold the selected text is ***Ctrl + B****.*

Using the Change Case Command

Word provides facilities to change to capital letters of any text by using the Change Case command.

1. Select the text for which you want to change capitalization.

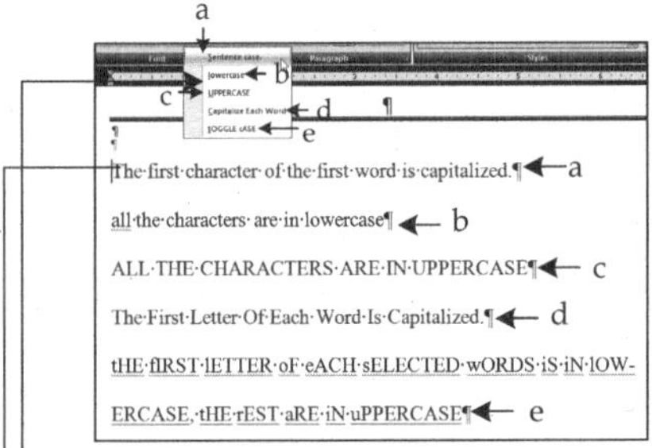

2. Click the **Home** tab of **Font** group. Click **Change Case** command.
3. The options offered by the Change case options are as follows:
   - **a.** Sentence case: The first character of the first word is capitalized.
   - **b.** lower case : All the characters are in lowercase.
   - **c.** UPPER CASE : All the characters are in upper-case.
   - **d.** Capitalize Each Word : The first letter of each word is capitalized.
   - **e.** tOGGLE cASE : The first letter of each selected word is in lowercase, the rest are in uppercase.

To remove character formatting

1. Select the character whose formatting you wish to remove.

2. Press ***Ctrl + Spacebar*** *or click* 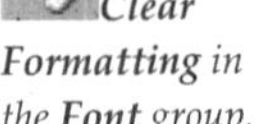 ***Clear Formatting*** *in the* ***Font*** *group.*

Word removes all the formatting applied with a character style.

Copying Character Formatting

Character formatting is very simple. You can use the **Format Painter** on the **Home** tab, such as underlining text while changing its font and font size. For example, you have formatted one block of text, again you may want to format another part of block text, exactly the same.

1. Select the text that has the format you want to copy.

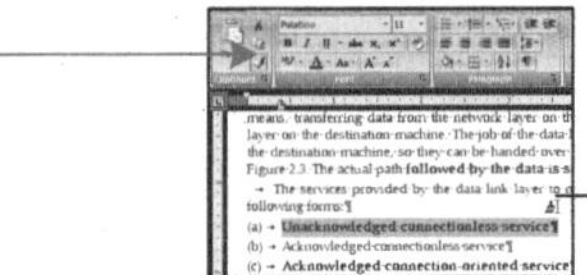

2. Click the **Home** tab of **Clipboard** group. Click the **Format painter** command.
3. When the mouse pointer changes to a paint brush icon with an I-beam, select the text you want to format.

Formatting Paragraphs

A paragraph can take the following characteristics. These are *alignment, Indents, Line spacing and Space before and after the paragraph.*

> **Notes:**
>
> *When you want to create a new line without creating a new paragraph, press **Shift + Enter** keys at the point where you want to create the new line.*

Align Text

The attribute *Alignment* of a paragraph refers to the position of the main document text on the page.

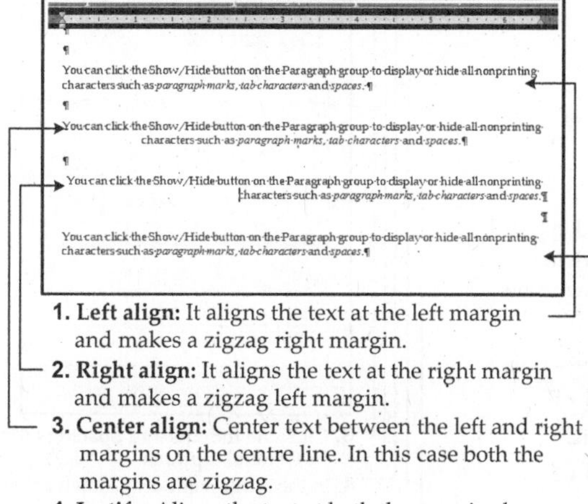

1. **Left align:** It aligns the text at the left margin and makes a zigzag right margin.
2. **Right align:** It aligns the text at the right margin and makes a zigzag left margin.
3. **Center align:** Center text between the left and right margins on the centre line. In this case both the margins are zigzag.
4. **Justify:** Aligns the text at both the margins by increasing the spacing between the words.

> *The shortcut to word underline is **Ctrl + Shift + W**.*

Indents

Indents are the white space added to the margins and thus decreasing the text area for paragraphs. So, when you have a "right margin and you want to add a right indent of 1.0", your text will be printed 2.0" from the right edge of the paper.

Once you change the indent, each new paragraph you start by pressing the **Enter** key will maintain the same indentation setting until you change it.

Line Spacing

Line spacing in a paragraph means the amount of space between the lines.

> *The keyboard shortcut for aligning text are:*
>
> *Left: Ctrl + L*
>
> *Center: Ctrl + E*
>
> *Right: Ctrl + R*
>
> *Justify: Ctrl +J*

Space before and after Paragraphs

There is a spacing box in the Paragraph dialog box which lets you define the amount of white space that Word 2010 must place before and after paragraphs. Space settings can be entered in *points* (pts), *inches* (in), *centimetres* (cm), or *lines* (li). Thus, 12 points would be entered as **12 pt**, 2 lines as **2 li**, etc.

Notes:

*The keyboard shortcut to open the **Font** dialog box is **Ctrl +D** Or **Ctrl + Shift + F**.*

The keyboard shortcuts to change fonts are:

Bold:

Ctrl + B

Italic:

Ctrl + I

Underlined:

Ctrl + U

*To **increase the font size** by one point press **Ctrl +]** keys together.*

*To **decrease the font size** by one point press **Ctrl + [** keys together.*

Using Paragraph Dialog box Launcher

1. Position the insertion point anywhere in the paragraph to be formatted or select multiple paragraphs.
2. Click the **Home** tab of **Paragraph** group. Click **Paragraph launcher** dialog box.

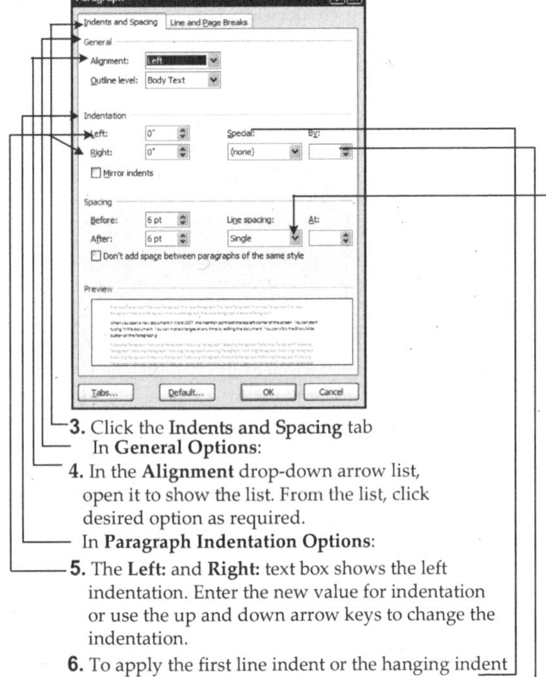

3. Click the **Indents and Spacing** tab
   In **General Options**:
4. In the **Alignment** drop-down arrow list, open it to show the list. From the list, click desired option as required.
   In **Paragraph Indentation Options**:
5. The **Left:** and **Right:** text box shows the left indentation. Enter the new value for indentation or use the up and down arrow keys to change the indentation.
6. To apply the first line indent or the hanging indent use the **Special:** list box. The options are:
   First line Indent: This indents only the first line of the paragraph.
   Hanging Indent: This indents all except first line of the paragraph.
7. In the **By:** text box, enter the indention or use the up and down arrow key to give the required indentation.
   In Spacing Options:
8. Line spacing drop-down has the options for controlling the line spacing.

Notes:

The keyboard shortcut key to indent paragraph

Ctrl + M

Ctrl + Shift + M

Ctrl + T

Ctrl + Shift + T

Ctrl + Q

The shortcut key to change the line spacing

***Ctrl + 1** creates single spaced lines*

***Ctrl + 2** creates double spaced lines*

***Ctrl + 5** creates one and half spaced lines*

***Ctrl + 0** add or remove one line space preceding a paragraph.*

The options are given below:

Single: Default value.

Double: Places a blank line between successive lines.

1.5 Lines: Leaves half the line space between the lines.

At Least: Indicate the minimum space between lines.

Exactly: Give the exact space between lines.

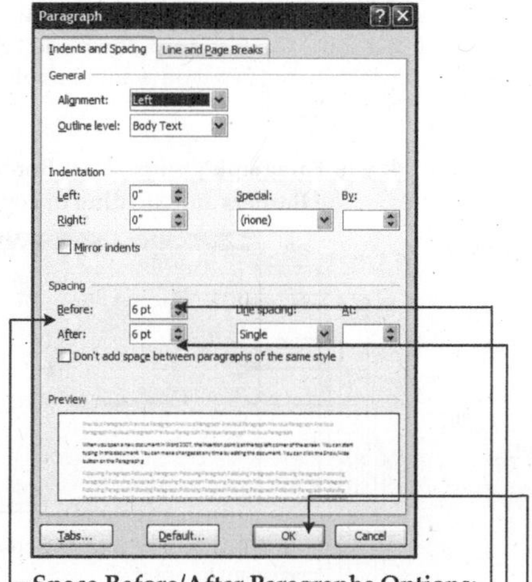

Space Before/After Paragraphs Options:

9. Type the space or select the space required in the **Before:** text box for adding space before the paragraph.
10. Type the space or select the space required in the **After:** text box for adding space before the paragraph.
11. Click **OK** press key to close the Paragraph dialog box.

Applying Borders

A *border* may be a box around a paragraph (or paragraphs) from all sides. It could be a line that sets a paragraph off on one or more sides. A border can include *shading,* which fills a paragraph with a pattern. Boxes and lines can be solid black and shading can be gray or in colour.

If a group of paragraphs is formatted with a box around them and you press Enter key at the end of the last paragraph, your new paragraph falls within the box. However, if you want to create a new paragraph outside the border, then move the insertion point outside the border before you press Enter key.

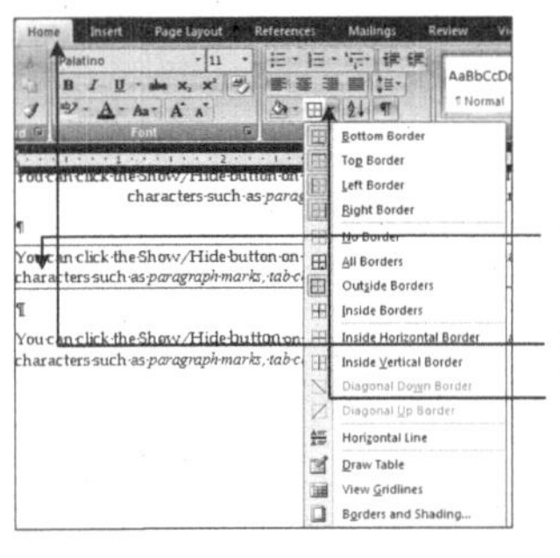

1. Position the insertion point anywhere in the paragraph.
2. Click the **Home** tab.
3. In the Paragraph group, click the borders drop-down and select the desired format you want to apply.

4. In **Paragraph** group, select **Borders and Shading...** option. The **Borders and Shading** dialog box appears.

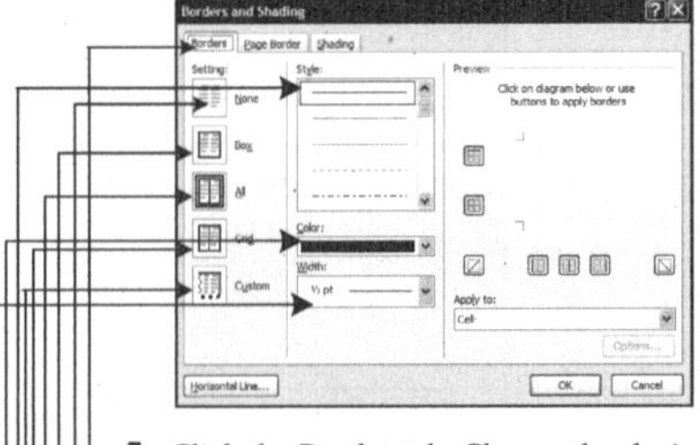

5. Click the Border tab. Choose the desired setting you want to apply.
   a. **None:** No box.
   b. **Box:** A box with identical lines on all four sides, of the selected text or paragraphs.
   c. **Shadow:** A box with a drop shadow on the bottom right corner.
   d. **3-D:** A "Picture frame" box.
   e. Custom Custom design borders on one or more sides of the selected paragraph(s).
6. After selecting the setting, choose the **Style:** in the style scroll list. Style determines the type of line used for border.
7. In the **Color:** dropdown list, choose the colour you want the border to be in. If you choose Auto option, the default colour for text is used.
8. In the **Width:** drop down list specify the width for the border.
9. The **Preview** box shows how the borders are applied to the selected text.
10. In **Apply to:** Choose width you want to apply in the border to a selected text or paragraph.
11. Click **OK** or press **Esc** key.

Notes:

*Double-click the **Format Painter** button if you want to change the format of multiple selections in your document.*

To remove or change a line or border:

1. Select the paragraph(s) for which you want to remove or change boxes or lines.

*2. Click the Borders and Shading option from the **Home** tab of **Paragraph** group.*

3. Select No border option.

Applying Shading

Shading can be applied in different percentages of black or the selected color and in patterns. Percentages of black appear as grays of various intensities. For each shade or pattern, you can select a foreground or background color.

1. Select the text or paragraph/paragraphs you want to apply shading.
2. In **Paragraph** group click **Border** down arrow and choose **Borders and Shading...** . In the **Borders and Shading** dialog box click the **Shading** tab property sheet.

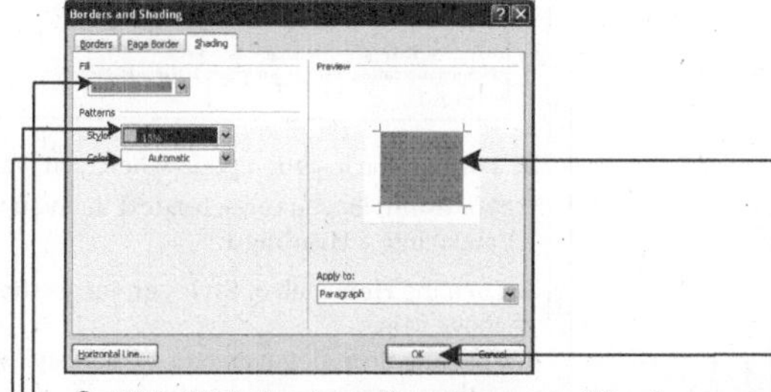

3. **Fill:** Click the drop-down arrow to fill color you want for the shading or click **No color** to remove shading color.
4. **Style:** In this drop down list click the shading style you want to apply "over" this fill color.
5. **Color:** In this drop down list, click a color for the line and dots in the selected shading pattern. The **Color:** box is not visible if you click color in the **Style:** box.
6. Select a color from the Fill list to color a percentage pattern or a pattern background. The effect of the selection option appears in the preview box.
7. Click OK.

Notes:

To remove shading using mouse:

1. Select the paragraph(s) from which you want to remove shading.

2. In Borders and Shading dialog box, select the Shading tab.

3. Choose No fill from the Fill group and also clear Style from the pattern group.

4. Click OK.

Applying Quick Formatting

In Word 2010, you can apply a specific style quickly and easily on the **Home** tab in the **Styles** group. For example, buttons for changing the font size, colour and other character attributes have been gathered in the **Font** group on the **Home** tab so that they are all easily accessible.

*To view the attributes of a particular style, click the **Styles Dialog Box Launcher**, and then rest your pointer over a style in the list.*

Applying a Style

Applying a style to a selection of text is easy as clicking a button in the Styles Gallery.

Notes:

*In **Full Screen Reading** and **Outline view**; you do not see the margins.*

1. Select the text to which you want to apply a style.

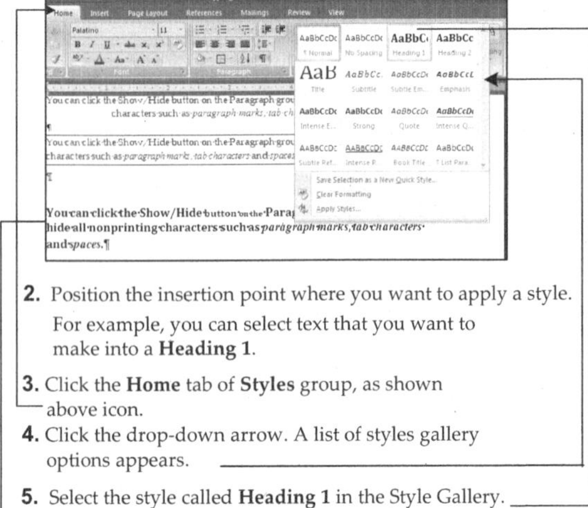

2. Position the insertion point where you want to apply a style.

   For example, you can select text that you want to make into a **Heading 1**.

3. Click the **Home** tab of **Styles** group, as shown above icon.
4. Click the drop-down arrow. A list of styles gallery options appears.
5. Select the style called **Heading 1** in the Style Gallery.
6. The selected changed to **Heading 1** options.

*To **Open Apply Styles** task pane press **Ctrl + Shift + S** keys together.*

Adding a new style to the Style Gallery

You might want to create a new style and add it to the Styles Gallery.

1. Select the text to which you want to create a new style.

   For example, you want the selected paragraph to be justified and font size will be 11 pt New Times Roman.

2. Select the paragraph, above the selection. The Mini toolbar appears. Click the **Font** type and size to format the text.
3. Right-click the selection, choose Styles. A sub menu appears. Click **Save Selection as a New Quick Style...** .

*To **Open Styles** task pane press **Alt +Ctrl + Shift + S** keys together.*

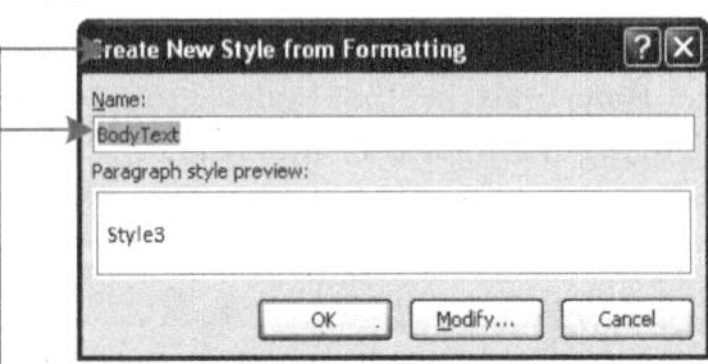

4. **Create New Style from Formatting** dialog box appears.
5. In the **Name:** box, give the style name to format.
   For example BodyText and then click OK.

Notes:

To remove a style from the styles gallery

1. Select the style you want to remove from the ***Style Gallery****.*

2. On the ***Home*** *tab on* ***Styles*** *group, right-click the style that you want to remove from the gallery.*

3. Click ***Remove*** *from* ***Quick Styles Gallery****.*

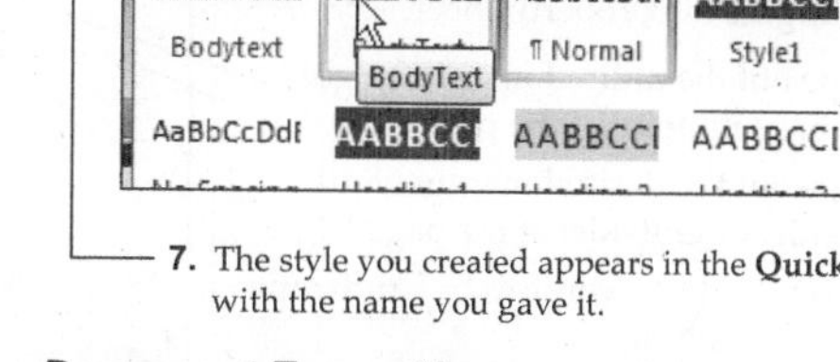

7. The style you created appears in the **Quick Style Gallery** with the name you gave it.

Document Formatting

Formatting a document in Word 2010 is the process of changing the appearance of a document as a whole. It involves the length of the *printed page, left margin, right margin,* etc.

Document Margins and Orientation

Word 2010 default margins are 1 inch at the top and bottom and 1 inch on the left and right. You can change the margins for the entire document or for different parts of the document.

You see the page as it will print. Always select the **Print Layout view** if you want to see headers, footers, page numbers, footnotes, etc.

Setting Document Margins

Page margins can quickly be changed using the ruler or they can be set to precise locations using page dialog box.

You can also select one of the two types of page orientations namely, portrait (vertical) and landscape (horizontal). You can change the paper size and page orientation for a section or for the entire document.

1. Select the sections for which you want to change margins. *Alternatively,* position the insertion point in the section whose margins you want to change.

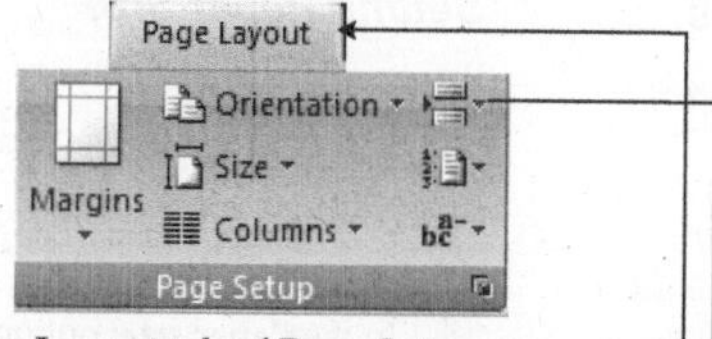

2. Click the **Page Layout** tab of **Page Setup** group.
3. In the top right corner, click **Insert Page and Section Breaks** drop-down arrow.

Indents are added to margin settings. That is, if you specify a 1.0" left margin and a 1/2" left indent, your text will print 1½ from the left edge. If you set a 1.0" right margin and indent the right edge of a paragraph 1.0", the text will stop 2.0" from the right edge of the page.

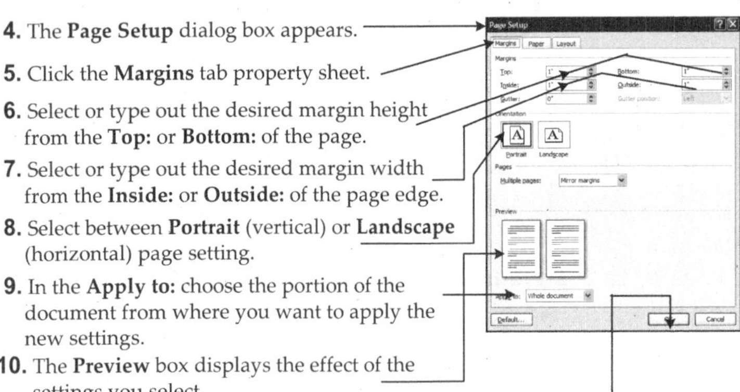

4. The **Page Setup** dialog box appears.
5. Click the **Margins** tab property sheet.
6. Select or type out the desired margin height from the **Top:** or **Bottom:** of the page.
7. Select or type out the desired margin width from the **Inside:** or **Outside:** of the page edge.
8. Select between **Portrait** (vertical) or **Landscape** (horizontal) page setting.
9. In the **Apply to:** choose the portion of the document from where you want to apply the new settings.
10. The **Preview** box displays the effect of the settings you select.
11. Click **OK.**

Set the margins using the Ruler

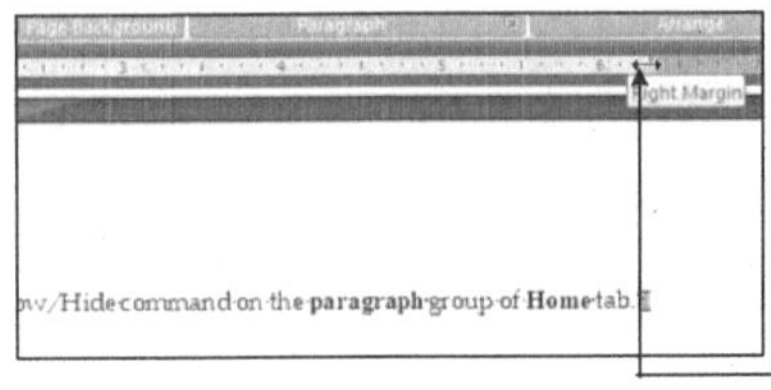

1. Switch to **Print Layout** view.
2. If the ruler is not displayed, click **View** tab. In the **Show** group, click the **Ruler** check box.
3. Position to the transition area on the ruler that is *where gray becomes white.*
4. The mouse pointer will become a two-headed arrow.
5. Drag the margin to the desired position with a mouse. The ruler's dimensions change as you drag.

Notes:

Section breaks differ from paragraph marks (¶), in that a section break controls the information below it, while a paragraph mark controls the information that appears before it or precedes it.

Setting Paper Size

Page margins are usually set according to paper size you use.

1. Select the text, in the section that you want to change.
2. In the **Page Setup** dialog box, click **Paper** tab.
   In the **Paper size:** options
3. Click the drop-down list, it offers different standard paper size. Select the desired size you want. Commonly used paper size is A4 and legal size A3.
4. Type or select the **Width:** and **Height:** of the paper you are using.
5. In the **Apply to:** select the portion of the document you want to print on the selected paper size.

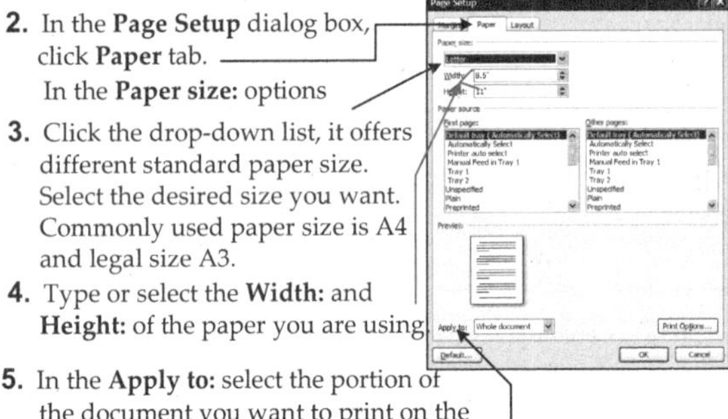

Notes:

Most printers require a minimum width for margin settings, because they can't print all the way to the edge of the page. If you try to set margins that are too narrow, Word 2010 displays the message ***One or more margins are set outside the printable area of the page.***

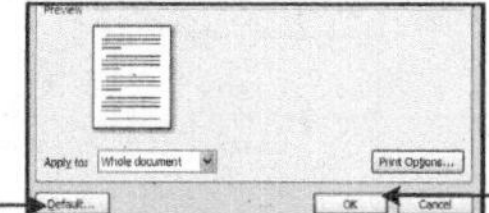

6. Click the **Default...** buttons if you want to save these settings as default settings, so they can apply to all pages printed hereafter.
7. Click **OK** button.

Inserting Page Break

1. Position the insertion point where you want the break to occur.

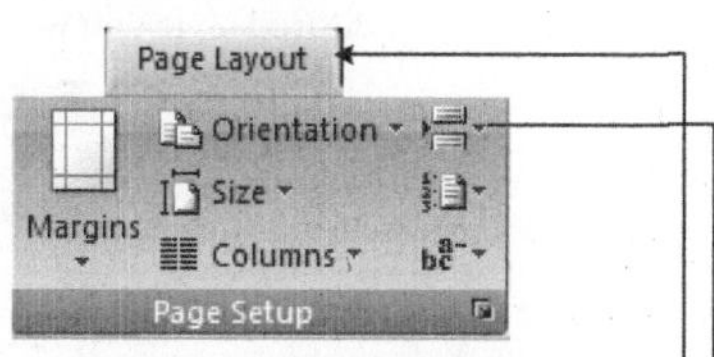

2. Click the **Page Layout** tab of **Page Setup** group.
3. In the top right corner, click **Insert Page and Section Breaks** drop-down arrow.
4. The list of options appear. Choose an desired options.
5. **Page** options mark the point which one page ends and the next page begins.
6. **Column** options indicates that the text following the column break will begin in the next column.
7. **Next page:** This selection would start the new section on a new page.
8. **Continuous page:** This selection would insert a section brek without starting it on a new page.

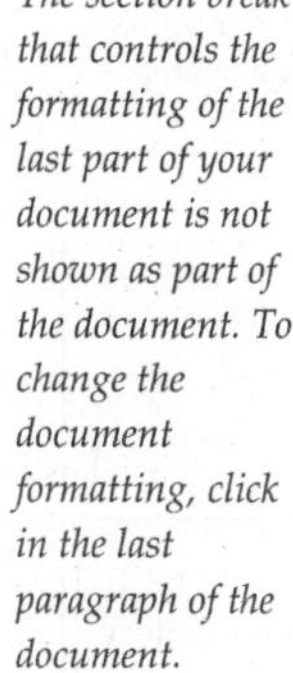

The section break that controls the formatting of the last part of your document is not shown as part of the document. To change the document formatting, click in the last paragraph of the document.

Inserting Header and Footer

You can insert a header or footer, and you can select the style you want from a gallery. Select the specified style to the document.

Headers and footers contain information at the top or bottom of the pages of a document. Word 2010 has the option of printing a different header or footer on the first page of a document or the section also.

Notes:

Deleting Page Breaks: *Select the page break. Now press the* ***Del*** *key. The Page Break is removed.*

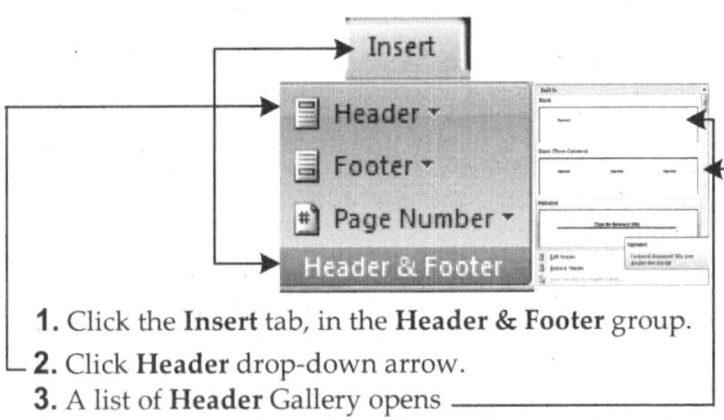

1. Click the **Insert** tab, in the **Header & Footer** group.
2. Click **Header** drop-down arrow.
3. A list of **Header** Gallery opens
4. Scroll through the gallery. You will notice the variety of headers that are available in the gallery. Select the desired style you want.

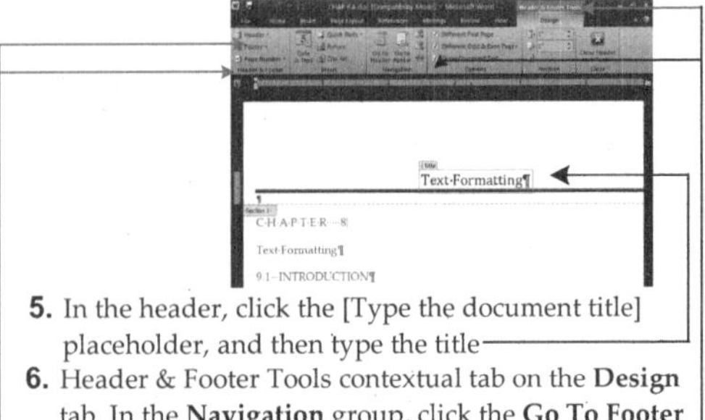

To quickly edit a header and footer, view the document in Print Layout view, and then double-click the header or footer.

5. In the header, click the [Type the document title] placeholder, and then type the title
6. Header & Footer Tools contextual tab on the **Design** tab. In the **Navigation** group, click the **Go To Footer** button. Word displays the footer area at the bottom of the page. (OR)
7. In the **Header & Footer** group, click the **Footer** button. Click the down arrow, a list of footer Gallery opens.

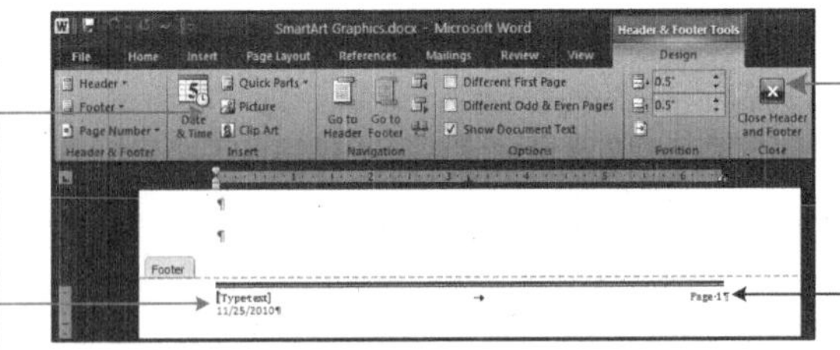

8. The page number and document name are included in the header gallery, if you want date and time to appear in the footer.
9. Word 2010 inserts the Footer pane in the bottom of the page with text and page number option in the Footer gallery list.
10. Word inserts **Date and Time** in the Footer by selecting **Date and Time** icon in the **Design** tab of **Insert** group.
11. After inserted header and footer in the document. Click the **Close Header and Footer** in the **Close** group.

Notes:

*To quickly edit a header and footer, view the document in **Print Layout** view, and then double-click the header or footer.*

Deleting Header and Footer

1. Position the insertion point in the section with the header or footer you want to delete.
2. Select the **Header/Footer** you want to delete, and then press **Del** key.
3. If you have different headers or footers in other sections of the document, click the **Show Next** or **Show Previous** button on the **Navigation** group to find the next header or footer you want to delete.

Insert Page Number

You can quickly add a page number from the gallery, or you can create a custom page number.

When you edit a header or footer, it changes throughout the entire document or section.

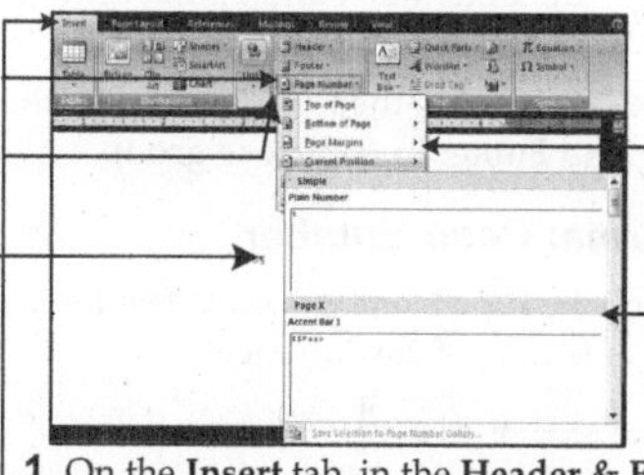

1. On the **Insert** tab, in the **Header & Footer** group, click **Page Number**.
2. The list of options appears, Click **Top of Page**, **Bottom of page**, or **Page Margins**, depending on where you to want page numbers to appear in the document.
3. Choose a page numbering design from the gallery. The gallery includes Page options such as **Bold numbers 1**, **Plain Number 1**, **thick line**, **Tildes**, etc. Select any options from the list.
4. You can see the Bottom of Page appears in the document.

To change the space between the text and header and footer

1. Double click the header and footer text in the document.

While working in Header/Footer box, the main document appears grayed. To work in the main document double click the main document.

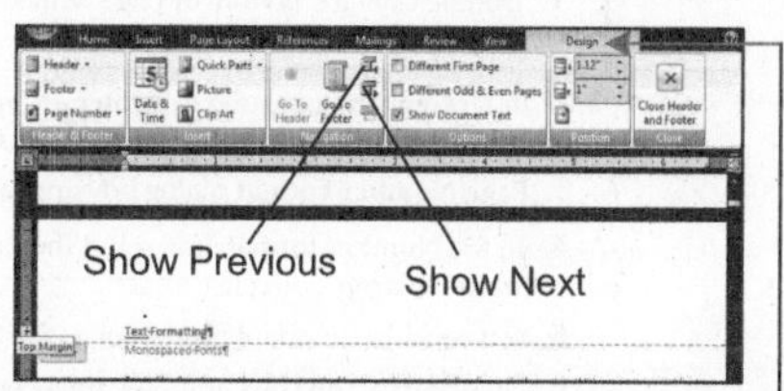

2. In the **Design** tab of **Navigation** group, click the **Show Next**, **Show Previous**, or switch between **Header and Footer** button to find the header or footer you want to adjust.

Notes:

You can format text in the header or footer by selecting the text and using the formatting options on the Mini toolbar.

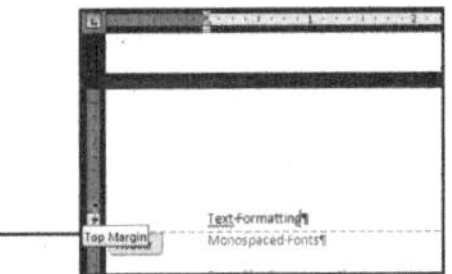

3. Point to either the top or the bottom margin boundary on the vertical ruler.
   When the mouse pointer becomes a double-headed arrow, do one of the following:
   - To add or reduce space between the top of the document text and a header, drag the top margin boundary down or up.
   - To add or reduce space between the bottom of the document text and a footer, drag the bottom margin boundary up or down.
4. To return to the document, click the **Close Header and Footer** in the **Close** group.

Format Page Number

Using the Page Number format feature to add page numbers to the top or bottom of the document.

If you created different first-page or odd and even headers or footers, or if you have sections that aren't linked, be sure to remove the page numbers from each different header or footer.

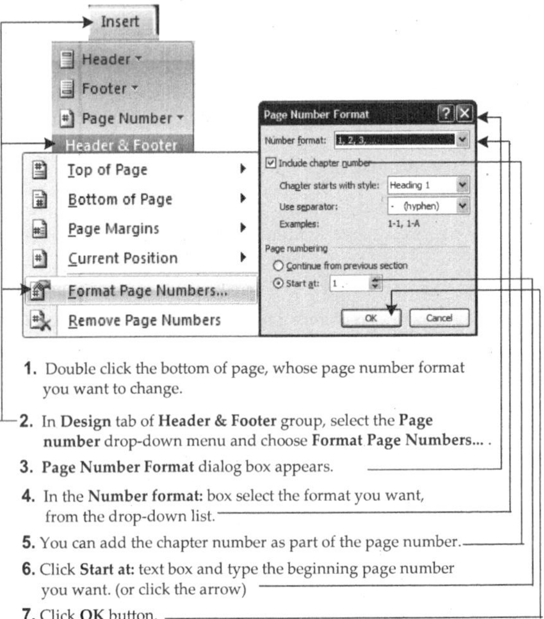

1. Double click the bottom of page, whose page number format you want to change.
2. In **Design** tab of **Header & Footer** group, select the **Page number** drop-down menu and choose **Format Page Numbers...** .
3. **Page Number Format** dialog box appears.
4. In the **Number format:** box select the format you want, from the drop-down list.
5. You can add the chapter number as part of the page number.
6. Click **Start at:** text box and type the beginning page number you want. (or click the arrow)
7. Click **OK** button.

Notes:

Change the Font and Size of Page Numbers

1. Double-click the header and footer of pages in your document.

2. Select the page number.

3. The Mini toolbar appears above the selected page number.

4. For example, you want to change the font, click a font name in the box. Or if you want to change the font size, click a font size in the box.

Start the Page Numbering with a Different Number

If, for example, you add a cover page to a document with page numbers, the second page is automatically numbered Page 2. You might want the document to begin with Page 1.

1. Double click the bottom page number in the document.
2. In the **Design** tab of **Header & Footer** group, click Page Number down arrow. Select **Format Page Numbers...** .
3. **Page Number Format** dialog box appears. In the page numbering section click **Start at:** radio button to enter the page number you want to start.
4. Click OK.

Removing Page Number

Word 2010 automatically removes or deletes page number when you click **Remove Page Numbers** or when you remove a single page number manually from the document.

1. In the **Design** tab, in the **Header & Footer** group, click **Page Number** down arrow.
2. Click **Remove Page Numbers.**

Dividing Text into Columns

When you type, Word 2010 normally displays your text to fill the area defined by the left and right margins. However, you can also divide a page into two or three columns, which can be especially for printing newletters.

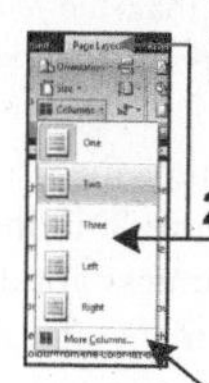

1. Select the text that you want to divide into columns. or press **Ctrl + A** to select entire document.
2. Click the **Page Layout** tab of **Page Setup** group. Click the **Columns** drop-down box. Select the number of columns you want.

Or click the **More Columns...** . The **Columns** dialog box appears.

Editing Columns

After you create two or three columns in the document, you may want to modify their widths, modify the spacing between columns, and choose whether to display a vertical line between columns.

1. Move the cursor to the text divided into columns that you want to modify.

Notes:

To remove columns

1. Position the insertion point or select text where you want to remove columns.

2. In the Columns dialog box, in the Presets group, select one column.

3. Click OK.

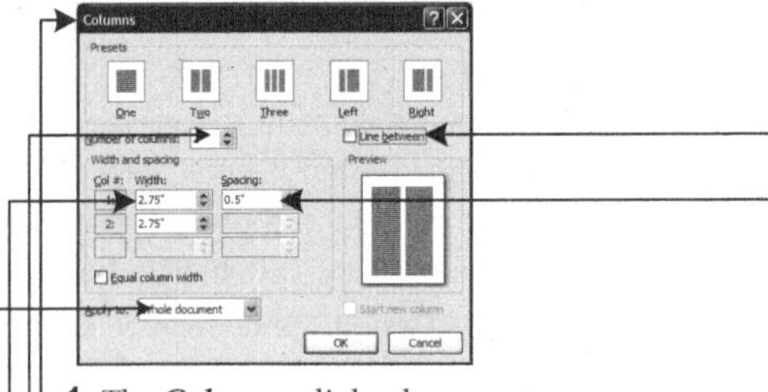

1. The **Columns** dialog box appears.
2. Click in the **Number of Columns** spinner box and click the up/down arrow to define how many columns you want.
3. Click in the **Width** spinner box and click the up/down arrow to define a width for column 1.
4. Click in the **Spacing** spinner box and click the up/down arrow to define the spacing width to the right column 1.
5. Select the **Line between** check box to display a vertical line between columns.
6. Click the **Apply To** list box and choose Whole Document.
7. Click OK.

Notes:

You can also remove page numbers by deleting a single page number from your document.

Delete a Footnote and Endnote

1. Click and drag over the superscript number in the body text of the document to select it

2. Press ***Delete.***

Inserting Footnote and Endnote

Word 2010 footnote feature enables you to *enter, edit,* and *view* footnotes/endnotes in a variety of formats. The only difference between footnotes and endnotes is that, the *footnotes appear at the bottom of the page* and *endnotes appear at the end of the section or document.*

1. Position the insertion point after the text where you want to insert a reference mark. Word 2010 inserts the reference mark at the insertion point, unless you have selected text, in which case it positions the mark after the selection.

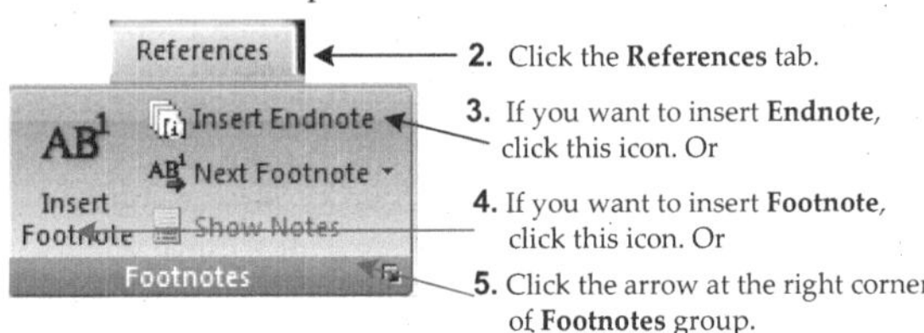

2. Click the **References** tab.
3. If you want to insert **Endnote**, click this icon. Or
4. If you want to insert **Footnote**, click this icon. Or
5. Click the arrow at the right corner of **Footnotes** group.

Notes:

The keyboard shortcut to insert Footnote is ***Alt + Ctrl + F*** *and Endnote is* ***Alt + Ctrl + D***

6. The **Footnote and Endnote** dialog box appears.
7. Select either the **Footnote** or the **Endnote** option.
8. Select the desired format in the **Number format:** drop-down list.
9. To customize the numbering, click **Custom mark:** and then click the **Symbol...** button. The **Symbol** dialog box opens, select the symbol you want to use for numbering and then click Ok. The selected character appears in the **Custom mark:** text box.
10. In **Start at:** spinner box, select the format according to, in **Number format**. Select the desired changes in the **Apply Changes to:** drop-down box. Click Insert button to insert the footnote.
11. Word 2010 inserts the footnote, type the text in the footnote or endnote.

If you are in Draft view, leave the note pane visible and press ***Show Notes*** *in the* ***Footnotes*** *group.*

Inserting Symbols

In Word 2010, you insert symbol and mathematical equations in the documents such as characters like copyright © or registered (®) symbols, Currency symbols (such as £) etc.

Notes:

If you are in ***Print Layout*** *view, you can* ***Navigate*** *next or previous footnote in the document of* ***References*** *tab of* ***Footnotes*** *group.*

1. Move the cursor where you want to insert a symbol in the document.

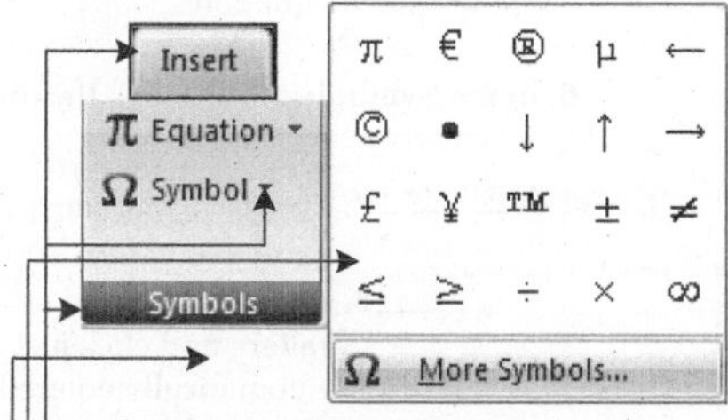

2. Click **Insert** tab of **Symbols** group, click the symbol drop-down arrow as shown above arrow.
3. A list of symbols appears, click the desired symbol you want. Word 2010 inserts your chosen symbol in the document.
4. If you want to see more options in the symbols, click the **More Symbols...** . A **Symbol** dialog box appears.

Notes:

When you want to delete a note, you work with the note reference mark in the document window, not the text in the note.

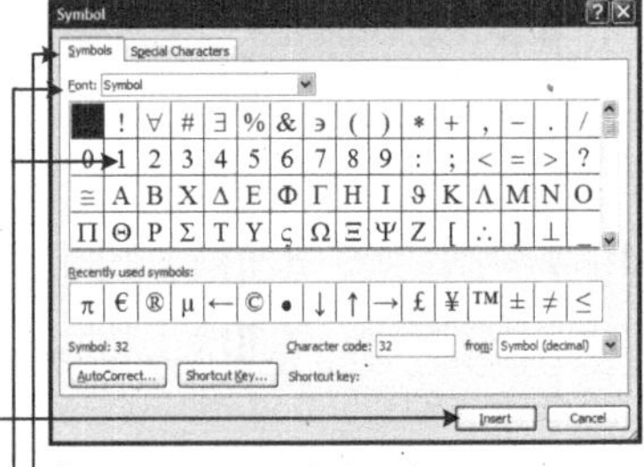

5. Click the Symbols tab.
6. Select the desired font in the **Font:** list, and you can see the selected symbol in the box.
7. If you click **Insert** button it will turn into **Close** button.

Inserting Equations

1. Move the cursor where you want to type equation in the document.

Equation placeholders do not appear in the document on the screen or in print.

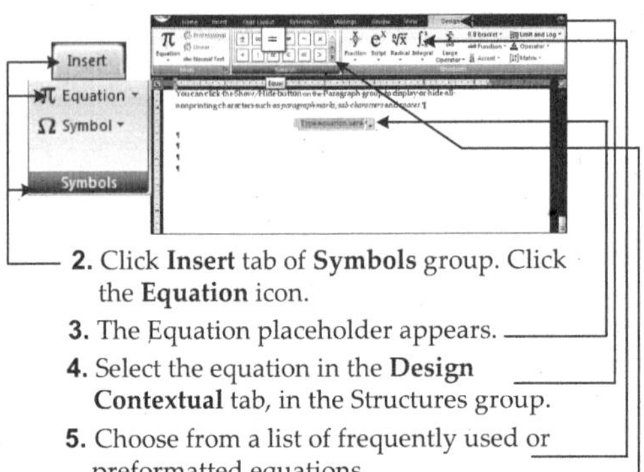

2. Click **Insert** tab of **Symbols** group. Click the **Equation** icon.
3. The Equation placeholder appears.
4. Select the equation in the **Design Contextual** tab, in the Structures group.
5. Choose from a list of frequently used or preformatted equations.

Or

6. In the **Symbols** group, click the drop-down arrow.

When you type an equation, Word 2010 automatically converts the equation into a professionally formatted equation.

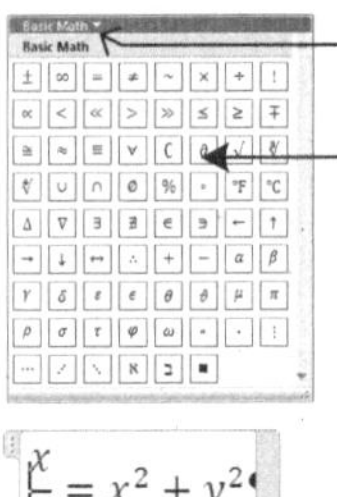

7. The Basic Mathematical sets are available in the drop-down list.
8. Select the desired symbol, in the basic gallery and click just once, it is automatically entered in the equation placeholder.

$\frac{x}{y} = x^2 + y^2$

9. After you complete the equation, you can see how it look in the document.

Notes:

*For symbols you use frequently, assign a shortcut key by clicking the Shortcut key button in the **Symbol** dialog box.*

*You can automatically insert some symbols with the **Autocorrect feature***

*Word 2010 templates to be stored in your default Templates folder. If you do not store the templates you create in this folder, Word 2010 will not display them in your **My Templates** list.*

Creating a New Template

To create a document based on one of the Word 2010 templates, for example, by adding your name and address and then save the document as a new template with the different name.

1. Click the **File** menu and choose **New...** . The **New Backstage** view appears.

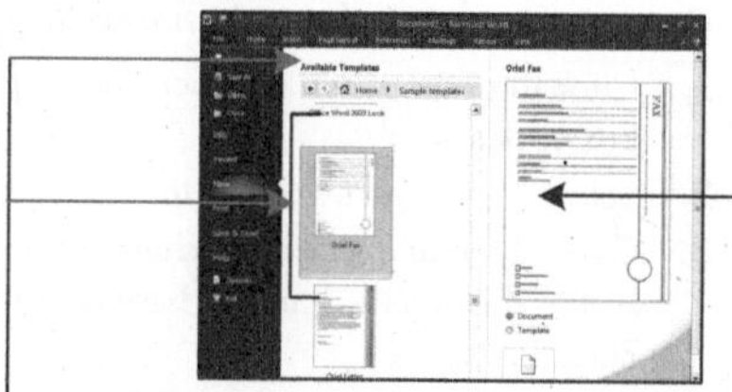

2. In **Available Templates**, select Sample template. A list of template appears. Select the desired template you want to create.
3. Make the changes that you want to the margin settings, page size and orientation, and other formats.
4. In the **Preview** box, you see a sample document for which the template is designed. For example, here we select **Oriel Letter** template. Double-click the selected template. Or
5. Click **Create** button.

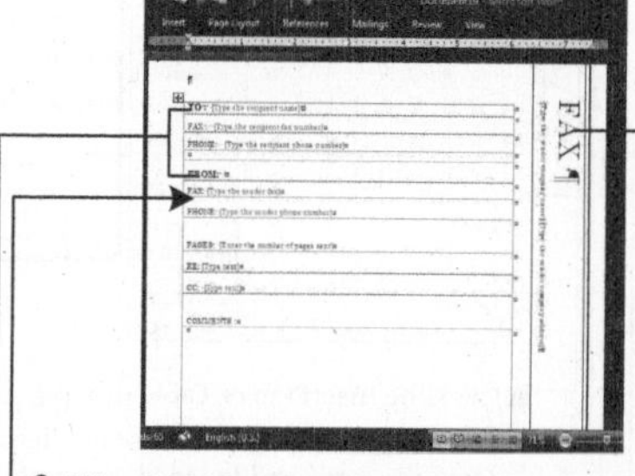

6. Word 2010 opens a new fax cover document based on the selected template, with placeholders for the text you need to apply.
7. In the document on the right side of the page, click the [Company name, address] placeholder.
8. Type the **To:** and **From:** address in the document.
9. After completing the Fax Letter, click the **File** menu and then Click Save **As...** .

Notes:

You can also save the template as a Word Macro-Enabled Template (.dotm file) or a Word 97-2003 Template (.dot file)

10. In **Save As** dialog box, click the **Navigation** pane, select **Trusted Templates**. Word 2010 displays a Templates folder.
11. Give file name in the **File name:** box, type Fax template.
12. Select Word Template in the **Save as type:** drop-down list.
13. Click **Save** button.

Create a template based on existing template

1. Click the **File** menu and then click **Open**. The **Open** dialog box appears.
2. Select the templates folder in the **Look in:** drop-down list.
3. Click Open and make the changes that you want to appear in the document that you base on the template. And then click **Save**.

Notes:

When the user interface (UI) is not displayed full size, the icons might not be displayed in the same order as before. For example, icons that were displayed on one row may be displayed three rows deep.

Creating a Table

Word 2010 allows you to create a table selecting the Insert Table grid on the insert tab or **Insert table...** using the **Table** options in the **Table** groups.

1. Position the insertion point where you want to insert a table.

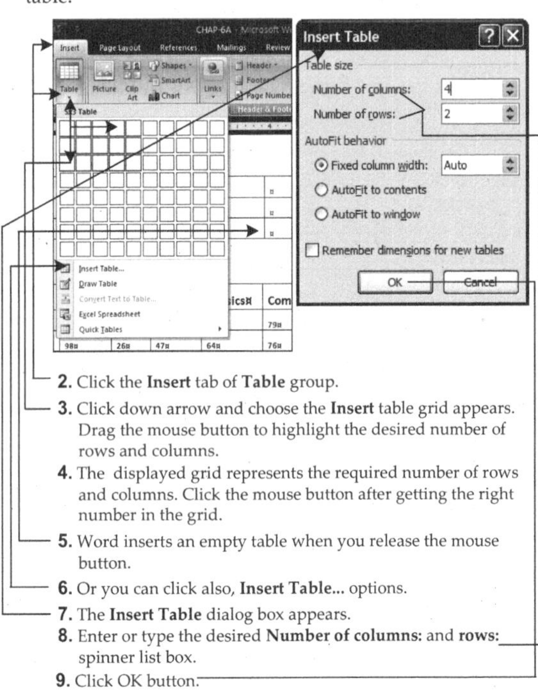

2. Click the **Insert** tab of **Table** group.
3. Click down arrow and choose the **Insert** table grid appears. Drag the mouse button to highlight the desired number of rows and columns.
4. The displayed grid represents the required number of rows and columns. Click the mouse button after getting the right number in the grid.
5. Word inserts an empty table when you release the mouse button.
6. Or you can click also, **Insert Table...** options.
7. The **Insert Table** dialog box appears.
8. Enter or type the desired **Number of columns:** and **rows:** spinner list box.
9. Click OK button.

Notes:

*The insertion point will move left and down to the next row when you press **Tab** key in the last column and insert a new row in the table.*

Selecting Columns

To select a column, move the mouse pointer to the area at the top of a column called the *column selection bar*. At the column selection bar the pointer changes to a large, down-pointing arrow.

Selecting Rows

By clicking any cell's selection bar will select the entire row. By holding the left most button and dragging it the rest of the rows also.

Selecting Adjacent Groups of Cells

To select groups of adjacent cells, either drag through the cells or click in one cell and press **Shift** + click in the others.

Selecting the Whole Table

To select a complete table, press down the **Alt** key and double click anywhere in the table.

Inserting Rows

To add a new row at the end of an existing table, position the insertion point anywhere in the last cell and press the **Tab** key. Word 2010 inserts a new row using the styles of the cells that are immediately above it.

Selecting a Cell

The area between the first character in a cell and the left edge of the cell is called the cell selection bar.

Clicking on this bar selects the contents of the entire cell.

Cell selection bar

Name	English
Anita	29
Geeta	98
Vineeta	68
Shashi	57
Sunita	55
Bindya	49

1. Position the insertion point below the row where you want the new row to be inserted.

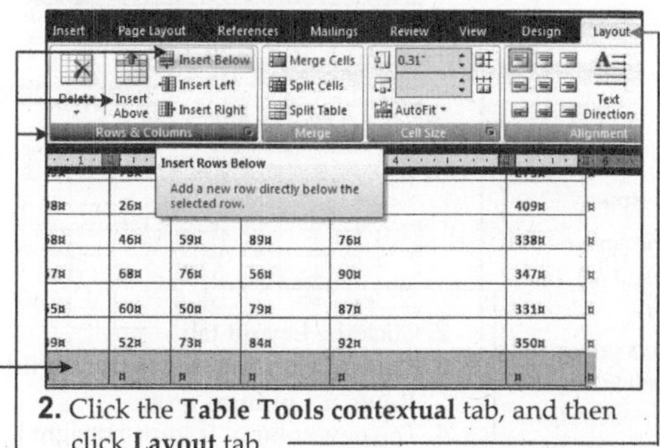

2. Click the **Table Tools contextual** tab, and then click **Layout** tab.
3. Click **Insert Above** or **Below** in the **Rows & Columns** group.
4. The new row is inserted below the selected row.

If you draw a table row or column line that you want to erase, click the ribbon's Eraser button and drag your mouse over the line you want to erase.

Notes:

*It will move right and up one row when you press **Shift + Tab** past the last column on the left.*

Changing Row Height

Word 2010 sets the height of each row automatically in order to accommodate the cell containing the tallest entry.

1. Click anywhere in the row where you want to change its height.

Maths	Physics	Computer science	Total
54	35	79	275
47	64	76	409
59	89	76	338
76	56	90	347
50	79	87	331
73	84	92	350

0.19"
1.5"
AutoFit
Cell Size

2. Move the pointer to the horizontal line. The pointer changes to up-and-down arrow. Use it to drag the row to the desired height.
3. Release the mouse button. Or
4. Click **Table Row Height** scroll box, to change the height of row in the cell size group.

Alternatively, right click and select Insert, click the small triangle, a sub menu options appears. Select the Insert Rows Above or Below option.

Inserting Columns

1. Select the column to which you wish the new column to appear.

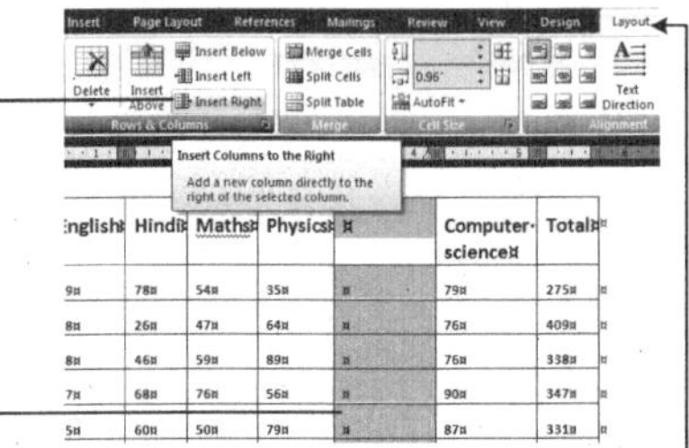

2. Click the **Layout** tab.
3. Click **Insert Columns to the Rigtht** options in the **Rows & Columns** group.
4. The new column is inserted right to the selected column.

Delete Rows

*Click the Layout Contextual tab. In **Rows & Columns** group, click **Delete** drop-down arrow. A list of options appears. Select **Delete Rows** option.*

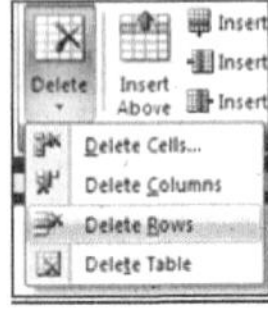

Alternatively, right click and select Insert. Click the small triangle. A sub menu options appears. Select the Insert Columns to Left or Right option.

Changing Column Width

1. Point to a column boundary.

Notes:

To insert a column at the right edge of a table.

1. Select an end-of-row marker.

*2. **Right** click and select Insert. A small triangle with sub menu options appears. Select the desired options you want to insert.*

Name	English	Hindi	Maths	Physics	Computer science	Total
Anita	29	78	54	35	79	275
Geeta	98	26	47	64	76	409
Vineeta	68	46	59	89	76	338
Shashi	57	68	76	56	90	347
Sunita	55	60	50	79	87	331
Bindya	49	52	73	84	92	350

2. The pointer will change shape to a double arrow. Drag the column width marker. Watch the dotted line as well as the ruler settings, then release the mouse button when it reaches the desired width.

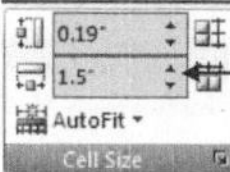

3. Click **Table Column Width** scroll box, to change the Table Column Width in the **Cell Size** group.

If you hold down the **Shift** key while dragging, the column to the right does not change size while the table's overall width increases.

Merging and Splitting Cells

1. Select the cells to be merged.

Use the Merge Cells feature to join multiple cells. Similarly, use the split feature to separate cells.

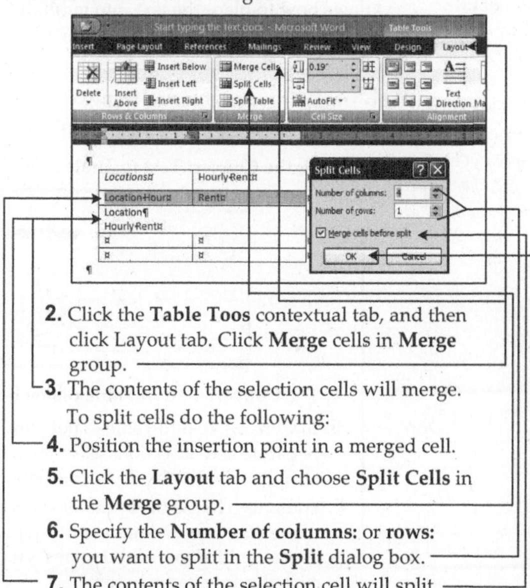

2. Click the **Table Toos** contextual tab, and then click Layout tab. Click **Merge** cells in **Merge** group.
3. The contents of the selection cells will merge.
   To split cells do the following:
4. Position the insertion point in a merged cell.
5. Click the **Layout** tab and choose **Split Cells** in the **Merge** group.
6. Specify the **Number of columns:** or **rows:** you want to split in the **Split** dialog box.
7. The contents of the selection cell will split
8. Click OK

Notes:

Deleting Columns

1. Select the column(s) to be deleted.

*2. Click the **Layout** tab. Click **Table** down arrow and choose **Delete Columns.***

Aligning Text in a Table Cell

You can align text in a table cell in nine different ways: Top Left (the default alignment), Top center, Top Right, Center Left, Center Right, Bottom Left, Bottom Center, and Bottom Right as shown icons in.

1. Click the cell that contains text that you want to align.

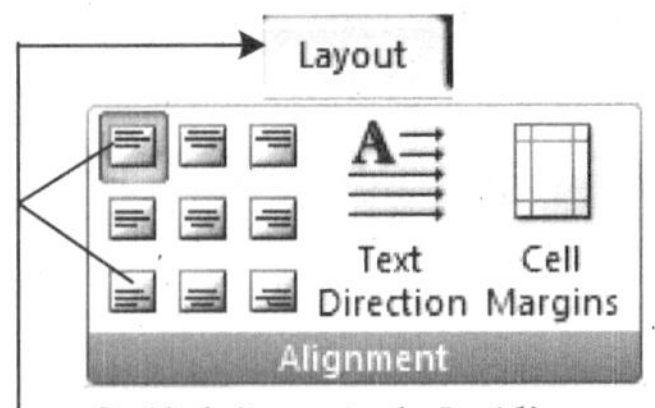

2. Click **Layout** tab. In **Alignment** group choose the Text direction options you want in the cells.

For example, you want the text to be Top Right, choose Align text to the top right corner of the cell in the **Alignment** group options.

Convert Text to a Table

If you have an existing text that you would like to turn into a table, you need to first separate text into block. So Word 2010 knows how to place the text into individual cells in a table. You can change the delimiter character to commas, tabs, or any other character, such as # or *.

The split Cells feature allows you to split selected cells into multiple cells. Data already entered in cells to be split can be merged, if desired. This rearranges the data to fill the new cells.

1. Select the text that you want to convert into a table.
2. Click **Insert** tab, click **Table**, pull-down menu appears.
3. Click the **Convert Text to Table...** command.

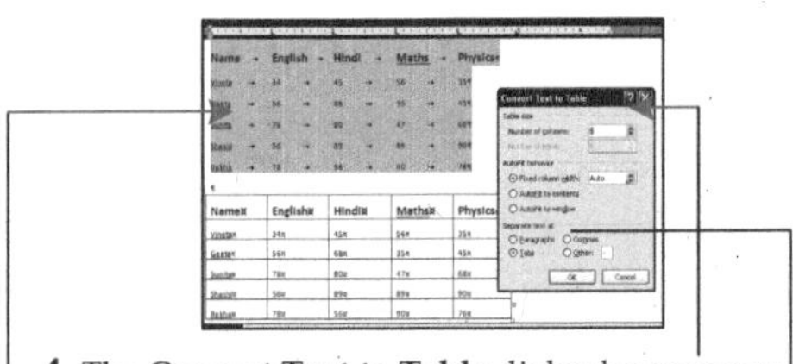

4. The **Convert Text to Table** dialog box appears.
5. In Convert Text to Table dialog box, in the Separate text at section, select the radio button such as Paragraphs, Tabs, or Commas.
6. You must choose the option that corresponds to the way you divided your text. For example, if you divided your text by tabs, you would click the Tabs radio button.
7. Click OK. Word 2010 converts your text into a table.

Formatting Table Styles

Notes:

Merging cells changes all selected cells into one. If there is information in the cells, it is also merged.

With Word 2010, you can quickly get started by creating a quick table, a preformatted table with sample data that you can customize it. You can then apply one of the **Table Styles** available on the Design contextual tab, which may include a variety of colours in rows and columns and also, you can add borders.

1. Select the entire table by pressing at the top corner of the arrow in the table or press **Alt + 5** on the numeric keypad with **Numlock** off.

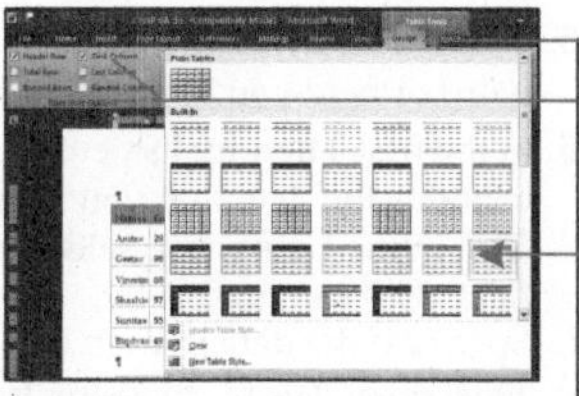

2. Click **Design** tab. In the **Table Style Options** group, click or clear check boxes, such as **Header Row** or **Banded Columns.**
3. Click the **More** button on the **Table Style** group.
4. A pull down menu of all available styles appears. As you move the mouse pointer over a table style, Word 2010 displays a live preview of how your table will look.
5. Click a table desired style. Word 2010 will format your table according to the style you select.

*If you hold down **Ctrl** key while dragging mouse, all columns to the right change size but the table's overall width will not change. Thus, the width of the columns on the right will only change.*

Sorting the Contents of a Table

Tables can not only organize data, but they can also arrange your data alphabetically. The Sort command can be used to arrange the rows in a specific order *ascending, descending,* etc. Word 2010 can sort lines of tabular text, items you have entered in tables, or even paragraphs in a document.

Word 2010 Sort Text command sorts the selected text alphabetically, numerically, or chronologically (date wise) as per your need.

1. Position the insertion point in the table you wish to sort. *Alternatively,* select the cells you want to sort.

2. Under Table Tools, on **Layout** tab. Click **Data** drop-down list. Click **Sort** icon.

Notes:

If you want the sort to be case-sensitive, or if you are sorting things not in a table, click the ***Options...*** *button in the Sort dialog box and make the choices accordingly in the* ***Sort Options*** *dialog box.*

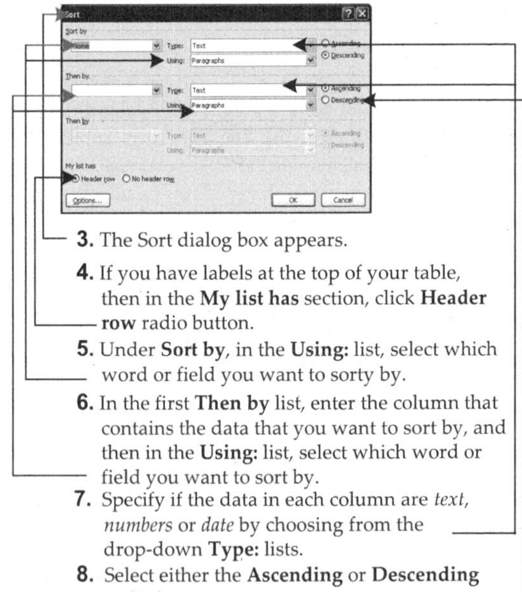

3. The Sort dialog box appears.
4. If you have labels at the top of your table, then in the **My list has** section, click **Header row** radio button.
5. Under **Sort by**, in the **Using:** list, select which word or field you want to sorty by.
6. In the first **Then by** list, enter the column that contains the data that you want to sort by, and then in the **Using:** list, select which word or field you want to sort by.
7. Specify if the data in each column are *text, numbers* or *date* by choosing from the drop-down **Type:** lists.
8. Select either the **Ascending** or **Descending** radio button.
9. Click OK. Word 2010 will sort the table based on the data in the column you selected.

Adding Borders

Borders can emphasize parts of your table, such as a particular row or column. To add a border to a table, you need to define the following:

1. Move the cursor to the row, column, cell or table where you want to add borders.

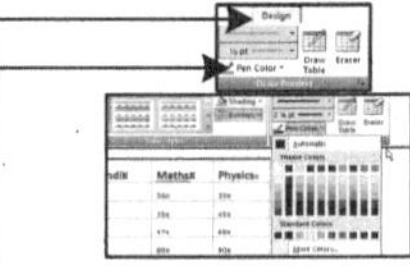

2. Click **Design** contextual tab, of **Draw Borders** group, click **Pen Color**. As seen below, color palette appears.
3. Click a color for your border you want to apply.

You can make the outline or the border of your shape look different by changing the color, the look of the line style, or the weight of the line.

Notes:

New column retains the format of the column, adjacent to which it is inserted but borders will not change.

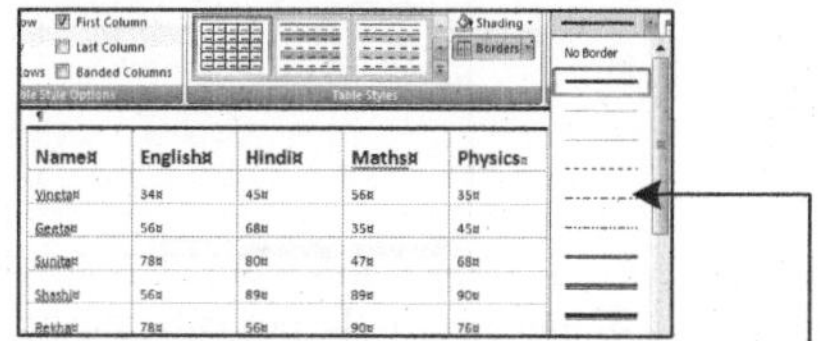

4. Click the **Line Style** list box. A pull down menu appears with different line styles, such as dotted lines or triple lines.
5. Click a desired line style you want to apply.

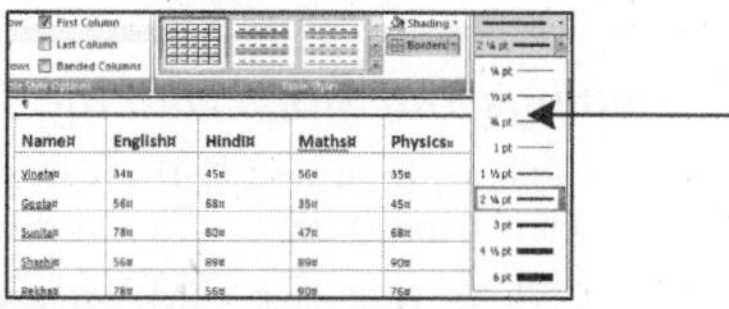

6. Click the **Line Weight** list box. A pull down menu appears with different line thickness such as 1/2 or 21/4, etc.
7. Click a desired line weight (thickness) you want to apply.
8. Word displays your chosen border in the color and thickness (weight) you chose.

A formula consists of an equal sign (=), followed by a function name (such as SUM), followed by parentheses containing the location of the cells on which you want to perform the calculation. For example, the formula =SUM(Left) totals the cells to the left of the cell containing the formula.

Performing Calculations in a Table

When you want to perform calculations on numbers in Word 2010 table, you can create *formula* that uses a built-in mathematical function.

1. Position the insertion point in the cell in which you want to enter the formula.

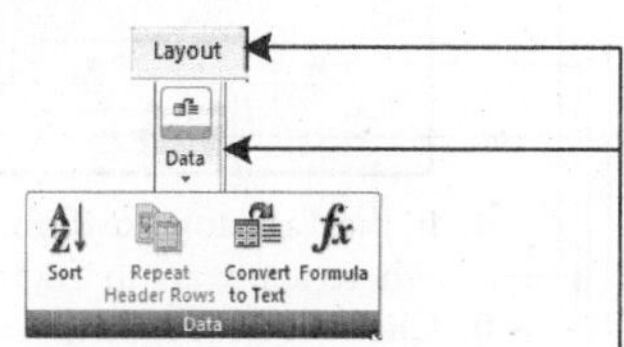

2. Click **Layout** tab. Click **Data** group. Click **Formula.** The **Formula** dialog box appears.

A new feature called the Table Wizard helps you to automate table creation.

Notes:

Setting tab stops with the ruler

1. With the ruler in view, click the button at the left edge of the horizontal ruler repeatedly until it shows the icon for the tab stop you want to insert. Tabs are Left, Right, Decimal and Centre.

2. Click on the ruler where you want to position a tab stop. If you make a mistake, drag the stop off the ruler and try again.

3. When you type, press the Tab key to move the insertion point to the new tab position.

To insert a tab in a table, press ***Ctrl + Tab.***

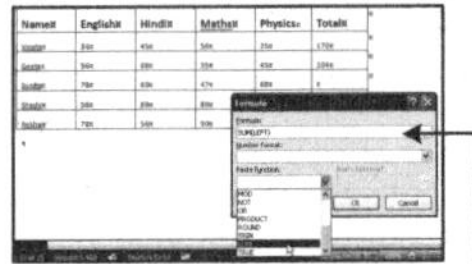

3. In the **Formula:** box enter the formula or In the **Paste function:** drop down list select the function you want to use and specify the range of cells to be used for the calculation.
4. In the **Number format:** drop down list, select the number format.
5. Click OK.

Settings Tab Stops with the Tabs Dialog Box

1. Position the insertion point in paragraph for which you want to insert tab.
2. Click the **Home** tab. Click **Paragraph Launcher**. Dialog box opens.
3. In **Paragraph** dialog box, click **Tabs...** button. **Tabs** dialog box appears.

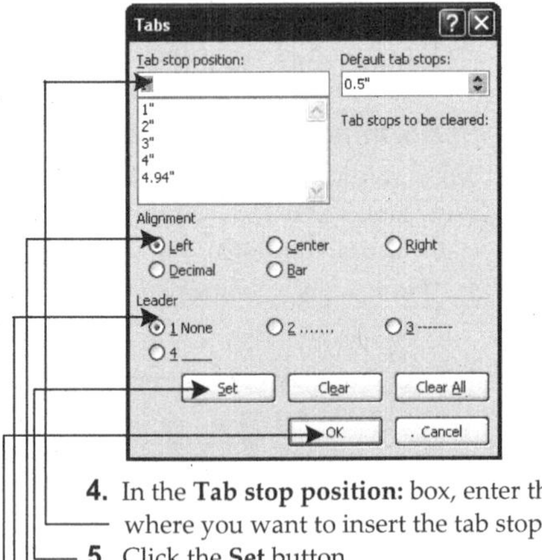

4. In the **Tab stop position:** box, enter the position where you want to insert the tab stop.
5. Click the **Set** button.
6. In the **Alignment** area select the type of tab you want to insert.
7. Specify the **Leader** options in front of the tab stop.
8. Click OK.

Notes:

When you open the main document in Word 2010 it brings with it the associated data source with which it was saved last. If you use a different main document, then remember to attach it with a new data source that you may want to use.

Mail Merge

Mail Merge is a mass-mailing facility that takes names, addresses and pertinent facts about recipients and merges the information into the form of a letter. Mail Merge printing (merge printing in short) uses two files: a data file that contains a listing of data items (or fields) arranged in some specific order and a master file that contains the standard text as well as the data variables which are replaced with specific data items from the data file during the merge operation performed by Word 2010.

Creating a Document for Mail-Merge

For mail-merge, you need to do the following:

- Create a data source
- Create main document.
- Insert fields into the main document.
- Check for design and data entry errors.
- Merge the data source document and the main document and finally, print merged documents.

Starting Mail Merge

Word 2010 has a step by step Mail Merge **W**izard that guides you through the steps for creating merged documents.

1. First create a blank document.

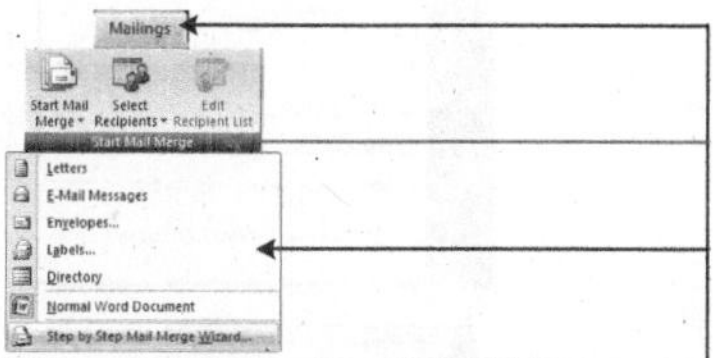

2. Click the **Mailings** tab in the **Start Mail Merge** group and click, down pointing arrow. A list options appears.
   It will be offering five choices: *Letters, E-Mail Messages, Envelopes, Labels* and *Directory*

Note that Letters, E-Mail Messages, Envelopes, Labels, and Catalogues are various types of documents you can produce using Mail Merge Wizard.

The first step in the mail merge process is to **Create the Main** document, because the type of main document governs the subsequent choices you can make in the **Mail Merge Helper**.

Notes:

Planning Data Source

Designing a data source document is one of the most important part of using the mail-merge feature. To begin with, you may want to create a data source document which has one field for the name of your friend; one field for the address and one field each for the city and pincode.

Creating Main Document

1. Click the **Mailings** tab in the **Start Mail Merge** group and click down pointing arrow and select **Step by Step Mail Merge Wizard...** .

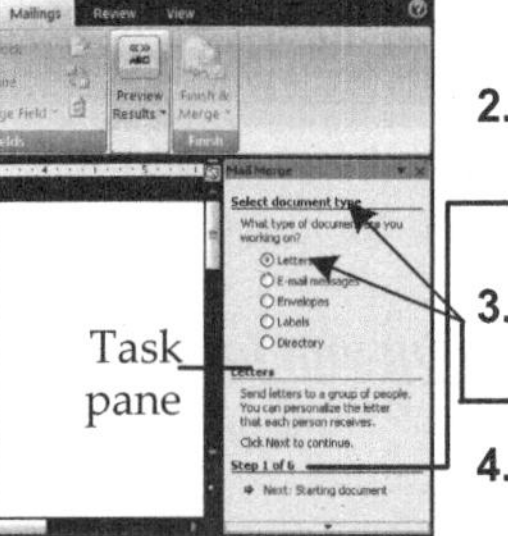

2. On the right hand side the Mail Merge task pane box appears. It shows Step 1 of the Wizard's six steps.
3. Under the **Select document type**, click Letters radio button.
4. Click **Next: Starting document**.

The wizard guides you through the rest of the mail process. The following are more details, listed in step-by-step order

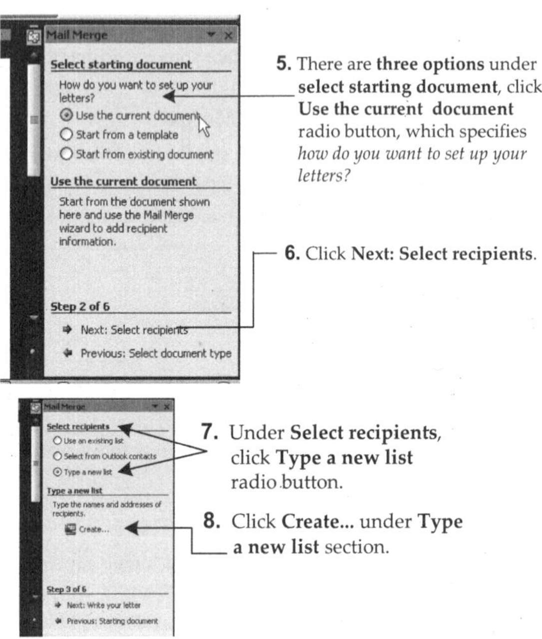

5. There are **three options** under **select starting document**, click **Use the current document** radio button, which specifies *how do you want to set up your letters?*
6. Click **Next: Select recipients**.
7. Under **Select recipients,** click **Type a new list** radio button.
8. Click **Create...** under **Type a new list** section.

Specifying Data Source

It contains the fields you specified in the data source. You can enter as many data records as are required. After entering data, click the close button to save the Address list.

Notes:

Adding and Removing Field names:

*As you may not require all the field names in the New Address List dialog box, so for each of the following field names, first select the field and then click the **Customize Columns...** button.*

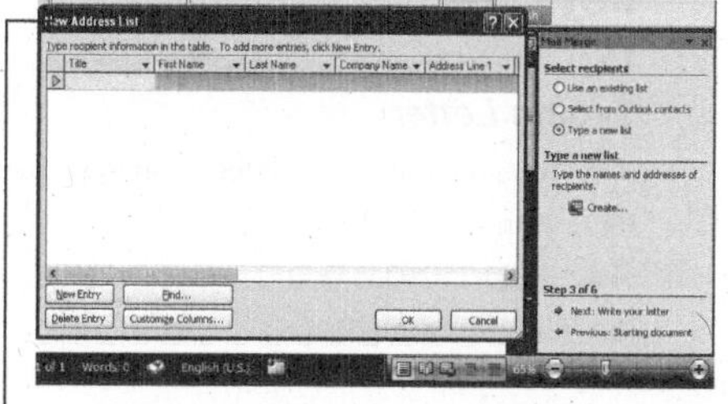

9. A **New Address List** dialog box appears. Type the information you want to include for the data source.

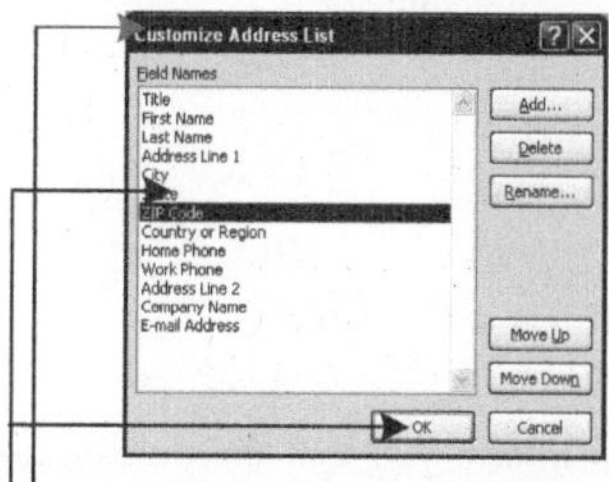

10. The **Customize Address List** dialog box appears.

11. Select the **Field names** order appears in the **Customize Address list** dialog box, then click OK.

Saving Data Source

When you have finished adding, removing and arranging fields, click OK to save your data source.

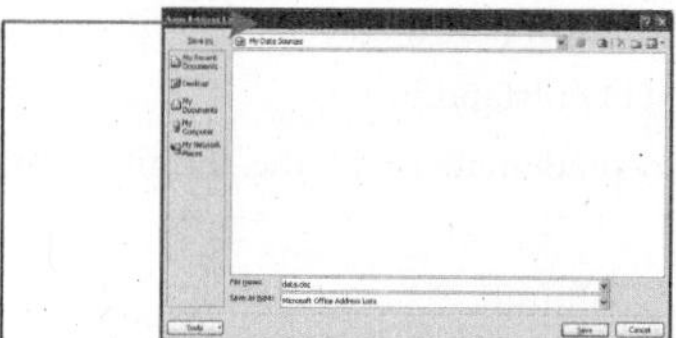

12. The **Save Address List** dialog box appears. Enter a name and location for your data source file, say, **Data.doc** in the **File name:** list box. Then click **Save** button to save the file.

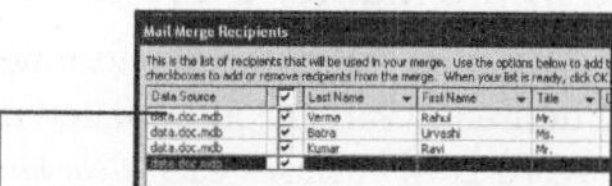

13. The Mail Merge Recipients dialog box appears. Select the receipients that will be used in your merge process.

Notes:

If you have installed address validation software, you can click Validate addresses in the Mail Merge Recipients dialog box to validate your recipients' addresses.

14. Click OK.

15. Click Next: Write your letter.

Typing Letter

Now type the following letter as an example:

Pitampura

New Delhi-110 034

Ref. Rahul/Comm/20

Dated: 3rd June, 2010

To

<<Title>> <<FirstName>>

<<LastName>>

<<Address1>>

<<City>>-<<Pin>>

Dear <<Title>> <<LastName>

I have to inform you that the meeting of the club committee will be held at the Club House, 36-N, Chanakyapuri, Vinay Marg on Tuesday 25th June, 2010 at 9.30 p.m. I hope you will make it convenient to attend the conference. The agenda for the conference is as under:

1. Confirmation of the minutes of the last meeting (enclosed).
2. Accounts and Internal Auditors Report for the months of Feb and March 2010 (enclosed).
3. Election of new members.
4. List of outstanding
5. Any other matter with the permission of the Chairman.

Yours faithfully,

P.K.Verma

(Secretary)

Inserting Fields Names in the Master Document

When you place the merge field names into a master document, you are essentially telling Word 2010 where you desire the variable information from the *data source* file to appear. You will see that Word 2010 encloses each *field name* in chevrons i.e. the marks represented as << >>.

Notes:

Resume a Mail Merge:

If you need to stop working on a mail merge, you can save the main document and resume the merge later. Word 2010 retains the data source and field information. If you were using the ***Mail Merge*** *task pane, Word 2010 returns to your place in the task pane when you resume the merge.*

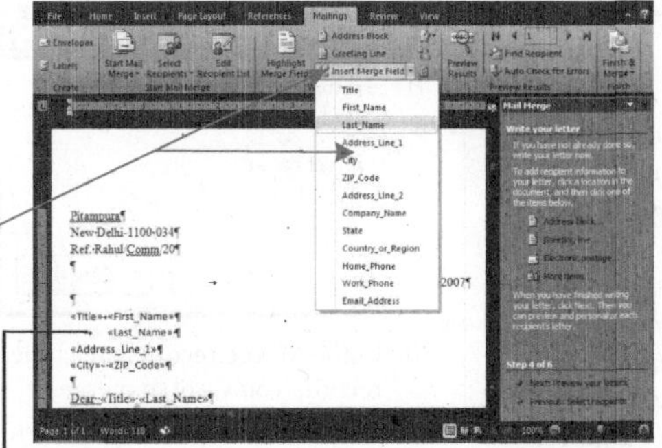

1. In the Mailing tab, click **Insert Merge Field** in the **Write & Insert Fields** group.
2. Click the down pointing arrow and choose the field names that you can insert in your master document appears. You select field names from this list.

Saving the Master Document

3. After you have completed the main document and inserted all of the merge fields, click Save As on the Office button.
4. Give the name of the document, and then click **Save** button.
5. Click **Next: Preview your letters.**

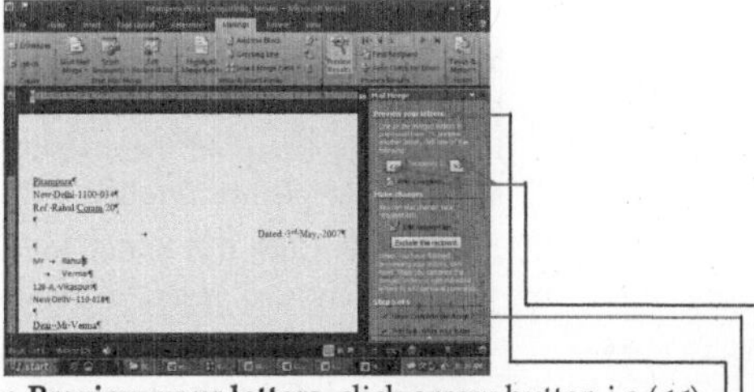

6. In the **Preview your letters**, click arrow button i.e (<<) to show the first record, and to go the second record click (>>) arrow button.
7. Click **Next: Complete the merge.**
8. To personalize individual documents, you actually complete the merge, and then edit the information you want in the resulting merged document.
9. Click **Edit individual letters...** . under **Make changes.** The **Merge to New Document** dialog box appears.

Notes:

*By default, Word 2010 embeds pictures in a document. You can reduce the size of a file by linking to a picture. In the **Insert Picture** dialog box, click the arrow next to **Insert**, and then click **Link to File**.*

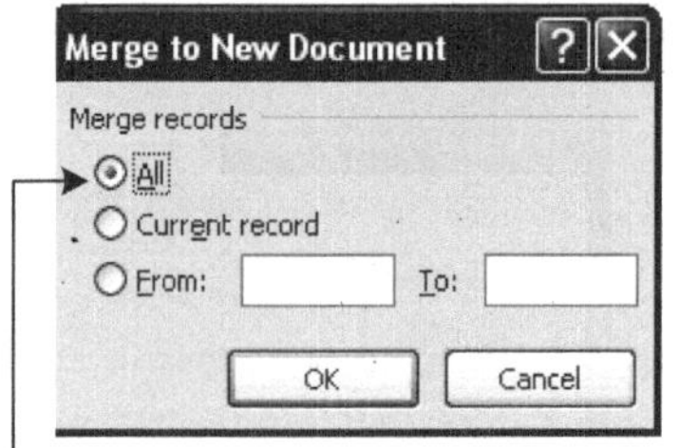

10. In the **Merge records** area, select the records you want to merge.
11. Click **All** radio button and then click OK.

Word 2010 creates and opens a new merged document. Your main document also remains open. You can switch back to it if you want to make a change to all the documents and then save all the merged documents. Click Office button and Save the file.

Printing the Merged Letters

If you want to print the letters, make sure that the printer is switched on and is in ready to print. Then click the print... under Merge. Or click **Finish & Merge** in **Finish** group. Click down pointing arrow and choose **Print Documents...** . The **Merge to Printer** dialog box appears. Select the records and click OK.

Insert Picture Command

You can insert scanned photographs or pictures created in any program into a Word 2010 document. Two button in the illustrations group on the Insert tab can be used to specify the source of the picture as follows:

- **Picture:** Click this button to insert a picture from a file. Or you can also insert a picture directly from the digital camera.
- **Clip Art:** Click this button to insert one of the hundreds of clip art images that come with Word 2010 such as photos and drawings of people, places and things etc.

To insert a Picture

1. Open the document in which you want to insert the graphics.
2. Position the insertion point where you want the graphics to appear.
3. Click the **Insert** tab and choose **Picture** icon in the **Illustration** group. **Insert Picture** dialog box of Word 2010 appears.

Notes:

Insert a linked picture from a Web page

1. Open the Word document.

2. On the Web page, right-click the picture you want, and then click ***Copy****.*

3. In the Word document, right-click where you want to insert the picture, and then click ***Paste****.*

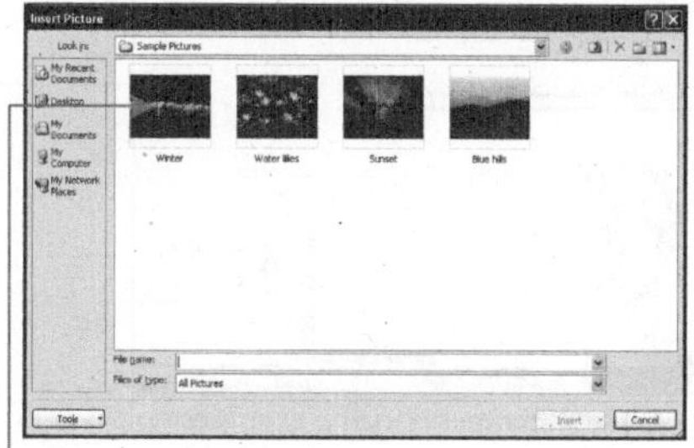

4. In **Insert Picture** dialog box, displaying the contents of your Sample Pictures folder.
5. Select the desired picture you want to insert in the document.

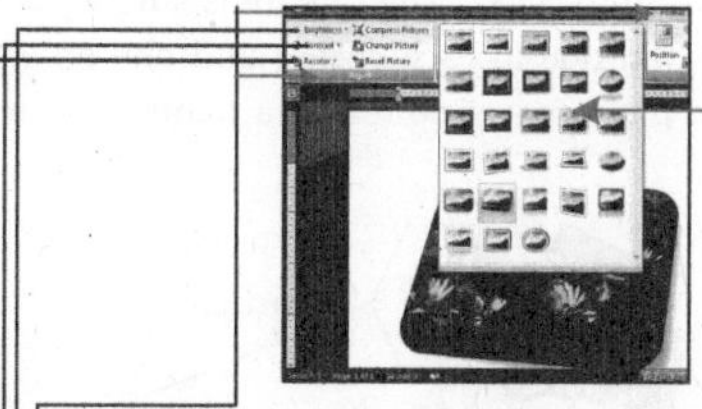

6. On the **Format** contextual tab, in the **Adjust** group, choose the desired option you want to apply in the picture.
   Brightness: It increase or decrease the brightness of the picture.
   Contrast: It increase or decreases the contrast of the picture.
   Recolor: Recolors the picture to give it a stylized effect such as grayscale or light.
7. In the **Picture Styles** group, click the **More** button. The **Picture Styles** gallery opens.
8. In the gallery, point to each thumbnail in turn to see its effect. Then, click the desired style you want to apply.

To insert a Clip Art

1. Open the document in which you want to insert the graphic.
2. Position the insertion point where you want the graphics to appear.
3. Click the **Insert** tab and choose **Clip Art** icon in the **Illustration** group.

4. In the **Clip Art task pane**, select the graphics you want to insert in the document.
5. Click the arrow right side of the picture. A pop up menu appears. Click **Insert**.

Resizing Graphics

Click the graphics you want to select. The picture is surrounded by a box containing eight handles. You will find one in each corner and one on each side of the outline box. When you position the mouse pointer on a handle, it turns into a two-headed arrow.

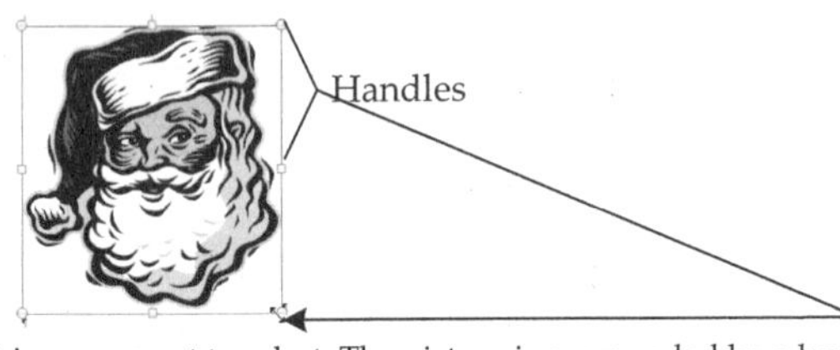

1. Click the graphics you want to select. The picture is surrounded by a box containing eight handles.
   You will find one in each corner and one on each side of the outline box.
2. When you position the mouse pointer on a handle, it turns into a two-headed arrow.
3. To increase or decrease the size of the entire graphic proportionally (*height* and *width* increases proportionally), drag a *corner* handle diagonally, releasing it when the image is of proposed size.
4. To distort a dimension, use the handles on the edges of the graphics.

Drawing in MS Word 2010

The Drawing feature allows you to create your own drawing or edit a pre-existing drawing.

1. Click the Insert tab, in the **illustrations** group, click **Shapes** button. Click the down pointing arrow and choose the different shapes such as *lines, Basic shapes, flowchart, Block arrows, callouts,* etc.

Notes:

Drawing features can be used to format Clip Art, text boxes, Word Art, and AutoShapes

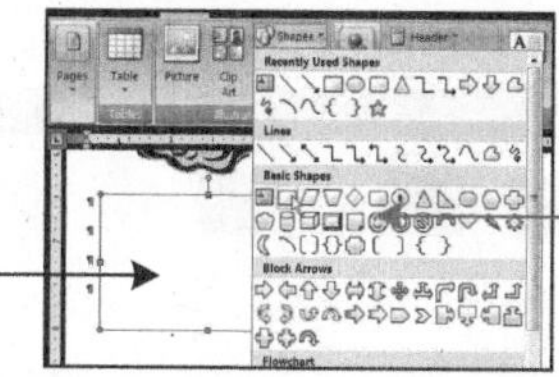

2. For example, to draw rectangle, under **Basic shapes:** click a rectangle button.
3. Click on the page to set the rectangle's upper left corner, and drag with your mouse to create a rectangle of the desired shape and size. (Holding down the key while you do this creates squares)

Change the Appearance of a Drawing

If you want to change the Outline, Shape fill and other formatting can be changed depending on the type of drawing you are editing.

1. Click the drawing object you want to change.
2. Click the **Format** tab in the **Shape Styles** group.
3. Click drop-down arrows for the effects you want to apply.

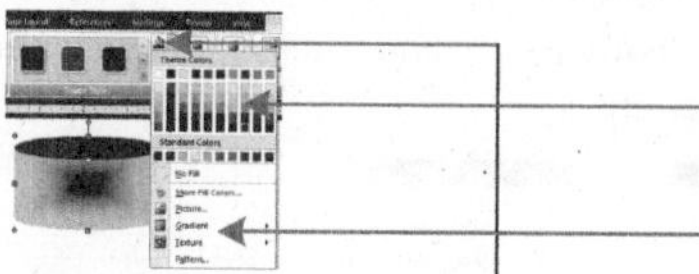

4. Click Shape fill drop-down arrow.
5. Choose the desired colour you want to apply.
6. If you want to apply Gradient or Texture, select the desired options you want to apply with the selected object.

To apply an Outline Fill

1. Click the drawing object you want to apply the Outline.
2. Click the **Format** tab, in the **Shape Styles** group.

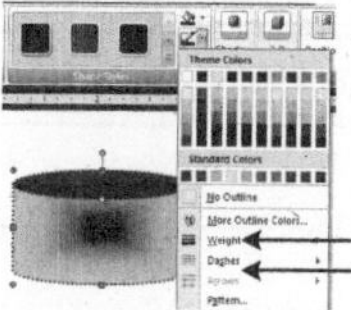

3. Click Outline drop-down arrow.
4. To apply line width, click the **Weight** option. A sub menu appears, choose the desired options you want to apply to the selected object.
5. To apply Dash style, click the **Dashes** option. A sub menu appears, choose the desired options you want to apply to the selected object.

Notes:

Add text to Shape

Right-click the shape that you want to add text to, click Add Text, and then type your text.

Applying Styles to Objects

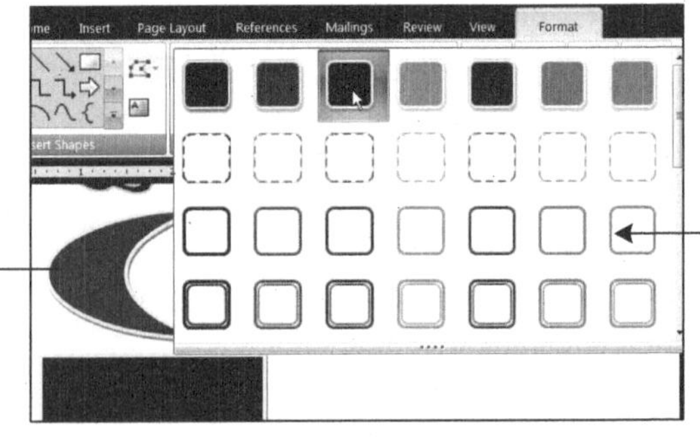

1. Click the Object you want to apply style. The selected objects are surrounded by small handles.
2. Click **Format** contextual tab, click **Shape Style** group. Click **More** button. A list of styles appears.

Rotate a Drawing

1. Select the object you want to rotate.
2. Click the **Format** tab and choose **Rotate** option in the **Arrange** group.

The text that you add becomes part of the shape — if you rotate or flip the shape, the text rotates or flips also.

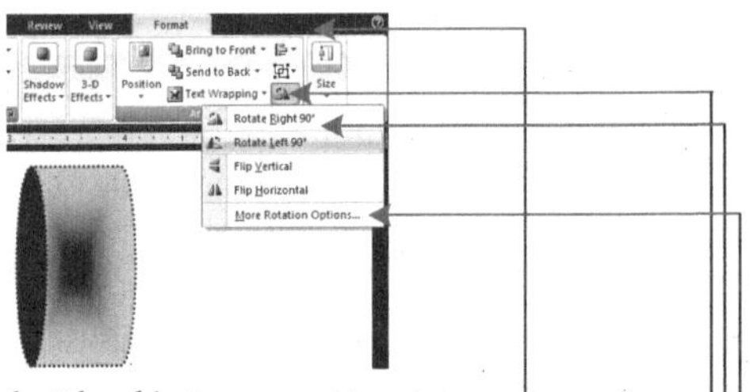

3. Select the object you want to rotate.
4. Click the **Format** tab. In **Arrange** group click **Rotate** drop-down arrow.
5. Select the desired option you want to rotate at right 90 degree and Left 90 degree.

Or

6. Click the **More Rotation Options...** .
7. The **Format Autoshapes** dialog box appears.

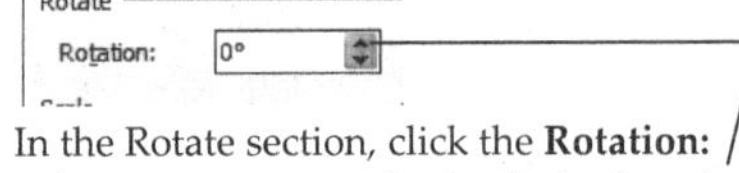

8. In the Rotate section, click the **Rotation:** spinner arrow to apply the desired angle.

Grouping an Object

Several objects can be combined into one object to make moving and editing easy.

1. Click the objects that you want to include in a group.
2. Click the **Format** tab and choose **Rotate** option in the **Arrange** group.

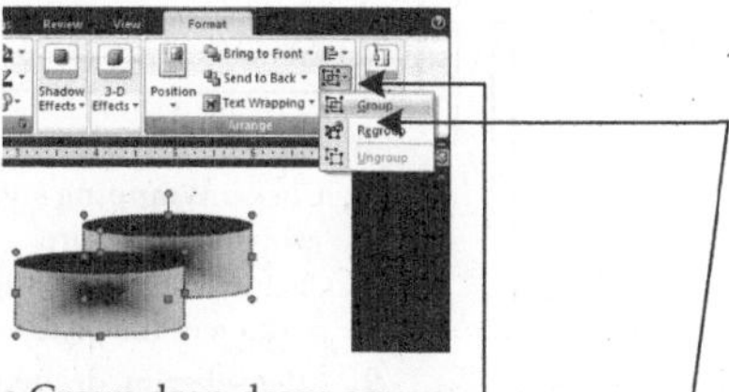

3. Click the Group drop-down arrow.
4. A list of options appears. Choose the Group option.
5. The selected object grouped into single object.

Notes:

Delete an object:

Click the shape that you want to delete, and then press Delete.

Wrap Text Around Images

By default, text appears only above and below any image you insert. You can make the text flow beside the image in several ways.

1. Select the image.
2. Click the **Format** tab. In the **Arrange** group, click **Text Wrapping** drop-down arrow.

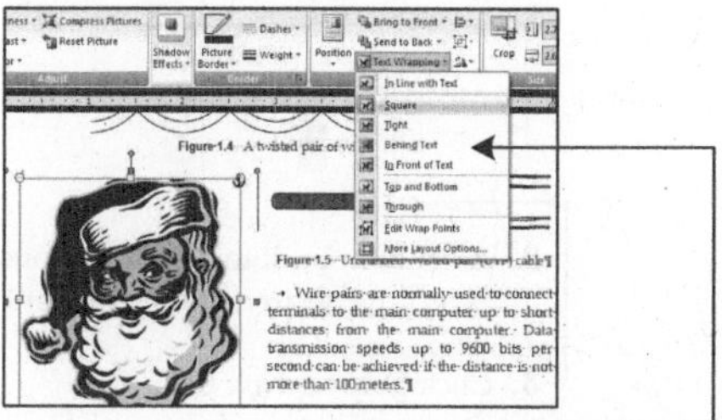

3. A list of text wrapping options appears. Select the desired option you want to position the image.

   Or

4. Right-click the image, then click Format Picture.
5. The **Format Picture** dialog box appears.

Notes:

You can change the distance of the surrounding text from the drawing by clicking the Advanced button in the Format Picture dialog box.

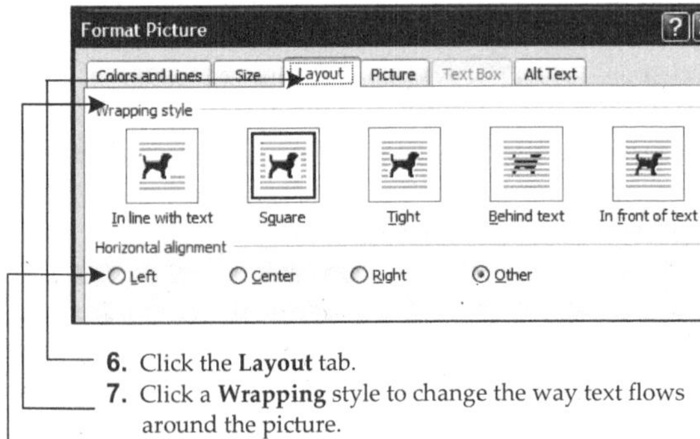

6. Click the **Layout** tab.
7. Click a **Wrapping** style to change the way text flows around the picture.
8. Click a **Horizontal alignment** option to change the position of the picture.
9. After selecting desired option, click OK.

Create a Text Box

The Text Box feature is used to format quotes, sidebars, and other text in an outlined or shaded box. The surrounding text can be set to flow around or through the text box in a variety of ways.

To create a text box do the following steps:

1. Click the Insert tab. In the Text group, click Text Box drop-down arrow.

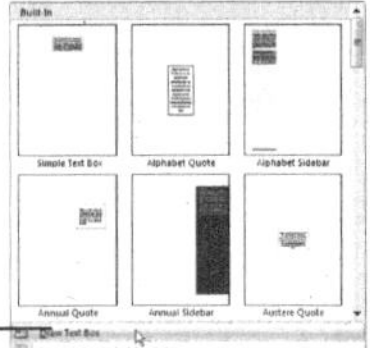

2. A list of in-built text style options appears. Select the desired style you want to apply.
   Or
3. Click Draw a Text Box.
4. The pointer turns into a large plus sign.
5. Click and drag to create a text box. Make the box as small or as large as you want it.

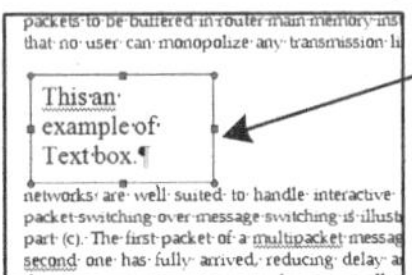

6. Type the desired text.
7. When finished, click outside body text.

Format a Text Box

1. Select the text box to be modified.
2. Click the **Format** contextual tab, click **Size** down pointing arrow and choose **Size Launcher** Dialog box.

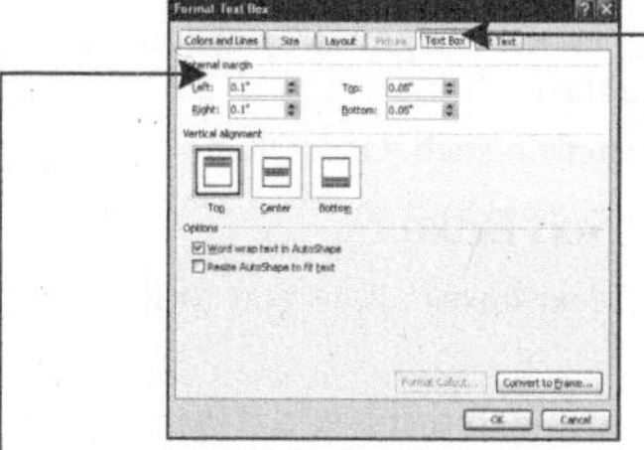

3. The **Format Text Box** dialog box appears.
4. Click the Text Box tab.
5. Type or scroll to the desired internal margins (the distance between the text and the outer border of an object.) i.e. left, right, top and bottom margins.

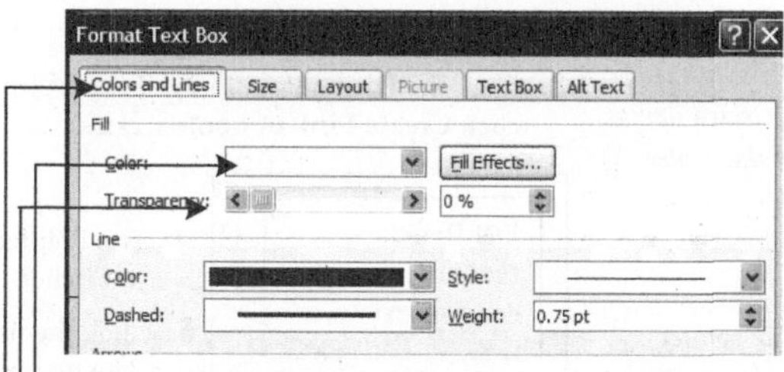

6. To change text box borders, click the **Colors and Lines** tab.
7. Click the **Color** drop-down arrow in the Fill area to change the color inside the text box.
8. Click and drag the **Transparency:** slider to lighten the chosen color.

9. Click the **Color** drop-down arrow in the **Line** area to change the color of the text box outline.
10. Click the **Dashed** drop-down arrow to choose a solid or a dashed outline.

Notes:

You can simultaneously undo multiple changes that you made to one dialog box option, as long as you did not make changes to another dialog box option in between.

Notes:

Change Text Box Size:

1. Select the text box.

2. Click one of the handles that appears at the corner and center of each edge of the box, and drag until the box is of the desired size.

Moving Objects

1. Select the item(s) to be removed.

2. Point to one of the selected items with the mouse pointer, avoiding the object's handles.

3. The pointer will change, to an arrow with four heads.

4. While the pointer has this shape, drag it with your mouse and watch as an outline of the object(s) proposed a new location.

5. Releasing the mouse button completes the move.

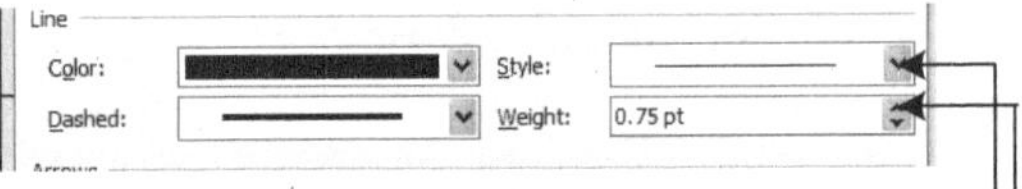

11. Click the **Style:** drop-down arrow to choose a single or double outline.

12. Click the **Weight:** drop-down arrow to set the width of the outline.

13. After finished, click OK.

Link Text Boxes

Linked text boxes allow you to flow text from one box to the next.

1. Create two text boxes. Type or paste with text in the First text box.
2. Click the first text box to select it.

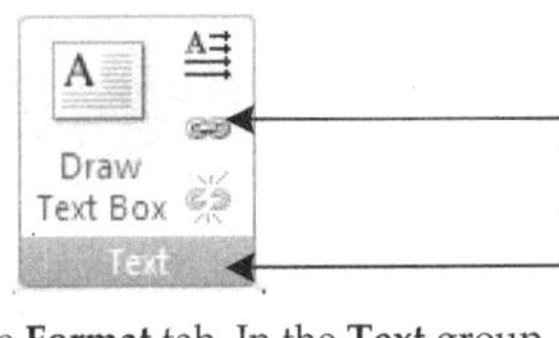

3. Click the **Format** tab. In the **Text** group click **Create Link** option.

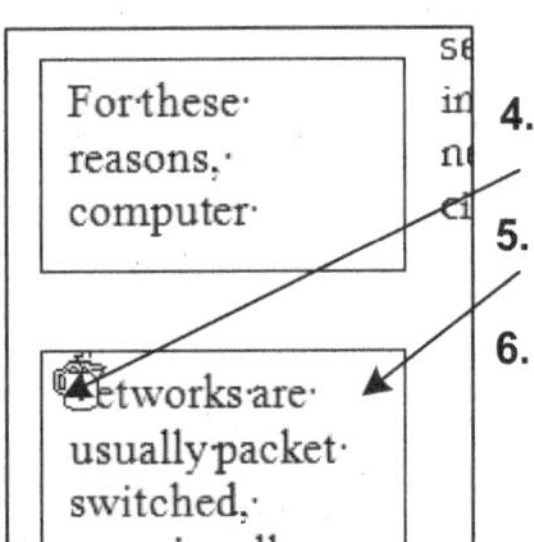

4. The Pointer changes to Pitcher.
5. Click the next text box. The text pours.
6. To remove the pitcher pointer, press Esc.

Break Links Between Text Boxes

1. Click the first box containing the link you want to break.
2. Click **Break Line** option in the **Text** group.

WordArt

WordArt is a gallery of text styles that you can add to MS Word 2010 documents to create decorative effects, such as shadowed or mirrored (reflected) text.

Add WordArt

To add WordArt do the following steps:

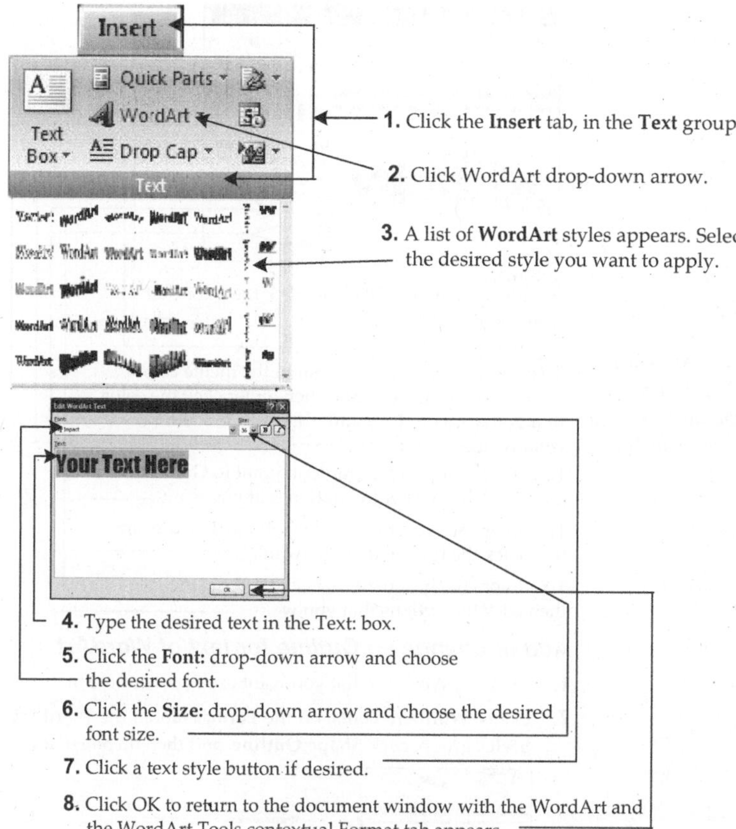

You can customize the shape surrounding the WordArt as well as the text in the WordArt.

Notes:

Delete the WordArt:

Select the WordArt that you want to remove, and then press Delete.

To edit WordArt, right-click the WordArt. From the pop-up menu that appears, choose Edit Text. The Edit WordArt Text dialog box appears so you can edit your text.

Add or change a fill for text of WordArt

1. Click the **WordArt** that you want to add a fill to.
2. Under **WordArt** Tools, on the **Format** tab, in the **WordArt Styles** group, click Shape Fill, and then do one of the

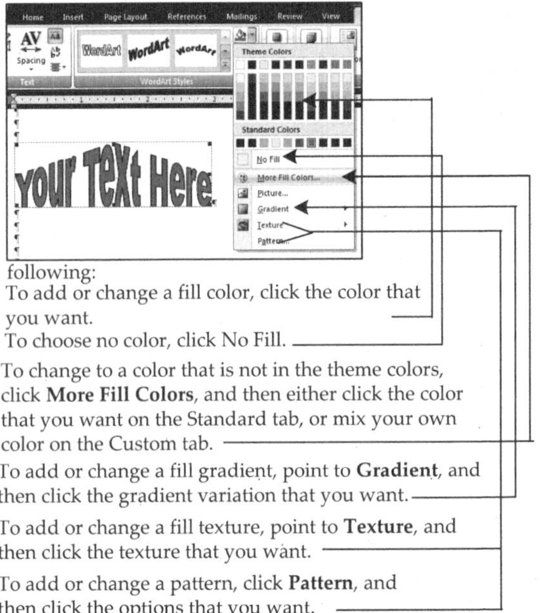

following:

To add or change a fill color, click the color that you want.

To choose no color, click No Fill.

To change to a color that is not in the theme colors, click **More Fill Colors**, and then either click the color that you want on the Standard tab, or mix your own color on the Custom tab.

To add or change a fill gradient, point to **Gradient**, and then click the gradient variation that you want.

To add or change a fill texture, point to **Texture**, and then click the texture that you want.

To add or change a pattern, click **Pattern**, and then click the options that you want.

Add or change an Outline for text of WordArt

1. Click the WordArt that you want to add an outline to.
2. Under **WordArt Tools**, on the **Format** tab, in the **WordArt Styles** group, click **Shape Outline**, and then do one of the

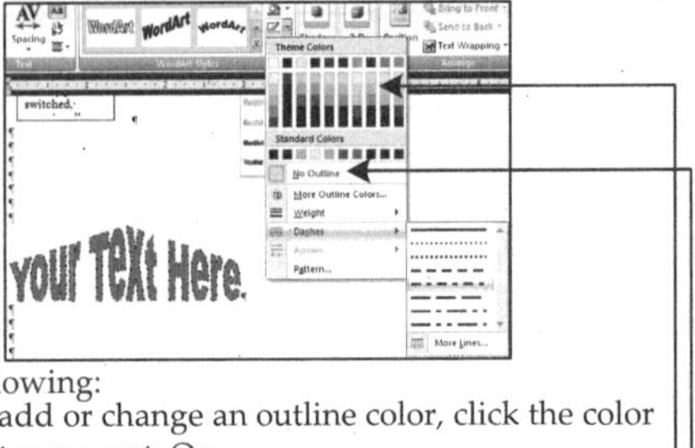

following:

To add or change an outline color, click the color that you want. Or

To choose no color, click **No Outline**.

Notes:

Delete a fill from text or WordArt:

1. Click the WordArt that you want to delete a fill from.

*2. Under **WordArt Tools**, on the **Format** tab, in the **WordArt Styles** group, click **Shape Fill**, and then click **No Fill**.*

To change WordArt Shape:

*1. Under WordArt Tools on the Format tab in the WordArt Styles choose **Change WordArt Shape**.*

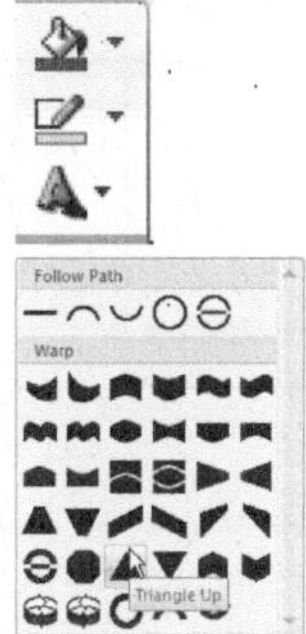

2. Choose the desired style you want to apply.

To add or change the thickness of the outline, point to **Weight**, and then click the thickness that you want.

To add or change the outline to dots or dashes, point to **Dashes**, and then click the style that you want.

To add or change the pattern, click Pattern, and then click the options that you want.

Add or change an effect for text of WordArt

1. Click the WordArt that you want to add an outline to.
2. Under **WordArt Tools**, on the **Format** tab, in the **WordArt Styles** group, click **Shape Outline**, and then do one of the

following:

To add or change a shadow, in the **Shadow Effects** group.

Click Shadow Effects drop-down arrow and then click the shadow style you want to apply.

To add a 3-D effect, click **3-D Effects**, click the second 3-D Effects, and then choose the options that you want.

Create Table of Contents from the Gallery

The easiest way to create a table of contents is to use the built-in heading styles. You can also create a table of contents that is based on the custom styles that you have applied.

To create a table of contents by applying heading styles — for example, Heading 1, Heading 2, and Heading 3 — to the text that you want to include in the table of contents. Word 2010 searches for those headings and then inserts the table of contents into your document.

Notes:

Word 2010 provides a gallery of automatic table of contents styles. Mark the table of contents entries, and then click the table of contents style that you want from the gallery of options.

1. Click where you want to insert the table of contents.

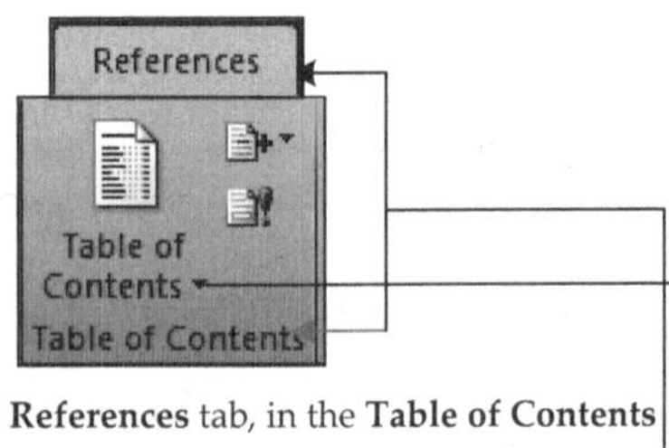

2. Click the **References** tab, in the **Table of Contents** group.
3. Click the down arrow.

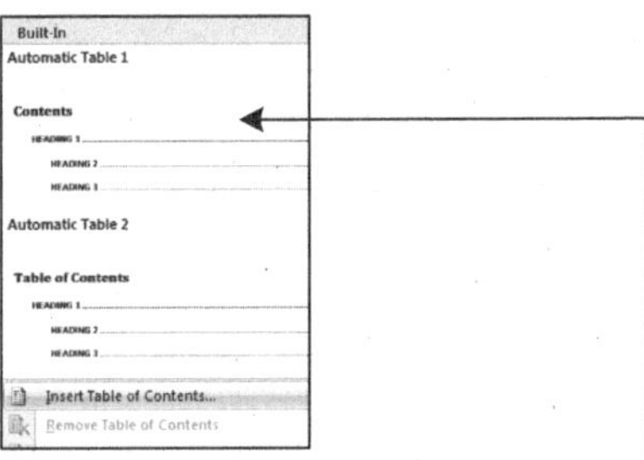

4. A list of Built-in styles appear. Click **Insert Table of Contents...** .

Delete a table of Contents

1. On the reference tab, in the Table of Contents group, click Table of Contents.

*2. Click **Remove Table of Contents**.*

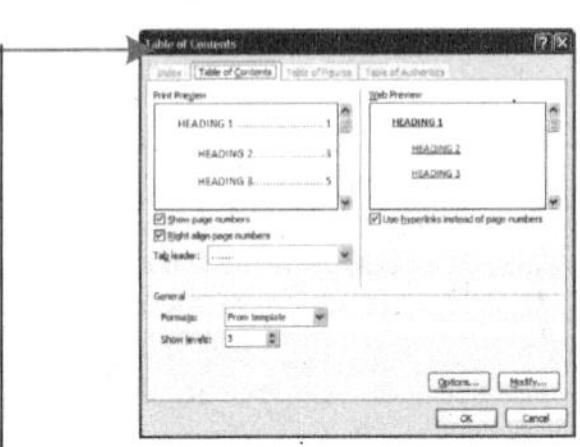

5. A list of Built-in styles appear. Click **Insert Table of Contents...** .

> **Notes:**
>
> *To use custom style in the table of contents, click Options in the Table of Contents dialog box.*
>
> *1. Under* ***Available styles****, find the style that you applied to the headings in the document.*
>
> *2. Under* ***TOC*** *level, next to the style name, type a number from 1 to 9 to indicate the level that you want the heading style to appear.*
>
> *3. Click OK.*

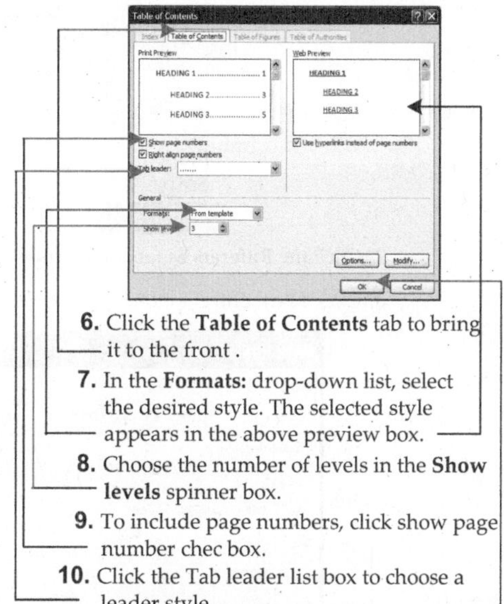

6. Click the **Table of Contents** tab to bring it to the front .
7. In the **Formats:** drop-down list, select the desired style. The selected style appears in the above preview box.
8. Choose the number of levels in the **Show levels** spinner box.
9. To include page numbers, click show page number chec box.
10. Click the Tab leader list box to choose a leader style.
11. When finished, click OK.

Update a Table of Contents

If you added or removed headings or other table of contents entries in your document, you can quickly update the table of contents.

1. Click the **References** tab, in the **Table of Contents** group.
2. Click Update Table.
3. Click Update page numbers only or Update entire table.

Mark Index Entries

Word 2010 can automatically create an index based on text you select.

1. Select the text you want to use as an index entry, or click the location to which you want an index entry to refer.

Notes:

To change the style of the page number, click bold or italic in the Mark index entry dialog box.

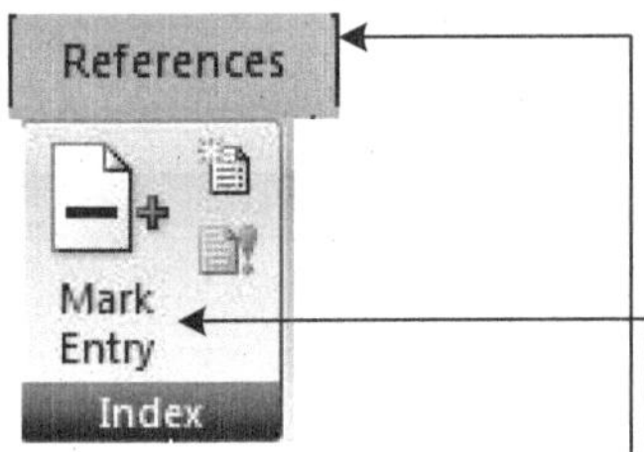

2. Click the **References** tab, in the **Index** group.

3. Click Mark Entry option.

Indexes come in handy when creating lengthy documents. Mark all commonly used concepts in the document.

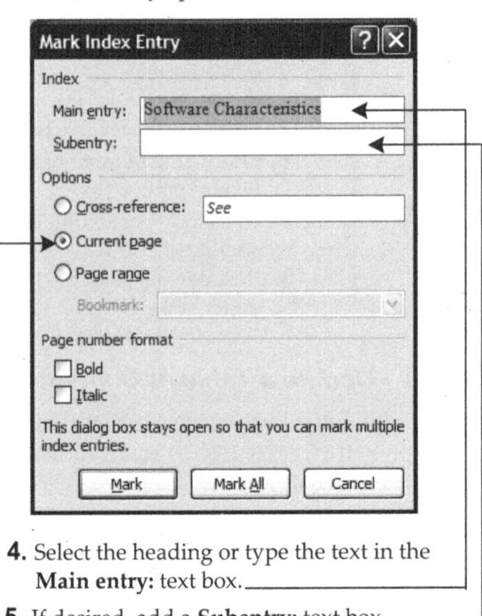

4. Select the heading or type the text in the **Main entry:** text box.

5. If desired, add a **Subentry:** text box.

6. Click the desired index option:
   - *Cross-reference* to refer to another index entry (type the entry in the text box).
   - *Current page* to refer to the current page only.
   - *Page range Bookmark* to list a range defined by a bookmark.

7. Click the Mark button. Or
   Click the Mark All button to mark all instances of the selected text in the document.

Notes:

Screenshot feature is available in Excel, Outlook, PowerPoint, and Word and you can use it to take a picture of all or part of the windows open on your computer. These screenshots are easy to read in printed documents and on PowerPoint slides that you project.

Inserting Index Entries

1. Click **Insert index,** where you want to begin the index into the document.

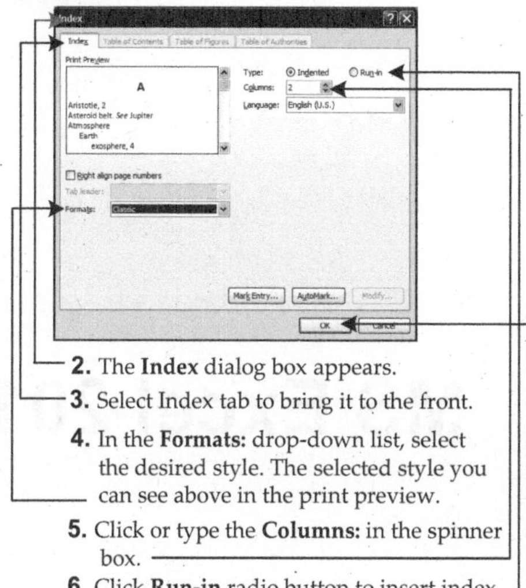

2. The **Index** dialog box appears.

3. Select Index tab to bring it to the front.

4. In the **Formats:** drop-down list, select the desired style. The selected style you can see above in the print preview.

5. Click or type the **Columns:** in the spinner box.

6. Click **Run-in** radio button to insert index entries in the document.

7. Clcik OK.

Insert a ScreenShot

You can quickly and easily add a screenshot to enhance the readability or capture information without leaving the program that you are working in.

1. Click the document that you want to add the screenshot to.

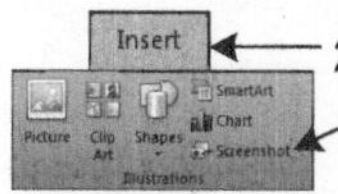

2. Click **Insert tab,** in the **Illustrations** group, click **Screenshot.**

Do one of the following options:

- To add the whole window, click the thumbnail in the **Available Windows** gallery.

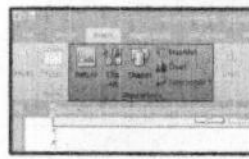

- To add part of the window, click Screen Clipping, and when the pointer becomes a cross, press and hold the left mouse button to select the area of your screen that you want to capture.

MS Excel 2010

Starting MS Excel 2010

MS Excel is a popular spreadsheet program, where you design worksheets using this software package. Excel 2010 uses a workbook-style presentation which is made up of several worksheets, like pages in a notebook. You can open Excel 2010 using Start button.

Notes:

*Excel 2010 needs **Windows Vista** or **Windows 7** as operating system to run on an IBM PC. However, Excel 2010 can also be used with **Windows XP** operating system, if **service pack 3** is installed on Windows XP.*

Excel 2010 is a popular spreadsheet program, where you design worksheets using this program.

Excel 2010 is a software package which accepts data in a tabular form, shows data in a tabular form and serves many functions to perform calculations.

Starting MS Excel 2010 in Windows 7

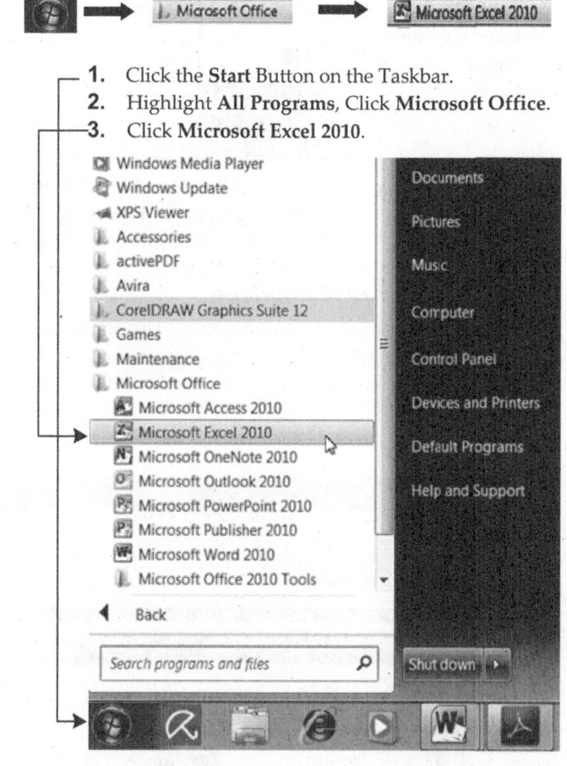

1. Click the **Start** Button on the Taskbar.
2. Highlight **All Programs**, Click **Microsoft Office**.
3. Click **Microsoft Excel 2010**.

Starting MS Excel 2010 in Windows XP

Excel 2010 has a grid of columns and rows into which you can enter numeral, text, etc. Each box in the grid is called a cell.

Notes:

A worksheet is a sheet made up of rows and columns. It refers to the actual document you create by using the spreadsheet program. The worksheet is always stored in a workbook.

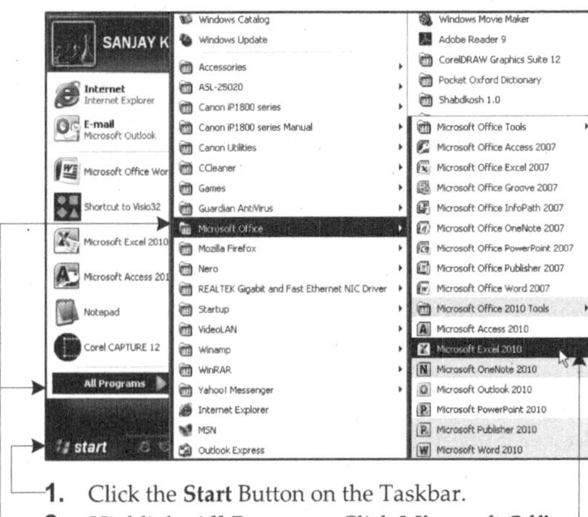

1. Click the **Start** Button on the Taskbar.
2. Highlight **All Programs**, Click **Microsoft Office**.
3. Click **Microsoft Excel 2010**.

About MS Excel 2010 Interface

Excel 2010 includes the Microsoft Office Fluent interface, which consists of a customizable visual system of tools and commands. It shows the elements of the Excel 2010 application window and an open Excel 2010 workbook in detail.

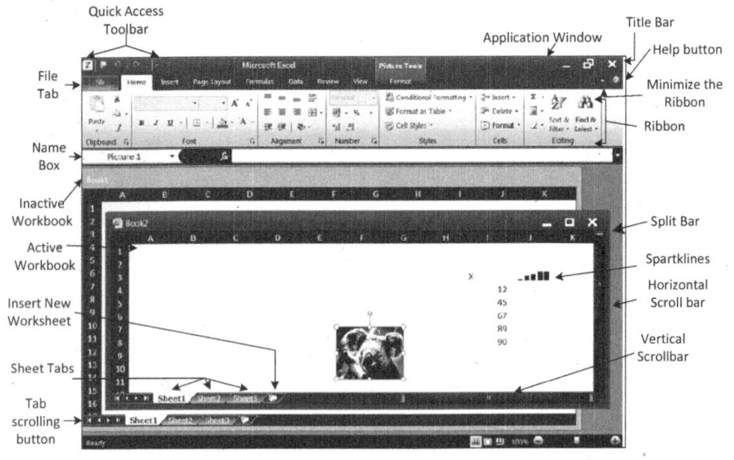

Row is a horizontal block of cells. The first row is numbered 1, the second 2, and so on. There can be a maximum of 1,048,576 rows in a worksheet.

Notes:

A column is a vertical block of cells. A worksheet contains 16,384 (Column A to Column XFD) columns. The first column is A, the second is B and so on until you reach Z. Then comes column AA through XFD which is the 16,384th column.

Cell is the intersection of a row and a column.

Formulas are equations that perform calculations on values in a worksheet. A formula always begins with = (equal) sign.

In Excel 2010, you can create your own tabs and groups and rename or change the order of the built-in tabs and groups.

Terms used in the Excel 2010 Worksheet:

Title Bar: At the top of an Excel 2010 window, there is the title bar. The left edge of this bar has the Application window control icon next to which the name of the open document is displayed. On the right edge of the title bar, *minimize, restore/maximize* and *close* buttons are placed.

Application Window: The window within which Excel 2010 runs.

Quick Access Toolbar: The buttons on the quick access toolbar represent a *command* or a *procedure.*

Active Workbook: The Excel 2010 workbook window that accepts entries and commands.

Inactive Workbook: A window that contains Excel 2010 information. It is not affected by commands. Such a window has a gray title bar and is behind the active workbook window.

Ribbon: Ribbon is displayed just below the title bar. In Ribbon, *Commands* are organized in logical *groups,* which are collected together under *tabs.* You can hide the Ribbon by double-clicking the active tab. Different types of Tabs described here under are available in the Ribbon of Excel 2010.

File Tab: It replaces the office button in Excel 2007. It contains commands like New, Open, Save, Save As, Print, etc.

Home Tab: It contains the button related to the worksheet contents.

Insert Tab: It contains the button related to the items which you can insert in your worksheet.

Page Layout Tab: It includes the button related to the appearance of the worksheet.

Formulas Tab: It contains the button related to functions.

Data Tab: It contains the button related to data.

Review Tab: It contains the button related to security and accurate data.

View Tab: It contains the button related to view of the worksheet i.e. how you want to view the worksheet?

Minimize the Ribbon: This button will minimize the Ribbon. To restore the Ribbon, again click on this button.

Scroll Bar: The scroll bar appears at the *left* for vertical scrolling and at the *bottom right* for horizontal scrolling.

To scroll one cell at a time, click the scroll button with arrows at the corners of the scroll bars.

To scroll more, drag the scroll button in the scroll bar.

Notes:

A window within the Excel 2010 application window in which a worksheet, chart, or dialog box is shown.

Shortcut menus are meant to display frequently used commands relating to the selected item or object.

A workbook is a collection of many worksheets. By default, a workbook opens with three worksheets and it can contain a maximum of 255 worksheets.

Split Bar: The split bar is located at the top of the *vertical* scroll bar and to the right of the *horizontal* scroll bar. Double click the split button on the vertical scroll bar. It splits the sheet horizontally.

Tab Scrolling Buttons: These are the arrow buttons to the left of the sheet tabs for scrolling the worksheet.

To scroll between sheet tabs, click an arrow for the direction you want to scroll.

To scroll one sheet tab at a time in left or right direction, click the middle tab scrolling buttons.

To scroll through a group of sheet tabs in left or right direction, click the tab scroll buttons at the left and right corner.

To display a list of the sheets in the workbook right click a tab scrolling button to display the menu.

Sparklines: Excel 2010 introduces this new feature which allows simple graphs to fit in a single cell.

Sheet Tabs: A tab is near to the bottom of a work book window that displays the name of a sheet. Click the sheet tab to move to the next sheet. To display the shortcut menu right click the sheet tab. To scroll through the sheet tabs, use the tab scrolling button.

Name Box: The *name box* is at the left end of the formula bar. It identifies the selected *cell, chart item* or *drawing object.*

Formula Bar: The *formula bar* displays the constant value or formula used in the active cell. The formula bar is also used for editing the cell contents.

Status Bar: Status bar appears at the bottom of the Excel 2010 window. It displays information regarding a selected command or an operation in progress. Note that the right side of the status bar shows zoom slider, different views tool such as Normal, Page.

Notes:

You can create a blank workbook or create new workbook based on an existing workbook, the default workbook template, or any other template.

Creating New Workbook

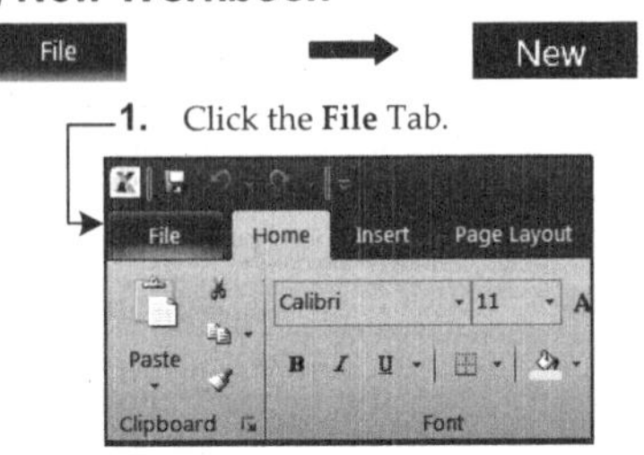

Notes:

*To create new workbook, you can also press **Ctrl + N** keys together.*

2. Select **New.**
3. Under **Available Templates**, double-click **Blank Workbook.**

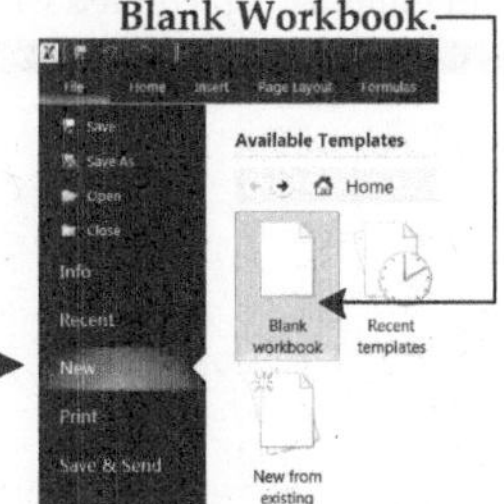

Opening a Workbook

Excel 2010 makes use of several workbooks and their worksheets. To work on any worksheet first of all, you have to open a workbook.

Notes:

You can open a workbook from open dialog box or from recently accessed list.

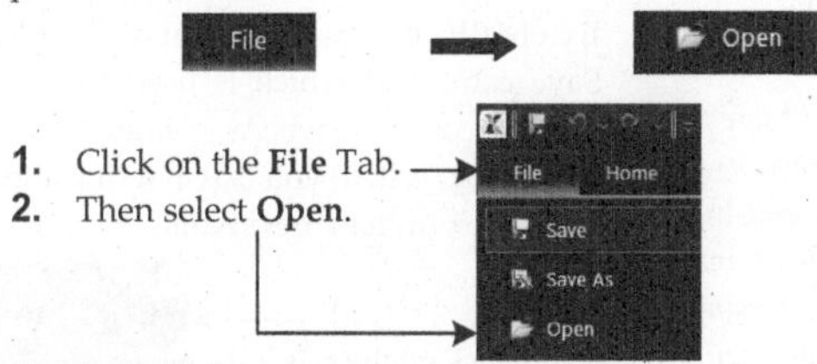

1. Click on the **File** Tab.
2. Then select **Open.**

In **Windows 7 operating system**, the Open dialog box appears as seen in the following screen.

3. In Open Dialog box, choose the drive, folder name that contains the workbooks. After finding the required workbook, select it.

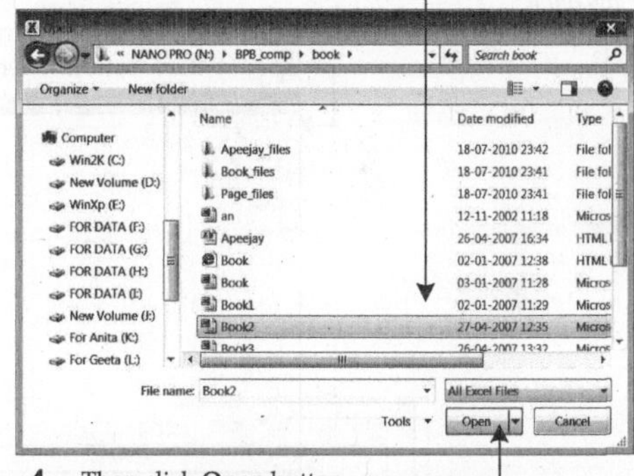

4. Then click **Open** button.

In **Windows XP with Service Pack 3 operating system**, the Open dialog box appears as shown below:

Notes:

*To open recent files choose recent files from the list of right side of the **Recent**.*

*Excel 2010 worksheet is saved with **.xlsx**.*

*You can also save your workbook by pressing (Save) button from the **Quick Launch Toolbar**.*

*To Open More than one Workbook Simultaneously repeat step 1 and 2 of opening a single workbook. Then, click the name of one file name and then hold down **Ctrl** key and click another file name and then press **Enter** key.*

3. In Open Dialog box, In Look in: choose the drive, folder name that contains the workbooks.
4. After finding the required workbook, select it.

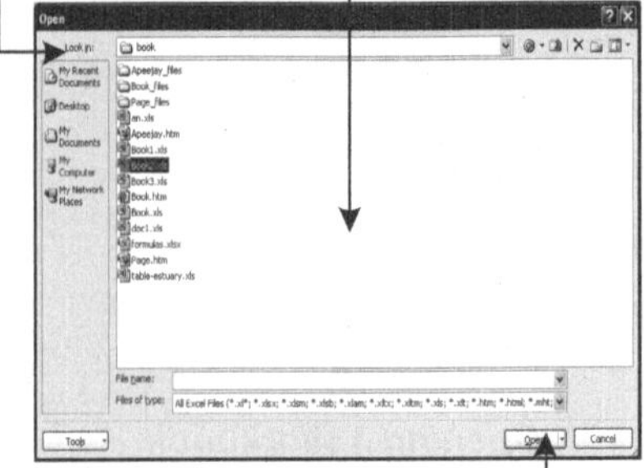

5. Then click **Open** button.

Saving a Workbook

Excel 2010 has two commands for saving workbooks. One is Save command which is used to save an existing workbook. Another one is Save As command which is used to save the workbook when you save it for the first time or save the workbook under a new name.

1. Click on the **File** Tab.
2. Then select **Save As**.

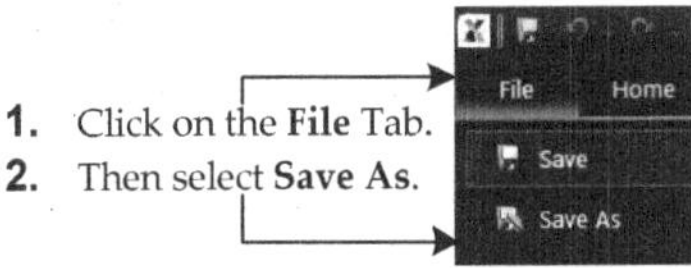

In **Windows 7 operating system**, Save As dialog box appears as seen in the following screen.

3. In Save As Dialog box, In **Save in:** drop down list specify the location where you want to save file.

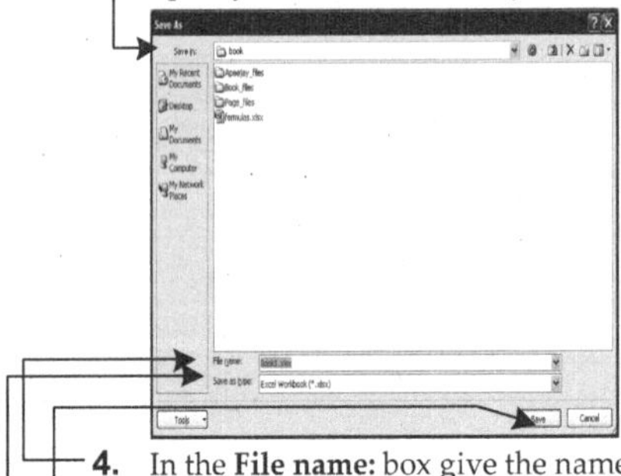

4. In the **File name:** box give the name of the file.
5. In the **Save as type:** box give the type of file.
6. Click **Save** button.

In **Windows XP with Service Pack 3 operating system**, Save As dialog box appears as seen in the figure below.

3. In Save As Dialog box, In **Save in:** drop down list specify the location where you want to save file.

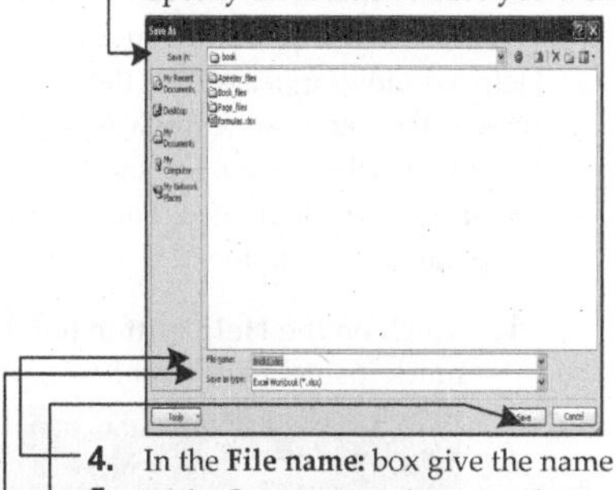

4. In the **File name:** box give the name of the file.
5. In the **Save as type:** box give the type of file.
6. Click **Save** button.

Closing a Workbook Window

When you finish using worksheet or chart, you need to close its window. If you have made any changes since the last time you saved the workbook, Excel 2010 displays an alert dialog box, asking whether you want to save your work before closing.

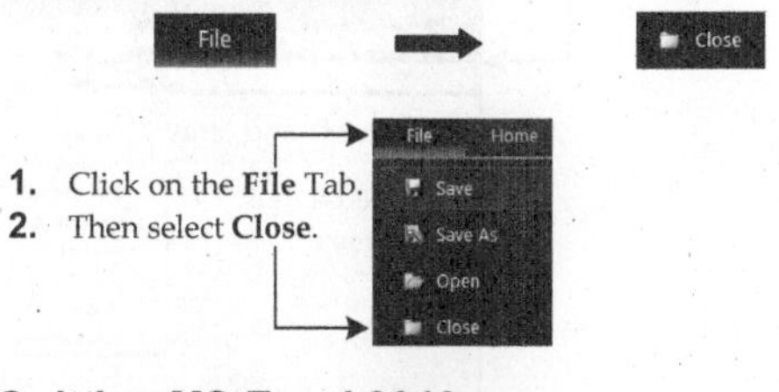

1. Click on the **File** Tab.
2. Then select **Close**.

Notes:

*In case **Alert** dialog box appears and if you click **Don't Save** a recent copy of this file then it will be temporarily available, or if you choose **Save** if you do want to save changes. Type a new file name and choose **Save**.*

*You can also quit from Excel by pressing **Close** button (X) in the top right corner or alternatively, press **Alt + F4** keys together or double-click the **Control icon** at the left of the title bar*

Quitting MS Excel 2010

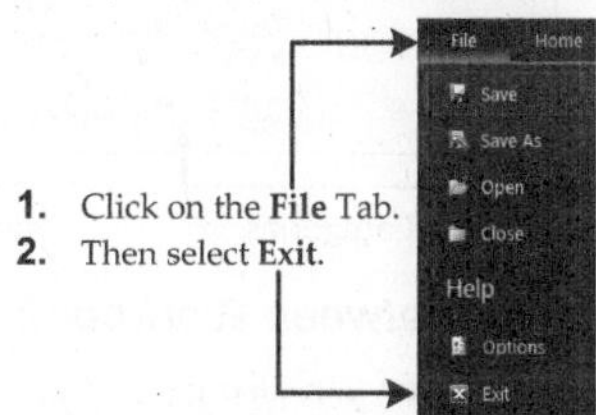

1. Click on the **File** Tab.
2. Then select **Exit**.
3. When all workbooks are closed, Excel 2010 window closes, and the application is terminated.

Notes:

The Search button shown in Help window is a drop down control that lets you specify what and where to search a file.

Getting Help

Office 2010 has been known for offering helpful advice. To take advantage of its full help feature set, make sure that you are connected online, when you request any help. The first time you use the Help feature in MS Office programs, the online Help window appears in a default location and size on your screen. You can change the way the Help window is displayed. After that, when you open the Help window, the settings that you made are maintained. Each program in MS Office 2010 has a separate Help window.

1. Click on the **Help** button (circle with question mark inside) or *Alternatively*, press **F1** key.

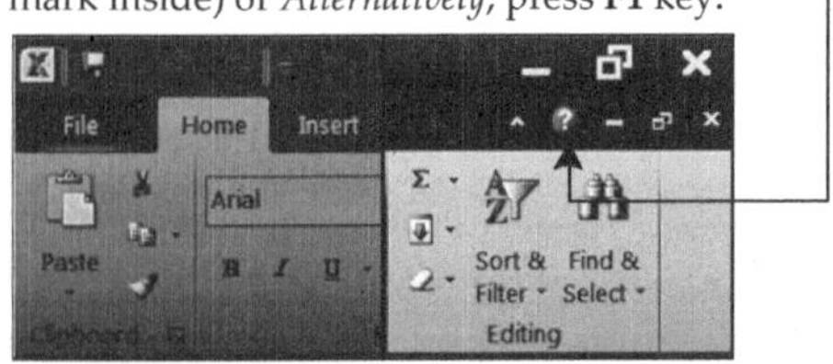

2. Type the particular word which you want to search in the search box and press **Enter** key.

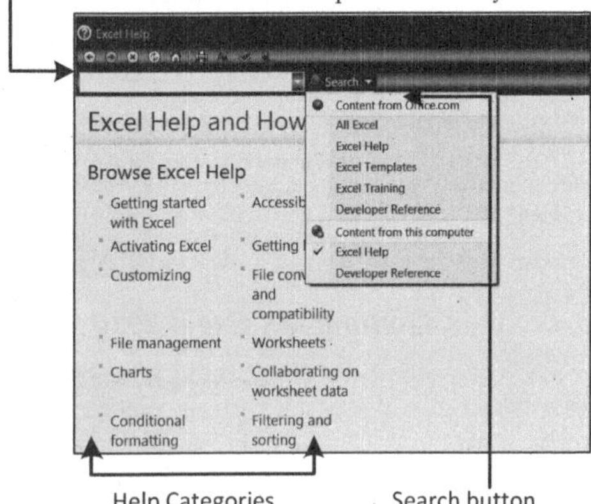

Switching between Workbook Windows

In Excel 2010, you can also get multiple workbooks open, each in its own document window. To work on a workbook you need to activate it.

1. Click on the **View Tab**.

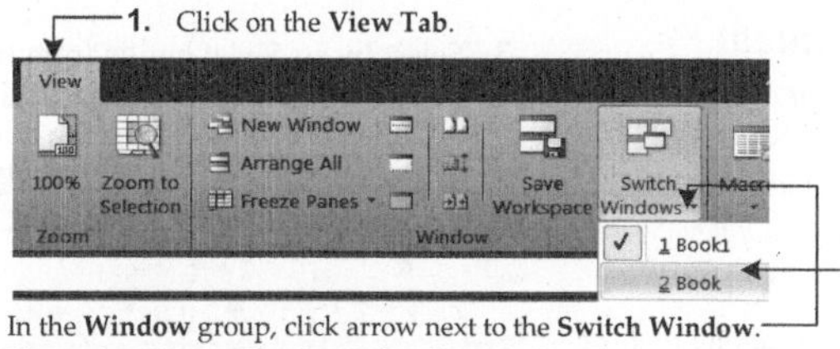

2. In the **Window** group, click arrow next to the **Switch Window**.
3. Then select the workbook window from the list of open windows.

Changing Default Number of Sheets in New Workbooks

Notes:

By default, a workbook opens with three worksheets and it can contain a maximum of 255 worksheets.

1. Click on the File Tab.
2. Then click Options.
3. Excel Options dialog box appears with **General** properties.

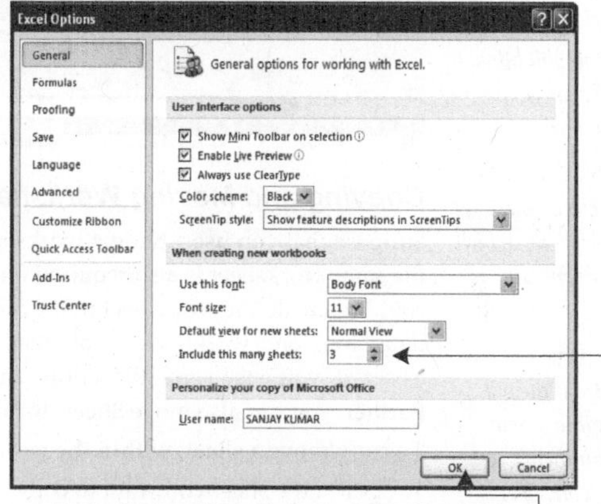

4. Enter the number of sheets in **Include this many sheets:** spinner box under the **When creating new workbooks** group.
5. Click **OK** to accept the settings.

Inserting and Deleting Sheets

Notes:

To insert or delete worksheet, position the mouse pointer on the tab of any sheet and then choose the desired option.

If you revise workbooks, you will want to *insert/delete* sheets from the workbook. Excel 2010 gives you the flexibility to easily insert and remove sheets.

To Insert a sheet in a workbook:

1. Activate the workbook into which you want to insert the sheet.
2. Select the existing sheet before which you want to insert the new sheet by clicking its sheet tab or by pressing **Ctrl + PgUp** or **Ctrl + PgDn** keys as the case may be.

Notes:

You can insert a new sheet in the workbook at any location you desire.

You cannot undo or get back a worksheet after deletion. Therefore, you should be very careful before you delete a worksheet.

Double clicking the sheet tab will allow you to change the sheet name.

An active sheet is the sheet in which you can operate.

If you move the sheet from the old location to a new location then a copy of the worksheet is left at the old location.

3. Select **Insert Sheet** option from **Insert** drop down list of the **Cells** group of the **Home Tab** Or, Press **Alt + Shift + F11** keys together to insert a new worksheet.

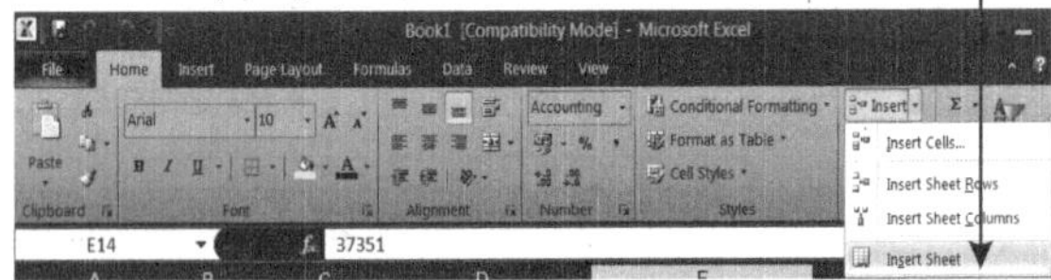

To Delete a sheet in a workbook:

1. Select the sheet you want to delete.
2. Click on the **Home tab**, in the **Cells** group. Select **Delete Sheet** from the **Delete drop down list.**

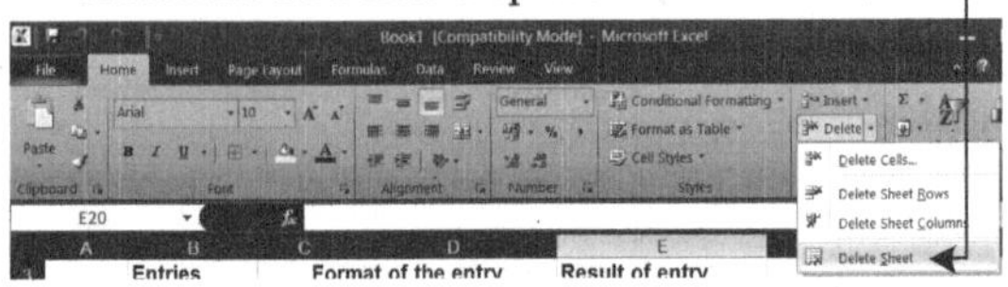

Copying and Moving Worksheets in a Workbook

Suppose that you use a budget worksheet in one workbook and the same worksheet is also required for another workbook. You could re-create the worksheet in the new workbook or copy the data from one workbook to another, but it would be much easier if you just copy the entire sheet of other workbook. Further, you can also move Sheets to new locations.

To copy/move a sheet, within the workbook:

1. Select the sheet you want to copy or move.
2. If you want to ***copy*** within the same workbook, press and hold down **Ctrl** key and drag the sheet tab to its new location.
3. However, if you want to ***move*** the sheet within the original workbook, drag the sheet tab to the location where you want to move the worksheet.

To copy worksheet between workbooks:

1. Open both the workbooks.
2. Click on the View Tab.
3. In **Window** group, click Arrange All button.
4. It will open up **Arrange Windows** Dialog box.

 ***If you want to add a sheet to the end of the workbook, you need to first insert it before an existing sheet and then move the new sheet to the end.***

Notes:

When a sheet is inserted at the new location, then name of the copied sheet will be that of the original sheet name. But, if sheet with the same name is already in the workbook, the name is followed by a number in parentheses indicating its ***copy*** *number.*

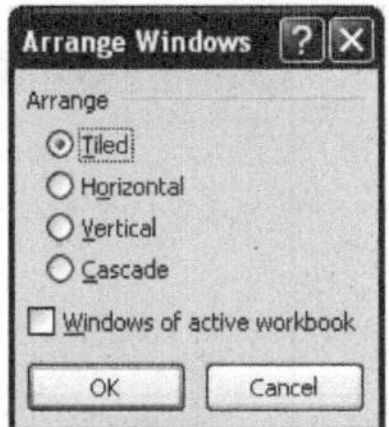

5. Select the desired arrangement.
6. Then Click **OK**.
7. ***To copy***: Press and hold down key and drag the sheet tab from one workbook onto the tabs in the other workbook.
8. ***To move***: One sheet to another workbook, drag the sheet tab onto the tabs at the bottom of the other workbook.

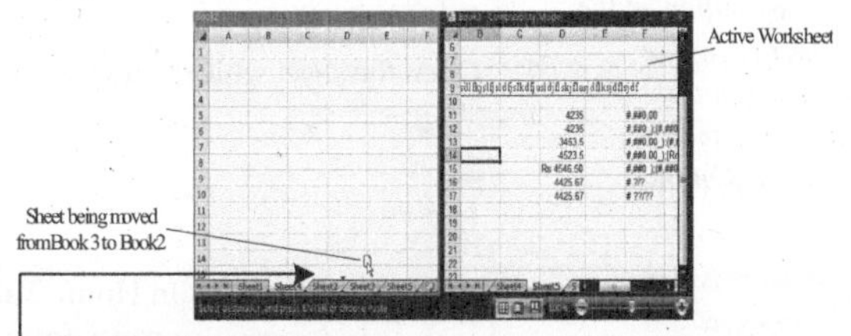

9. A black triangle appears above the receiving tabs, to show the location for the copy's insertion.
10. Release the mouse button.

Create a New Workbook and Copy the Sheet

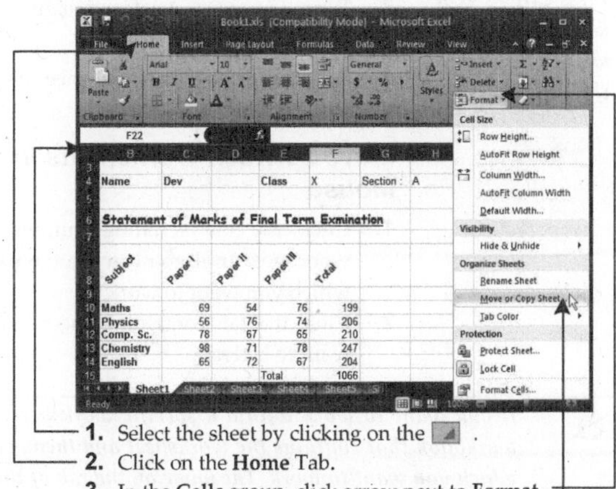

1. Select the sheet by clicking on the .
2. Click on the **Home** Tab.
3. In the **Cells** group, click arrow next to **Format**.
4. Then choose **Move or Copy Sheet...** .

It will open Move or Copy dialog box.

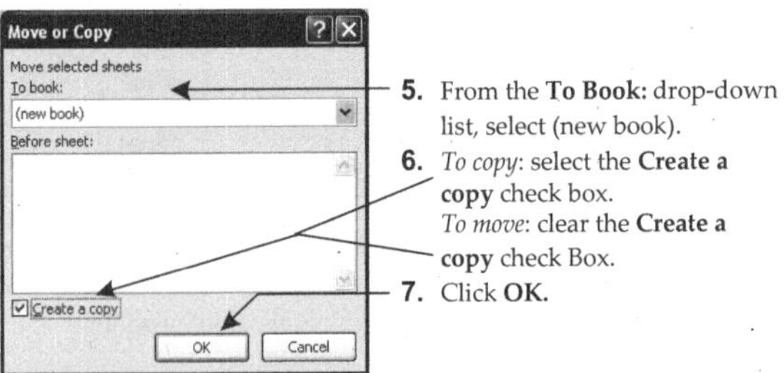

5. From the **To Book:** drop-down list, select (new book).
6. *To copy*: select the **Create a copy** check box.
   To move: clear the **Create a copy** check Box.
7. Click **OK.**

Notes:

To rename sheet, click the right mouse button on the sheet tab whose name you want to rename, and then choose ***Rename.***

To move between worksheets:

Press ***Ctrl + Pgup*** *keys together to activate previous sheet, and*

Press ***Ctrl + PgDn*** *keys together to activate the next sheet.*

Renaming a Sheet

The names assigned to worksheets in a workbook by default are Sheet 1, Sheet 2, etc. However, you can also name the sheets as per your needs.

1. Open the sheet which you want to rename.

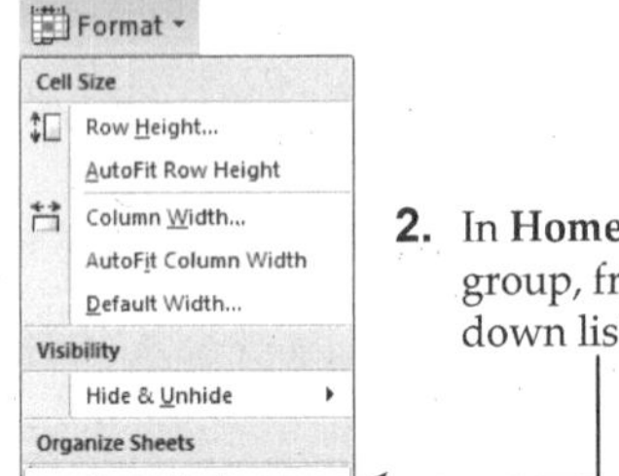

2. In **Home Tab**, under the **Cells** group, from the **Format** drop down list, select **Rename Sheet.**
3. Type the new sheet name, using up to 31 characters including spaces.
4. Press **Enter** key. The new sheet name appears on the sheet tab.

Move between Worksheets in a workbook using Mouse

1. Click the tab scrolling buttons to scroll through the workbook until you can see the name of the worksheet in which you want to work.
2. Click the tab containing the name of the worksheet you want to activate.

If you want to work within a specific worksheet, then activate first the workbook that contains the worksheet and then activate the worksheet in which you want to work. The name on the tab of the active sheet is in bold letters. You can switch between worksheets by using either the keyboard or a mouse.

Notes:

When you select a group of sheets, the word **|Group|** *is displayed in the title bar which indicates that a group of sheets is selected.*

To ***deselect*** *the group, click any sheet tab that is not selected.*

Grouping Sheets

You can perform operations on several sheets at one time by creating a *group selection.* This group selection is useful to edit or format a group of sheets *identically* or to reorganize a group of sheets. You can group the worksheets and then add text or format them all at once.

1. Select the first sheet tab.

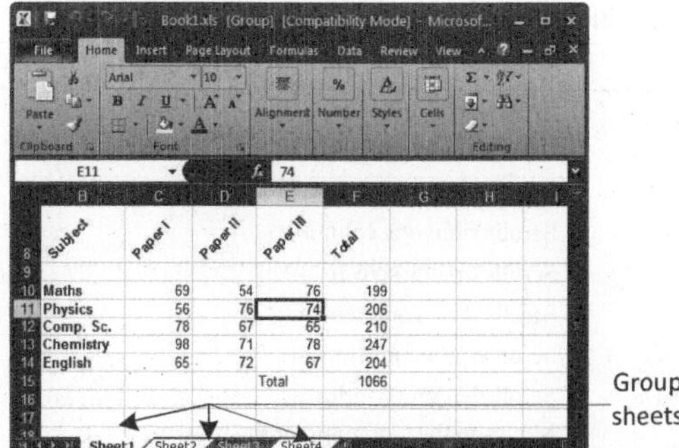

2. To select a group of adjacent sheets, press and hold down **Shift** key, while selecting the last sheet tab in the group. All sheets in between, including the first and last sheet you clicked are selected.

   OR

   To select a group of non-adjacent sheets, hold down **Ctrl** key and click the next sheet tab you want to select. Do this for each sheet tab you want to select.

Controlling the Display of Sheet Tabs

Excel gives you the flexibility to control the display of the sheet tabs at the bottom of the workbook. You can edit or choose the option to display the names of the sheet or turn off the display as per your convenience.

1. Click on the File Tab.
2. Then click Options.
3. Excel Options dialog box appears with **Advanced** properties.

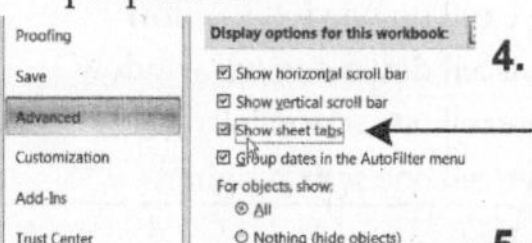

4. Click on the **Show sheet tabs** check box under the **Display options for this workbook** group.
5. Then click OK button.

Notes:

The vertical and horizontal scroll boxes give you the position in worksheet.

Scrolling with Mouse

To scroll the window with the mouse, use the scroll bars located at the right and bottom of each worksheet. The arrows in the scroll bars show the direction the window moves over the worksheet. Click the arrow to scroll in that direction.

Scrolling with Keyboard

When you scroll using a keyboard, the cell selected by you changes as you scroll. Following table shows some keys to scroll.

Key	Movement
↑	Scrolls up one row.
↓	Scrolls down one row.
←	Scrolls left one column.
→	Scrolls right one column.
PgUp	Scrolls up one screen.
PgDn	Scrolls down one screen.
Alt + PgUp	Scrolls right one window.
Alt + PgDn	Scrolls left one window.
Home	Moves to the beginning of the row.
Ctrl + Home	Moves to the beginning of the worksheet.

Selecting a Single Cell using Keyboard

Before you can *enter*, *edit* or *modify* the contents of a cell, you must select or activate the cell or cells you want to change. Following table shows keys to select a cell.

Key	Movement
↑	Moves the active cell up one cell.
↓	Moves the active cell down one cell.
→	Moves the active cell right one cell.
←	Moves the active cell left one cell.
Tab	Enters data and moves the active cell right.
Shift + Tab	Enters data and moves the active cell left.
Enter	Enters data and moves the active cell down.
Shift + Enter	Enters data and moves the active cell up in the selected range.
Ctrl + Arrow	Moves the active cell in the direction indicated by arrow until the edge of a block of data is reached
Home	Moves the active cell to column A of the current row
Ctrl + Home	Moves the active cell to the first cell in the worksheet (cell A1)
Ctrl + End	Moves the active cell to the last cell in the used portion of the worksheet
PgUp	Moves the active cell up one full window
PgDn	Moves the active cell down one full window
Alt + PgUp	Moves the active cell one screen left
Alt + PgDn	Moves the active cell one screen right

Notes:

To select a single cell using mouse, move the mouse pointer over the cell and click the cell.

*The single cell that receives the data or formula you enter is the **active cell**. A selection of multiple cells is referred to as a **range**.*

*If you want to see the active cell, but it is not visible in the window, press **Ctrl + Backspace** keys together.*

*To select a large range of cells using **Go To** command, type a range address in the Reference: box, such as **A5:F12**, and then click **OK**.*

Selecting a Range of cells

Select a range of cells when you want to apply a command to all the selected cells or want to enter data into the cells in the range.

1. Click the cell at one corner of the range.

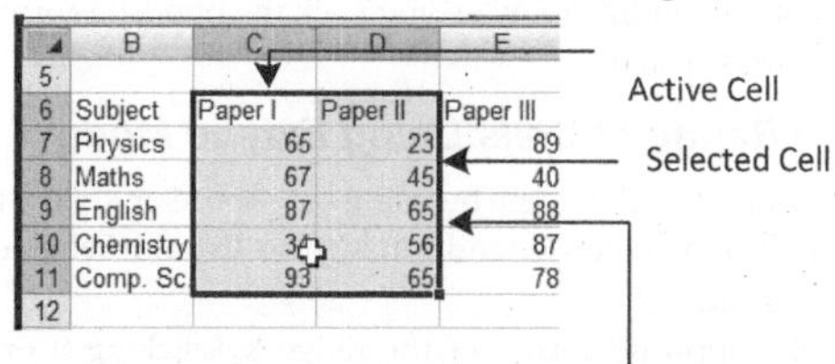

2. Drag keeping mouse button pressed, to the opposite corner of the range and release the mouse button.
3. A rectangular range of cells is selected.

Selecting Range of Cells Using Go To Command

The Go To... command moves you to any cell or address in the sheet you request. If you choose a named cell or a range of cells, with Go To, the entire range is selected.

1. Select one corner of the range.
2. Click on the **Home tab**.

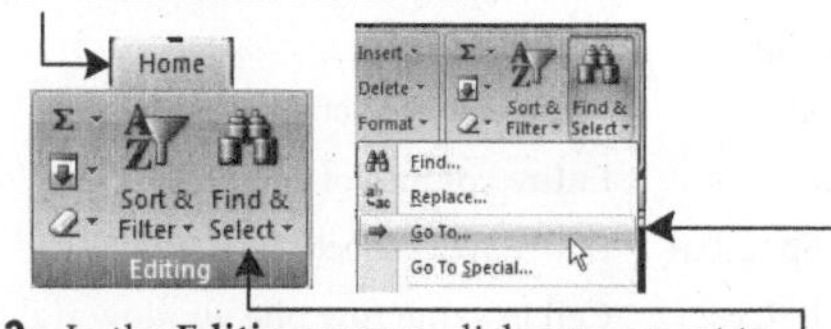

3. In the **Editing** group, click arrow next to **Find & Select**.
4. Then click **Go To...** or press **F5** key or press **Ctrl + G**. The Go To dialog box appears.

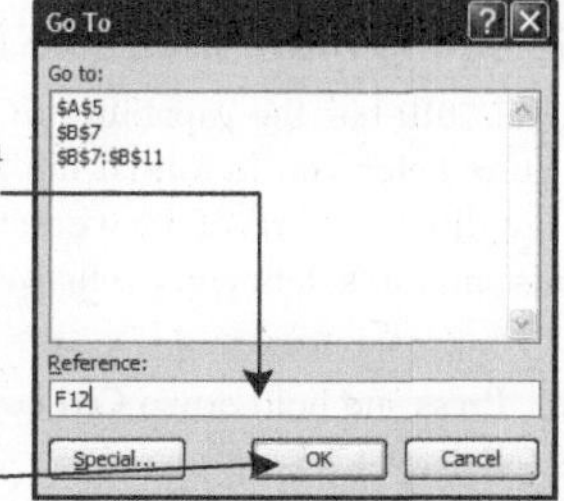

5. Type the cell reference of the opposite corner in the **Reference:** text box.
6. Hold down **Shift** key when you click the **OK** button, or press **Enter** key.

Selecting Range of Cells Using Mouse

Select the cell on one corner of the range. Scroll the window so that the opposite corner appears. (Do not click in the worksheet. The original corner must remain active).

or

Press and hold down **Shift** key as you click the opposite corner. All cells between the two corners are selected.

Selecting Range of Cells Using Extend Mode

1. Select a corner of the range by using the mouse or keyboard.
2. Press **F8** key to enter Extend mode. The **Extend Selection** indicator appears in the status bar.
3. Select the opposite corner of the range by clicking it or moving to it with the movement keys.
4. Press **F8** key again to turn off Extend mode.

Selecting Range of Cells using Keyboard

Following table shows some keyboard shortcut for selecting ranges of cells.

Key	Extend Selection from Active Cell to
F8	Activate Extend
Shift + Arrow Key	Next cell selected.
Shift + Home	Beginning of row
Shift + Ctrl + Home	Beginning of worksheet (A1)
Shift + Ctrl + End	End of screen
Shift + Spacebar	Entire row of active cell
Ctrl + Spacebar	Entire column of active cell
Shift + Ctrl + Spacebar	Entire worksheet
Shift + Ctrl + PgUp	Cell in same row one window right
Shift + Ctrl + PgDn	Cell in same row one window left
Shift + Ctrl + arrow key	arrow Edge of the next block of data in key the direction of the arrow key

Selecting more than one Range of Cells

Excel 2010 has the capability to select multiple nonadjacent ranges at a time. This feature helps you to format multiple ranges with a single command. You may even print different parts of the worksheet with a single print command. Similarly, you can erase multiple data-entry cells with one keystroke.

1. Select the first range of cell.
2. Press and hold down **Ctrl** key as you select each additional range of cells.
3. Release **Ctrl** key.

Following figure shows an example of selecting multiple ranges of cells.

4		Name:	Dev	Class	XII		Section	A
5								
6		Subject	Paper I	Paper II	Paper III		Total	
7		Physics	65	67	89		221	
8		Maths	67	63	40		170	
9		English	87	65	88		240	
10		Chemist	34	56	87		177	
11		Comp. S	93	65	78		236	
12								
13		Total maks obtained by a Dev in Class XII					1044	

Notes:

When you select a range of cells, Excel 2010 displays the sum of the selected ranges in the status bar.

AutoCalculate

1. Right-click the Status bar.
2. From the pop-up list that appears, select the function you want to use for AutoCalculate.
3. Then, select the range you want. Excel 2010 displays the appropriate results in the Status bar.

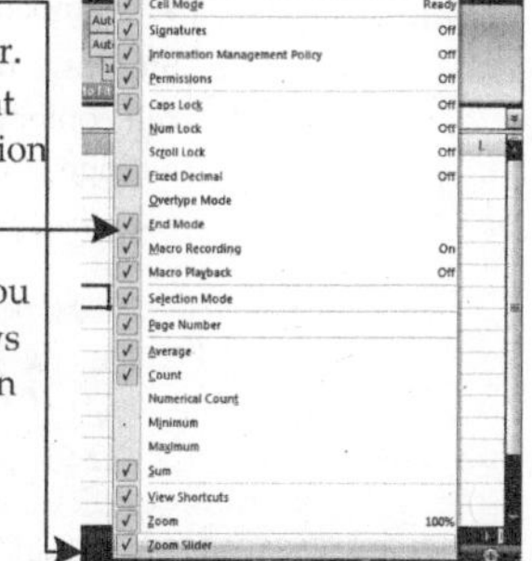

Selecting Entire Row/Column with Mouse

Some operations are quicker if you select an entire row or column at one time. For example, formatting is simple and more efficient if you select and format the entire row or column instead of formatting each cell in the row or a column

To select single row or column, click the row or column's heading. The complete row or column is selected.

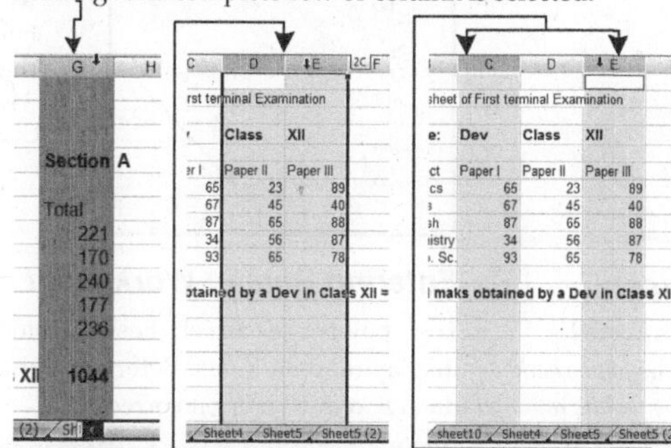

To select adjacent rows or columns, drag across the headings or by clicking the first row and pressing the **Shift +clicking** the last row or column.

To select multiple nonadjacent rows and columns, hold down the **Ctrl** key as you click each heading

Notes:

Excel 2010 has a very useful command that enables you to select cells by contents or the relationship to formulas.

Selecting Cells by Type of Contents

This command is useful if you need to select the following:

1. Cells containing values within an area of formulas
2. Related formulas
3. Comments
4. A rectangular region that surrounds all touching filled cells
5. Array formulas
6. Errors
7. Embedded, graphical or charting objects

Suppose, we want to check the entire worksheet for a specific cell content such as Formula then select that single cell or select a range of cells to check cells within a range.

1. Click on the **Home tab.**

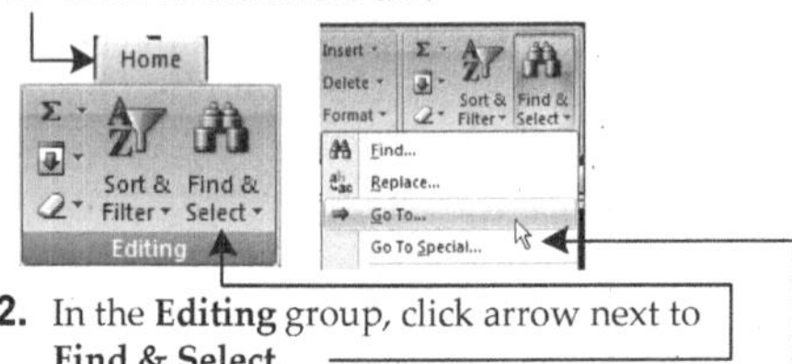

2. In the **Editing** group, click arrow next to **Find & Select.**
3. Then click **Go To Special... . Go To Special** dialog box appears.

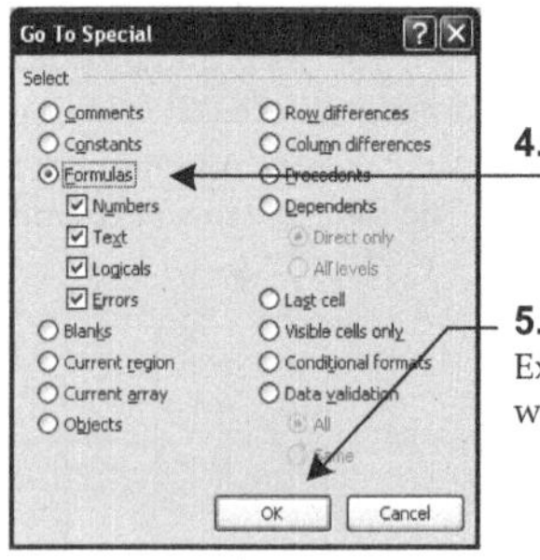

4. Select the option from **Go To Special** dialog box. Here, we select **Formulas** radio button.
5. Then click **OK** button.

Excel will select the range or cell which contain the formula.

Notes:

The active cell appears with a dark border and its row and column headings appear to be raised to easily identify the cell address.

Entering Data in Worksheet

The power of Excel lies in storing, manipulating, and displaying data items. Before you can manipulate and display data, you must enter it correctly.

When you see the message *Ready* in the status bar then you can enter data items in a worksheet. You can enter different types of data in a cell of the Excel worksheet.

Notes:

*If you make mistake before finalizing data entry, press **Backspace** key to delete the character to the left of the insertion point. To erase everything that you have typed, click **cancel button** from the formula bar or press **Esc** key.*

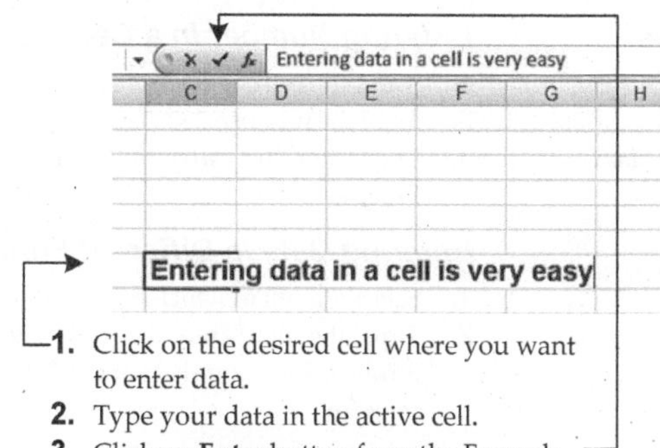

1. Click on the desired cell where you want to enter data.
2. Type your data in the active cell.
3. Click on **Enter** button from the Formula bar or press **Enter** key or **Tab** key.

If Edit directly in-cell feature is turned off, the entry you type appears in the cell but the cursor appears in the formula bar.

Turn On In-Cell Editing Option

To enter and edit data directly in the cell, you need to turn on the in-cell editing option, if not done already.

1. Click on the File Tab.
2. Then click Options.
3. Excel Options dialog box appears with **Advanced** properties.

Text in a cell can include any combination of letters, numbers and keyboard symbols

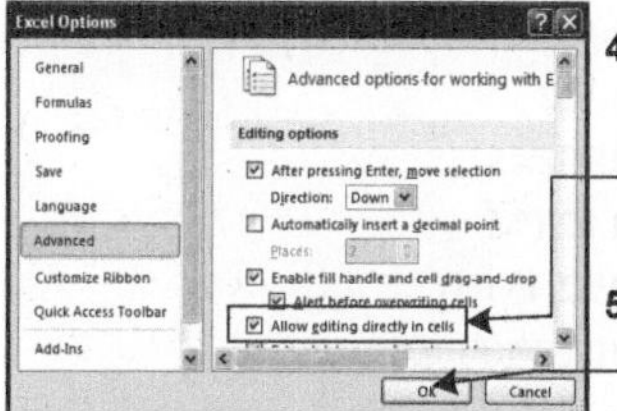

4. Click on the check box i.e. Allow editing directly in cells under the **Editing options** group. The option is *on* when a check mark appears.
5. Click **OK** to accept the settings you change.

A cell can contain up to a maximum of 32,000 characters.

Entering Text in a Cell

1. Select the cell.
2. Type the text entry.
3. Then click the ***Enter*** button in the formula bar or press **Enter** key.

By using fixed decimal representation feature of Excel 2010, you can automatically add decimals to every value entered in a worksheet.

To enter numbers as text, type an apostrophe (') followed by number for example, '45,000. *Alternatively*, you may place an equal sign in front of the numbers and enclose the number in quotation marks. For example, to enter the number 45,000 as text, type ="45,000".

Notice that in a cell with the General format, numbers entered as text will align on the left, just like text. When you enter a number as text, you can still use the number if it is needed in a numeric formula.

Entering Number in a Cell

1. Select the cell.
2. Type the number.
3. Then click the ***Enter*** button in the formula bar or press **Enter** key.

Entering Date in Different Formats in Worksheet

1. Select the cell in which you want to enter the date.
2. Type the date into the cell with any of the following formats. For example to enter 9th October 2010, type:

   10/09/10

   09-Oct-10

   9-Oct (The year from the system date is used)

   Oct-10 (Only the month and year are shown)

   10/09/10 09:45

In any of the above date formats, you can use either /, -, or space to separate different elements.

Entering Time in Different Formats in Worksheet

1. Select the cell in which you want to enter the time.
2. Type the time in any of the following formats. For example to enter 1:32 PM type:

   13.32

   13:32:45

   1:32 PM

   1:32:45 PM

   10/09/10 13:32

Moving the Active Cell when Entering Data

To quicken the data-entry process, select the range in which you want to enter data. The active cell would move automatically after pressing a data entry key i.e. **Entry** button (check mark) in the formula bar. This feature is especially convenient for data-entry in the forms and in the lists. To enter data in a selected area, press the appropriate key as per the options given below:

Key	Action
Tab	Enters data and moves right in the selected area.
Shift + Tab	Enters data and moves left in the selected area.
Enter	Enters data and moves down in the selected area.
Shift + Enter	Enters data and moves up in the selected area.

Notes:

You can enter integers, such as 145; decimal fractions, such as 145.437; integer fractions, such as 1 1/2; or scientific notation, such as 1.45437E+2.

When a formatted number does not fit within a cell, number signs like hash (####) are shown.

Leave a space before the AM or PM. Do not mix a 24-hour clock time with an AM or PM. As the last format shows, you can combine the date or time during entry.

*To enter the current date select the cell and press **Ctrl + ;** keys together.*

*To enter the current time select the cell and press **Ctrl + :** keys together.*

*To format a date in the default date format, press **Ctrl + #** keys together.*

Notes:

To format a time in the default time format, press Ctrl + @ keys together.

You can enter different types of series in two ways:
1. Using the mouse to drag the fill handle.
2. Using a command that gives you the capability to create many types of series.

Dragging the fill handle to the right and down fills the series in increasing order; dragging the fill handle up or left fills the series in decreasing order.

*The **fill handle** is the small square located at the lower right corner of a selection.*

The area enclosed with the gray border fills with a series of numbers determined by the first two cells you selected.

When the active cell reaches the edge of the selected area, it automatically wraps around to the next appropriate cell. Suppose you press **Tab** key repeatedly, the active cell reaches the right edge and then jumps to the first cell in the next row of the left edge.

Autofill Feature

Excel 2010 makes it very easy to enter a series of dates, number or text. For example, you can insert column heading like *Jan, Feb, Mar,* etc. or enter number at equal intervals such as *2, 4, 6, 8,* etc. very easily.

Creating Linear Series:

1. Enter the first two elements of data in the series in adjacent cells, namely 1 and 3 in cells B6 and C6. Excel uses these two data items to determine the amount of increment in each step and the starting number for the series.

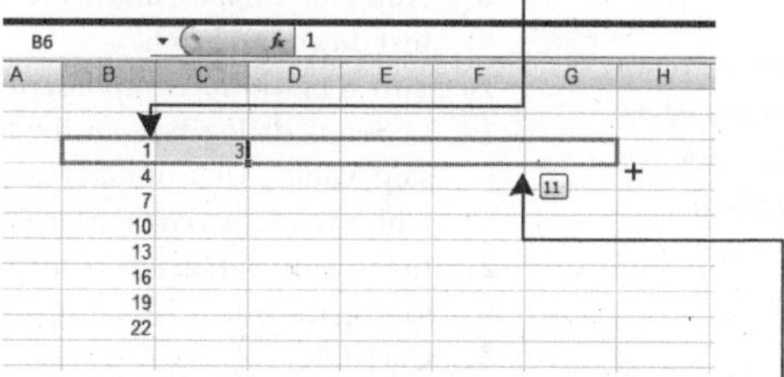

2. Select these two cells and then drag the fill handle down or right to fill in increasing and drag the fill handle up or left to fill in decreasing order.
3. Release the mouse button.

Create a Number Series using Fill Series Dialog Box:

1. In the first cell, enter the *first number.*
2. Select the range of cells you want filled.
3. Click on the **Home tab.**

4. In the **Editing** group, click arrow next to **Fill.**
5. Then choose **Series...** to display the Series dialog box.

Notes:

*When the series reaches either the end of the selected range or the **Stop Value**, Excel stops filling the cell. If you use a negative **Step Value**, the **Stop value** must be less than the starting value.*

*In **Linear or growth** series, the **Step Value** may be positive or negative.*

While creating Data series, note that Weekday gives you dates without Saturdays and Sundays.

*The **AutoFill** feature in Excel recognizes key words, such as days of the week, month names, and Quarterly abbreviations. Excel extends a series to repeat correctly, namely, Qtr1 follows Qtr4 and then the series continues.*

6. Click the Rows or Columns option that matches the type of range you want filled.
7. Select the Trend check box if you want selected values to be replaced by values for a linear or exponential best-fit.

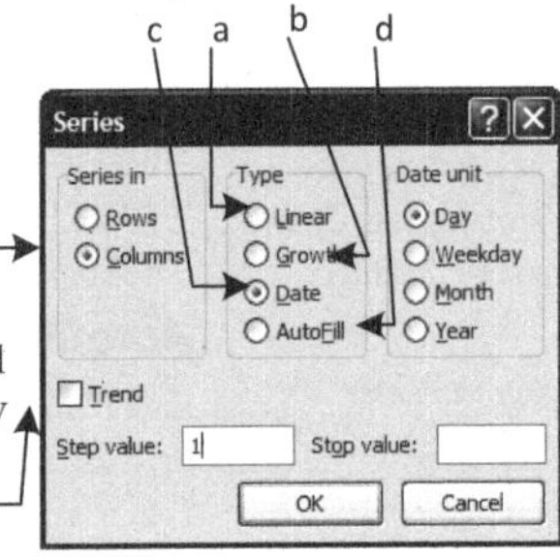

a. Linear: Adds the Step Value to the preceding number in the series.

b. Growth: Multiplies the Step Value by the preceding number in the series.

c. Date: Enables the Date Unit group so that the increment applies to a Day, Weekday, Month, or Year.

d. AutoFill: Creates automatic series that may include text dates and labels.

To create a Linear or Growth series:

1. In Series dialog box, in the Step value: box enter the step value. This number is the constant amount by which the series changes from cell to cell.
2. In the **Stop value:** box enter a value at which you want to stop the fill.
3. Click OK.

To create a Date Series:

1. Click the **Date unit** area of the **Series** dialog box and the select either *Day, Weekday, Month,* or *Year* to designate the date increment.
2. To specify the increment amount, enter the Step value in the Step value box. If the starting value is **12/1/09**, and you choose Month as the Date Unit and 2 as the Step Value, the second date in the series becomes **2/1/10**.

Add Data in a Custom List for use with AutoFill

1. Click on the File Tab.
2. Then click Options.
3. Excel Options dialog box appears with **Advanced** properties.

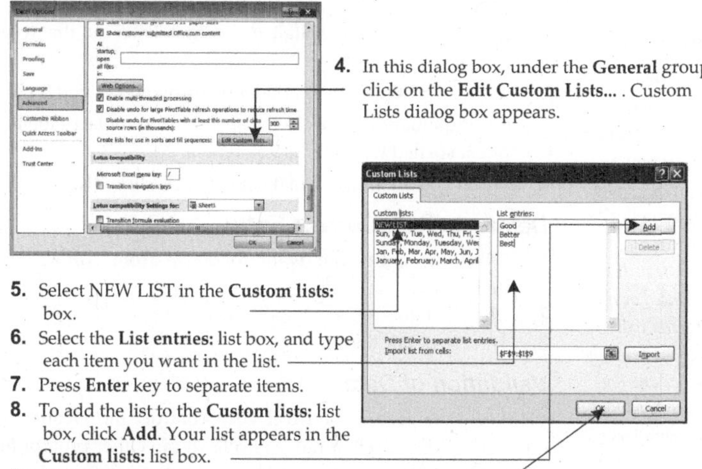

4. In this dialog box, under the **General** group, click on the **Edit Custom Lists...** . Custom Lists dialog box appears.

5. Select NEW LIST in the **Custom lists:** box.
6. Select the **List entries:** list box, and type each item you want in the list.
7. Press **Enter** key to separate items.
8. To add the list to the **Custom lists:** list box, click **Add**. Your list appears in the **Custom lists:** list box.
9. Click **OK** .

AutoCorrect Feature

Excel 2010 has the AutoCorrect feature that recognizes common typing errors and automatically corrects them as you type. AutoCorrect will also correct two initial capitals. You can also use AutoCorrect to expand abbreviations. When you type *incl*, AutoCorrect will expand it to the full word *include*.

To add AutoCorrect Entry Manually:

1. Click the **File Tab** and then click **Options**. Excel Options dialog box appears. In this dialog box, Click on **Proofing** button on the left side. Under **AutoCorrect options** group, click on the **AutoCorrect Options...** .

Options ➡ Proofing ➡ AutoCorrect Options...

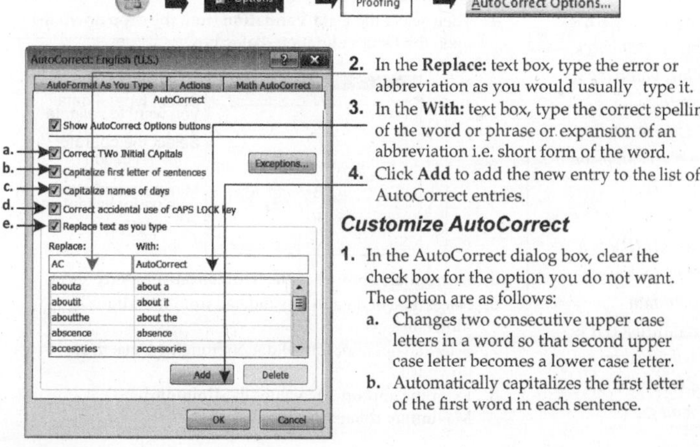

2. In the **Replace:** text box, type the error or abbreviation as you would usually type it.
3. In the **With:** text box, type the correct spelling of the word or phrase or expansion of an abbreviation i.e. short form of the word.
4. Click **Add** to add the new entry to the list of AutoCorrect entries.

Customize AutoCorrect

1. In the AutoCorrect dialog box, clear the check box for the option you do not want. The option are as follows:
   a. Changes two consecutive upper case letters in a word so that second upper case letter becomes a lower case letter.
   b. Automatically capitalizes the first letter of the first word in each sentence.

Notes:

AutoCorrect *feature working both as a correction tool because it recognizes common typing errors. It automatically corrects text. It can also be used as a short hand tool where you enter the abbreviations for long words so that on entering the abbreviation, it is replaced with the actual word.*

You can add your own AutoCorrect entries and also delete any features already available which you do not want to use.

You can also add AutoCorrect entries during a spell check. For this, you have to choose the AutoCorrect button when Excel stops on the mistake.

Data validity *is a check to determine whether data entered into a cell is valid, defined by a set of criteria that you may set.*

c. Automatically capitalize the first letter of the week day.

d. CAPS LOCK key is accidently turned on as you type.

e. Automatically checks the spelling and replaces the text if spelled wrongly, as you type.

2. When you are finished making changes, click **OK**.

Delete an AutoCorrect Entry

1. Select the entry you want to delete from AutoCorrect dialog box.
2. Click **Delete**
3. Then click **OK** button.

Validation of Data

Validate Data feature of Excel 2010 controls the creation of input criteria for a cell or range of cells. It can either prompt the user for the correct information or can display an error message if the data entered does not match the criteria.

To Specify the Data Validation Settings:

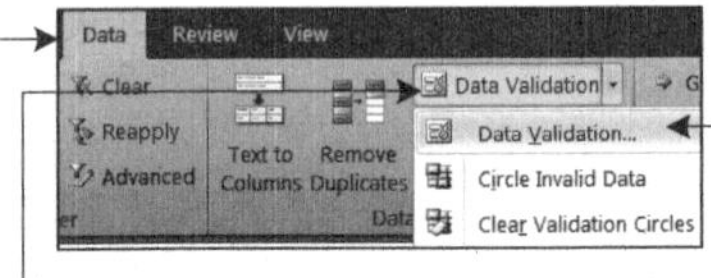

1. Select a cell or range of cells for which you want to validate data.
2. Click on the **Data Tab**.
3. Then click arrow next to **Data Validation** button under the **Data Tools** group.
4. Then select the **Data Validation** from the drop down list to open the Data Validation dialog box.

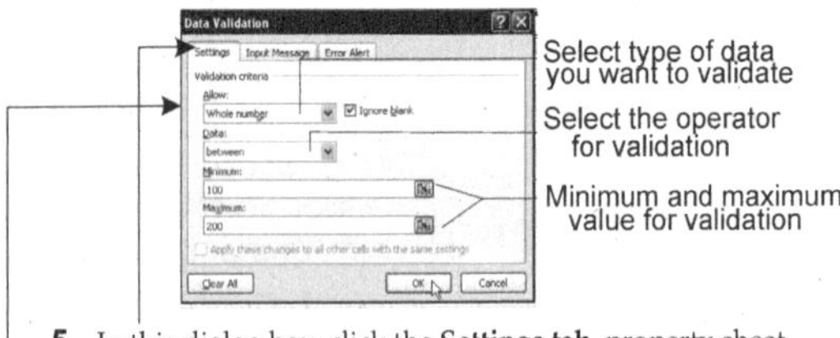

5. In this dialog box, click the **Settings tab** property sheet.
6. Select type of data to be validated from the **Allow:** drop -down list..
7. Select an operator for validation from the **Data:** drop-down list.
8. Enter the appropriate values in **Minimum:** and **Maximum:** collapsable box.

To Specify an Input Message:

1. Click the **Input Message** tab in Data Validation dialog box after specifying the settings property sheet.

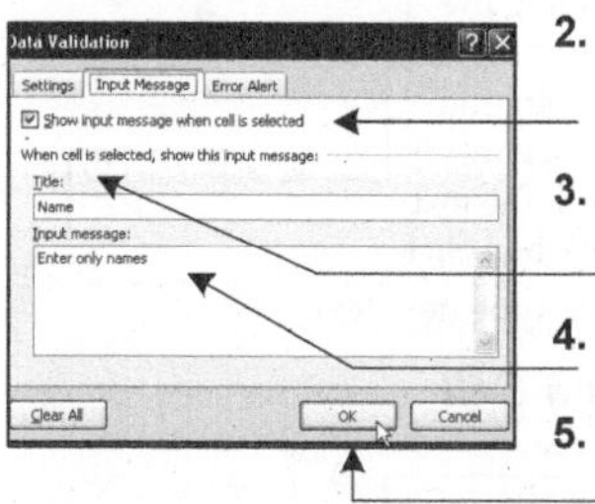

2. Click the **Show input message when cell is selected** so that the check box is ticked.
3. In the **Title:** box enter a title for the message. This is displayed in Bold in the message box.
4. Type the text of the message in the **Input message:** box.
5. Click **OK** to save settings.

To Specify an Error Alert:

1. Click the **Error Alert tab** in the Data Validation dialog box after specifying your settings property sheet.

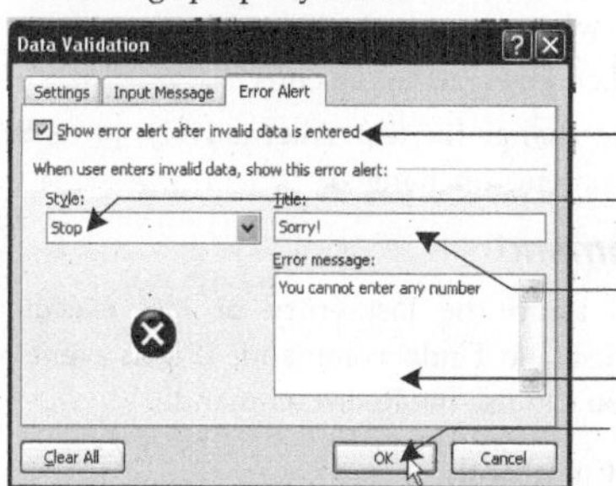

2. Click the **Show error alert after invalid data is entered.**
3. Select a **Style:** for the message from the dropdown list.
4. Enter a Title for the message in the **Title:** box.
5. Enter the text for the error message in the **Error message:** box.
6. Click **OK.**

Notes:

With AutoComplete feature of Excel 2010 for repeated words you only have to type just few letters and the complete word is displayed. To accept the word press ***Enter*** *key.*

AutoComplete

Excel includes a feature called AutoComplete to make it easy to enter repeated text items in a column.

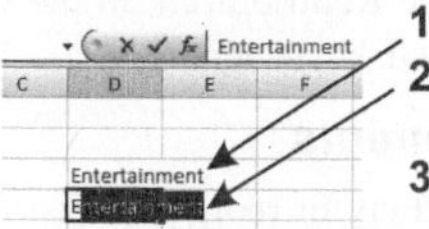

1. First time, type the complete name.
2. Next time you have to type only first letter.
3. Then press any **arrow key** or **Enter** key.

Excel 2010 matches and completes the entry automatically.

Editing Data

While editing a cell entry, you can edit the text either in the formula bar or in the cell itself.

 ***A flashing insertion point indicates where typing and editing will take place.***

Notes:

To use the Undo command, you must choose it immediately after executed action you want to undo.

To undoing or redoing multiple actions, select the Undo or Redo buttons on the Quick Access toolbar. These buttons have a small arrow downward the right. When you click this arrow, a drop-down list of the previous actions that can be undone or redone are displayed as shown below:

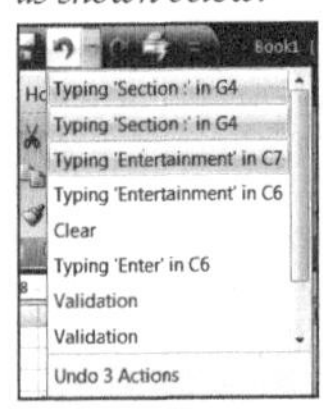

Editing Cell Entry in the Formula Bar

1. Select the cell containing the data you want to edit.
2. Move the insertion point into the text in the formula bar.
3. Position the pointer in the text you want to edit and then click.
4. Edit the cell entry or type new text.

Insertion point

Editing Cell contents

Editing Ce

Editing Directly in a Cell

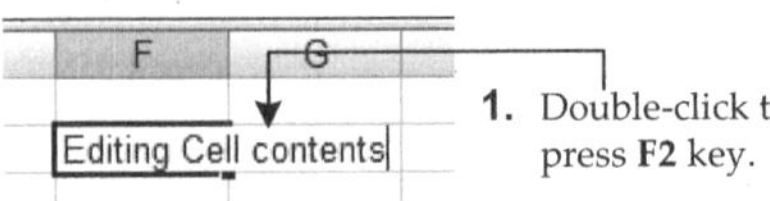

1. Double-click the selected cell or press **F2** key.
2. Press the **arrow** keys to move the *I-beam* that marks the insertion point to where you want to edit.
3. Make the desired changes to the cell entry.
4. Press **Enter** key to change the text. Alternatively, press **Esc** key to leave the contents unchanged.

Undo/Redo Command

When you want to undo the last entry or last executed command, you can use the Undo command. If you want to redo the last entry, you can use the Redo command.

Undo Last Executed Command:

1. Click on the **Undo** button on the **Quick Access** toolbar or press **Ctrl + Z** keys together.

Redo Last Executed Command:

1. Click on the **Redo** button on the **Quick Access** toolbar or press **Ctrl + Y** keys together.

Moving and Copying Cell Contents

Cutting and pasting is a valuable function for reorganizing a worksheet. You may *cut* a range of cells to *paste* them elsewhere. This operation can move cell contents, format, and any note attached to the moved cells. You can also copy a range of cells and paste it into another location.

1. Select the cell or range of cells you want to move.
2. Move the mouse pointer over the selection's border. The pointer changes to an arrow.

B	C	D	E	F	G	H
Subject	Paper I	Paper II	Paper III	Total		G10:H14
Maths	69	54	76	199		
Physics	56	76	74	206		
Comp. Sc	78	67	65	210		
Chemistry	98	71	78	247		
English	65	72	67	204		
			Total	1066		

3. Drag the pointer and the gray outline of the selection to the new location.
4. Release the mouse button when the gray outline is where you want to place the selected range.

Notes:

As you move range of cell, you can see the range reference where the selection will be pasted.

Using the drag-and-drop method, you can make only a single copy. You cannot copy to multiple locations.

*If you release the **Ctrl** key before you release the mouse button, the copy operation becomes a move operation. The plus (+) sign next to the arrow disappears.*

*To move or copy data to another application such as **Word**, you cannot use drag and drop technique. For this, you can use menu commands or shortcut keys*

Copying Cell Contents by Dragging and Dropping

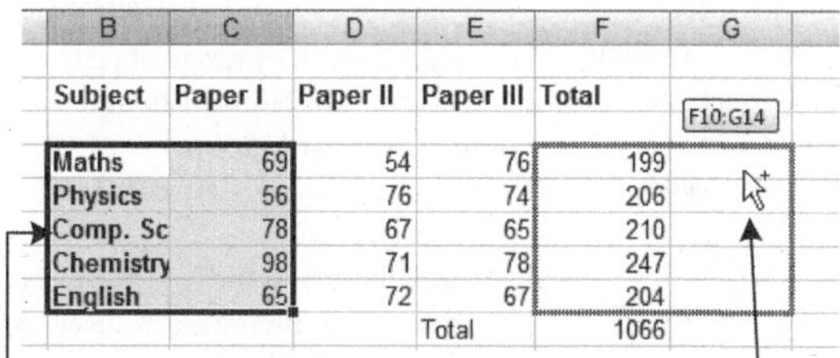

B	C	D	E	F	G
Subject	Paper I	Paper II	Paper III	Total	F10:G14
Maths	69	54	76	199	
Physics	56	76	74	206	
Comp. Sc	78	67	65	210	
Chemistry	98	71	78	247	
English	65	72	67	204	
			Total	1066	

1. Select the range of cells you want to copy.
2. Hold down the **Ctrl** key and move the pointer over an edge of the selection. The pointer becomes an arrow with a **+ (plus)** sign.
3. Continue holding down **Ctrl** key as you drag the edge of the selection to where you want to copy.

Moving Cell Contents with Ribbon

1. Select the cell or range of cells you want to move.

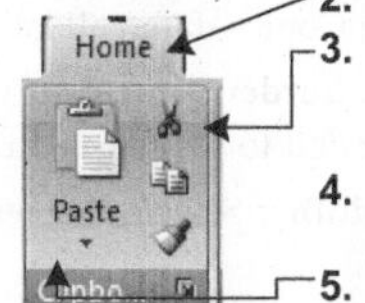

2. Click on the **Home Tab.**
3. Then click **Cut** button under the **Clipboard** group, or press **Ctrl** + **X** keys together.
4. Select the cell at the upper-left corner, where you want to paste the selected cells.
5. Click **Paste** button under the **Clipboard** group.

Copying Cell Contents with Ribbon

1. Select the cell or range of cells you want to move.

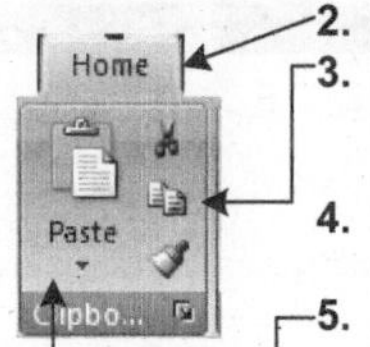

2. Click on the **Home Tab.**
3. Then click **Copy** button under the **Clipboard** group, or press **Ctrl** + **C** keys together.
4. Select the cell at the upper-left corner, where you want the duplicate to appear.
5. Click **Paste** button under the **Clipboard** group.

To move and insert data, select the cell or range of cells you want to move. Then move the mouse pointer over the selection's border, pointer changes to an arrow. Press and hold down the Shift key and drag the pointer to where you want the data inserted.

Notes:

To copy a picture of the selected cell (s) instead of actual contents, click the down arrow of ***Copy button*** *and then select* ***Copy as Picture...*** *option.*

Paste button *of the* ***Clipboard group*** *places the contents of the clipboard where the cursor is. The drop-down arrow of the Paste button called* ***Paste Preview*** *(shown below). It describes various ways to paste data. Point an option for a description, click to select it.*

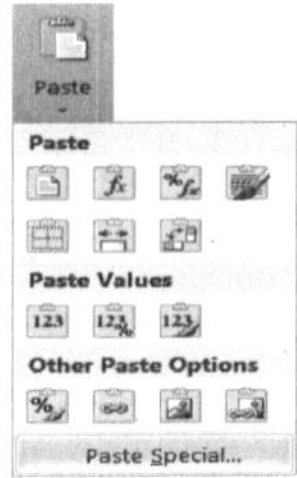

Using Paste Special Feature

Paste Special feature is very useful to copy and paste part of a cell's attributes, such as the format or value, but not both. With this command, you can reorient database layouts into worksheet layouts and vice versa.

1. Select the cell or range of cells.
2. Click on the **Home** Tab and then click **Copy** button under the **Clipboard** group.
3. Select the upper-left corner of the worksheet where you want to paste.
4. Click the arrow next to **Paste** button under the **Clipboard** group and then select Paste **S**pecial... to display Paste Special dialog box.
5. In this dialog box, select the desired option from Paste group according to your need.
   - **(a) All:** Transfers all the original contents and characteristics.
   - **(b) Formulas:** Transfers only the formulas.
   - **(c) Values:** Transfers only the values and formula results.
   - **(d) Formats:** Transfers only the cell formats.
   - **(e) Comments:** Transfers only note contents.
   - **(f) Validation:** Copies data validation rules.
   - **(g) All except border:** Transfers everything except any borders applied to the selected range.
   - **(h) Column widths:** Selects the width of one column to another.
   - **(i) Formulas and number formats:** Paste formulas but not values with their number format
   - **(j) Values and number formats:** Paste only values with their number format.

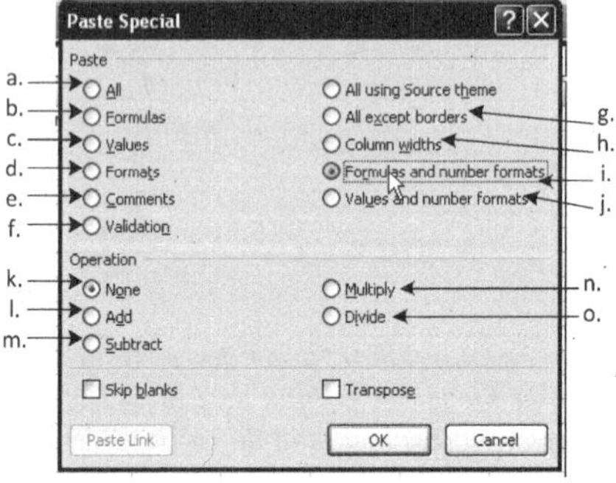

Notes:

*While moving or copying cell contents with menu command press **Ctrl + V** keys together to paste and retain the copy in clipboard memory or press **Enter** key to paste only one time.*

*You can also drag a selected range to another worksheet in the workbook. To do so, hold down the **Alt** key and then drag the selection to the sheet tab. The sheet pops up and you can then drag the selection to the location you want on the sheet.*

You can also drag a selected range to another worksheet in the workbook. To do so, hold down the Alt key and then drag the selection to the sheet tab. The sheet pops up and you can then drag the selection to the location you want on the sheet.

Select the desired option from Operation group according to your need.

(k) **None:** Replaces the receiving cell.

(l) **Add:** Adds to the receiving cell into which they are being pasted.

(m) **Subtract:** Subtracts from the receiving cell into which they are being pasted.

(n) **Multiply:** Multiplies by the receiving cell into which they are being pasted.

(o) **Divide:** Divides into the receiving cell into which they are being pasted.

6. Select the **Skip Blanks check box** if you do not want to paste blank cells which you have selected when you copy a range.
7. Select the **Transpose check box** to change rows to columns or to change columns to rows.
8. Click **OK**.

Inserting Cells, Rows or Columns

Sometimes you may need to insert cells, rows, or columns to make room for new formulas or data. You can insert cells, rows, or columns as easily as you can delete them.

Inserting Cells:

1. Select a cell or range of cells where you need new cells inserted.
2. Click on the **Home** Tab.
3. In **Cells** group, click arrow next **Insert**.
4. Then select **Insert Cells...** from the **Insert** drop-down list.

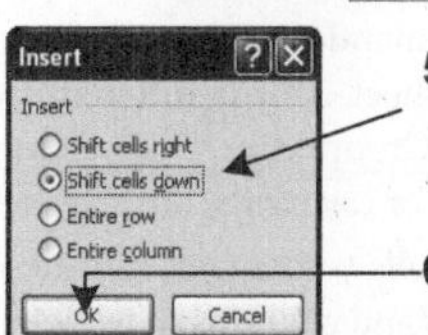

5. To insert cells, select the direction you want selected cells to be inserted.
6. Click Ok.

Inserting *Rows* or *Column:*

1. Select cell in the *rows* or *columns* where you want to insert *new* rows or columns.
2. Select **Insert Sheet Rows** from **Insert** drop down list of the **Cells** group of the **Home** Tab to insert rows.
3. Select **Insert Sheet Columns** from **Insert** drop down list of the **Cells** group of the **Home** Tab to insert columns.

Clearing Cell Contents

You can clear or erase everything in a cell or erase the format only, or erase the formulas only, or erase the comments only.

To clear the contents of a cell, select the cells and then press **Del** key. Only the contents are deleted. Formats and notes will remain intact.

1. Select the cell or range of cells you want to clear.

2. Click on the **Home** Tab.
3. Then click arrow next to **Clear** button under the **Editing** group and then select the option that you want.
4. Select the command according to your need.
   a. **All:** Clears cell contents and notes; returns the format to General format.
   b. **Formats:** Returns the format to General format.
   c. **Contents:** Clears contents but does not change formats or notes.
   d. **Comments:** Clears comments but does not change contents or formats.
   e. **Hyperlink:** Clears hyperlinks but does not change contents or formats.
   f. **Remove Hyperlinks:** Clears hyperlinks and formatting.

Deleting Cells, Rows or Columns

The Delete command completely removes *cells, rows,* or *columns* from the worksheet. This is different from the Clear command in the Editing Group. The Clear command removes the cell's *contents, format,* or *comments,* but it leaves the cell intact.

1. Select the cells or range of cells to be deleted, or select cells in the rows and columns to be deleted.

Notes:

*To fill multiple rows or columns at one time, select all the original cells and then use the **Ctrl+drag** procedure to fill the cells at one time.*

*To open Insert dialog box, you can press **Ctrl + + (plus)** keys or click the right mouse button and select Insert... .*

To clear the contents of a cell or range of cells, using shortcut menu, select the cell(s), click the right mouse button and choose Clear Contents.

*If you accidentally clear a cell's contents, immediately press **Ctrl + Z** keys together. This will undo your most recent edit action.*

2. Click on the **Home** Tab.
3. In **Cells** group, click arrow next **Delete.**
4. Then select **Delete Cells...** from the **Delete** drop-down list.

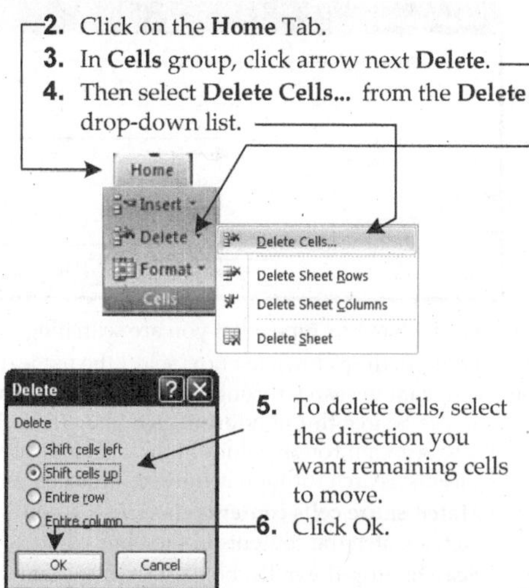

5. To delete cells, select the direction you want remaining cells to move.
6. Click Ok.

Notes:

Find cannot be used with comparative operators, such as =, <, and >=. Entering <12 in the Find What Box: searches for the text <12 rather than for numbers less than 12.

Using Find/Replace Feature

Find feature enable you to find *text, numbers,* or *formula* that are anywhere in the worksheet. ***Replace*** enables you to find and replace in a worksheet.

Find Text or Value

1. Select the cells in which you want to search or select a single cell to search the entire worksheet.
2. Click on the **Home tab.**

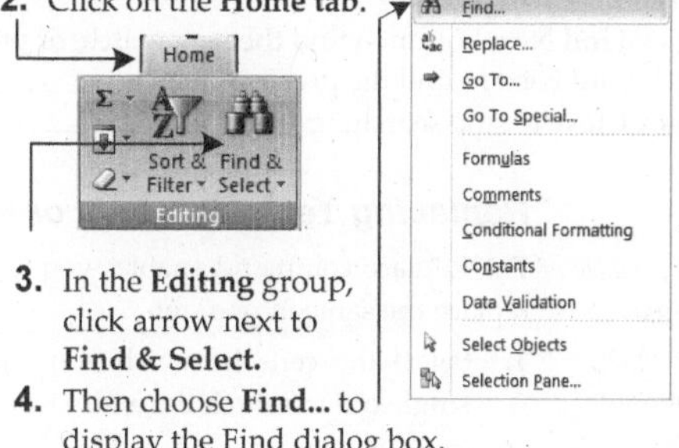

3. In the **Editing** group, click arrow next to **Find & Select.**
4. Then choose **Find...** to display the Find dialog box.

You can use Find command to locate formulas that contain a unique term, a specific text label, a cell note containing a specific word, or error values. The Find feature is especially helpful when you are correcting a worksheet you may not be familiar with.

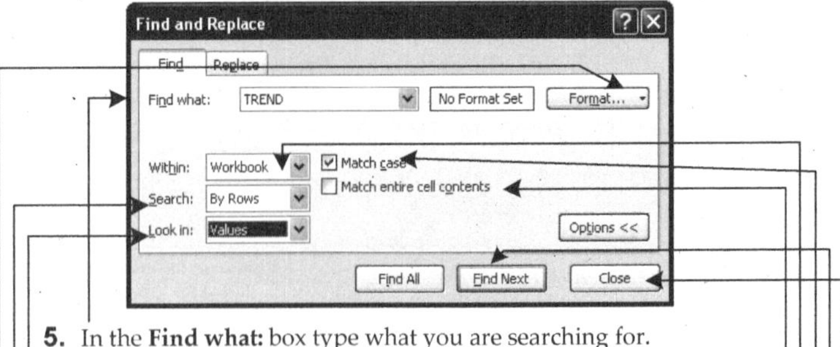

5. In the **Find what:** box type what you are searching for.
6. In the **Look in:** drop-down list box, select the name of the items you want to search through. The item are as under:
   a. *Formulas:* Search through formulas in the cells indicated.
   b. *Values:* Search through values in the cells indicated.
   c. *Comments:* Search through comments attached to the cells.
7. Select **Match entire cells contents** check box if you want the entire cell contents match the contents in the **Find what:** text box. .
8. In the **Search:** drop-down list box, select the option that describes the direction.
   a. *By Rows:* Searches across rows starting at the current cell.
   b. *By Columns:* Searches columns starting at the current cell.
9. In the **Within:** drop-down list box, select the option that describes the area.
   a. *Sheet:* Search within the worksheet.
   b. *Workbook:* Search in full workbook.
10. Select **Match case** check box if you want to exactly match upper or lowercase.
    Click on **Format...** button if you perform search on the particular format.
11. Click **Find Next** button to find the next match, or press **Shift** and click **Find Next** to find the previous match.
12. Click **Close** to stop searching.

Notes:

Click on the Replace Tab in the Find dialog box to open Replace dialog box.

*You can also use wildcard such as ? (to find single character), * (to find any number of characters).*

Replacing Text, Numbers or Formulas

The Replace command enables you to locate an entry and then replace the same in one step.

1. Select the cells in which you want to search or select a single cell to search the entire worksheet.
2. Click on the **Home tab.**

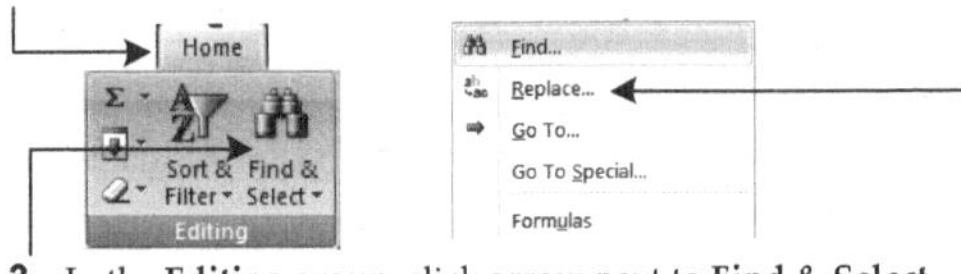

3. In the **Editing** group, click arrow next to **Find & Select.**
4. Then choose **Replace...** to display the Replace dialog box.

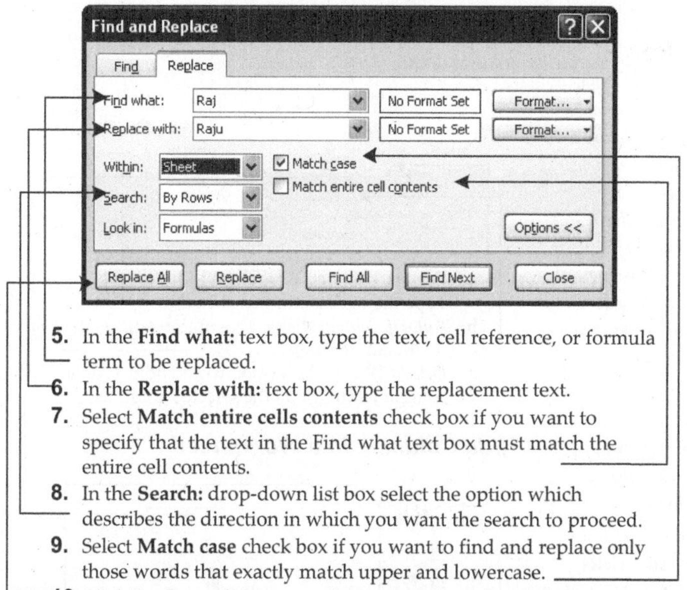

5. In the **Find what:** text box, type the text, cell reference, or formula term to be replaced.
6. In the **Replace with:** text box, type the replacement text.
7. Select **Match entire cells contents** check box if you want to specify that the text in the Find what text box must match the entire cell contents.
8. In the **Search:** drop-down list box select the option which describes the direction in which you want the search to proceed.
9. Select **Match case** check box if you want to find and replace only those words that exactly match upper and lowercase.
10. Click **Replace All** button to find and replace all matches.

Notes:

To improve the appearance of a worksheet or table in it, you can adjust columns width and rows height. If need be, you can even hide confidential data.

Adjusting Columns Width

You can adjust the width of one or more columns to get better look in a worksheet.

To adjust column width with mouse:

1. Select the columns to change the width.
2. Move the pointer onto the column separator to the right of the column heading. Pointer changes to a two-headed, horizontal arrow.
3. Drag the column left or right until the column is of the required width.
4. Release the mouse button.

To adjust column width using command button:

1. Select the columns that you want to change the width.
2. Click on the **Home** Tab.
3. In the **Cells** group, click arrow next to **Format**.

It pops up menu. Use one of the following options to adjust column width:

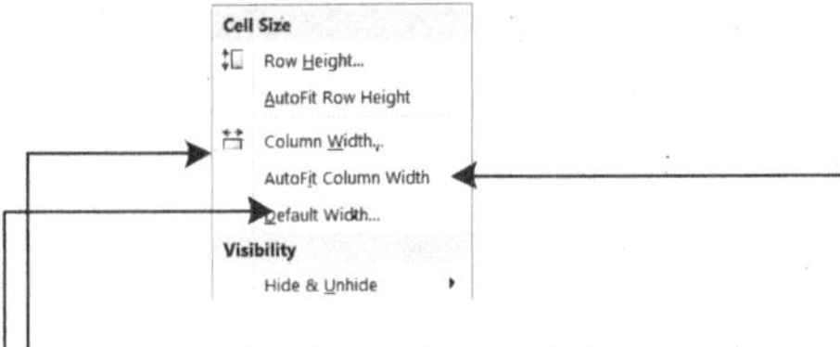

a. *Column Width...:* Column Width dialog box appears. Type the width and then click OK.
b. *AutoFit Column Width:* This option adjusts the column width automatically.
c. *Default Width:* This option would adjust to the Default column width for all the selected columns.

Hide Columns in a Worksheet

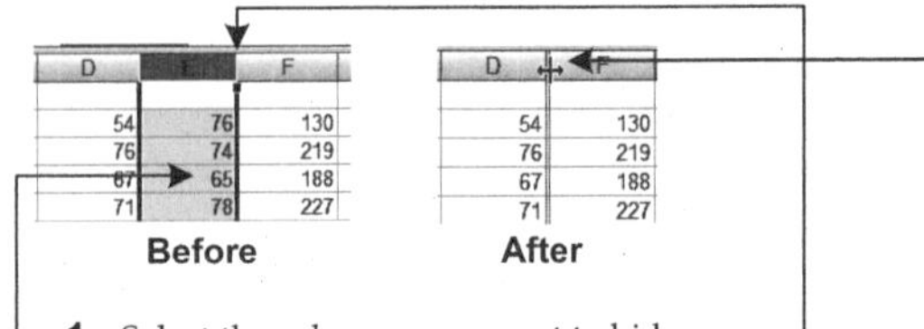

1. Select the columns you want to hide.
2. Move the mouse pointer over the column separator line i.e. on the right of the column you want to hide.
3. The mouse pointer changes to a two-headed pointer. Drag the column separator left until crosses the separator on its left.

Unhide Columns in a Worksheet

D	F
54	130
76	219
67	188
71	227

Before

D	E	F
54	130	
76	219	
67	188	
71	227	

After

1. Move the pointer over the column separator on the right of a hidden column. The mouse pointer changes to a two-headed pointer with space between the two heads.
2. Move the pointer so that its left tip touches the column separator. Drag the column separator to the right, and then release it.

Notes:

If you work on a large worksheet, you may not require to print or view whole worksheet at one time. For this reason, you can hide columns temporarily so that they do not print or appear on the screen.

To hide column using Ribbon,

1. Select the columns.

2. Under ***Home*** *Tab, click* ***Cells*** *group and then click arrow next to* ***Format****.*

3. Here, select ***Hide & Unhide*** *and then select* ***Hide Columns****.*

To unhide column using Ribbon,

1. Select the columns between which hidden columns appear.

2. Under ***Home*** *Tab, click* ***Cells*** *group and then click arrow next to* ***Format****.*

3. Here, select ***Hide & Unhide*** *and then select* ***Unhide Columns****.*

Adjusting Row's Height

You can adjust row height in a worksheet to create enough space for *titles, subtotals, grand totals,* etc.

To adjust row height with mouse:

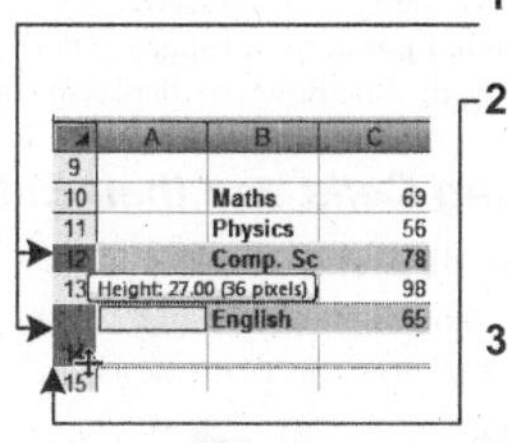

1. Select the rows for which you want to adjust the height.
2. Move the mouse pointer to the line directly under the header of the row you want to change. The mouse pointer changes to a two headed vertical arrow.
3. Drag the two-headed arrow pointer up or down until the row is of the required height.
4. Then release the mouse button.

To adjust row height using command button:

1. Select the row (s).
2. Click on the **Home** Tab.
3. In the **Cells** group, click arrow next to **Format**.
4. It pops up menu. Use one of the following options to adjust row height.

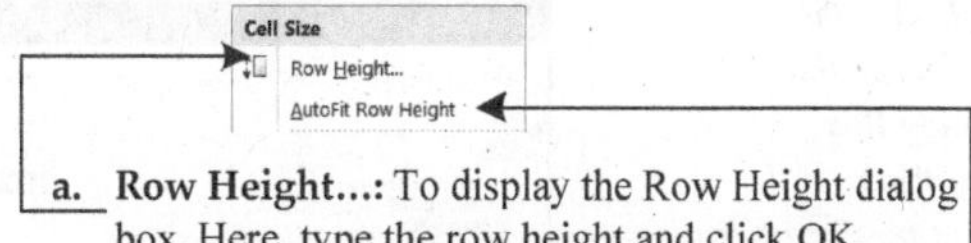

a. **Row Height...:** To display the Row Height dialog box. Here, type the row height and click OK.
b. **AutoFit Row Height:** Excel adjusts rows height automatically.

Hide Rows in a Worksheet

1. Select a row or rows which you want to hide, in a worksheet.

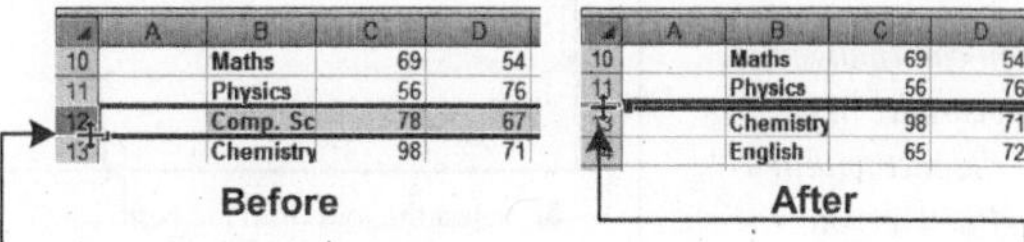

2. Move the mouse pointer over the row to separate till it changes to double arrow.
3. Now drag till the row is hidden or all the selected rows are hidden.

Notes:

To hide column using Ribbon,
1. Select the rows.
2. Under ***Home*** *Tab, click* ***Cells*** *group and then click arrow next to* ***Format****. Here, select* ***Hide & Unhide*** *and then select* ***Hide Rows****.*

Unhide Rows in a Worksheet

	A	B	C	D
10		Maths	69	54
11		Physics	56	76
13		Chemistry	98	71
14		English	65	72

	A	B	C	D
10	Height: 12.00 (16 pixels)		69	54
11		Physics	56	76
12		Chemistry	98	71
13		English	65	72

1. Move the pointer over the row number that is under the hidden rows.
2. Move the pointer up slowly until it changes to a double-headed pointer with space in between the two headings.
3. Drag the line down to display the hidden rows.

Formatting Cells and their Entries

You can use different character fonts and styles in an Excel 2010 worksheet. You can also change font colours and if you have a colour printer, you can print worksheet with these colours.

Notes:

There are two methods to format cells in a worksheet.
1. By using Dialog Box Launcher
2. By using Ribbon command.

*You can open **Format Cells** dialog box by pressing keys **Ctrl + 1** or by clicking on the **Dialog Box Launcher** i.e. the small icon that appears on the bottom right corner of the **Font** group i.e. Font of the **Home** tab.*

You can change the appearance of part of the text within a cell just as you change the appearance of a cell or range of cells.

Format Entries within a Cell or a Range of Cells using Dialog Box Launcher

1. Select the cell, range, or multiple ranges.
2. Under **Home** Tab, click **Cells** group.
3. Click arrow next to **Format.** Here, select **Format Cells...** .
4. In **Format Cells** dialog box, click on the **Font tab**.

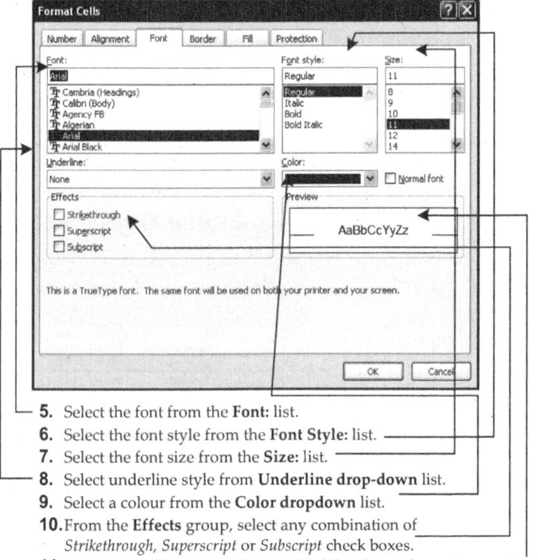

5. Select the font from the **Font:** list.
6. Select the font style from the **Font Style:** list.
7. Select the font size from the **Size:** list.
8. Select underline style from **Underline drop-down** list.
9. Select a colour from the **Color dropdown** list.
10. From the **Effects** group, select any combination of *Strikethrough*, *Superscript* or *Subscript* check boxes.
11. The **Preview box** shows the result of the chosen formatting options.
12. Click OK.

Notes:

Fonts of various typefaces are used in printed materials. Font height is measured in points, and there are 72 points in an inch. Fonts also appear in different styles: plain, bold, italic, underline and strike- through. Excel 2010 can use up to 256 different fonts in a worksheet.

Format Cell Entries using Ribbon Command

1. Select cell, ranges, or multiple ranges.

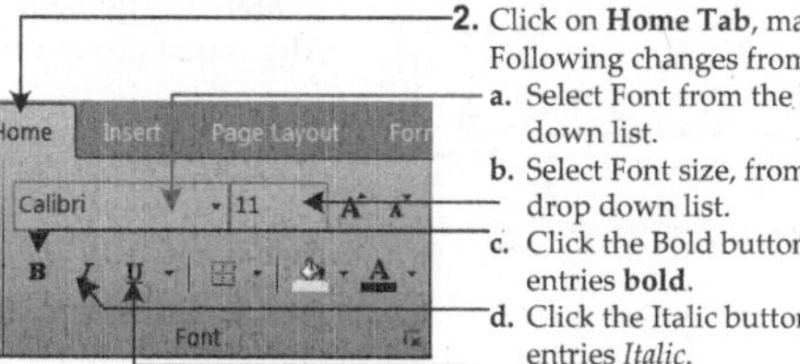

2. Click on **Home Tab**, make the Following changes from **Font group**:
   a. Select Font from the **Font:** drop down list.
   b. Select Font size, from the **Font Size:** drop down list.
   c. Click the Bold button to make the entries **bold**.
   d. Click the Italic button to make the entries *Italic*.
   e. Click Underline to make the entries underlined.

Align Cell Contents using Dialog Box Launcher

1. Select the cell or range of cells you want to format.
2. Under **Home** Tab, click **Cells** group.
3. Click arrow next to **Format.** Here, select **Format Cells...** .
4. In **Format Cells** dialog box, click on the **Alignment tab.**

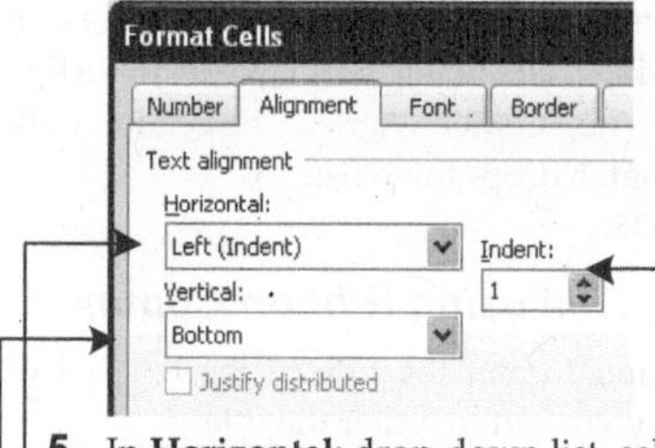

5. In **Horizontal:** drop-down list, select one of the following alignment options.
   a. *General:* Aligns text to the left and numbers to the right.
   b. *Left (Indent):* Aligns cell contents at the left edge.
   c. *Center:* Center aligns the cell contents.
   d. *Right:* Align cell contents at the right edge.
   e. *Fill:* To repeat the text to fill the cell.
   f. *Justify:* To wrap the cell contents into multiple lines within the cell and also align cell contents to both edges.
   g. *Center across Selection:* To align cell contents in the Center.
6. In the **Vertical:** drop-down list, select one of the following alignment options.
   a. *Top:* To align the entry with the top of the cell.
   b. *Center:* To center the entry between the top and the bottom edges of the cell.
   c. *Bottom:* To align the entry with the bottom of the cell.
   d. *Justify:* To align cell contents to both edges.
7. Click OK.
8. To indent text in a cell, choose the Left (Indent) option in the **Horizontal** group in step 5 and enter a value in the **Indent:** box.

Aligning Entries in the Cell

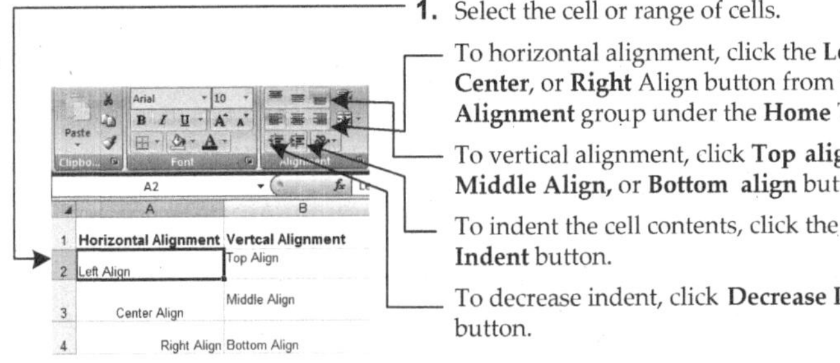

1. Select the cell or range of cells.

To horizontal alignment, click the **Left**, **Center**, or **Right** Align button from the **Alignment** group under the **Home** Tab.

To vertical alignment, click **Top align**, **Middle Align**, or **Bottom align** button.

To indent the cell contents, click the **Increase Indent** button.

To decrease indent, click **Decrease Indent** button.

Notes:

Aligning a title across a selection of cells enables you to center a heading over a table or report

To open Format cells dialog box with alignment tab, press ***Ctrl + 1*** *keys together or click on the* ***Alignment group*** *from the* ***Home tab*** *and then click on the* ***Dialog Box Launcher.***

The Merge and Center button does two things in one step. First, it merges the selected cells and then it centers the text in the left-most cell within the merged cell.

Center a Title Across Cells using Dialog box Launcher

1. Type and format the title in the left cell of the range in which you want the title centered.
2. Select the cells across which you want to center the text.
3. Under **Home** Tab, click **Cells** group.
4. Click arrow next to **Format.** Here, select **Format Cells... .**
5. In **Format Cells** dialog box, click on the **Alignment tab.**
6. Select the Center Across Selection option from the Horizontal: drop-down list.
7. Click **OK**.

Center a Title using Ribbon Command

1. Type and format the title in the left cell of the range in which you want to center the title.
2. Select the range.
3. Click the **Merge and Center** button of **Alignment** group under the **Home** Tab.

Merging Cells

1. Type and format the title in the left cell of the range in which you want to center the title

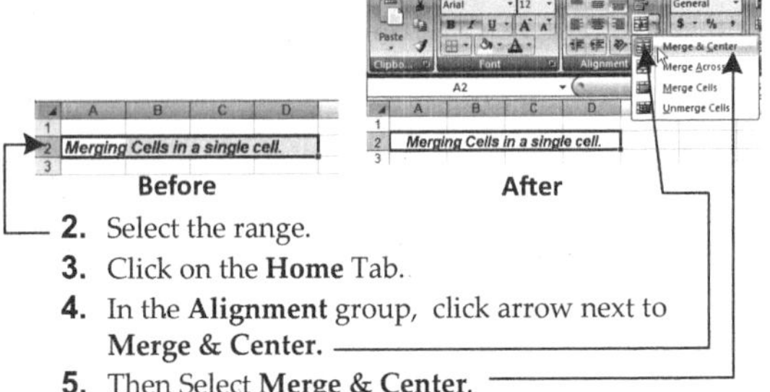

2. Select the range.
3. Click on the **Home** Tab.
4. In the **Alignment** group, click arrow next to **Merge & Center.**
5. Then Select **Merge & Center.**

Notes:

Excel 2010 gives you the option to wrap the text and to adjust it like a paragraph fitting within a cell. The cell's height increases to accommodate many such lines.

*To wrap text in a cell, press **Alt + Enter** keys together to enter a line break, as you type in text. Wrap text option is automatically applied to the cell.*

When the cell entry is larger than the size of the cell then you can use the shrink option to fit within the cell. Shrink option will reduce the size of the contents so as to fit within the cell.

Text is seen in horizontal and read from left to right. But, Excel gives you the option to align text so that the letters can be stacked so that you can read text from top to bottom.

Wrapping Text so as to Fit within a Cell

1. Select the cell or range of cells containing the text you want to wrap.

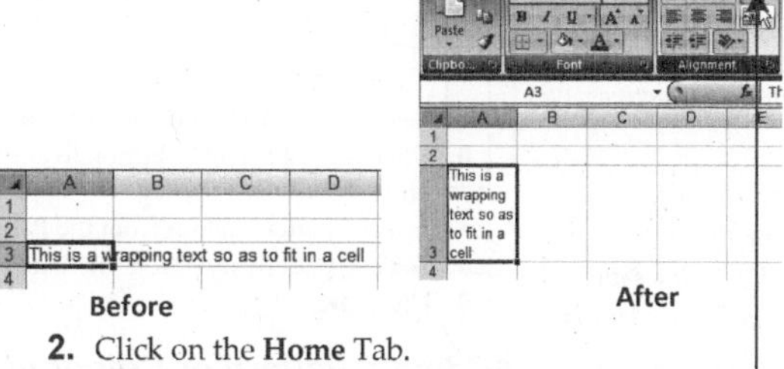

2. Click on the **Home** Tab.
3. In the **Alignment** group, click on the **Wrap Text** button.

Shrinking Text so as to Fit within a Cell

1. Select the cell or range of cells containing the text you want to shrink.
2. Under **Home** Tab, click **Cells** group.
3. Click arrow next to **Format.** Here, select **Format Cells...** .
4. In **Format Cells** dialog box, click on the **Alignment tab**.
5. Select the **Shrink to fit** check box.
6. Click **OK**.

Rotating Numbers and Text

1. Select the cells containing the title or label to be rotated.

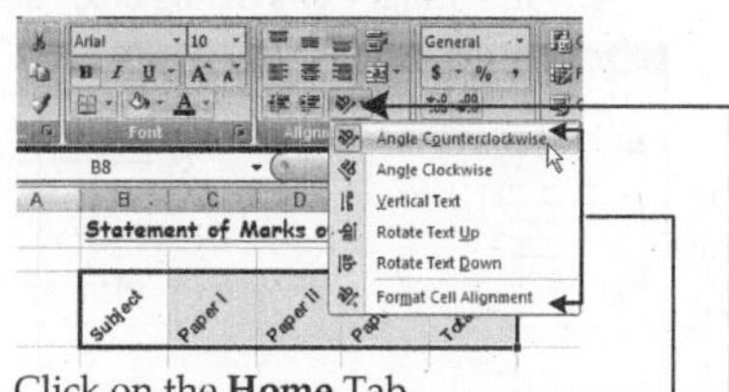

2. Click on the **Home** Tab.
3. In the **Alignment** group, click arrow next to **Orientation** button.
4. Then click on the desired option.

Adding Colour or Pattern using Dialog Box

1. Select the cell(s) to which you want to add colour/pattern.
2. Under **Home** Tab, click **Cells** group.
3. Click arrow next to **Format.** Here, select **Format Cells...** .
4. In **Format Cells** dialog box, click on the **Fill** tab. The Fill tab property sheet appears

Notes:

Shading, borders and colours in a worksheet would enable you to make worksheet or reports appear attractive.

You can place border around cell(s) or lines and double lines. This is to add emphasis as well as to define data-entry areas. This also helps to mark total and subtotal, to appear distinct.

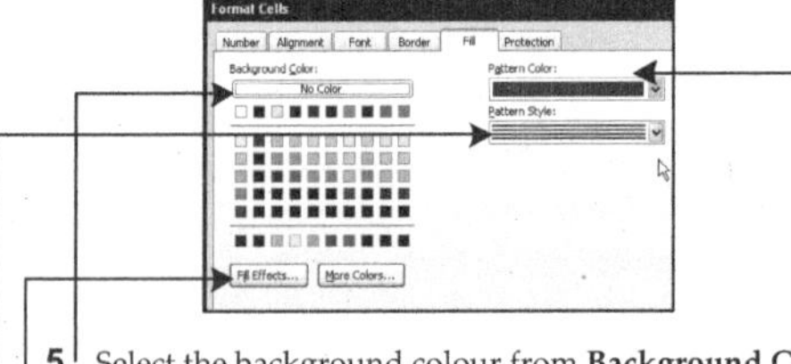

5. Select the background colour from **Background Color:** group.
6. Click on **Fill Effects...** button to apply different shading style and set the transparency.
7. Select a pattern colour from the **Pattern Color:** drop-down list.
8. Select a pattern style from the **Pattern Style:** drop-down list.
9. Click **OK**.

Adding a Pattern or Colour using Ribbon

1. Select the cell or range of cells you want to apply colour pattern.
2. Click on the **Home** Tab.
3. In **Font** group, click arrow next to the **Fill Color** button.
4. Click the colour you want to use.

Adding Borders using Dialog Box

1. Select the cell(s) or range of cells.
2. Under **Home** Tab, click **Cells** group.
3. Click arrow next to **Format.** Here, select **Format Cells...** .
4. In **Format Cells** dialog box, click on the **Border** tab.

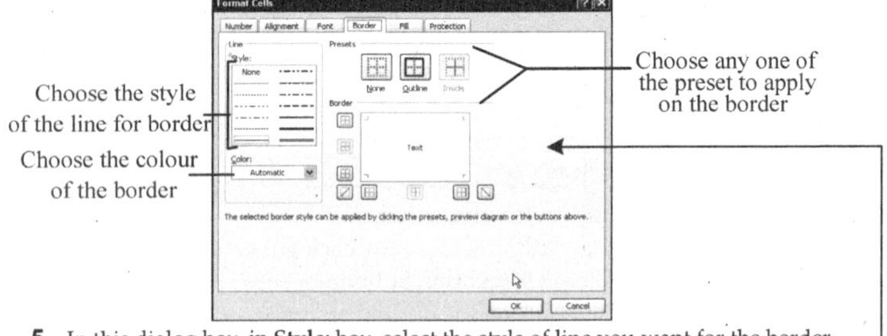

5. In this dialog box, in **Style:** box, select the style of line you want for the border.
6. In the **Color:** drop down list, select the colour of the border.
7. In the **Border** area, select the sides of the cell or range that you want to apply border to.
8. To outline the selected cell or range with one action, click the **Outline** button in the Presets area.
9. To apply border to all cells in the selection, click the **Inside** button.
10. To remove all borders, click the **None** button.
11. Click **OK**.

Adding Borders using Ribbon

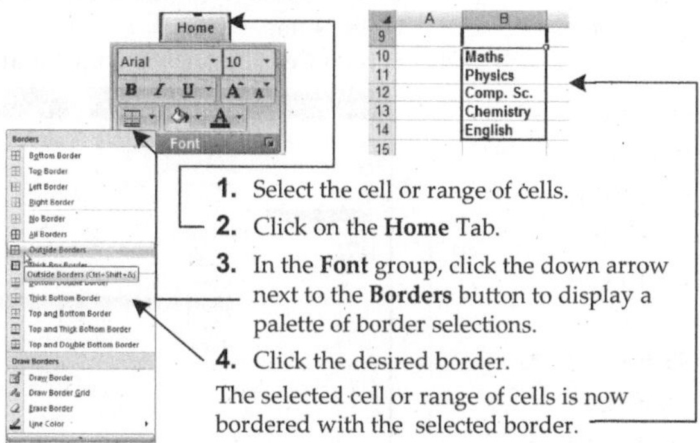

1. Select the cell or range of cells.
2. Click on the **Home** Tab.
3. In the **Font** group, click the down arrow next to the **Borders** button to display a palette of border selections.
4. Click the desired border.

The selected cell or range of cells is now bordered with the selected border.

Copying Formats from Cells to Other Cells

Excel 2010 gives a way to use format (appearance) which you created for a cell or range of cells.

The *Format Painter* button is designed to let you copy the formatting information from selected cell or range of cells. You can then apply that format to another cell or group of cells. Note that all format information attached to the selected cells would be copied.

1. Select the cell you want to copy from (the source cell).

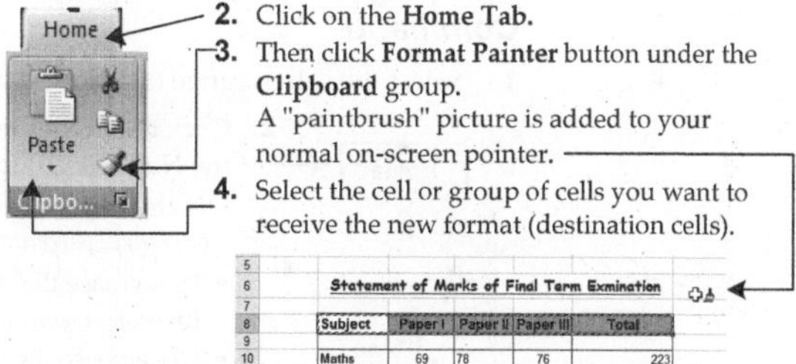

2. Click on the **Home Tab.**
3. Then click **Format Painter** button under the **Clipboard** group.
   A "paintbrush" picture is added to your normal on-screen pointer.
4. Select the cell or group of cells you want to receive the new format (destination cells).

Notes:

You can copy the format to one or more than one cell or range of cells by double clicking the Format Painter button while selecting the first cell or range of cells to which you want to copy the formatting and releasing the mouse button. Then select each additional cell or range of cells to which you want to copy the format and release the mouse button.

Numeric Formatting

Numbers, dates and *time* are stored in cells as pure numbers without formatting. Excel 2010 examines the format of the number you enter, to determine whether the application can format a cell for you according to the type of data entered.

Applying Numeric Formatting using Dialog Box Launcher

1. Select the cell or range of cells you want to format.
2. Click on the **Home** tab.

Notes:

Shortcut keys for format cells are:

General:

Shift + Ctrl + ~

Number:

Shift + Ctrl + !

Currency:

Shift + Ctrl + $

Percent:

Shift + Ctrl + %

Scientific:

Shift + Ctrl + ^

If the active cell contains a number, the Sample area shows you the appearance of the numeric format.

3. In the **Number** group, click the **Dialog Box Launcher** i.e. the small icon ( ) that appears on the bottom right corner of the Number group.
4. **Format Cells** dialog box with **Number** Tab appears.

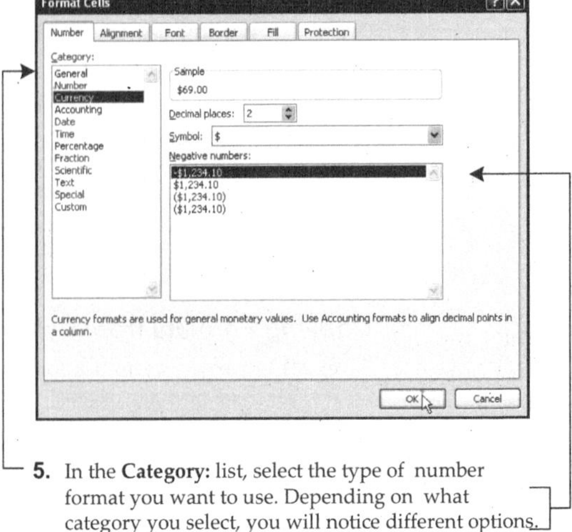

5. In the **Category:** list, select the type of number format you want to use. Depending on what category you select, you will notice different options.
6. Click OK.

Applying Numeric Formatting using Ribbon Command

1. Select the cell or range of cells you want to format.

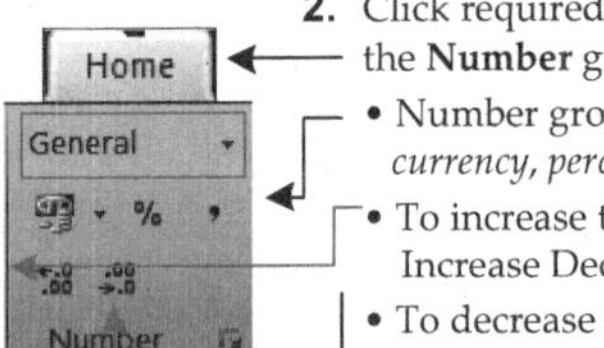

2. Click required formatting button from the **Number** group of the **Home Tab**.
   - Number group offers buttons for *currency*, *percentage*, or *comma* format.
   - To increase the decimal places, click the Increase Decimal button.
   - To decrease the decimal places, click the Decrease Decimal button.

Enter Date/Time using Shortcut keys

1. Select the cell.
2. Press one of the following keys:

Ctrl + ;	**Inserts current date.**
Ctrl + Shift + :	**Inserts current time.**
Shift + Ctrl + @	**Formats in h:mm AM/PM**
Shift + Ctrl + #	**Formats in d-mmm-yy.**

Notes:

The procedure for protecting a worksheet and its contents involves two commands:

1. The first command formats the cells or objects that you want protected.

2. The second command turns on protection for a sheet or the entire workbook.

Protecting cell is not useful unless you turn on the Protect Sheet Feature.

Protecting Workbook

With Excel 2010, you can protect cells, graphical objects, sheets, windows, and even on entire workbook. To prevent unauthorized people from changing the protection status or the display of hidden information, you can also use the facility for password.

Protecting Cell's Contents

1. Select the cell or range of cells that you want to protect or whose contents you want to hide from the formula bar.
2. Under the **Home** Tab, click **Cells** group.
3. Then click arrow next to **Format.** Here, select **Format Cells... .**
4. In **Format Cells** dialog box, click on the **Protection tab**.

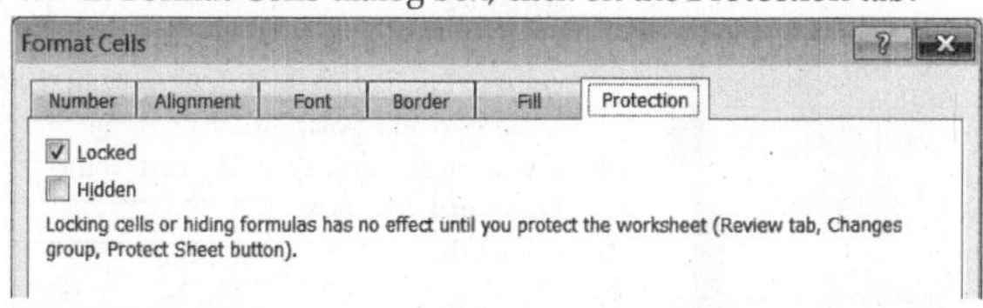

5. Select the check box whichever you want.
6. Click **OK**.

Unprotecting Cell's Contents

1. Select the cell or range of cells that you want to protect or whose contents you want to hide from the formula bar.
2. Under the **Home** Tab, click **Cells** group.
3. Then click arrow next to **Format.** Here, select **Format Cells... .**
4. In **Format Cells** dialog box, click on the **Protection tab**.
5. Clear the check box according to the requirement.
6. Click **OK**.

Protecting Worksheet

1. Click on the **Review** Tab.
2. In **Changes** group click **Protect Sheet**. It will display Protect Sheet dialog box.
3. Here, In **Allow all user of this Worksheet to:** list box, select the elements that you want users to be able to change.
4. If you prefer, enter a password in the **Password to unprotect sheet:** text box.
5. Click **OK**.

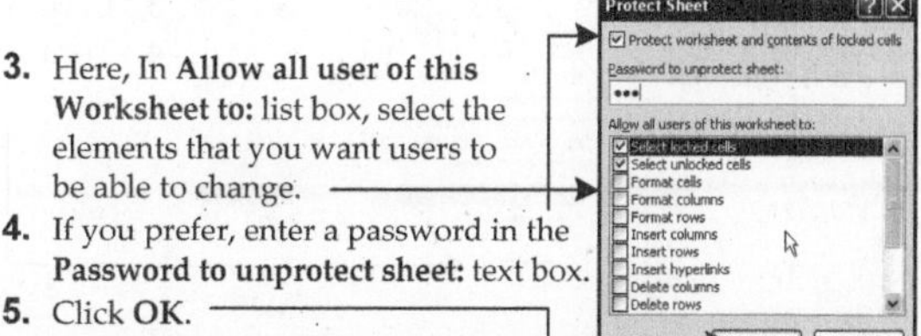

Notes:

When the user interface (UI) is not displayed in full size, the icons might not be displayed in the same order as before. For example, icons that were displayed on one row may be displayed three rows deep as shown below:

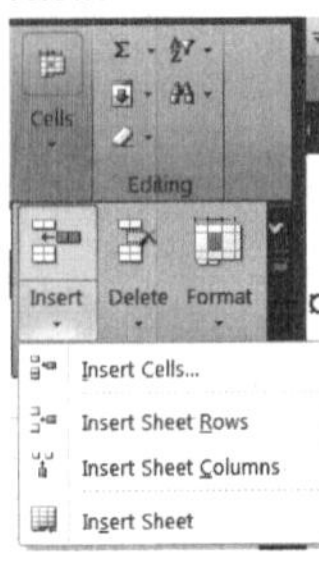

A style is a defined set of formatting characteristics, such as fonts and font sizes, number formats, cell borders, and cell shading.

To prevent anyone from making changes to specific cells, you can also use a cell style that locks cells.

Unprotecting Worksheet

1. Click on the **Review** Tab.
2. In **Changes** group click **Unprotect Sheet**. It will display Unprotect Sheet dialog box.
3. In this dialog box, type the password, if you gave any.
4. Then click OK.

Protecting Workbook

1. Click on the **Review** Tab.
2. In **Changes** group click **Protect Workbook**. It will display Protect Workbook dialog box.

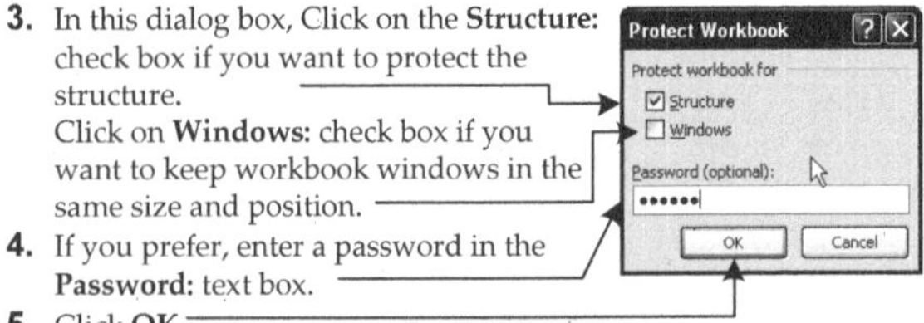

3. In this dialog box, Click on the **Structure:** check box if you want to protect the structure.
   Click on **Windows:** check box if you want to keep workbook windows in the same size and position.
4. If you prefer, enter a password in the **Password:** text box.
5. Click **OK**.

Applying Cell Style

To apply several formats in one step, and to ensure that cells have consistent formatting, you can use style facility available in Excel 2010.

1. Select the cells that you want to format.
2. In the **Home** Tab, under **Styles** group.
3. Click arrow next to Cell Styles and click the cell style that you want to apply.

Create Custom Cell Style

1. In the **Home** Tab, under **Styles** group.
2. Click arrow next to Cell Styles and click the cell style that you want to apply.

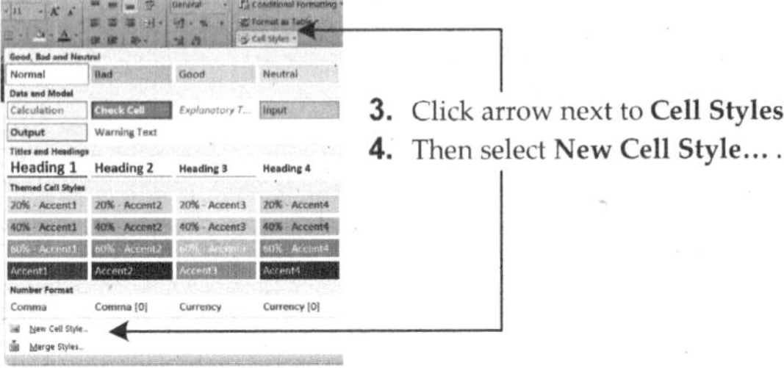

3. Click arrow next to **Cell Styles**.
4. Then select **New Cell Style...** .

Notes:

Excel 2010 has several built-in cell styles. You can apply, modify or duplicate a cell style to create your own, custom cell style.

Conditional format changes the appearance of a cell range based on a condition. If the condition is true, the cell range is formatted based on that condition, otherwise, the cell range is not formatted.

Conditional formatting helps you to highlight interesting cells or ranges of cells, emphasize unusual values by using data bars, colour scales and icon sets.

A color scale helps you to compare a range of cells by using a gradation of two or three colours. The shade of the colour represents higher, middle or lower values.

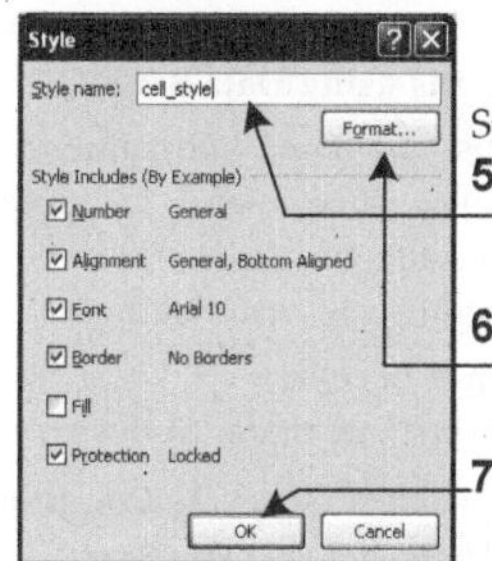

Style dialog box appears.

5. In this dialog box, type the name for the new cell style in the **Style name:** box.
6. Click on the **Format...** button to select the formatting according to your requirements.
7. Then click **OK**.

Applying Table Style at the Time of Table Creation

1. Select range of cells.
2. In the **Home** Tab, under **Styles** group.
3. Click arrow next to Format as Table and Click the table style from the Light, Medium or Dark that you want to use.

Conditional Formatting

Conditional formatting is the process of formatting cells automatically based on the data they contain. When the data changes and triggers a predetermined condition, Excel 2010 automatically changes the cell's format.

Formatting Cells using Color Scale:

Color scales in Excel 2010 are visual guides that help you understand data distribution and variation.

1. Select range of cells.
2. In the **Home** Tab, under **Styles** group.
3. Click arrow next to **Conditional Formatting**.
4. Then click on **Color Scales**.
5. Select the color scale that you want to apply.

After selecting color scale data will look like.

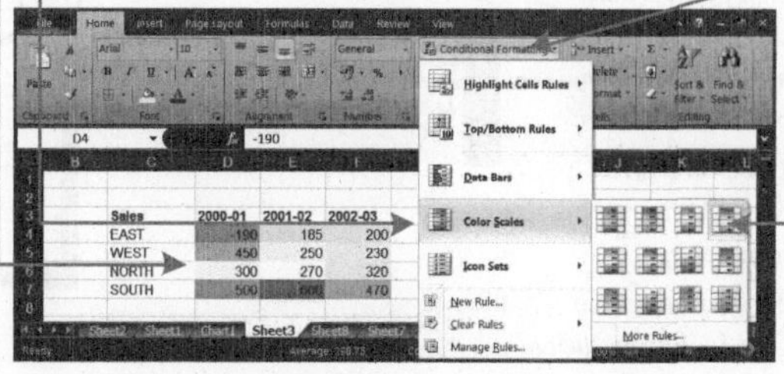

If one or more cells in the range contain a formula that returns an error, the conditional formatting is not applied to the entire range.

Notes:

Excel 2010 comes with new formatting options for data bars. You can apply solid fills or borders to the data bar, or set the bar direction from right-to-left instead of left-to-right. In addition, data bars for negative values appear on the opposite side of an axis from positive values as shown in the Figure.

In Excel 2010, you can access more icons sets, including triangles, stars, and boxes. You can also mix and match icons from different sets and more easily. Hide icons from view—for example, you might choose to show icons only for high profit values and omit them for middle and lower values. To do this:

*1. Select **More Rules...** from the Icon Set list.*

*2. Then select **No Cell Icon** from the **icon drop-down list** next to the icon*

Formatting Cells using Data Bars

Data bar helps you to see the value of a cell relative to other cells. It will be very useful in spotting higher and lower numbers especially with large values of data items, namely, top and bottom selling toys in a holiday sales report.

1. Select range of cells.
2. In the **Home** Tab, under **Styles** group.
3. Click arrow next to **Conditional Formatting.**
4. Then click on **Data Bars.**
5. Select the specific type of data bar.

After selecting Data bar data will be look like.

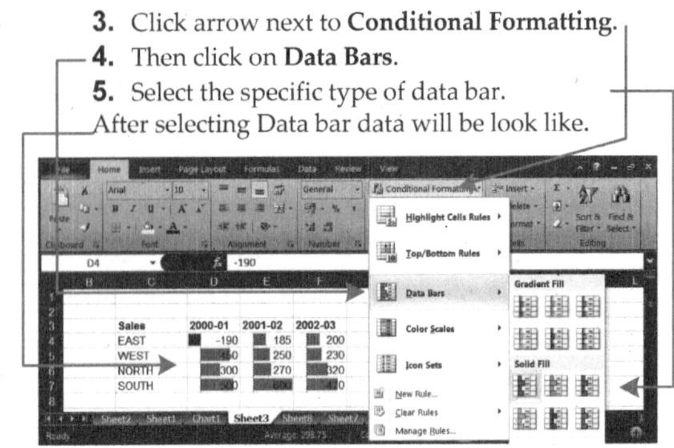

Formatting Cells by Icon Sets:

Icon set helps you to annotate and classify data into three to five categories separated by a threshold value. Each icon represents a range of values.

1. Select range of cells.
2. In the **Home** Tab, under **Styles** group.
3. Click arrow next to **Conditional Formatting.**
4. Then click on **Icon Sets.**
5. Select the icon set which you want.

After selection, icon sets will be look like.

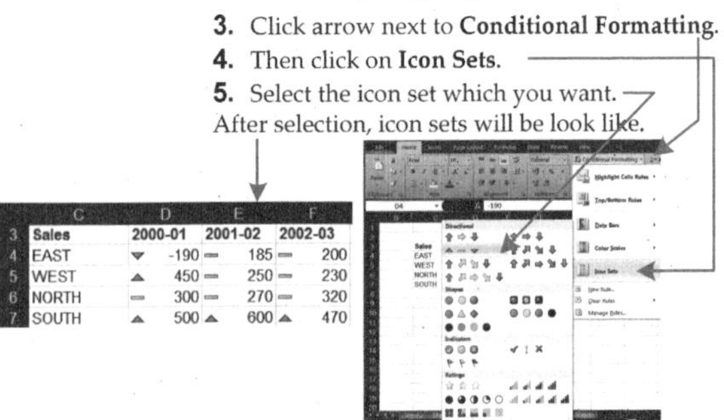

Sales	2000-01	2001-02	2002-03
EAST	-190	185	200
WEST	450	250	230
NORTH	300	270	320
SOUTH	500	600	470

Notes:

*Names are **Case-Retentive**, but not **Case-Sensitive**. For example, when you define the name SALES, then define the name Sales again then the second name will replace the first reference.*

The same name cannot be used to define cells or range on different sheets in the same workbook. You may use the same name to designate related cells in different worksheets.

To use the same name to define cells or ranges on more than one sheet in a workbook, you need to create sheet-level names.

Sheet-level names i.e. local names take precedence over book-level i.e. global names.

Applying Names to Workbook / Worksheet

Names can be given at *workbook level* (i.e. *global names*). They can also be applied at the *worksheet level* (i.e local names).

Names that you define globally (i.e. at the workbook level) apply to all the sheets in that workbook. But, the area of the local name is limited only to the sheet.

Define a Name Globally using New Name Dialog Box

1. Select range of cell(s) you want to name.
2. Click under Formulas Tab and then in the Defined Names group.

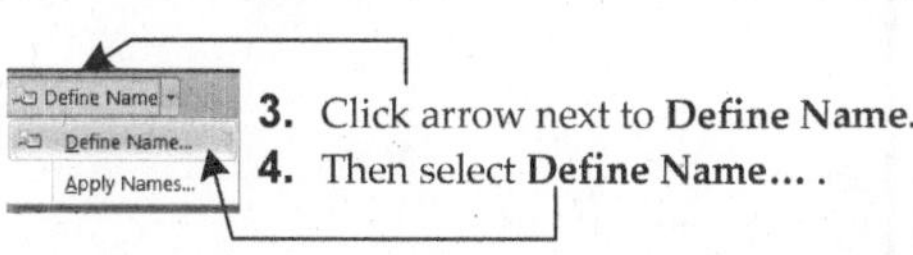

3. Click arrow next to **Define Name**.
4. Then select **Define Name...** .

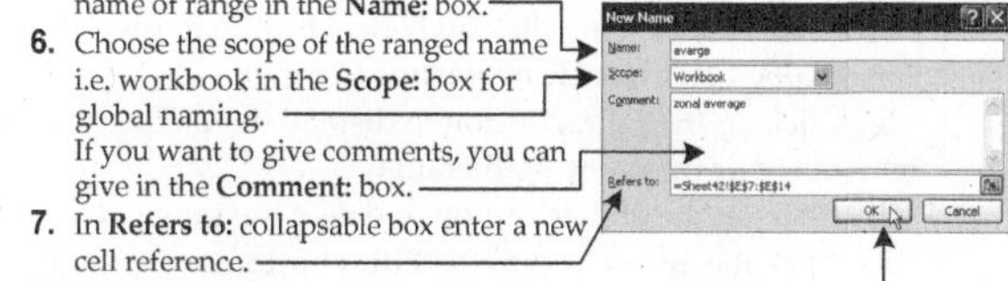

5. In the New Name dialog box, type the name of range in the **Name:** box.
6. Choose the scope of the ranged name i.e. workbook in the **Scope:** box for global naming.
   If you want to give comments, you can give in the **Comment:** box.
7. In **Refers to:** collapsable box enter a new cell reference.
8. Then click **OK** button.

Define a Name Locally using New Name Dialog Box

1. Select range of cell(s) you want to name.

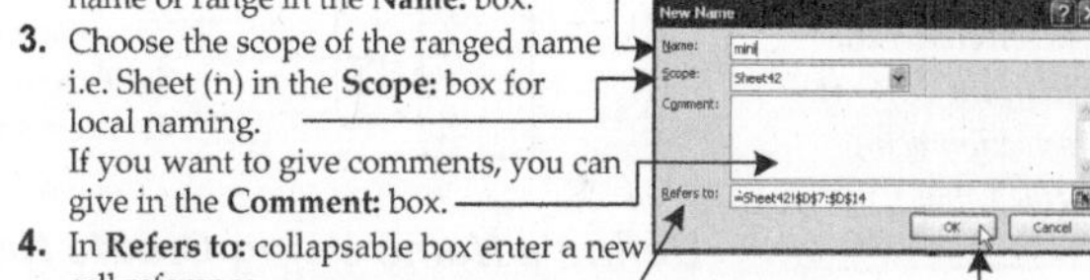

2. In the New Name dialog box, type the name of range in the **Name:** box.
3. Choose the scope of the ranged name i.e. Sheet (n) in the **Scope:** box for local naming.
   If you want to give comments, you can give in the **Comment:** box.
4. In **Refers to:** collapsable box enter a new cell reference.
5. Then click **OK** button.

Define a Name Globally/Locally Using Name Manager

1. Select range of cell(s) you want to name.
2. Click under Formulas Tab.
3. Then in the Defined Names group, click Name Manager. Name Manager dialog box appears.

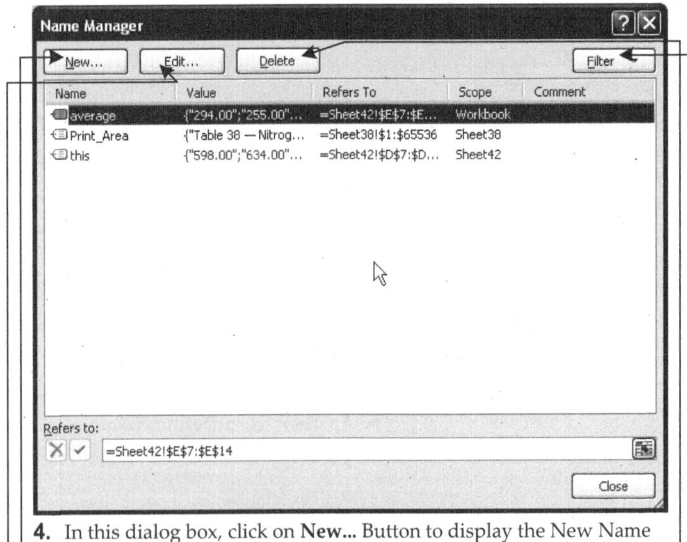

4. In this dialog box, click on **New...** Button to display the New Name dialog box to create new name to range.
5. Click on the **Edit...** Button to display the dialog box for editing the range or the name of the range.
6. Click on the **Delete** button to delete the range.
7. Click the arrow next to the **Filter** button and choose the option.

Notes:

If you enter a name that is already used, the cell or range of cells with that name is selected, rather than the current selection being given that name.

Define a Name Using the Name Box

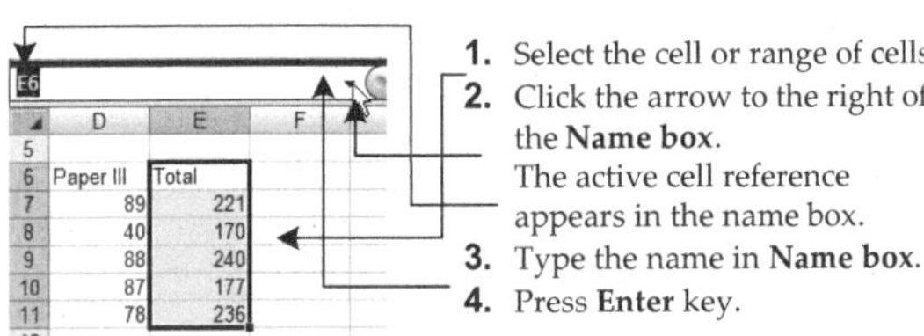

1. Select the cell or range of cells.
2. Click the arrow to the right of the **Name box.**
   The active cell reference appears in the name box.
3. Type the name in **Name box.**
4. Press **Enter** key.

Define a Name Using Create Names from Selection Dialog Box

1. Select range of cell(s) you want to name.
2. Click under Formulas Tab.
3. Then in the Defined Names group, click Create from Selection. A Create Names from Selection dialog box appears.

When you try to assign a name that is already assigned earlier, a warning message is shown to you.

Notes:

*To select non adjacent cell(s) or ranges, make the first selection then press and hold down **Ctrl** key and make other selections in the same manner as when you name a simple range.*

*After you have deleted a name, note that clicking **Cancel** does not undelete it. Any cell referring to a deleted name will display the #NAME? Error, since the name will no longer be valid.*

Excel 2010 gives you the option to display formulas on a worksheet or the results of the formulas.

*The shortcut key for switching between viewing formulas and the results of formulas is **Ctrl + '** keys pressed together.*

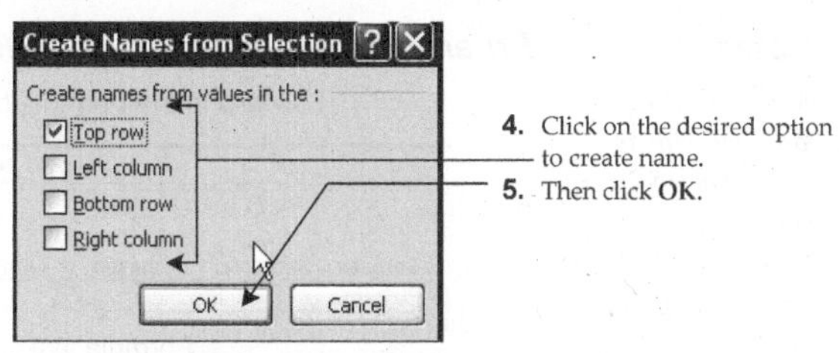

4. Click on the desired option to create name.

5. Then click **OK**.

Changing and Deleting Names

1. Select from the list box the name you want to change.

2. In **Name Manager** dialog box, to change the name, click on **Edit...** Button.
To change the cells reference, select the **Refers to:** box.
To delete a name, select the name you want to delete and click **Delete...** Button

3. Click OK.

Using Formulas

Formulas in Excel 2010 always begin with an equal sign (=) and can include following types of data items:

a. *numeric* and text values (constants)

b. arithmetic operator, comparison operators, text operators, functions, parentheses

c. cell references and names

Controlling the Display of the Formula Result

1. Click on the File Tab.

2. Then click Options.

3. Excel Options dialog box appears with Advanced properties.

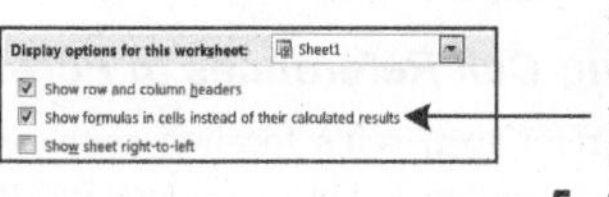

4. Click on the **Show formulas in cells instead of their calculated results** check box under the **Display options for this worksheet** group.

5. Then click **OK** button.

When you display formulas, Excel 2010 automatically doubles the width of all columns

8	Subject	Paper I	Paper II	Paper III	Total
9					
10	Maths	69	54	76	=C10+D10+E10
11	Physics	56	76	74	=C11+D11+E11
12	Comp. Sc.	78	67	65	=C12+D12+E12
13	Chemistry	98	71	78	=C13+D13+E13
14	English	65	72	67	=C14+D14+E14
15				Total	=F10+F11+F12+F13+F14

Notes:

*Always start the formulas with an equal sign (=). If you forget the equal sign, Excel 2010 does not interpret the entry as a formula. Suppose, you enter B12*D15 (no equal sign), then B12*D15 is actually entered into the cell as text.*

Always separate terms in a formula with operators or parentheses.

When you point to a cell to include it in a formula, you actually move the pointer to the cell you want it in the formula.

Entering Formula in the Formula Bar

Formula in the Formula bar

SUM | =B7+C7+D7

	A	B	C	D	E
5					
6	Subject	Semester I	Semester II	Semester III	Total
7	Physics	65	67	89	=B7+C7+D7
8					

Formula in the cell

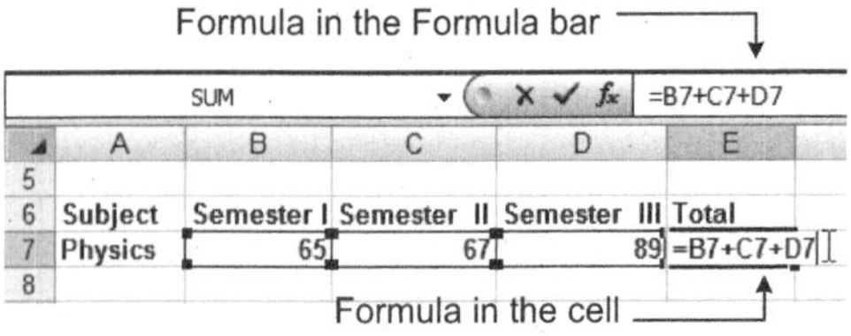

1. Select the cell in which you want to enter the formula.
2. Then type an equal sign (=).
3. Type a *value, cell reference, function,* or *name.*
4. If the formula is complete, press Enter key or click the Enter box (✓) in the formula bar. If the formula is incomplete, go to step 5.
5. Type an operator such as + or - signs.
6. Return to step 3.

Entering Formula in the Cell

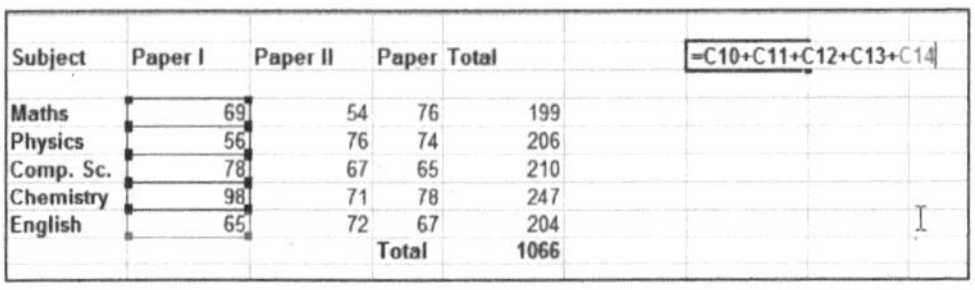

Subject	Paper I	Paper II	Paper	Total		=C10+C11+C12+C13+C14
Maths	69	54	76	199		
Physics	56	76	74	206		
Comp. Sc.	78	67	65	210		
Chemistry	98	71	78	247		
English	65	72	67	204		
			Total	1066		

1. Double click the cells or select the cell and press **F2** key in which you want to enter the formula.
2. Then type an equal sign (=).
3. Type a *value, cell reference, function,* or *name.*
4. If the formula is complete, press Enter key or click the Enter box (✓) in the formula bar. If the formula is incomplete, go to step 5.
5. Type an operator such as + or - signs.
6. Return to step 3.

Notes:

Difference between relative and absolute reference is that in absolute reference, the cell location is fixed once for all. In the relative reference it depends on the location where your pointer is.

Using Cell References in Formulas

You refer to a cell's location with a *relative* reference or an *absolute* reference. Let us understand the difference in the two types of cell references.

Suppose that you are in your office, and you want someone to take a letter to the post office. Using a relative reference, you tell the person. "Go out the front door; turn left cross the road and move two building then turn right and go to the second building." These directions are relative to your office location at the time you give the instructions. If you move to a different location, these directions are no longer valid.

To make sure that the letter gets to the mailbox no matter where you are, then you give different set of directions. You must say something like this" "Take this letter to the I.P. ESTATE post office." No matter where you are when you speak, the post office is at one absolute location: I.P ESTATE.

Notes:

*Each time you press key, Excel 2010 cycles through all combinations of relative and absolute references. Press **F4** key four times, for example, and you cycle from B22 through B22, B$22, $B22, and B22.*

Using Relative References

Excel 2010 uses relative referencing for cell addresses when you enter a formula. In following figure, the formula in cell G9 is = D9+E9+F9. All these references are relative.

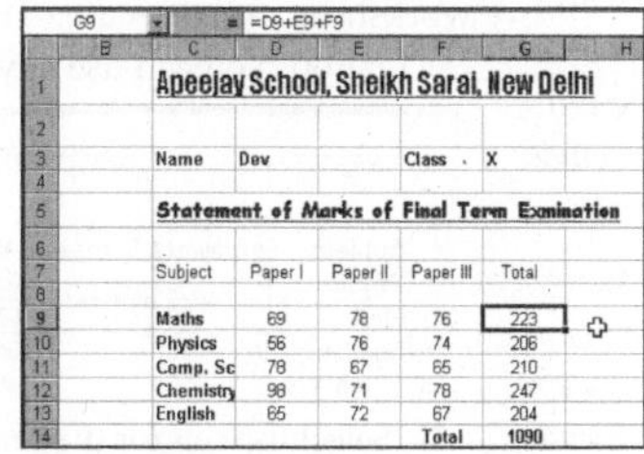
G9 =D9+E9+F9

Apeejay School, Sheikh Sarai, New Delhi

Name Dev Class . X

Statement of Marks of Final Term Examination

Subject	Paper I	Paper II	Paper III	Total
Maths	69	78	76	223
Physics	56	76	74	206
Comp. Sc	78	67	65	210
Chemistry	98	71	78	247
English	65	72	67	204
			Total	1090

The formula, translated into English, would read as follows:

"In cell G9, add the number in the 9th column to the left (D9), second column to the left (E9) and the adjacent column on the left (F9)" in the same row.

Suppose you copy formula across Column G, the formulas adjust their cell references to their new positions. The copied formulas are as follows:

G10 = D10+E10+F10

G11 = D11+E11+F11

G12 = D12+E12+F12

You will notice that the formulas change to give the cell references with relative position from the cell that contains the formula.

Notes:

Indicate absolute references by putting a dollar sign ($) in front of the column letter or row number that you want to freeze or both.

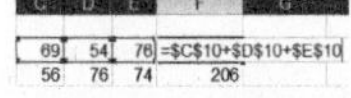

Using Absolute References

You use absolute references only to keep the cell reference values from changing as and when you copy a formula to a new location in a worksheet.

1. Type an equal sign (=) and the cell reference you want it to be absolute.
2. Press **F4** key, the absolute reference key, until the correct combination of dollar signs appears.
3. Type the next operator and continue to enter the formula, also.

Notes:

*To create mixed references type dollar signs or specific row and column numbers without brackets or press **F4** key.*

The easiest method to enter cell references in a formula is by pointing to the cell you want to include in a formula.

Cell reference in a formula changes after you copy the formula to a new location or after you fill a range with a formula.

When you move a formula from one cell to other, the cell references within the formula do not change. But when you copy a formula, then absolute cell references do not change and relative cell references will change.

To copy formula into adjacent cells using fill handle, select the cell that contains the formula and then drag the fill handle over the range you want to fill.

Using Mixed References

In some cases, you may want either the row to stay fixed or the column to stay fixed when copying the cells from one place to other in a worksheet. In such cases, use a mixed reference. Such references contain both absolute and relative reference. For example, the reference $B5 prevents the column from changing, but the row changes relative to a new copied location.

Entering Cell Reference

Cell references allow you to use values from different parts of a worksheet and execute. This enables you to do the desired calculation. You can use any cell or group of cells in a formula.

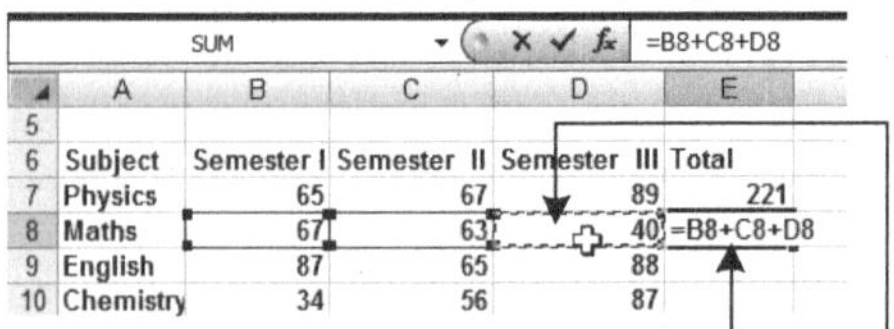

1. Select the cell for the formula.
2. Type an equal sign (=).
3. Point to the cell you want it in the formula and click, or press the arrow keys to move the dashed marquee to the cell you want in the formula.

The address of the cell you point to appears at the cursor location in the formula bar.

Moving or Copying Formulas

1. Select the cell that contains the formula you want to move or copy.
2. Point to the border of the selection.
3. To move the cell, drag the selection to the upper-left cell of the paste area. Excel 2010 replaces any existing data in the pasted area.
4. To copy the cell, hold down **Ctrl** key as you drag the mouse.

Using Operators in Formulas

Operators are used in formulas to execute operations on the values taken by formulas.

Operators	Signs
Arithmetic	+, , *, /, %, ^
Text	& (ampersand)
Comparative	=, <, <=, >, >=, <>
Reference	Colon (:), comma(,), space ()

Arithmetic Operator

Following table shows how to use each of the arithmetic operators.

Operator	Formula	Result	Type of Operation
+	=5+2	7	Addition of 5 with 2
–	=5–2	3	Subtraction of 2 from 5
–	–5	–5	Negation (negative of the number)
*	=5*2	10	Multiplication of 5 with 2
/	5/2	2.5	Division of 5 by 2
%	5%	.05	Percentage
^	=5^2	25	Exponentiation (to the power of)

Text Concatenation Operator

The ampersand (&) operator, joins text within quotation marks or text contained in referenced cells. Joining text is known as *concatenation*. Following table shows how to use each of the Text Concatenation operators.

Operator	Formula	Result	Type of Operation
&	=A12&""&C15	Ms.Gibbs	Text in A12 and C15 is joined

Comparison Operators

To compare values, you can create formulas using comparison operators. These operators return a TRUE or FALSE result, depending on how the formula evaluates the condition. Examples of comparison operators in formulas are shown in the following table:

Formula	Type of Operation
=A12<15	TRUE if the contents of cell A12 is less than 15; FALSE if the contents of cell A12 is 15 or more.
=B36>=15	TRUE if the contents of cell B36 is 15 or more; FALSE if the contents of cell B36 is less than 15.

Reference Operator

Reference operators make no changes to constants or cell contents (See Following Table)

Operator	Formula	Result	Type of Operation
:	SUM (A7:A11)	Range	Evaluates as a single reference.
,	SUM (A7:A11, B11)	Union	Evaluates two references as a single reference
Space	SUM (A9:A11 A7:A11)	Intersect	Evaluates cells common to both references (if no cells are common to both, then #NULL results.
Space	=Yr10 Sales	Intersect	Cell contents at the intersect of the column named Yr10 and the row named Sales

Range Operator

Use the range operator (:) to reduce your work in formulas. If you want a formula to refer to all cells in column B, type B:B. Similarly, the range that includes all cells in rows 5 through 12 is entered as 5:12.

Evaluation (Precedence) of Formulas

Excel 2010 follows a set of rules when applying operators in a formula. Working from the first calculation to the last, Excel 2010 evaluates operators in the order shown in the following table.

Operator	Definition
:	Range
Space	Intersect
,	Union
–	Negation
%	Percentage
^	Exponentiation
* and /	Multiplication and division
+ and –	Addition and subtraction
&	Text joining
=, <, and <= >, >=,	Comparisons

If you want to change the order in which calculations are performed then enclose in parentheses the terms you want Excel 2010 to calculate first.

For example, you will notice the difference between the results of the following formulas:

Formula	Result
=6+21/3	13
=(6+21)/3	9

Entering Functions In a Worksheet

You can operate a function by using following methods:

1. **Enter Function directly:** You can type the function name and the required arguments in the formula bar. To use this method you need to remember the name of the function and the arguments to be passed.
2. **Insert the function:** This is an easier method because Excel 2010 inserts the function and asks you to fill in the parameters only.

Entering a Function Directly

1. Activate the cell.
2. Type the function and the argument in the formula bar.

Notes:

Reference operators enable you to combine absolute and relative references and named ranges. Reference operators are valuable for joining cells (union) or referring to a common area shared between different ranges.

Notes:

Functions are pre-defined formulas or programs that perform calculations in Excel on specific values, called arguments. Each function takes specific types of arguments such as numbers, references, text, or logical values.

Using the Insert Function

Use the Insert Function to make your job much easier. The Insert Function guides you through the process and explains each function as well as each argument within a function

1. Select the cell where you want to enter the function.

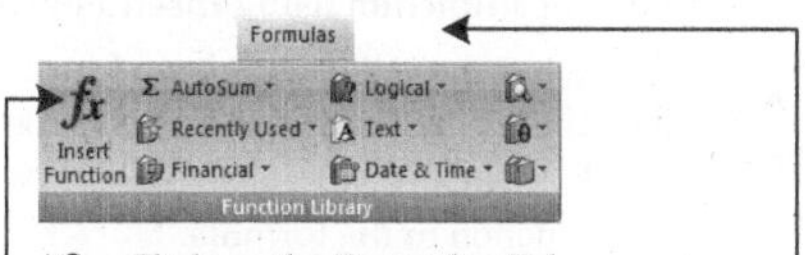

2. Click on the **Formulas** Tab.
3. Then click on the **Insert Function**.

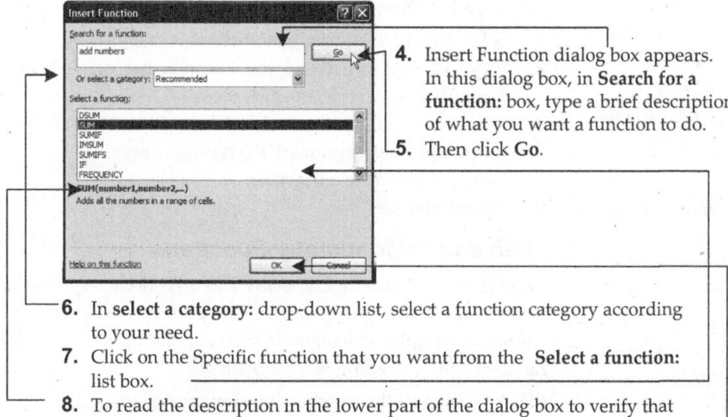

4. Insert Function dialog box appears. In this dialog box, in **Search for a function:** box, type a brief description of what you want a function to do.
5. Then click **Go**.
6. In **select a category:** drop-down list, select a function category according to your need.
7. Click on the Specific function that you want from the **Select a function:** list box.
8. To read the description in the lower part of the dialog box to verify that this is the function you want.
9. Then click **OK** or **Double click the function** whichever you want to use. It will display a dialog box **Function Arguments.**

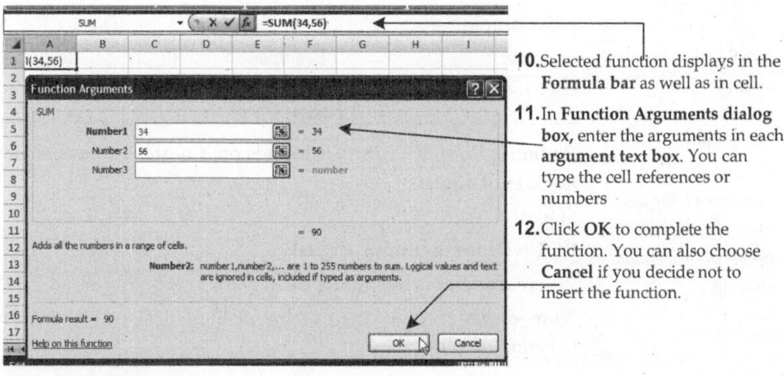

10. Selected function displays in the **Formula bar** as well as in cell.
11. In **Function Arguments dialog box,** enter the arguments in each **argument text box**. You can type the cell references or numbers
12. Click **OK** to complete the function. You can also choose **Cancel** if you decide not to insert the function.

Editing a Function

After you enter function into a formula in the formula bar, if need be, you can edit it in two ways. You can use Insert Function to step through the functions in a formula, or you can manually edit the formula and functions.

Editing a function using Insert Function

1. Select the cell containing a function.
2. Under the **Formulas** tab, click on the **Insert Function**. The Function Arguments dialog box appears and shows the function in the formula.
3. Change any arguments necessary in the function.
4. When you finish making changes, click **OK**.

Editing a Function Manually

1. Select the cell containing a function.
2. Press **F2** key to activate the Formula bar or click in the Formula bar.
3. Select the argument in the formula you want to change.
4. Enter the new argument by typing, dragging, pasting a name, or inserting a function.
5. Press **Enter** key.

Math and Trigonometry Functions

Excel 2010 includes many math and trigonometry functions. Mathematical functions are used to perform wide variety of simple or complex calculations such as totaling the value for a range of cells, rounding of a number.

SUM( ): Adds all the numbers in a range of cells.

Syntax:

SUM(number1,number2,...)

Where **number1**, **number2**,... are upto 255 arguments for which you want the total value or the sum of numbers.

For example,

Function	*Example*	*Result*
SUM() FUNCTION	=SUM(3, 2)	5
	=SUM("3",2, TRUE)	6

Round( ): Round( ) function rounds off a number to a specified number of digits.

Syntax:

ROUND(number,num_digits)

Where **number** is the number you want to round.

Num_digits specifies the number of digits to which you want to round off a number.

Notes:

*You can also display the **Insert Function dialog box** by clicking on the **Insert Function** button on the center of the formula bar i.e. fx or by pressing **Shift** + **F3** keys together*

*In the Insert Function, use the **Most Recently Used** category to quickly get to functions you use very often.*

*You can move across arguments by pressing **Ctrl** + → or **Ctrl** + ← keys together. To select as you move, hold down **Shift** key.*

Select a term or argument in the formula bar by double-clicking it.

Excel 2010 includes a set of more accurate statistical and other functions. Certain existing functions have also been renamed to better describe what they do.

For example,

Function	Example	Result
ROUND() FUNCTION	=ROUND(3.27, 1)	3.3
	=ROUND(-1.475, 0)	-1
	=ROUND(31.5, -1)	30

Rounddown( ): Rounddown( ) function rounds a number down towards zero.

Syntax:

ROUNDDOWN(number,num_digits)

Where **number** is the number you want to round.

Num_digits specifies the number of digits to which you want to round a number.

For example,

Function	Example	Result
ROUNDOWN() FUNCTION	=ROUNDDOWN(3.27, 1)	3.2
	=ROUNDDOWN(-1.475, 0)	-1
	=ROUNDDOWN(31.5, -1)	30

Roundup( ): Roundup( ) function rounds a number up away from 0 (zero).

Syntax:

ROUNDUP(number,num_digits)

Where **number** is the number you want to round.

Num_digits specifies the number of digits to which you want to round a number.

For example,

Function	Example	Result
ROUNDUP() FUNCTION	=ROUNDUP(3.27, 1)	3.3
	ROUNDUP(-1.475, 0)	-2
	=ROUNDUP(31.5, -1)	40

ABS( ): ABS( ) function returns the absolute value of a number. The absolute value of a number is the number without any + or sign.

Syntax:

ABS(num)

Where **num** is the real number of which you want the absolute value.

For example,

Function	Example	Result
ABS() FUNCTION	=ABS(-5)	5

SQRT( ): SQRT( ) returns a positive square root of a number.

Syntax:

SQRT(num)

Where **num** is the number for which you want the square root. If number is negative, SQRT returns the #NUM! because square root of a negative number is not defined.

For example,

Function	Example	Result
SQRT() FUNCTION	=SQRT(ABS(-16))	4

TRUNC( ): TRUNC( ) function truncates a number to an integer value by removing the fractional part of the number.

Syntax:

TRUNC(num,num_digits)

Where **num** is the number you want to truncate.

Num_digits is a number specifying the precision of the truncation. The default value for num_digits is 0 (zero).

For example,

Function	*Example*	*Result*
TRUNC() FUNCTION	=TRUNC(-8.9)	-8
	=TRUNC(8.9654, 2)	8.96

SUMIF(): SUMIF() adds the cells specified by a given criteria. It is used when we want to calculate a sum based on a string of text or a number within a range.

Syntax:

SUMIF(range,criteria,sum_range)

Where **Range** is the range of cells you want evaluated.

Criteria is a number, expression, or text that defines which cells will be added.

Sum_range are the actual cells to be summed. The cells in sum_range are summed only if their corresponding cells in range match the criteria. If sum_range is omitted, the cells in the range are summed.

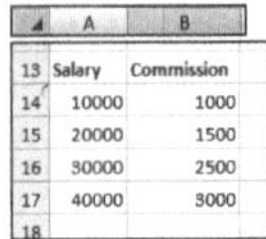

	A	B
13	Salary	Commission
14	10000	1000
15	20000	1500
16	30000	2500
17	40000	3000
18		

For example,

Function	*Example*	*Result*
SUMIF() FUNCTION	=SUMIF(A14:A17,">12000",B14:B17)	7000

Logical Functions

Logical functions are used when we want to check whether a given condition is true or false.

IF( ): IF( ) function used to determine whether a condition specified with in braces is true or false. It returns one value if a specified condition evaluates to TRUE and another value if it evaluates to FALSE.

Syntax:

IF(logical_test,value_if_true,value_if_false)

Where **Logical_test** is a value or expression that can be evaluated to TRUE or FALSE.

Value_if_true is the value that is returned if logical_test is TRUE.

Value_if_false is the value that is returned if logical_test is FALSE.

In Excel 2010, up to 64 IF() functions can be nested to construct more elaborate tests.

Notes:

If you have to share your worksheet with other people who do not have Excel 2010 installed, you can use the compatibility functions instead of the renamed functions. Earlier versions of Excel recognize the old names and provide the expected results.

When averaging cells, keep in mind the difference between empty cells and those containing the value zero, especially if you have cleared the Zero values check box from the ***Advanced*** *properties of the* ***Excel Options****. Empty cells are not counted, but zero values are counted and evaluated.*

For example,

	A	B	C	D	E	F	G
1			**Month**	**Actual Expense**	**Predicted Expenses**		
2	56		Jan	1000	800		
3	50		Feb	500	800		
4	65		March	500	975		
5	34						
6	67						
7	80		**LOGICAL FUNCTION**		**EXAMPLES**		**RESULT**
8							
9	99		IF() FUNCTION		=IF(A10>50, "PASS", "FAIL")		PASS
10	56				=IF(D2>E2,"Over Budget", "OK")		Over Budget
11	78				=IF(Marks>=89,"A", IF(Marks>=79, "B", IF(Marks>=69,"C", IF (MARKS>=59,"D", "F"))))		B

TRUE( ): TRUE( ) returns the logical value TRUE and it takes no arguments.

Syntax:

TRUE( )

FALSE( ): FALSE( ) function is same as TRUE( ) but it returns the logical value FALSE.

Syntax:

FALSE( )

Statistical Functions

Statistical functions are used to perform statistical analysis on ranges of data. It includes simple as well as complex statistical functions such as *average, min, max, standard deviation, slopes* etc.

MAX( ): Max function returns the largest value in a set of values stored in the cells.

Syntax:

MAX(number1,number2,...)

Where **number1,number2,...** are up to 255 numbers for which you want to find the maximum value.

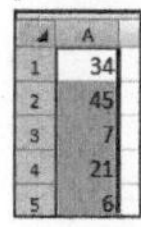

	A
1	34
2	45
3	7
4	21
5	6

For example,

Function	*Example*	*Result*
MAX() FUNCTION	=MAX(A1:A5)	45
	=MAX(A1:A5,75)	75

MIN( ): Min function returns the smallest number in a set of values.

Syntax:

MIN(number1,number2, ...)

Where **number1,number2,...** are upto 255 numbers for which you may want to find the minimum value.

For example,

Function	*Example*	*Result*
MIN() FUNCTION	=MIN(A1:A5)	6
	=MIN(A1:A5,0)	0

Average( ): The Average function returns the average (arithmetic mean) of the arguments which are passed in function as an argument.

Syntax:

AVERAGE(number1,number2,...)

Where **number1, number2,...** are upto 255 numeric arguments for which you want the average.

For example,

Function	*Example*	*Result*
AVERAGE() FUNCTION	=AVERAGE(A1:A5)	22.6
	=AVERAGE(SCORE)	22.6
	=AVERAGE(SCORE,B2)	19

Count( ): Count function counts the number of cells that contain numbers and the numbers within the list of arguments. Use COUNT to get the number of entries in a number field in a range or an array of numbers.

Syntax:

COUNT(value1,value2,...)

Where **value1, value2,...** are upto 255 arguments that can contain or refer to a variety of different types of data, but only numbers are counted.

	I
1	Sales
2	1/5/2007
3	19
4	62.24
5	TRUE
6	#DIV/0!
7	

For example,

Function	*Example*	*Result*
COUNT() FUNCTION	=COUNT(I1:I7)	3
	=COUNT(I4:I7)	1
	=COUNT(I1:I7,2)	4

COUNTIF(): COUNTIF() counts the number of cells within a range that meets the given criteria.

Syntax:

COUNTIF(range,criteria)

Where **Range** is the range of cells from which you want to count cells.

Criteria is a number, expression, or text that defines which cells meet the criteria and they will be counted.

	H
8	SALARY
9	10000
10	20000
11	30000
12	40000
13	
14	
15	
16	MOTHER
17	FATHER
18	SON
19	DAUGHTER
20	SON
21	

For example,

Function	*Example*	*Result*
COUNTIF() FUNCTION	=COUNTIF(H9:H12,">12000")	3
	=COUNTIF(H16:H20,"SON")	2
	=COUNTIF(A1:A4,">=10")	3

Date and Time Functions

With date and time functions, you can analyze and work or calculate with date and time values in formulas. For example, if you need to use the current date in a formula, you can use the TODAY ( ) function, which returns the current date.

Today ( ): It returns the current date of the system. (See Figure below)

Syntax:

TODAY( )

Now(): Returns the current date and time. (See Figure below)

Syntax:

NOW( )

Day(): It returns the day of a date passed as a arguments. The day is given as an integer ranging from 1 to 31. (See Figure below)

Syntax:

DAY(serial_number)

Where **serial_number** is the date of the day you are trying to find. Dates may be entered as text strings within quotation marks.

4	DATE AND TIME FUNCTION	EXAMPLES	RESULT
5	TODAY() FUNCTION	=TODAY()	02-11-2010
6	NOW() FUNCTION	=NOW()	02-11-2010 12:53
7	DAY() FUNCTION	=DAY("4-JAN")	4
8		=DAY("15-APRIL-2007")	15
9		=DAY("4/15/2007")	#VALUE!
10	MONTH() FUNCTION	=MONTH("6-SEPT")	9
11	YEAR() FUNCTION	=YEAR(TODAY())	2010
12		=YEAR("2007/5/1")	2007

Month(): It returns the month of a date which is passed as arguments. The month is given as an integer, ranging from 1 (January) to 12 (December). (See Figure above)

Syntax:

MONTH(serial_number)

Where **serial_number** is the date of the month you are trying to find.

Year(): Returns the year corresponding to a date. (See Figure above)

Syntax:

YEAR(serial_number)

Where **serial_number** is the date of the year you want to find.

Text and Data Functions

With text functions, you can use text strings in formulas. You can also change the case of the string, find out the length of a text string or you can join two strings etc.

Concatenate( ): Joins two or more text strings into one text string. (See Figure below)

Syntax:

CONCATENATE (text1,text2,...)

Where **text1, text2,...** are 2 to 255 text items to be joined into a single text item. The "**&**" operator can also be used to join text items.

LEFT( ): LEFT returns the first character or characters in a text string, based on the number of characters specified as arguments. (See Figure below)

Syntax:

LEFT(text,num_chars)

Where **text** is the text string.

num_chars specifies the number of characters to be extracted. By default, it is assumed to be 1.

RIGHT( ): It is same as LEFT but it returns the last character or characters in a text string, based on the number of characters specified as arguments. (See Figure below)

Syntax:

RIGHT(text,num_chars)

Where **text** is the text string.

num_chars specifies the number of characters to be extracted

4	**TEXT AND DATA FUNCTION**	**EXAMPLES**	**RESULT**
5	CONCATENATE() FUNCTION	=CONCATENATE("TOTAL", " VALUE")	TOTAL VALUE
6			
7	LEFT() FUNCTION	=LEFT("PROJECT",4)	PROJ
8		=LEFT("PROJECT")	P
9			
10	RIGHT() FUNCTION	=RIGHT("PROJECT",4)	JECT
11		=RIGHT("PROJECT")	T

Financial Function

Financial functions perform common business calculations. For example, determination of the payment for a loan.

SLN( ): Returns the straight-line depreciation of an asset for one period. (See Figure below)

Syntax:

SLN(cost,Last_value,life)

Where **Cost** is the initial cost of the asset.

Last_value is the value at the end of depreciation.

Life is the number of years in which the asset is being depreciated (the useful life of the asset).

For example,

16	FINANCIAL FUNCTION		
17			
18	SLN() FUNCTION	=SLN(100000,7500,10)	$9,250.00
19			

Goal Seek (What-If Analysis)

Notes:

With Goal seek, you specify the value you want a formula to calculate, and then Excel 2010 changes the data in the formulas cell reference to tell you what values you need to achieve that goal.

In Excel 2007, you could have up to 32,000 data points in a data series for 2-D charts. But, in Excel 2010, the number of data points in a data series is limited only by available memory.

Goal Seek is part of a suite of commands sometimes called what-if analysis i.e. process of changing the values in cells to see how those changes affect the outcome of formulas on the worksheet.

1. Under the Data tab, in the Data Tools group, click arrow next to What-If Analysis.
2. Then click on the Goal Seek... to display the Goal Seek dialog box.

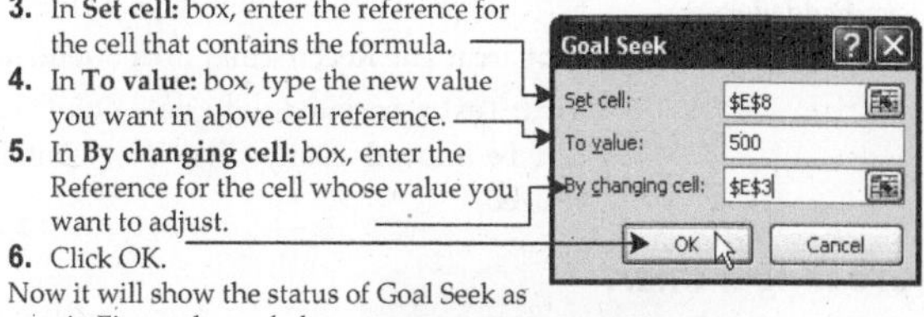

Now it will show the status of Goal Seek as seen in Figure shown below.

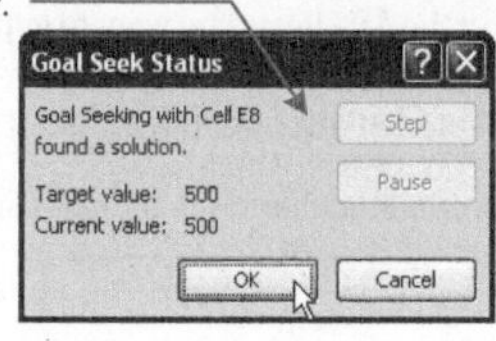

Working with Charts

With Excel 2010, you can instantly access formatting options by double-clicking a chart element.

You can create different types of charts using Excel 2010 that will help you to analyze data in a worksheet and give you a visual presentation of results. There are two types of charts namely, *embedded charts* and charts that appear in a *chart sheet*.

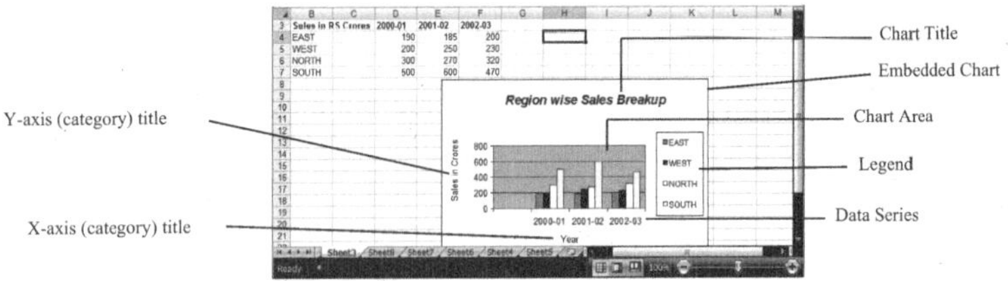

Notes:

Embedded charts are required when you want a chart side-by-side with the data for the chart.

*o quickly create a chart, select data and press **F11** key to insert a chart in a **chart sheet**, using the default chart type. But, when you press **Alt + F1** keys together, the chart is displayed as an **embedded chart**.*

An *embedded chart* appears in a worksheet next to tables or text. A chart can be created by itself in its own chart sheet within a workbook

Chart Terminologies

An Excel 2010 chart may contain objects that you may like to modify individually. These objects are described as under:

Axis (*x-axis* and *y-axis*): The horizontal or x-axis along the bottom of charts is also referred to as *category* axis. The vertical or y-axis against which data points are measured is also referred to as *value* axis. This axis contains the scale against which data is plotted.

Data point: A single piece of data.

Data series: A collection of data points.

Legend: The name of each data series is used as a legend title.

Marker: An object that represents a data point in a chart such as bar, pie and symbols. Markers that belong to the same data series appear in the same shape, symbol and colour.

Plot area: The Rectangular area bounded by the two axes.

Text: Text associated with data points or free-floating text that can be moved easily. The box containing the text can be resized.

Creating a Chart

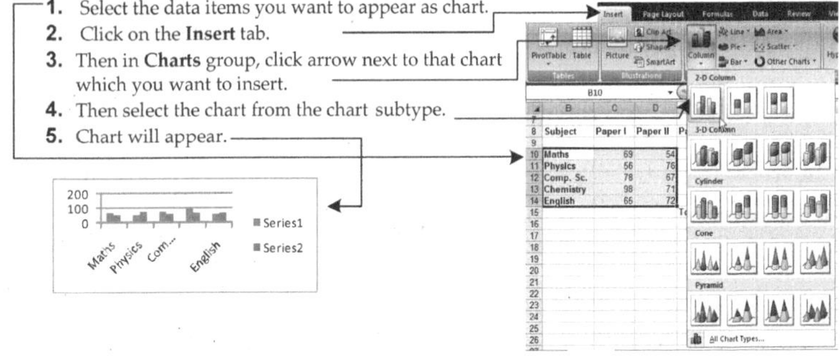

Notes:

When you create a chart, chart tools become available and the ***Design, Layout*** *and* ***Format*** *tabs are displayed. You can use command on these tabs to modify the chart so that data is presented the way you want.*

To change the size or proportion of chart, click the black handles along the borders (the pointer changes to a double-headed arrow). Now drag it until the chart is sized the way you want.

Column chart compares separate (noncontinuous) items as they vary over time. Column charts are used for comparing different items by placing them side-by-side. Cylinder, cone and pyramid charts are available in the same cluster.

Changing Location of a Chart

1. Click the embedded chart or the chart sheet whichever you want to move.

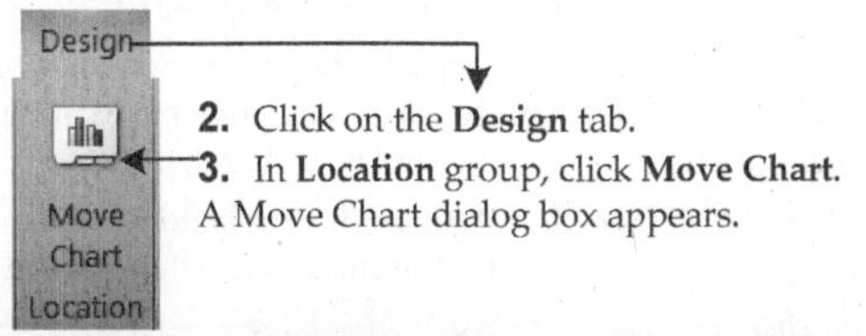

2. Click on the **Design** tab.
3. In **Location** group, click **Move Chart.** A Move Chart dialog box appears.

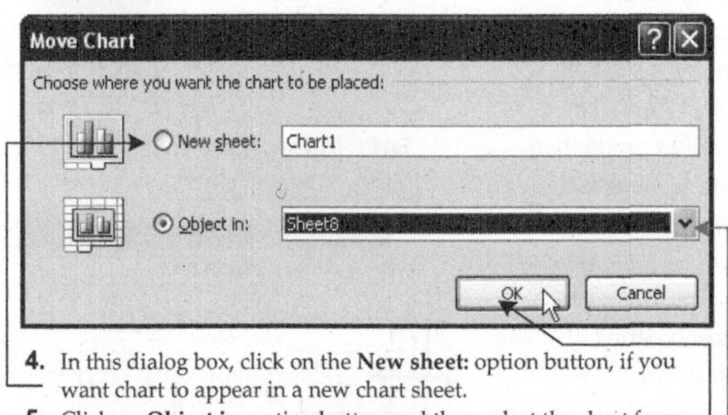

4. In this dialog box, click on the **New sheet:** option button, if you want chart to appear in a new chart sheet.
5. Click on **Object in:** option button and then select the sheet from the drop down list, if you want to embed a chart in particular sheet.
6. Click OK button.

Changing the Type of Chart

Excel 2010 offers you eleven different chart types and within each of these general types, you can select any subtypes. The easiest way to create charts is to select a chart type and sub-type you want. Thereafter, you may customize this chart according to your requirement.

1. Activate the chart by positioning the mouse pointer on the tab and clicking the tab for the *chart sheet*. In case, the *chart is embedded*, then click the chart itself.

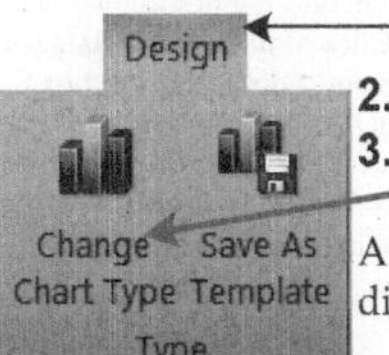

2. Click on the **Design** tab.
3. In **Type** group, click **Change Chart Type.** A Change Chart dialog box showing different chart types appears.

Excel 2010's 3D charts are attractive and effective for data representation. They are used to add visual depth and impact to the presentation of report.

Notes:

A bar chart is similar to a column chart except that categories are on the vertical (Y) axis and the values on the horizontal (X) axis.

A line chart compares trends over a period of time. Line chart is used in production, sales, or stock market situations to show the trend of revenue or sales over a period of time.

A pie chart compares the sizes of pieces in a whole unit. This type of chart is used when the parts total 100% for a single series of data.

A scatter chart or XY chart is useful for trends of collection of revenue in a company over uneven intervals plotted on the x-axis.

4. Select a chart type from the left side's list.
5. Select a sub-type from the right side's list.
6. Click **OK** to close the Change Chart dialog box.

Changing Data Source

You can add data to an existing chart. You can even add new data series or data points to existing series or change the range of data used by a chart.

1. Activate the embedded chart or activate the chart sheet for the chart to which you want to add data.

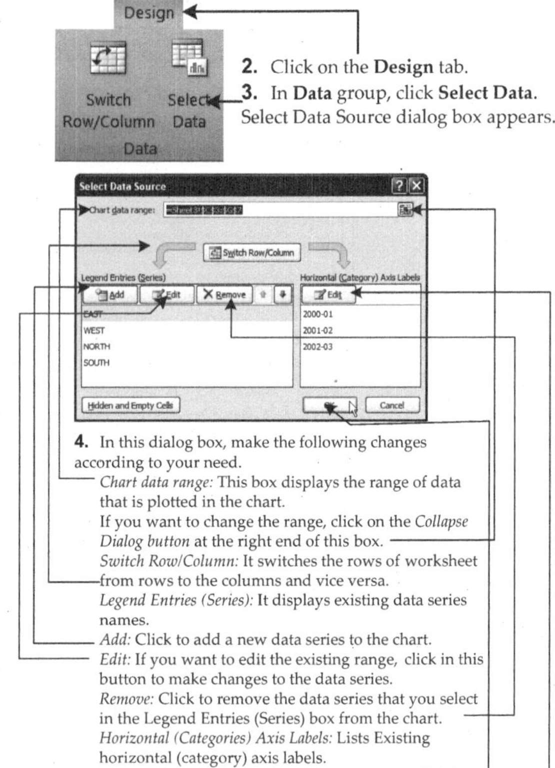

2. Click on the **Design** tab.
3. In **Data** group, click **Select Data.** Select Data Source dialog box appears.
4. In this dialog box, make the following changes according to your need.
   Chart data range: This box displays the range of data that is plotted in the chart. If you want to change the range, click on the *Collapse Dialog button* at the right end of this box.
   Switch Row/Column: It switches the rows of worksheet from rows to the columns and vice versa.
   Legend Entries (Series): It displays existing data series names.
   Add: Click to add a new data series to the chart.
   Edit: If you want to edit the existing range, click in this button to make changes to the data series.
   Remove: Click to remove the data series that you select in the Legend Entries (Series) box from the chart.
   Horizontal (Categories) Axis Labels: Lists Existing horizontal (category) axis labels.
   Edit: Click to modify the horizontal (category) labels.
5. After making changes, click **OK**.

An area chart compares the continuous changes in volume of multiple data series. This type of chart sums the data from all individual series to create top line that encloses area, giving view of how different series contribute to total volume.

Notes:

When you create a chart, Excel 2010 automatically includes labels along the category and value axes. This happens only if you had selected data and included cells containing labels.

Doughnut charts, similar to pie charts compare the sizes of pieces in a whole unit. The arrangement of the doughnut chart enables you to show more than one data series.

Radar charts are used to show the relationship between individual data series and between a specific series and the whole of the other.

Surface charts show high and low points along a surface. Surface charts are an excellent way to visually locate high and low points resulting from two changing variables.

Inserting Title in a Chart

1. Activate the Chart to which you want to add a title.

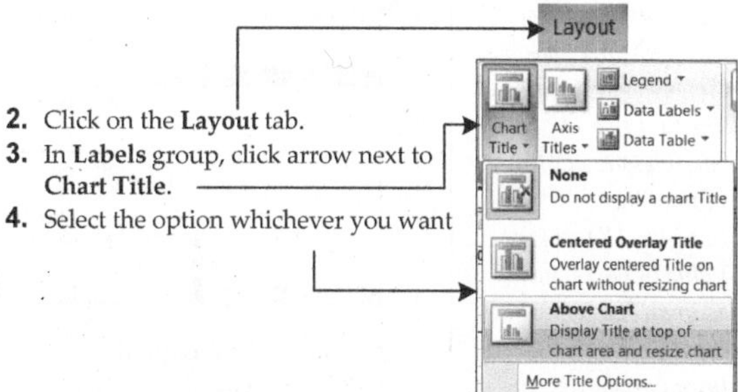

2. Click on the **Layout** tab.
3. In **Labels** group, click arrow next to **Chart Title.**
4. Select the option whichever you want

Editing Title in a Chart

1. Click the *title* to select it.
2. Then click inside the box that contains the text.
3. The insertion point appears where you click.
4. You can then use the arrow keys to move around the text or the **Backspace** and **Delete** keys to delete characters. You can press letter keys on the keyboard to enter the new text.

Inserting Floating Text to a Chart

1. Activate the chart by selecting it.

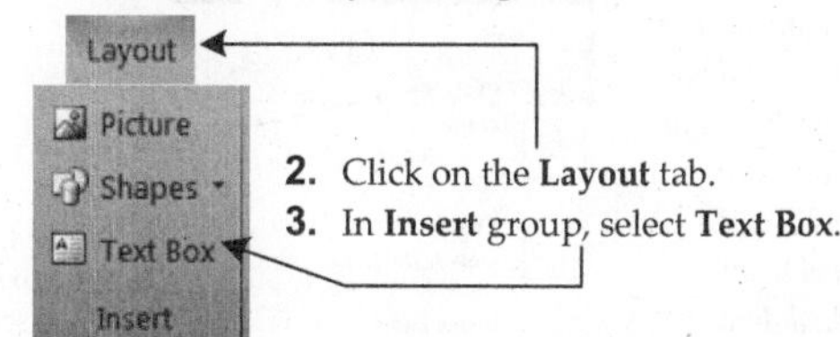

2. Click on the **Layout** tab.
3. In **Insert** group, select **Text Box.**
4. Cursor will change and now you can click the outside border of the chart or click one of the data series.
5. Type the text in text box and then click outside the text box when the text is complete.

Modifying the Axes

Excel 2010 creates a Category (X) axis and Value (Y) axis at the time of creating a chart.

1. Activate the chart where you want to remove an axis.

Notes:

A bubble chart allows you to represent three variables on a two-dimensional surface. The first two variables are plotted against the Category (X) and Value (Y) axes, just as in an XY (Scatter) chart. The third variable is represented by the size of the bubble.

Stock charts display stock prices over time. You can display high, low and closing prices and volume of stocks traded.

To add data label to an individual data series click the data series you want to add label. To add data label to an individual data point select the data point. Now right click and choose Add Data Labels.

In Excel 2010, you can use the macro recorder to record formatting changes to charts and other objects.

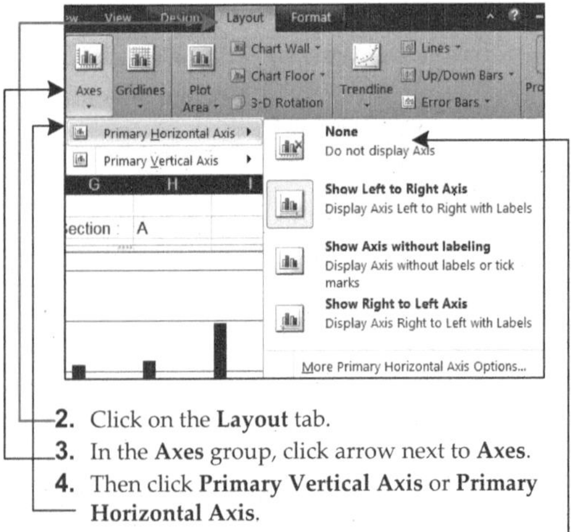

2. Click on the **Layout** tab.
3. In the **Axes** group, click arrow next to **Axes**.
4. Then click **Primary Vertical Axis** or **Primary Horizontal Axis**.
5. After that click **None**.

Inserting Data Labels

You can insert a label that can either be the value for that data point, or the category axis label associated with the data point. You can as well attach labels to many data points. This would help a viewer interpret data in a chart easily.

1. Activate the chart to which you want to add data labels.

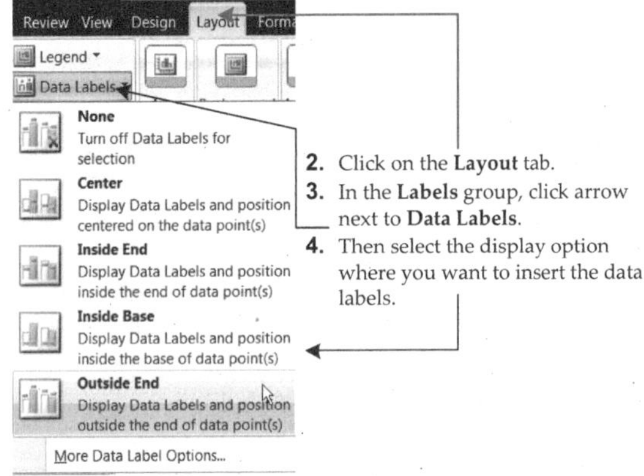

2. Click on the **Layout** tab.
3. In the **Labels** group, click arrow next to **Data Labels**.
4. Then select the display option where you want to insert the data labels.

Inserting Legends

Legend describes the symbols used in a chart. Excel 2010 creates legends from the labels on the shorter side of the worksheet data series.

Notes:

***Gridlines** help you to compare markers and in reading values accurately.*

Drawing gridlines in a chart helps you to compare values more easily.

Backstage view is where you manage your files and the data about them — creating, saving, inspecting for hidden metadata or personal information, and setting options.

*In Excel 2010, you can preview and print your Excel files in one location — on the **Print** tab in the Microsoft Office Backstage view.*

*To go back to your workbook and make changes before you print it, click the **File** tab.*

1. Activate the chart.

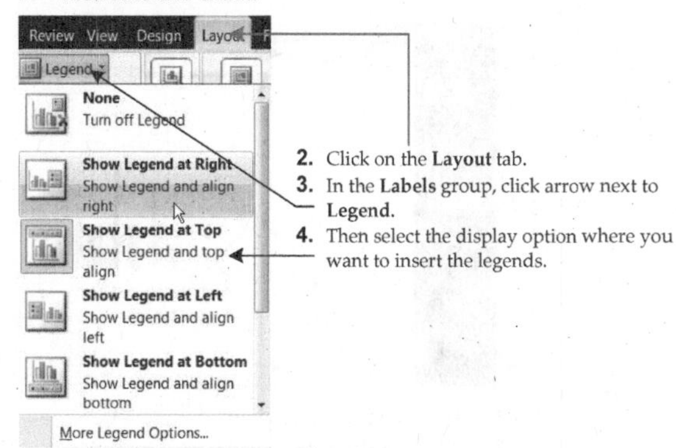

2. Click on the **Layout** tab.
3. In the **Labels** group, click arrow next to **Legend.**
4. Then select the display option where you want to insert the legends.

Inserting Gridlines to Chart

1. Activate the chart you want to add gridlines to.

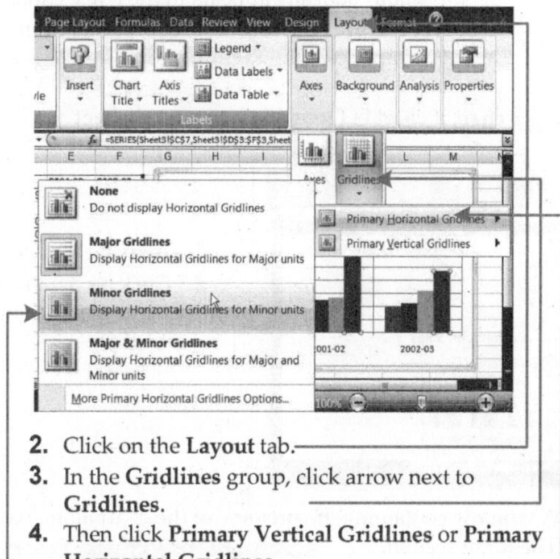

2. Click on the **Layout** tab.
3. In the **Gridlines** group, click arrow next to **Gridlines.**
4. Then click **Primary Vertical Gridlines** or **Primary Horizontal Gridlines.**
5. After that click the option according to your requirement.

Previewing Charts

After creating a chart and before printing, it is a good practice to see the full page view (preview) of the chart.

When you preview a worksheet in Excel, it opens in the MS Office Backstage view. In this view, you can change the page setup and layout before you print.

Preview a chart if chart is in a Chart sheet

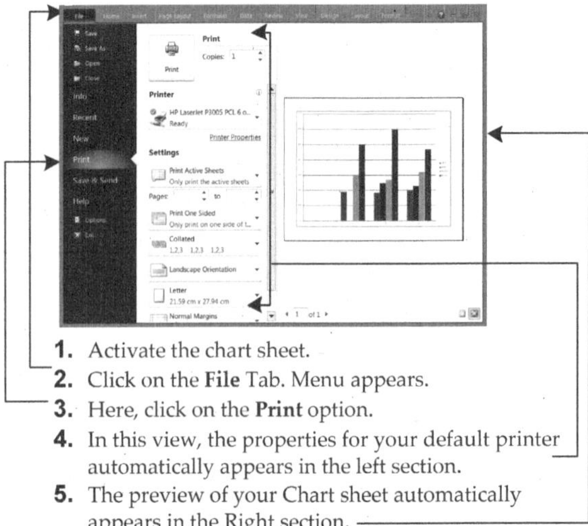

1. Activate the chart sheet.
2. Click on the **File** Tab. Menu appears.
3. Here, click on the **Print** option.
4. In this view, the properties for your default printer automatically appears in the left section.
5. The preview of your Chart sheet automatically appears in the Right section.

Preview a chart if chart is Embedded on a worksheet

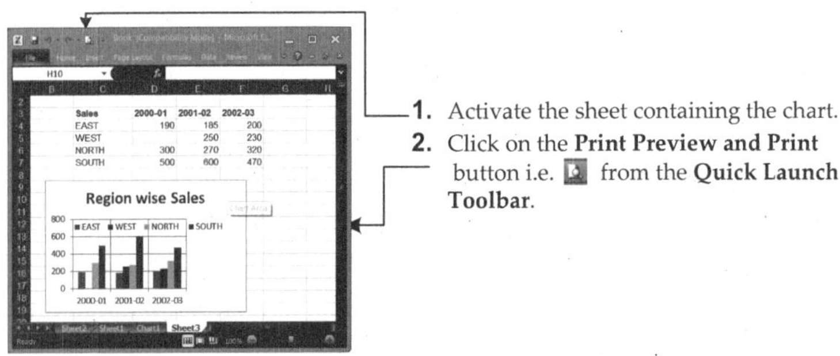

1. Activate the sheet containing the chart.
2. Click on the **Print Preview and Print** button i.e. [icon] from the **Quick Launch Toolbar**.

3. A window containing the preview of the chart along with data appears in The Right section.

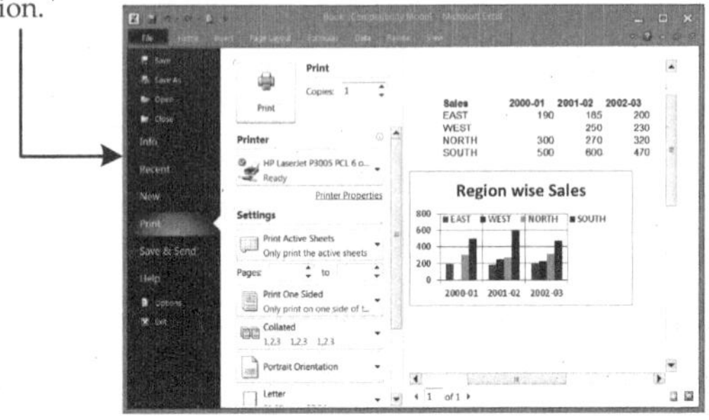

Using Sparklines

A sparkline is a tiny chart in a worksheet cell that provides a visual representation of data. Sparklines are used to show trends in a series of values, such as seasonal increases or decreases or to highlight maximum and minimum values.

Create a Sparkline

1. Select an empty cell or group of empty cells in which you want to insert one or more sparklines.
2. Click on the Insert tab.
3. In the Sparklines group, click the type of sparkline that you want to create: such as **Line**, **Column**, or **Win/Loss**. A **Data Range** dialog box appears.

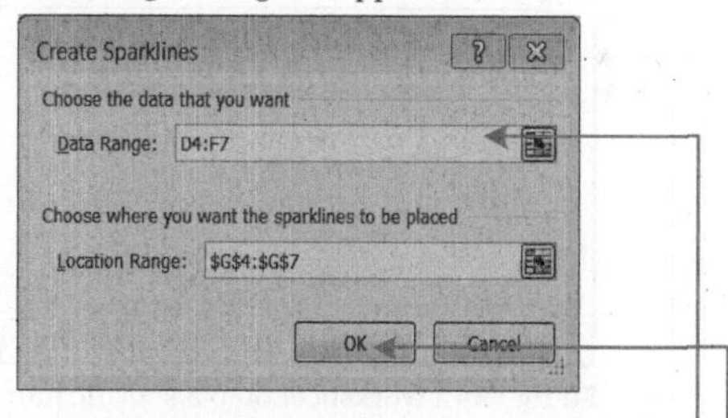

4. In **Data Range** dialog box, type the range of the cells In the **Data Range:** box or click on The collapsable button to select the range that contains the data on which you want to base the sparklines.
5. Click **OK** button.

Setting Up Worksheet for Printing

Before you print worksheet, it is better that you change the page setup as per the printer and paper which is used for printing a worksheet. Page Setup dialog box in Excel 2010 involves four tabs namely, *Page, Margins, Header/Footer* and *Sheet*.

Setting Page Options in Page Setup Dialog Box

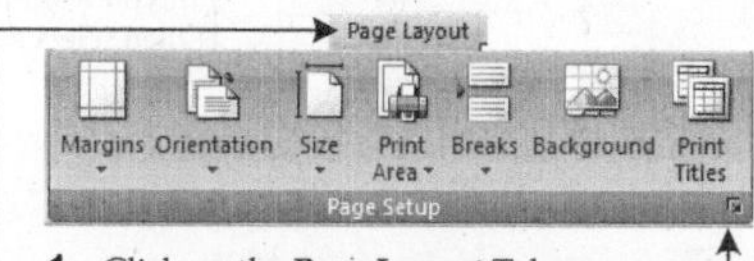

1. Click on the **Page Layout** Tab.
2. Then, in **Page Setup group**, click on the **Dialog box launcher** button to display the **Page Setup dialog box with Page tab.**

Notes:

Sparklines, the tiny charts that fit in a cell—to visually summarize trends alongside data. Sparklines show trends in a small amount of space. So, they are especially useful for dashboards or other places where you need to show a snapshot of your business in an easy-to-understand visual format.

In Excel 2007 and Excel 97-2003, sparklines that show trends in a series of values are not displayed on the worksheet. However, all sparklines remain available in the workbook and are applied when the workbook is opened again in Excel 2010.

When you choose ***Fit To:*** *option, Excel 2010 ignores any page breaks you have set, and fits the entire worksheet or print area to the specified number of pages.*

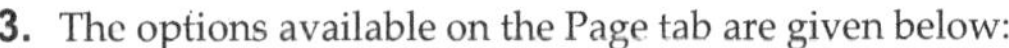

3. The options available on the Page tab are given below:

   Orientation: Portrait (meaning page length is more than the page width). Landscape (meaning page width is more than the page length).

   Scaling Adjust to: Allows you to enlarge or reduce the printed worksheet. You can reduce it to 10% to fit more of the worksheet on a page. You can also enlarge it to 400% to enhance details.

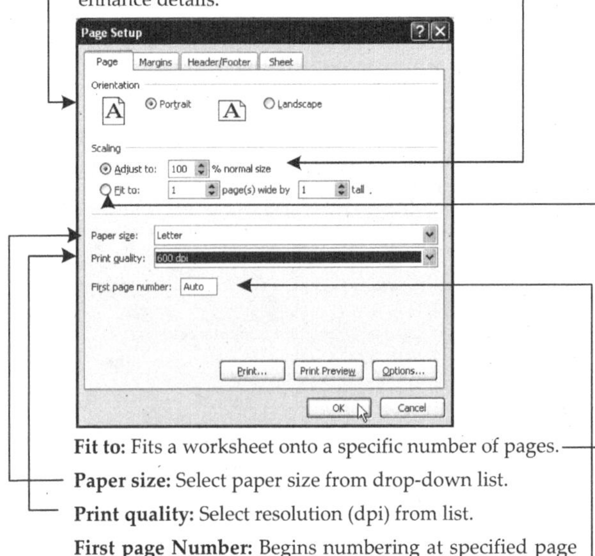

Fit to: Fits a worksheet onto a specific number of pages.

Paper size: Select paper size from drop-down list.

Print quality: Select resolution (dpi) from list.

First page Number: Begins numbering at specified page number.

Notes:

*You can also set the orientation from Ribbon by clicking the orientation option from the **Page Setup** group of **Page Layout** Tab.*

Setting the Margins in a Worksheet

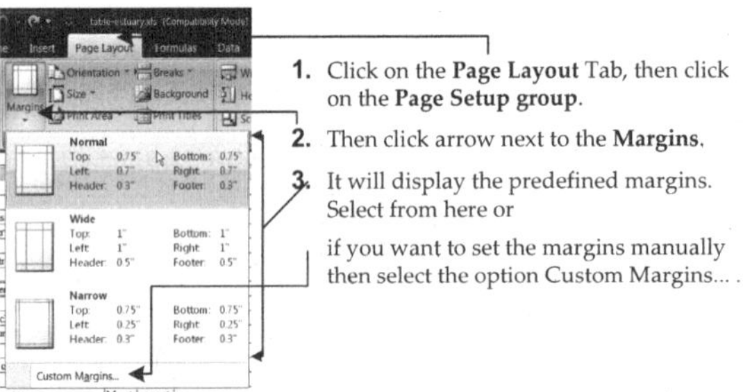

1. Click on the **Page Layout** Tab, then click on the **Page Setup group**.
2. Then click arrow next to the **Margins**.
3. It will display the predefined margins. Select from here or

   if you want to set the margins manually then select the option Custom Margins... .

To set the margins and select the position of headers, footers and print area, you have to click on the Margins tab in the Page Setup dialog box.

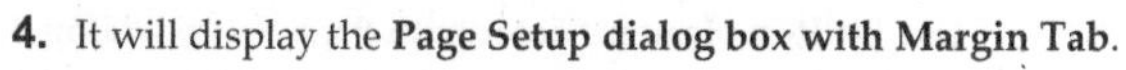

4. It will display the **Page Setup dialog box with Margin Tab**.

   Following Options are available in Margin Tab:

   Top: Give the distance between the top edge of the page.

   Left: Give the distance between the left edge of the page and the data printed on a page.

   Right: Give the distance between the right edge of the page and the data printed on a page.

   Bottom: Give the distance between the bottom edge of the page and the data printed on a page.

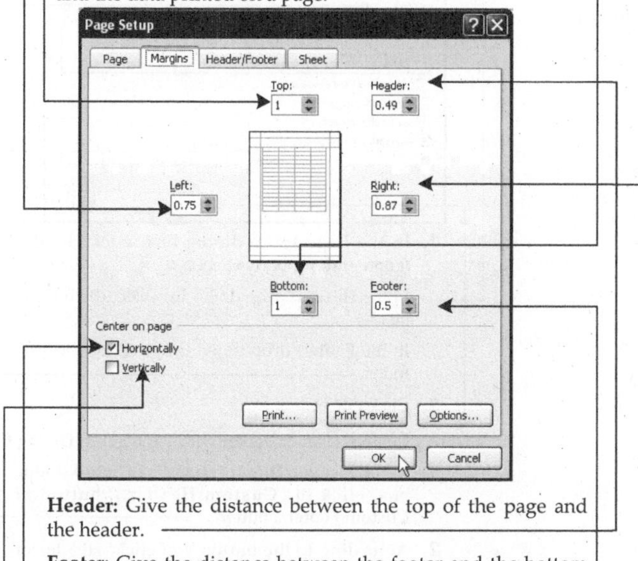

   Header: Give the distance between the top of the page and the header.

   Footer: Give the distance between the footer and the bottom of the page.

   Center on Page: Use this option to center the print area vertically or horizontally between margins.

   Horizontally: Give this option to horizontally center the page.

   Vertically: Give this option to vertically center the page.

Notes:

You can preview the worksheet as an area on the dialog box showing how the margins are set.

Setting Headers and Footers

You can use headers for company's name and report titles, etc. The footers are commonly used for page numbering and printing date/time.

If need be, you can use the built-in header/footer option in Excel 2010 or you can specify custom headers/footers.

Notes:

Headers and footers are not actually a part of the worksheet. They are part of the printed page. Therefore, they are allotted separate space on the printed page.

Use Built-in Header/Footer with Page Setup Dialog Box

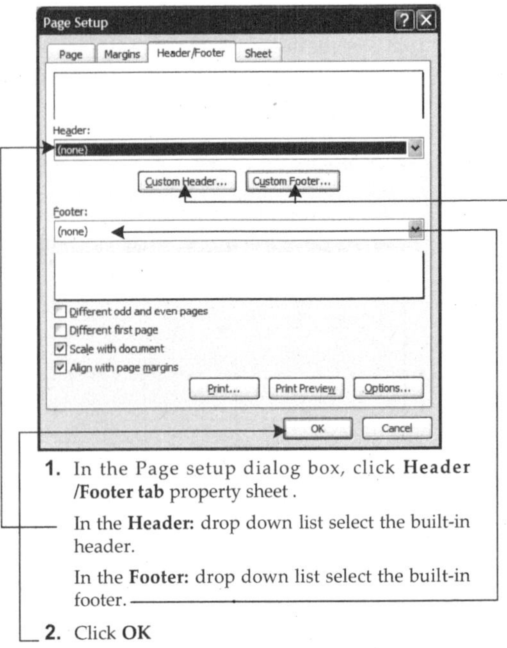

1. In the Page setup dialog box, click **Header /Footer tab** property sheet .

   In the **Header:** drop down list select the built-in header.

   In the **Footer:** drop down list select the built-in footer.
2. Click **OK**

Create a Custom Header/Footer with Page Setup Dialog Box

1. In the **Header/Footer tab** of Page Setup dialog box, click the **Custom Header...** button or **Custom Footer...** button.
2. According to the button you click, Header or Footer dialog box appears. Select the options according to your need.

Setting Sheet Options

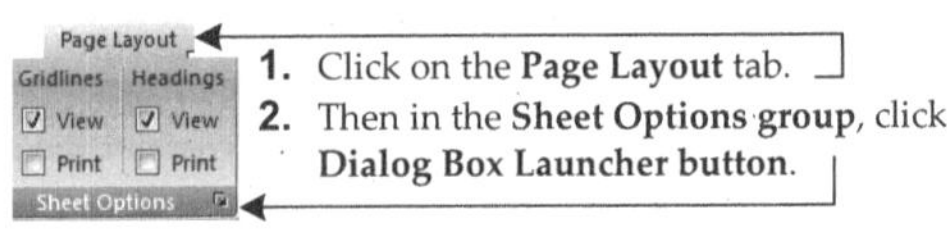

1. Click on the **Page Layout** tab.
2. Then in the **Sheet Options group**, click **Dialog Box Launcher button**.

It will display the Sheet Tab of the Page Setup dialog box. The Sheet tab options with function are given below:

Print area: Select area of worksheet you want to print.

*Print titles-*Appears rows or columns on each page when printing a multiple-page document.

Rows to repeat on top: You can specify the number of rows you want to repeat on each page.

Columns to repeat at left: You can specify the columns you want to repeat on each page.

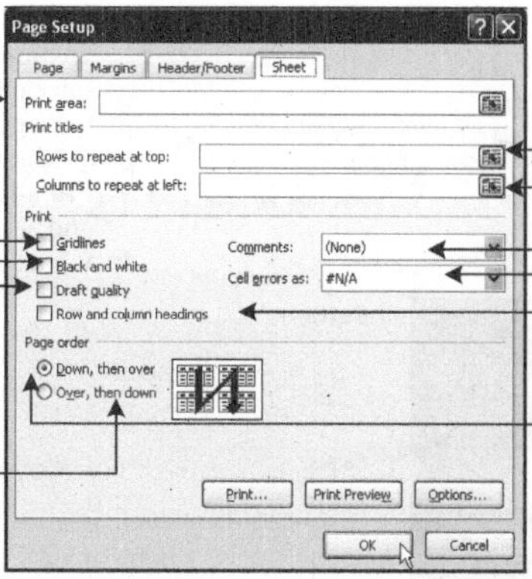

Print Options- Select print options:

Gridlines: Turns gridlines on/off (on the printed pages).

Black and white: Prints all pages in black and white.

Draft quality: Gridlines, graphics will not be printed.

Row and column headings: Includes row and column headings on every printed page.

Comments: This allows printing cell comments.

Cell errors as: This allows options for cells errors i.e. Displayed, Blank, (hyphen), or #N/A.

*Page order Options-*Select page order for multiple-page worksheet.

Down, then over: This option would print the page from top to bottom and then left to right.

Over, then down: This option would print the page from left to right and then from top to bottom.

Notes:

You can also print a workbook to a file instead of to a printer. This is useful when you need to print the workbook on a different type of printer from the one that you originally used to print it.

Printing Worksheet

You can set *margins* and *fonts* and include *headers/footers* as well as *titles* while printing a worksheet. You can even print multiple copies of the entire worksheet or a part of it.

1. Click on the **File** Tab. Menu appears.
2. Here, click on the **Print** option.

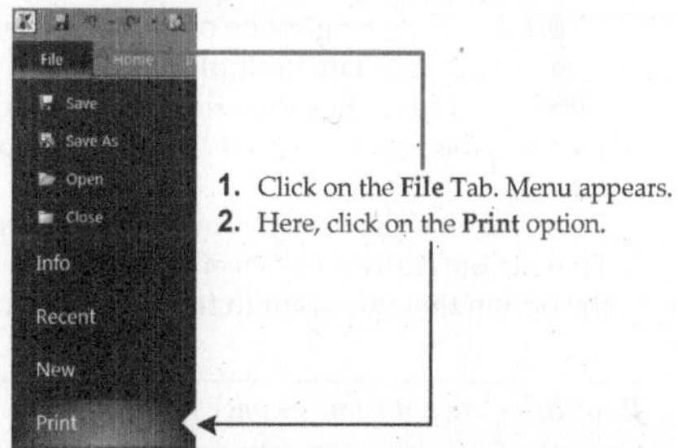

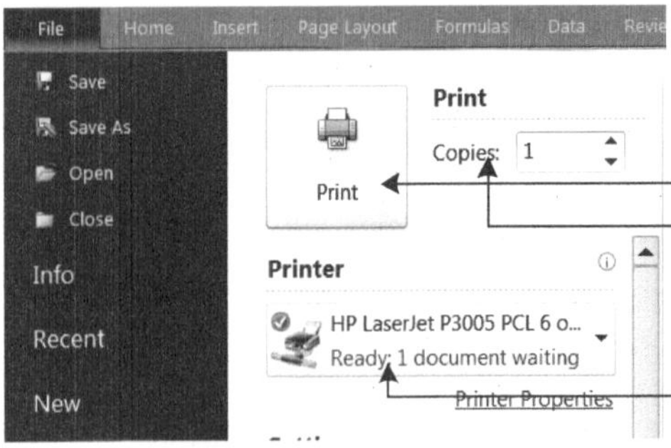

Print options are described as under:

In ***Print Area***, Click on the **Print** button to directly send the entire workbook for printing.

In **Copies:** spinner box specify the number of copies of the selected pages in a worksheet to be printed.

To change the printer, click the drop-down box under **Printer**, and select the printer that you want.

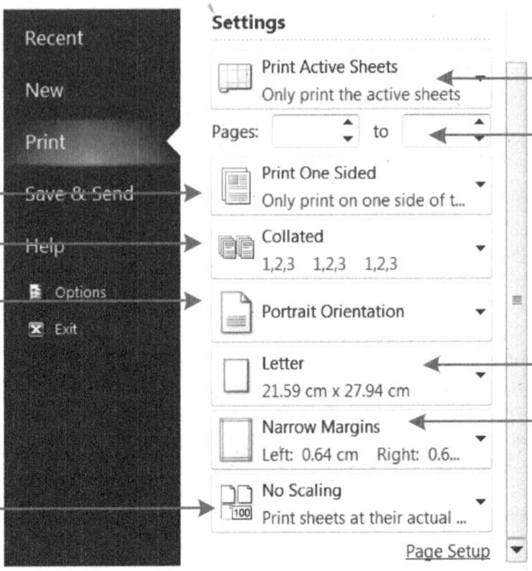

To make page setup changes, select the options that you want under **Settings**.

To print the selection, the active sheet or sheets, or the entire workbook.

To print pages you wish to print.

To print only on single side or on both side.

Allows you to collate multiple copies.

Allows you to change the orientation i.e. portrait or landscape.

To select the paper size, select from the Paper Size drop-down box .

To set the margin, select from the Margins drop-down box.

To scale the entire worksheet to fit on a single printed page, click the option that you want in the scale options drop-down box.

Print titles are not same as page headers. However, they can be used for similar purposes. Also, a page can be set up both print titles or page headers or both.

Creating Hyperlink

1. Click on Insert Tab.

2. In the Links group, click on Hyperlink. The **Insert Hyperlink** dialog box appears

Hyperlink to a New File:

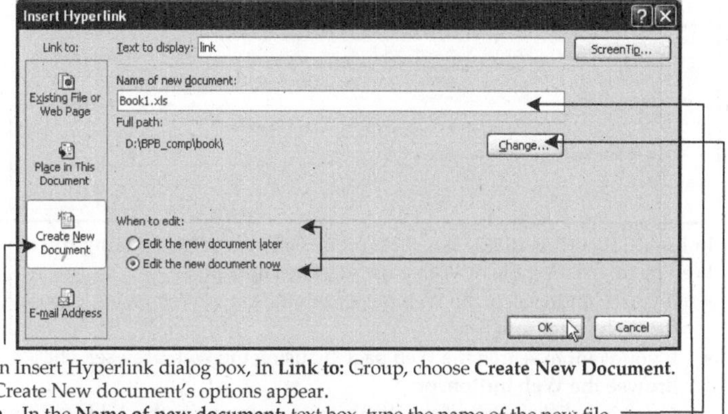

In Insert Hyperlink dialog box, In **Link to:** Group, choose **Create New Document.** Create New document's options appear.

- In the **Name of new document:** text box, type the name of the new file.
- If you want to change path of the file click on the **Change...** button.
- Under **When to edit:** Option, click the option for opening a file now or later. Click **OK** button.

Hyperlink to an Existing File:

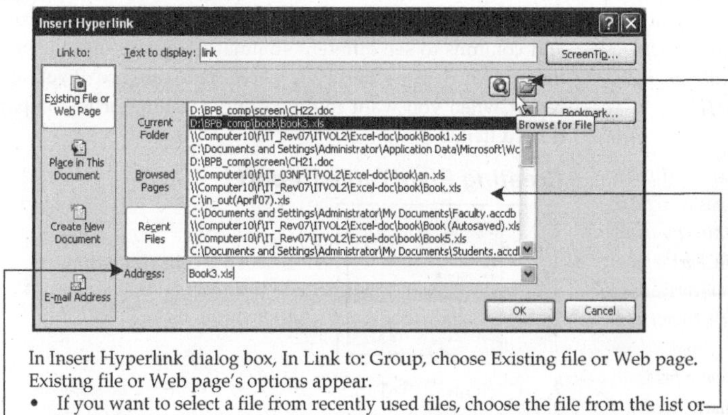

In Insert Hyperlink dialog box, In Link to: Group, choose Existing file or Web page. Existing file or Web page's options appear.

- If you want to select a file from recently used files, choose the file from the list or
- If you do not know the file path, you select the **Browse for File** button.

Alternatively,

- If you know the name and path of the file, you type it in the **Address:** box.

Hyperlink is a shortcut, coloured, underlined text or a graphic that specifies the link to a location that is stored on a Web, Word or any other location. When we click this link the specified file would open automatically.

Hyperlink to a Web page:

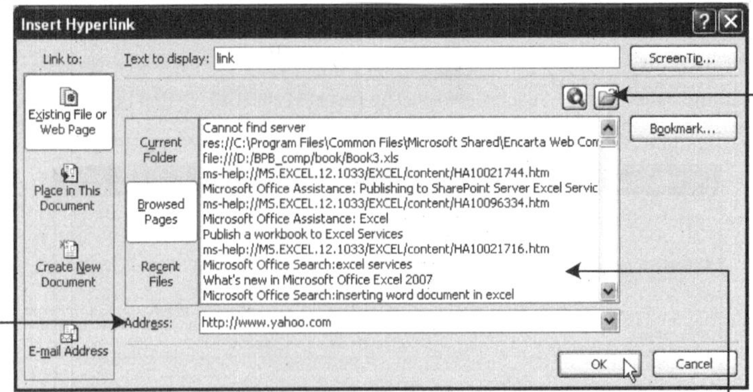

In Insert Hyperlink dialog box, In **Link to:** Group, choose **Existing file or Web page.** Existing file or Web page's options appear.

- If you want to select the Web page from the list of Web pages, choose the Web page from list or
- If you want to search the Web page by using the Web browser, click **Browse the Web button.** or
- If you know the name of the Web page, you type it in the **Address:** box.

Notes:

In Excel 2010, multithreading help speed up data retrieval, sorting, and filtering in PivotTables.

In Excel 2010, it is now easier to filter data directly in a PivotChart report and to reorganize the chart's layout by adding and removing fields. Similarly, with a single click, you can hide all field buttons on the PivotChart.

PivotTable

A PivotTable is an *interactive* table that lets you analyze and view large size of data in a list or database form so that it can be easily understood and analysed. You can rotate its rows and columns to see different summaries, details and views of the source data as per your need. You can use PivotTable report when you want to do sorting, totalling or to compare related items.

Creating PivotTable Report

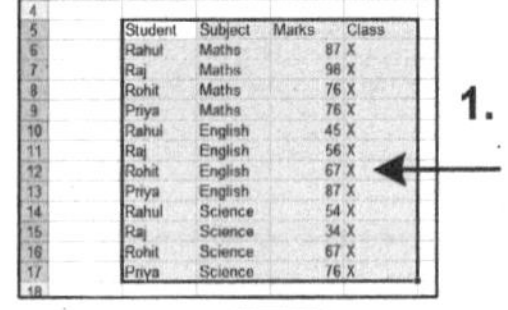

Student	Subject	Marks	Class
Rahul	Maths	87	X
Raj	Maths	98	X
Rohit	Maths	76	X
Priya	Maths	76	X
Rahul	English	45	X
Raj	English	56	X
Rohit	English	67	X
Priya	English	87	X
Rahul	Science	54	X
Raj	Science	34	X
Rohit	Science	67	X
Priya	Science	76	X

1. Select the cells (including column labels) that you want to include in the PivotTable.
2. Click on Insert Tab.
3. In the Tables group, click arrow next to.

4. Then choose **PivotTable** from the drop-down menu. The Create PivotTable dialog box appears.

Notes:

In Excel 2010, it is possible to fill down labels in a PivotTable so that you can more easily use the PivotTable. You can also repeat labels in PivotTables to display item captions of nested fields in all rows and columns.

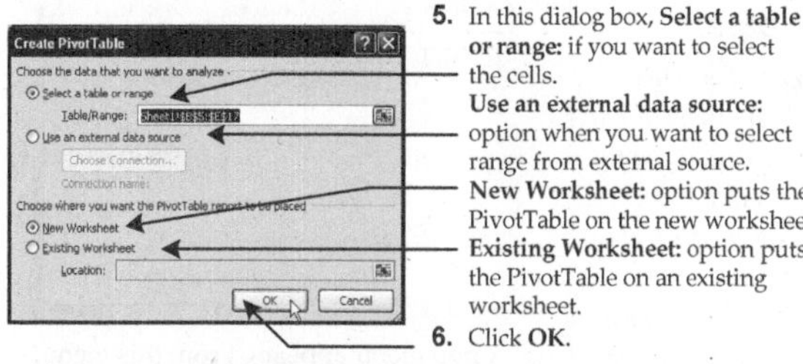

5. In this dialog box, **Select a table or range:** if you want to select the cells.
   Use an external data source: option when you want to select range from external source.
   New Worksheet: option puts the PivotTable on the new worksheet.
   Existing Worksheet: option puts the PivotTable on an existing worksheet.
6. Click **OK**.

After that, an empty PivotTable report is added to the location that you entered with the PivotTable field list so that you can start adding fields.

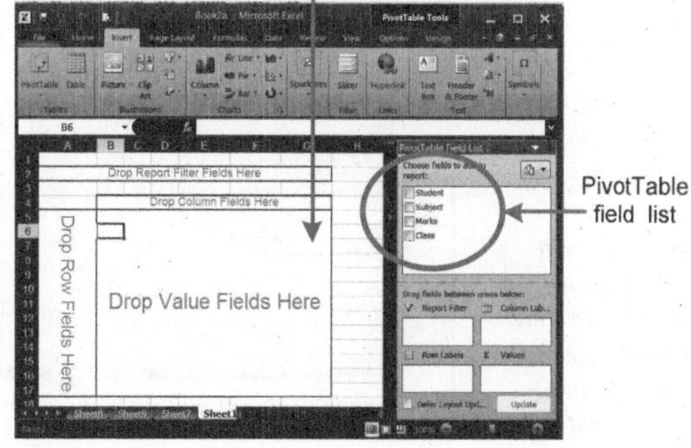

Mark one or more check boxes inside the PivotTable Field List pane. Each time you select another check box, Excel 2010 modifies how data appears in your PivotTable

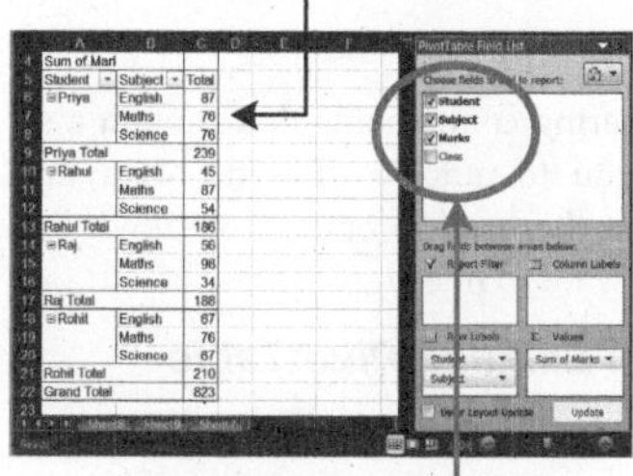

PivotTable with Student, Subject and Marks fields selected

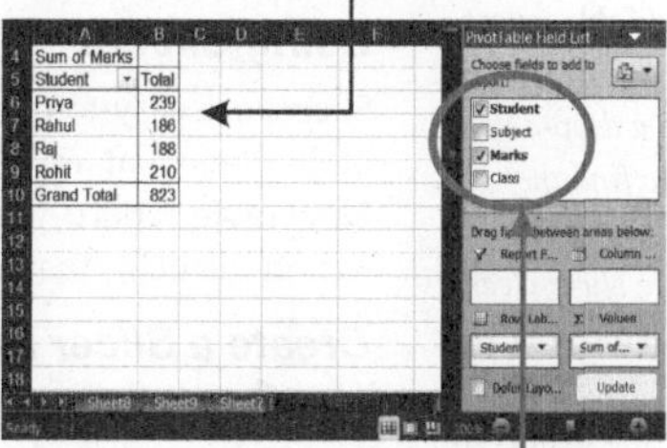

PivotTable with Student and Marks fields selected

Filtering a PivotTable

1. Click on the PivotTable you want to filter.

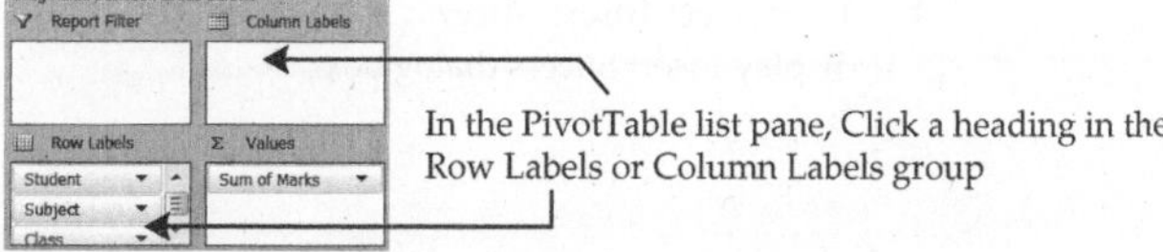

Notes:

With the help of slicers (new in Excel 2010), you can filter data in a PivotTable with the click of a button and to quickly see which filters are applied without having to open additional menus.

Slicers are typically associated with the PivotTable in which they are created. However, you can also create stand-alone slicers that are referenced from Online Analytical Processing (OLAP)

In regular PivotTable report filter, you have to open a drop-down list to find the filtering details. But, a slicer clearly labels the filter that is applied and provides details so that you can easily understand the data that is displayed in the filtered PivotTable report.

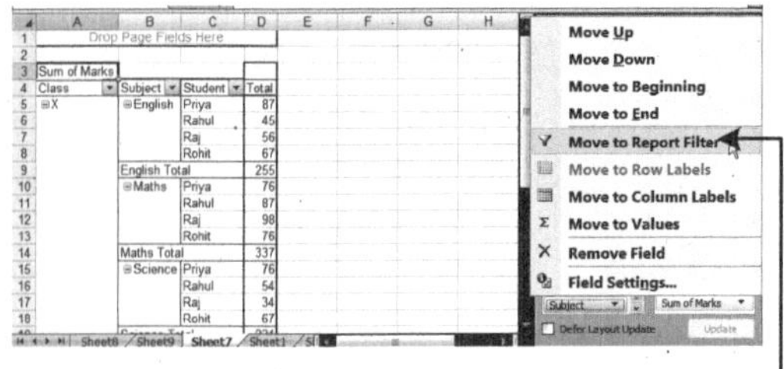

A pop menu appears, From this menu, select **Move to Report Filter**.

Excel 2010 moves your chosen label into the **Report Filter group** in the **Pivot Table Field List pane** and displays a filter list box at the top of your PivotTable (Here, we have selected **Subject** from Row Label)

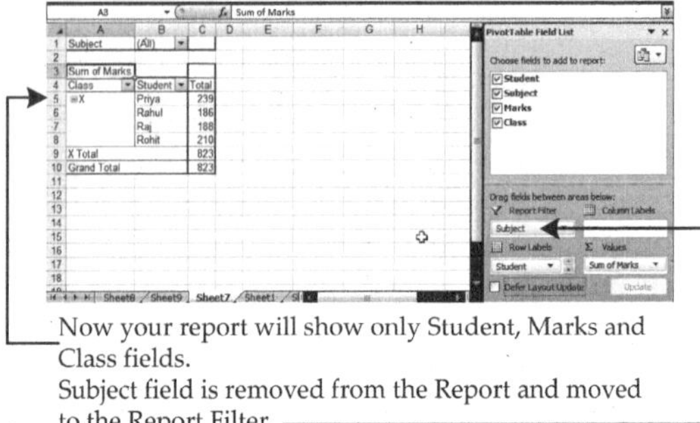

Now your report will show only Student, Marks and Class fields.

Subject field is removed from the Report and moved to the Report Filter.

Using Slicers

Slicers are easy-to-use filtering components that contain a set of buttons that enable you to quickly filter the data in a PivotTable report, without the need to open drop-down lists to find the items that you want to filter.

Create a Slicer in An Existing PivotTable

1. Click anywhere in the PivotTable report.
2. Click on Options Tab.
3. In the Sort & Filter group, click arrow next Insert Slicer.
4. Then select **Insert Slicer...** (Insert Slicer... Slicer Connections...). It will display Insert Slicers dialog box.

Notes:

*When you click on the PivotTable, it will display the **PivotTable** Tools, adding an **Options** and a **Design** tab.*

*To select more than one item in a slicer to filter, hold down **Ctrl** key and then click the items on which you want to filter.*

*A PivotTable can have both **local** and **shared slicers.***

*Slicers that are connected to and used in more than one PivotTable are called **shared slicers**. Slicers that are used in one PivotTable only are called **local slicers**.*

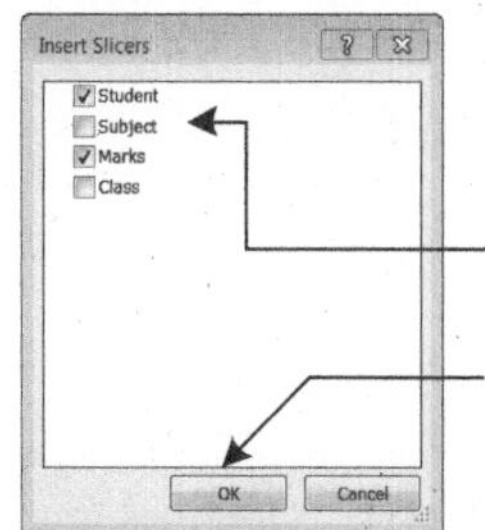

5. In the Insert Slicers dialog box, select the check box of the PivotTable fields for which you want to create a slicer.
6. Click **OK** button.

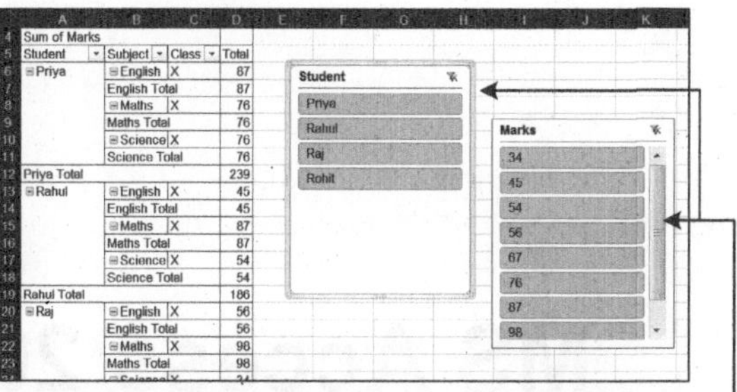

7. A slicer is displayed for every field that you selected. (Here, we selected Student and Marks field)
8. In each slicer, click the items on which you want to filter.

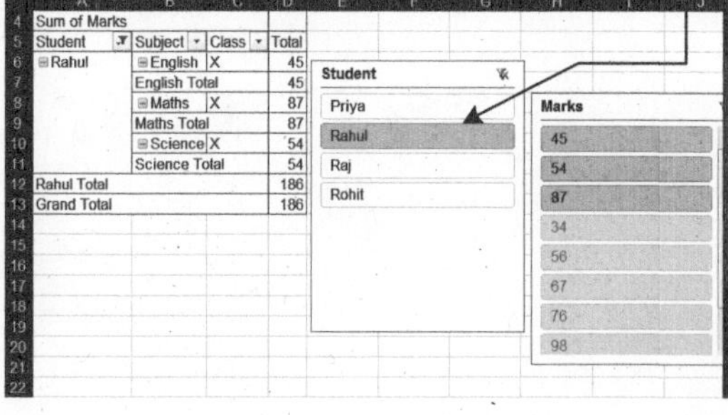

MS Access 2010

Getting Started

Access 2010 is a software package for database management. Access 2010 is an easy to use with full featured database development application. With the help of Access 2010, you can build web databases and publish them to a SharePoint site. SharePoint visitors can use your database application in a web browser, using SharePoint permissions to determine who can see what.

Notes:

*Access 2010 needs **Windows Vista** or **Windows 7** as operating system to run on an IBM PC. However, Access 2010 can also be used with **Windows XP** operating system, if **service pack 3** is installed on Windows XP.*

When you first start Access 2010, or if you close a database without closing Access, Microsoft Office Backstage view is displayed.

***Backstage view** is a starting point from where you can create a new database, open an existing database, view featured content from Office.com*

Starting MS Access 2010 using Start Button

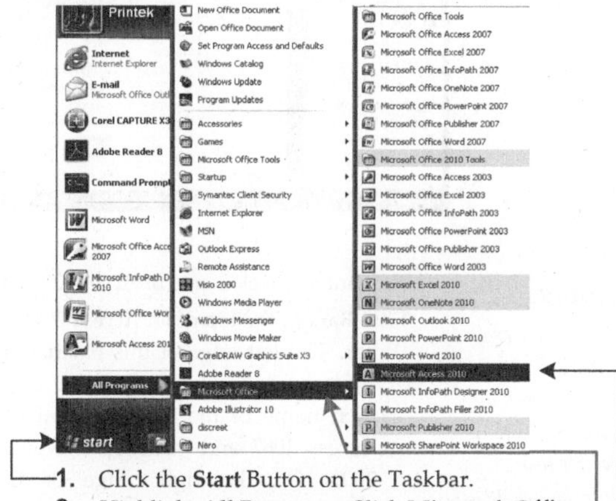

1. Click the **Start** Button on the Taskbar.
2. Highlight **All Programs**, Click **Microsoft Office**.
3. Click **Microsoft Access 2010**.
4. A starting page of Access is displayed.

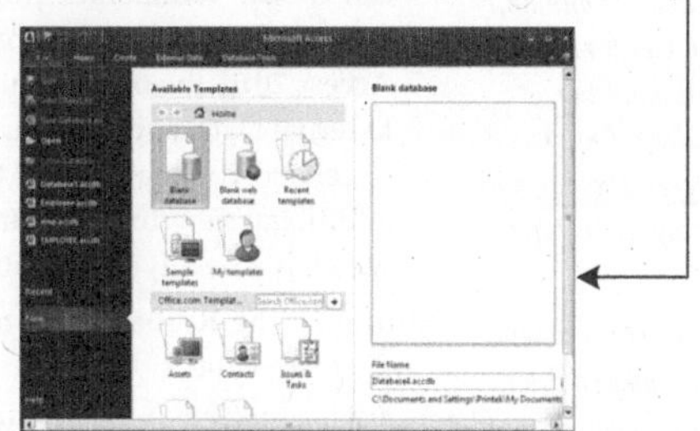

Access 2010 databases consist not only of the basic data items, but also of related items you use to work with them. Every database may contain six different types of objects. These objects are Tables, Queries, Forms, Reports, Macros and Modules.

About MS Access 2010 Interface

Access 2010 includes new user interface with significant changes from prior versions, especially versions prior to Access 2007. This new interface is the result of extensive research and usability testing, and it is designed to make it easier to find the commands.

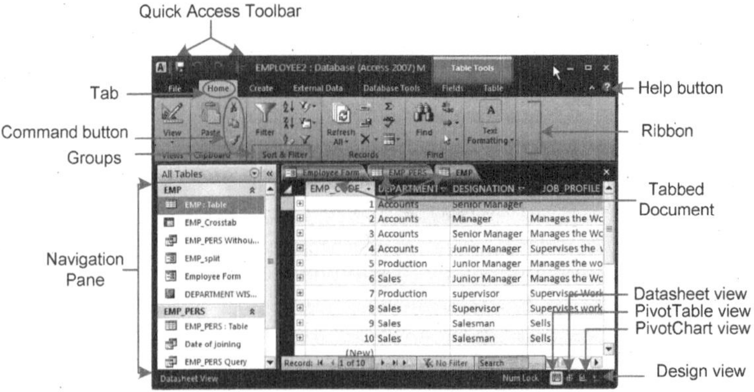

Notes:

The new user interface makes it easy to work in Access 2010. Major new interface elements in Access 2010 are Backstage view, Ribbon, Command tab, Contextual command tab, Gallery, Quick Access Toolbar and Navigation Pane.

Layout view *lets you make common design changes while you view a live form or report.*

New Interface elements of Access 2010 are given below:

Title Bar: At the top of an Access 2010 window, there is the title bar. The left edge of this bar has the Application window control icon next to which the Quick Access Toolbar, and then name of the database and database format Such as Access 2007 and other options are Access 2000 & Access 2003. On the right edge of the title bar, *minimize, restore/maximize* and *close* buttons are placed.

Ribbon: The area at the top of the program window where you can choose commands. In Ribbon, *Commands* are organized in logical *groups,* which are collected together under *tabs.* In Access 2010, the main command tabs are File, Home, Create, External Data, and Database Tools. Each tab contains groups of related commands and these groups surface some of the additional new user interface elements, such as the gallery, which is a new type of control that presents choices visually.

Minimize the Ribbon: This button will minimize the Ribbon. To restore the Ribbon, again click on this button.

Backstage view: Backstage view is new in Access 2010. It contains commands and information that apply to an entire database This view occupies the **File** tab on the ribbon and contains many commands such as *New, Open, Save, Save As, Print,* etc.

Quick Access Toolbar: A single standard toolbar that appears in the ribbon and offers single-click access to most needed commands.

Navigation Pane: The area on the left side of the window that displays your database objects. When you open a database or create a new one, the names of your database objects appear in the Navigation Pane. It replaces the Database window from earlier versions of Access.

Tabbed documents: Tabbed document is start with Access 2007. With the help of this, you can display your database objects in tabbed documents instead of overlapping windows. Now tables, queries, forms, reports, pages, and macros are displayed as tabbed documents.

Status bar: The bar at the bottom of the program window that displays status information and includes buttons that allow you to change your view i.e. *form view, PivotTable view, PivotChart view, layout view* and *design view.*

Notes:

Access 2010 can format text more easily by using the ***mini toolbar****. When you select text, the mini toolbar automatically appears above the selected text. You can use it to apply bold, italic, font size, color, and so on. If you do not want to use the mini toolbar, just move your pointer a few pixels away and the mini toolbar disappears.*

Creating New Database

Access 2010 gives you two ways to create a new database. These are as follows:

1. Creating a blank database
2. Creating a database using template that is installed with Access
3. Creating a database using template from Office.com

Creating a Blank Database

A blank database is a file that does not contain any objects or data. It is an empty shell that you can use to add new ***tables, queries, forms,*** *and* ***reports****.*

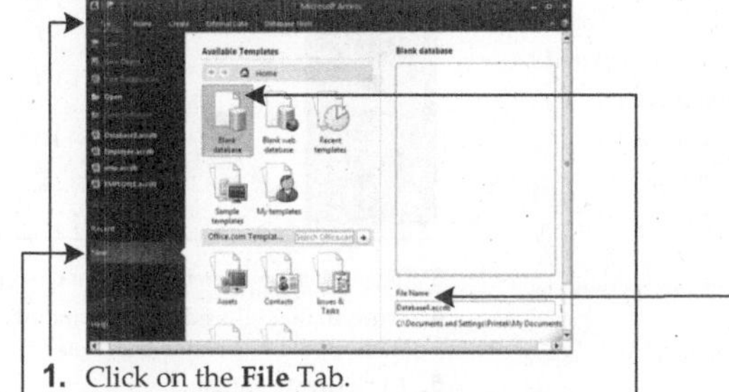

1. Click on the **File** Tab.
2. Click **New** and then click **Blank Database.**
3. In the **Blank Database right pane**, type a file name (say *Database1.accdb*) in the **File Name:** box.
   If you want to change the location of the file, click on the **Browse button** .
4. Click **Create**.

You can also press ***Ctrl + N*** *keys together to start a new database from anywhere in Access. After you give the database a name, Access closes the database that you were working on and opens a blank database window.*

Notes:

A template is a ready-to-use database containing all the tables, queries, forms, and reports needed to perform a specific task.

Access 2010 includes a suite of prebuilt tracking applications in the form of templates that you can use to get started quickly and refine them to track information in your way.

Access 2010 also supports creating web databases. So that you can use a web database with a web browser. Access 2010 is not required unless you want to make design changes.

5. Access creates and opens the database with an empty table named **Table1** in **Datasheet view.**

6. The cursor is placed in the first empty cell in the **Click to Add** column to add data.

Creating a Database using Template

Access provides you with a variety of templates that you can use to speed up the database creation process.

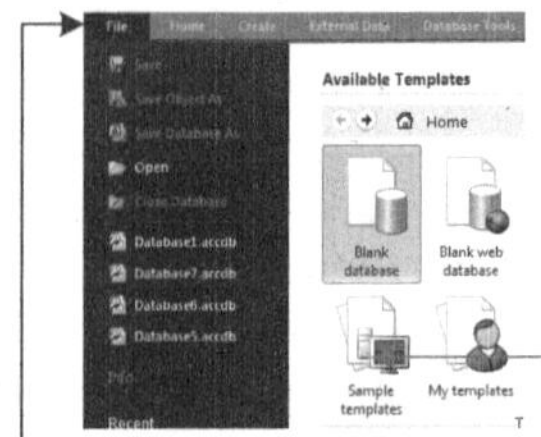

1. Click on the **File** Tab.
2. Then click on **New**, In **Available Templates,** click on the **Sample templates**.

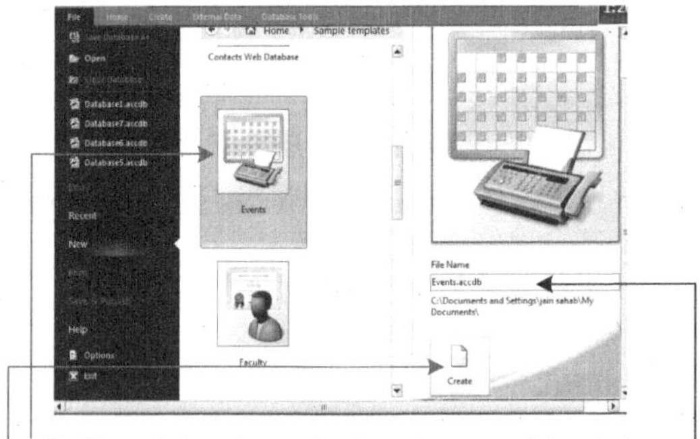

3. Then, click on the *template* from the center of the window.
4. Now, in the right side of the window, Access suggests a file name in the **File Name** box. You can change the file name.
5. Click **Create** button.
6. Access creates the database and then opens it.

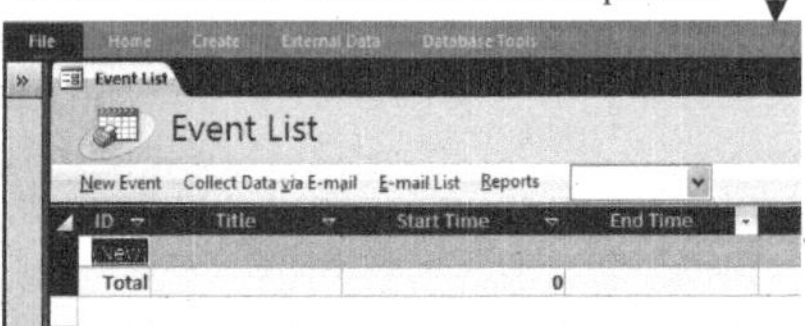

Notes:

In order to make data entry easier, you can create objects called Forms. Forms provide you with a "template" that you fill in whenever you enter the information for the record.

*You can also open database by clicking on the **Recent** option from the **File Tab** and then select the database from the right pane.*

You can also paste data from Microsoft Excel tables into a new datasheet — Access 2010 creates all of the fields and recognizes the data types automatically.

Access 2010 has a feature that you can use to perform several actions with a single command. Such a feature, called Macros operate by running a series of actions that can do various jobs again and again by just typing single word command only.

Open an Existing Database

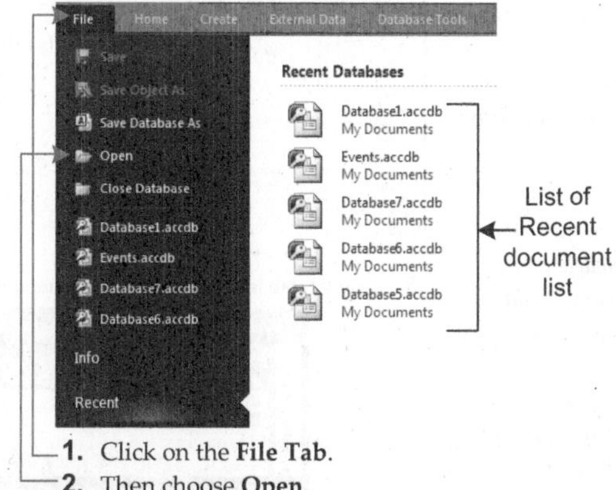

1. Click on the **File Tab**.
2. Then choose **Open**.

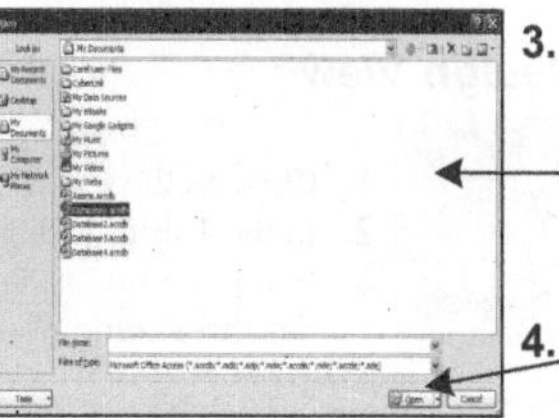

3. In Open Dialog box, choose the *drive, folder name* that contains the workbooks. After finding the required workbook, select it.
4. Then click **Open** button.

Create a Table in Blank Database

When you create a new blank database, a new empty table is automatically inserted for you. You can then enter data to start defining your fields.

Create a Table in an Existing Database

1. Open the blank database named as **Database1.accdb** that we created earlier.

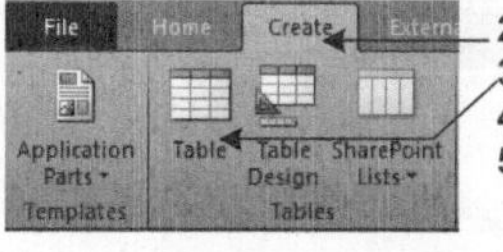

2. Click on the **Create** Tab.
3. In the **Tables** group, click **Table**.
4. A new table is inserted in the database.
5. Double click on the **Click to Add** Column to add a field (such as Name, Address, etc.)
6. Now, type data in the cell below the **Click to Add**column header.

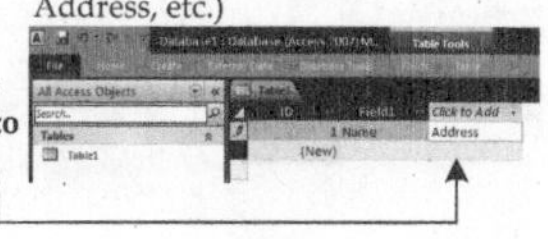

Notes:

Access 2010 offers easy access to both end-user help and developer help from the same Help viewer window.

In Access 2010, you use models when you want to add pre-built parts to your database. Models can include tables and database objects, such as queries and forms.

Create a Table based on Template

1. Open the database in which you want to create table.

2. Click on the Create Tab.
3. In the Templates group, click Application Parts button.
4. Select any one template from *Quick Start* Section. (Here , we select Contacts.)
5. A new table is inserted based on the table template you selected.

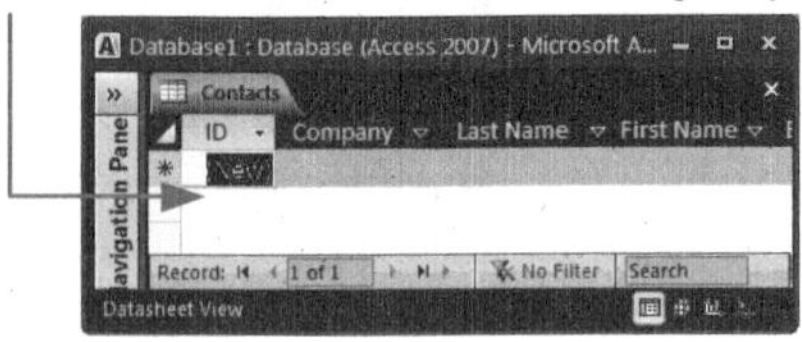

Create a Table using Design View

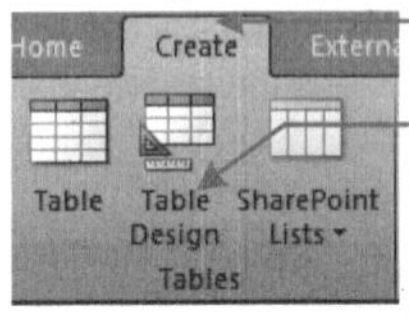

1. Click on the **Create** Tab.
2. In the **Tables** group, click **Table Design**.
3. You will find **Design** Tab and a grid that has three columns across the top.

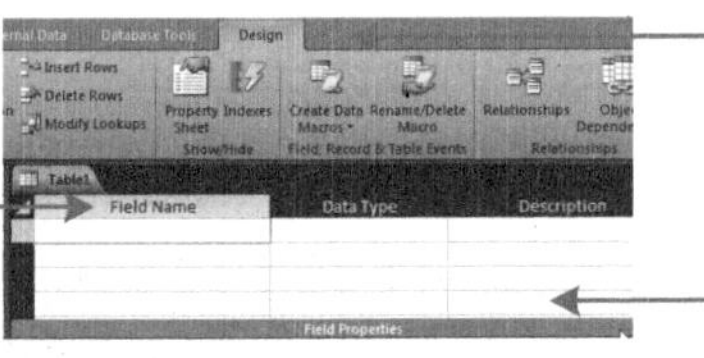

4. Under the **Field Name** column, type the name of the field which you want to insert into the Table.

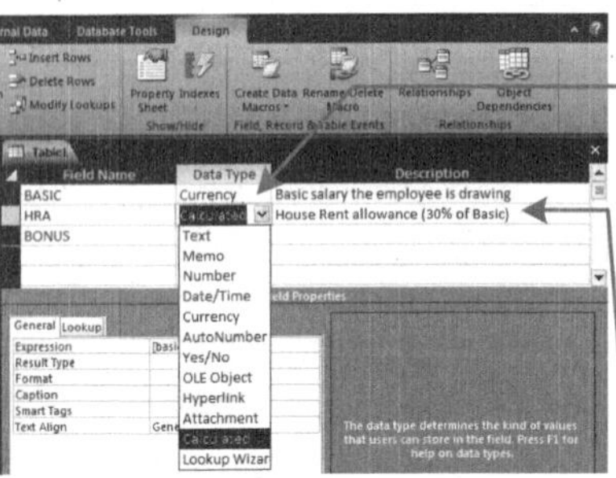

5. Move to the **Data Type** column and select a data type for the newly entered field.

When you select Calculated data type, An Expression builder opens up. Here, type the calculation you want to perform. In this example, we type **Basic * 30/100** in Expression builder.

6. Type a small description about the field in **Description** column. You may leave it blank also.

In Access 2010, new data type (Calculated) lets you create a field that is based on a calculation of other fields in the same table.

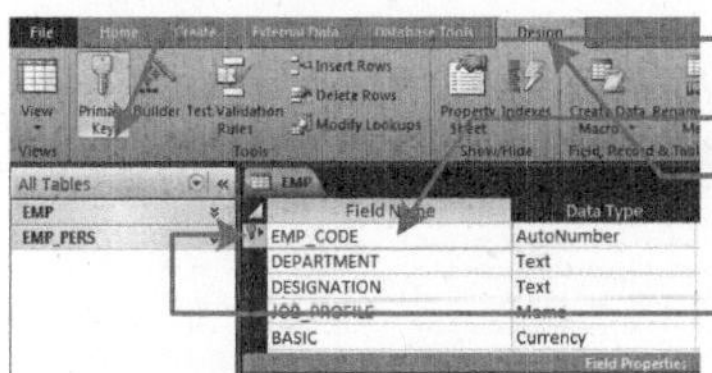

7. To set a field as the primary key, click the field.
8. Then click on the **Design** Tab.
9. In the **Tools** group, click **Primary Key**.

This field will now be assigned as the primary key.

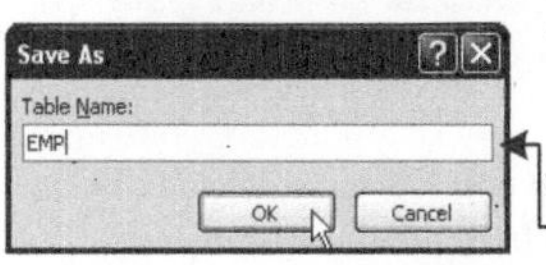

10. Click on the File Tab and then choose **Save** (Save) option and type a name for this Table.
11. Save As dialog box appears, Here, we have assigned the name **EMP** to the table.

Notes:

Each field in a table has a set of properties that you use to customize how a field's data is stored, handled, or displayed.

*To set the primary key for a table you have to use **Design view**.*

When you enter data in the new column, Access 2010 uses the information you type to recognize the appropriate data type for the field.

When data entered in a record is complete, it would get saved automatically.

Opening Table

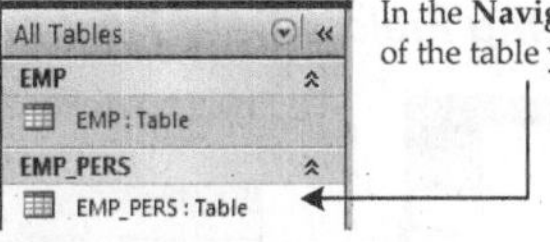

In the **Navigation Pane**, double click the name of the table you want to work on..

Add Data in the Table

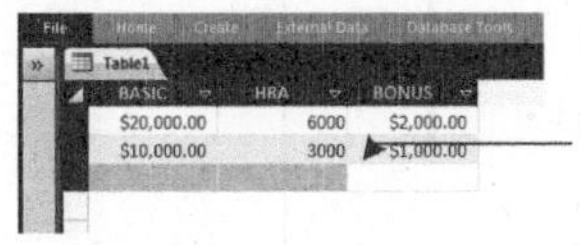

1. Open the table.
2. By default, Access 2010 opens the table in **Datasheet view**.
3. Click on the first field and then enter data.
4. After entering data in the first field, press **tab** to move cursor to the second field. Type in the second field and so on.

Edit Data in the Table

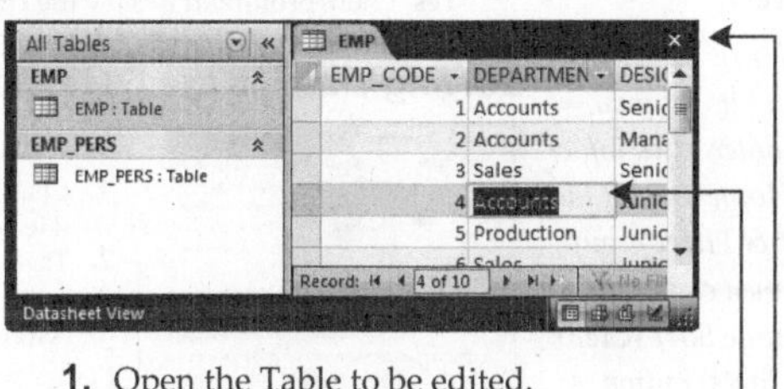

1. Open the Table to be edited.
2. *Double click* the field you want to edit.
3. Make changes in the field(s).
4. Click the **Close** button. Changes you applied will get automatically saved.

Data Type Properties are available for each field. For example, if data type property is set to Text, then the Field Size can be between 0 and 255 bytes (the default setting is 50).

Notes:

To change the position of a column in datasheet view, click on its header and drag it to the desired location.

Delete a Record in a Table

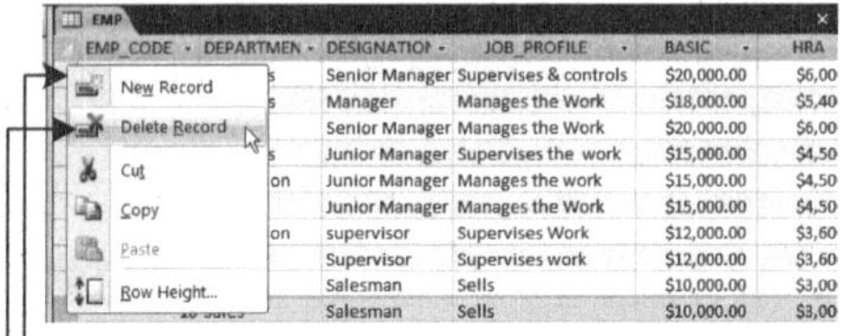

1. Open the Table.
2. Right click the record which is to be deleted.
3. Click **Delete Record** from the shortcut menu You will observe a dialog box. Click **Yes**.
4. The record is deleted.

Changing Field's Data Type

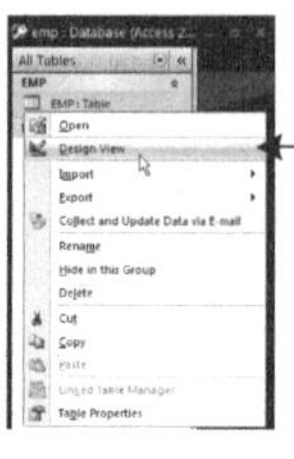

1. In the **Navigation Pane**, right click the table name and then choose **Design View**.

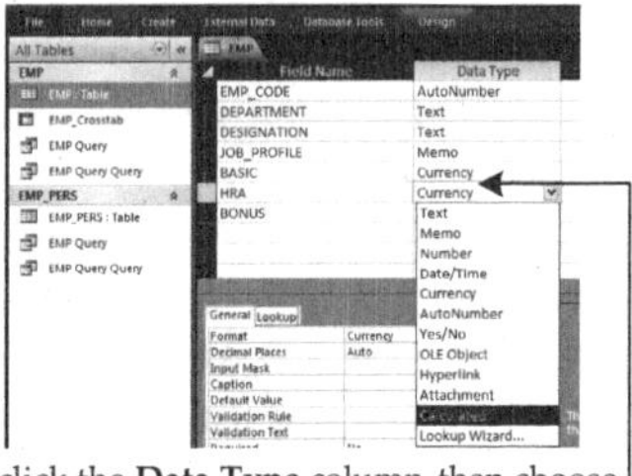

2. Move to the field and click the **Data Type** column, then choose the new data type you want.
3. Click **Close** button on the right side of the tab and choose **Yes** when prompted to save the changes.

Notes:

To return the data back to its original sort order, click under the ***Home*** *Tab, in the* ***Sort & Filter*** *group and then click on the* ***Remove Sort (Clear All Sorts)*** *button.*

You can sort on any type of data type except Memo, Hyperlink and OLE Objects.

Sorting Data in the Datasheet

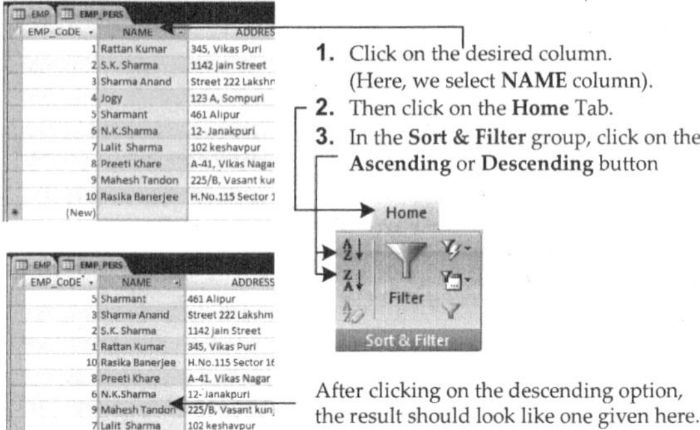

1. Click on the desired column. (Here, we select **NAME** column).
2. Then click on the **Home** Tab.
3. In the **Sort & Filter** group, click on the **Ascending** or **Descending** button

After clicking on the descending option, the result should look like one given here.

Create another table EMP_PERS, using the methods described earlier. This table will contain fields such as EMP_CODE, NAME, ADDRESS, PHONE, EMAIL DOJ. We will be using these two tables named EMP and EMP_PERS in our further study of Access 2010 such as in Relationship. Also add sample data to the Access Table just created.

Notes:

***Relationships** are those attributes defined from one table to another in the same database.*

*Field or group of fields that is the unique identifier for a table is called the **primary key**. But, In a relation, the column whose data values correspond to the values of a key column in another relation is called a **Foreign key**.*

There are three types of relation-ships that can be established among tables. These are:
1. One to one Relationship,
2. One to many Relationship,
3. Many to many Relationship

Create Relationships between Tables

Here, we create the relationship between two tables i.e. **EMP** and **EMP_PERS** tables.

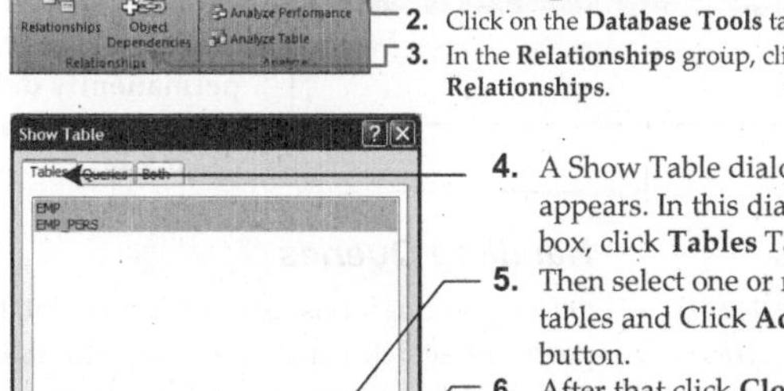

1. Open the database which contain **EMP** and **EMP_PERS** tables.
2. Click on the **Database Tools** tab.
3. In the **Relationships** group, click **Relationships**.
4. A Show Table dialog box appears. In this dialog box, click **Tables** Tab.
5. Then select one or more tables and Click **Add** button.
6. After that click **Close** button.

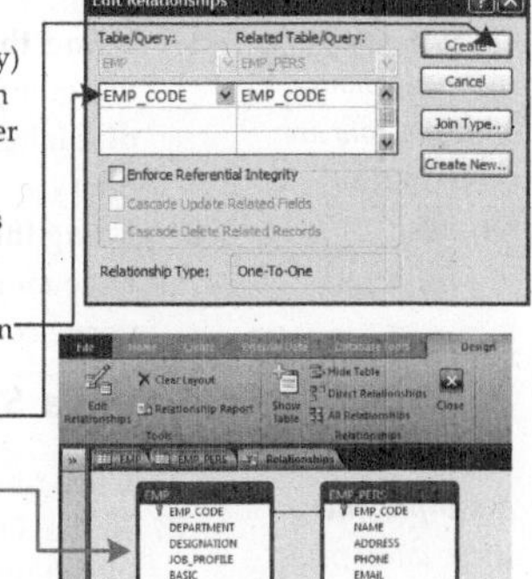

7. Now drag fields (primary key) from one table to the common field (foreign key) in the other table.
8. After that **Edit Relationships** dialog box appears. In this dialog box, verify the fields name shown that are common field for the relationship.
9. Then Click **Create New.**

Access makes a relationship between tables by lines.

Delete Relationships

1. Open the database which contain the tables whose relationship you want to delete.
2. Under the **Database** Tools, in the **Relationships** group, click **Relationships**. A Relationships window appears.

If you create relationship first time then the Show Table dialog box automatically appears. If it does not appear, click under the Design tab, in the Relationships group, click Show Table.

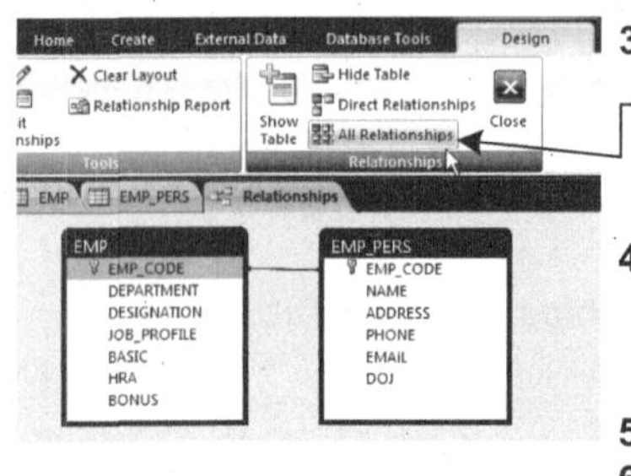

3. Click Under the **Design** Tab, in the **Relationships** group, then click **All Relationships**. All tablesthat have relationships are displayed, showing relationship lines.
4. Click the line of that relationship which you want to delete. *When you select the line, the relationship line appears thicker.*
5. After that Press **Del** key.
6. Access displays the confirmation dialog box showing the message "**Are you sure you want to permanently delete the selected relationship from your database?**"
7. Click **Yes**.

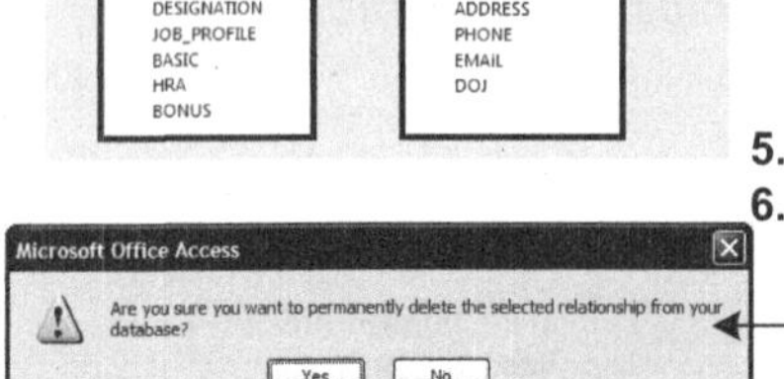

Handling Queries

Notes:

Queries that are used to retrieve data from a table or to make calculations are called ***select queries****. Queries that add, change, or delete data are called* ***action queries***

Queries are questions you ask from a database. Access 2010 has powerful search capabilities. For example, suppose from the **EMP_PERS** database, you want to know how many Employees have surname *Sharma*? Such an enquiry can be easily put to Access and you will get the answer very fast. Access lets you create queries in two ways:

1. **Using the query wizard:** When you create a query using the query wizard, the wizard guides you through a series of dialog boxes where you make the selection for the query.
2. **Using the design view:** When you use the design view you have more control over the query and Access 2010 lets you create complete queries in the design view.

Create a Simple Query using the Query Wizard

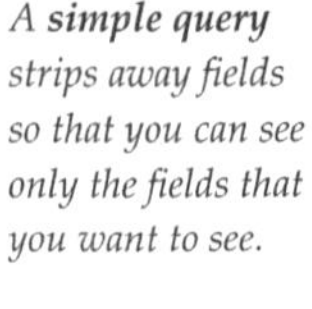

A ***simple query*** *strips away fields so that you can see only the fields that you want to see.*

1. Click under the **Create** tab.
2. In the **Queries group**, click **Query Wizard**.

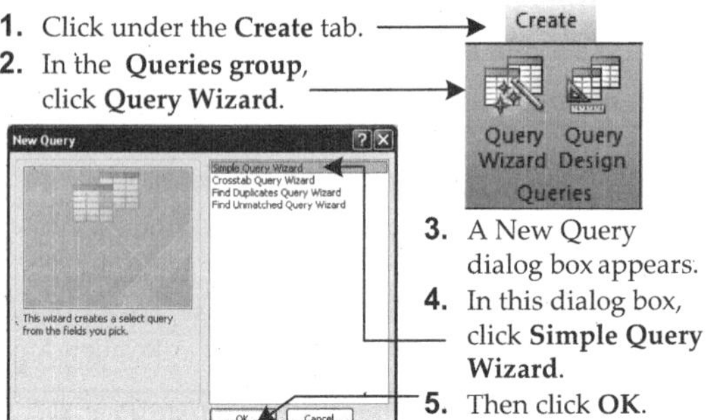

3. A New Query dialog box appears.
4. In this dialog box, click **Simple Query Wizard**.
5. Then click **OK**.

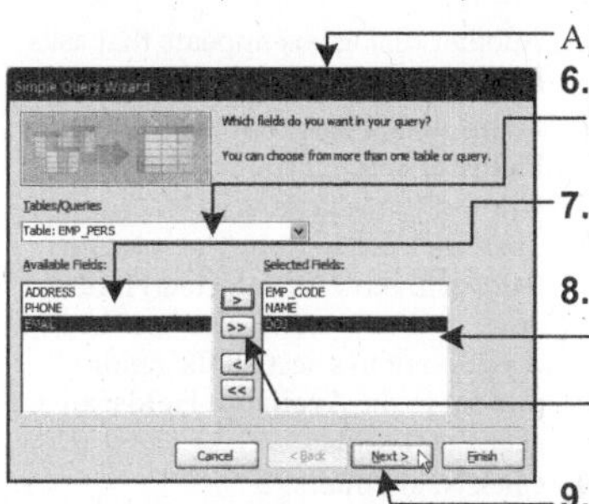

A Simple Query Wizard dialog box appears.

6. In this dialog box, from the **Table/Queries:** list box, select any previously, made query or table.
7. From the **Available Fields:** area select the fields which you want in your query.
8. Then click [>] button. The selected fields will move to **Selected Fields:** area. If you want to select all the fields present in the **Available Fields:** area, click [>>] button.
9. Click **Next** button.

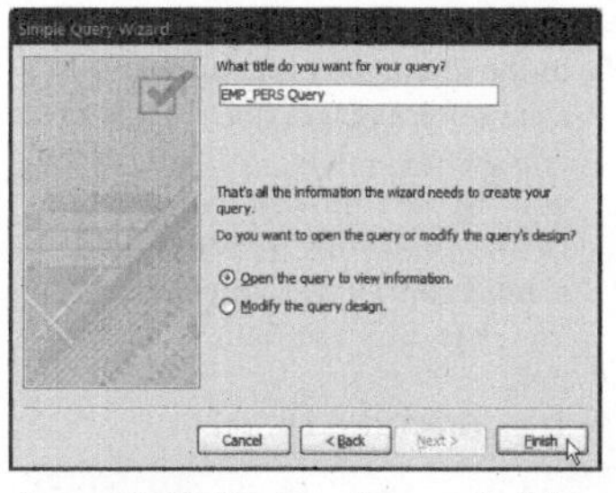

10. In the dialog box that appears type a title for your Query.
11. Then click **Finish** button.

Access 2007 displays the result of the query in a Datasheet View

EMP | EMP_PERS | EMP Query Query

Navigation Pane

EMP_CODE	NAME	DOJ
1	Rattan Kumar	2/28/2001
2	S.K. Sharma	3/13/1999
3	Sharma Anand	4/23/2000
4	Jogy	5/23/1992
5	Sharmant	5/23/2000
6	N.K.Sharma	12/29/1995
7	Lalit Sharma	2/1/1989
8	Preeti Khare	8/6/1998
9	Mahesh Tandon	4/12/2001
10	Rasika Banerjee	1/2/2002
(New)		

Notes:

*A **crosstab query** is a type of **select query** which is used to combine two or more fields to calculate and display a calculation based on a third field.*

*To remove a field from the **Selected Fields:** area click the [<] button. To remove all the fields, click the [<<] button.*

Create Crosstab Query using the Query Wizard

1. Click under the **Create** tab.
2. In the **Queries** group, click **Query Wizard**.
3. A New Query dialog box appears. In this dialog box, click **Crosstab Query Wizard.**
4. Then click **OK**.
5. In Crosstab Query Wizard dialog box, click on the table name.
6. Then click **Next** button.

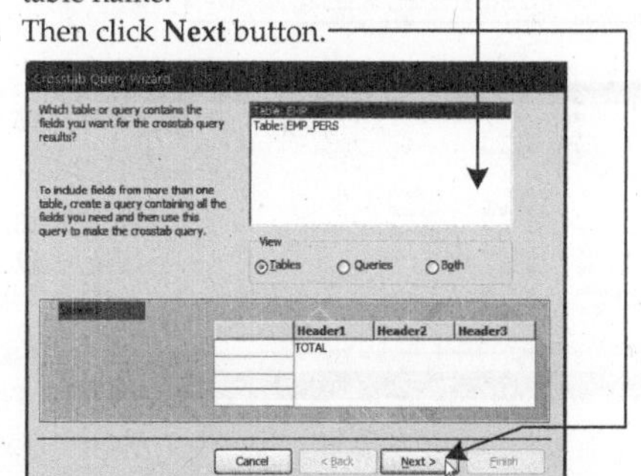

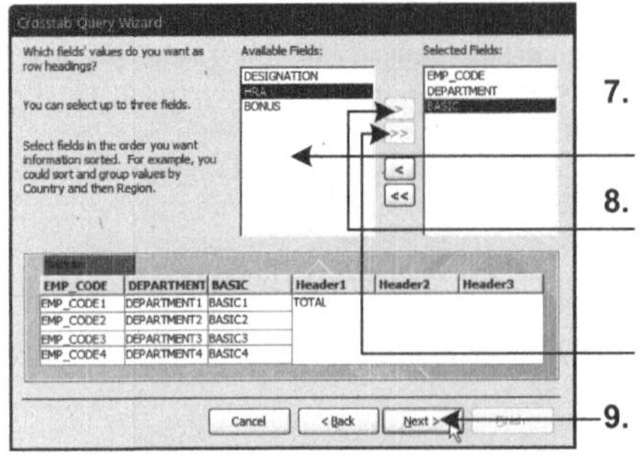

Another dialog box appears that asks for the fields.

7. In this dialog box, from the **Available Fields:** area select the fields which you want in your query.
8. Then click [>] button. The selected fields will move to **Selected Fields:** area.
   If you want to select all the fields present in the **Available Fields:** area, click [>>] button.
9. Click **Next** button.

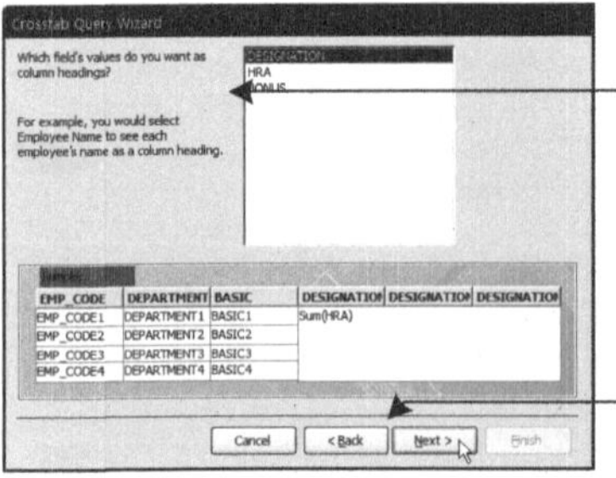

10. In the dialog box that appears, asking for a single field to use to crosstabulate data with the field you choose from last dialog box. In this dialog box, selected field should consist text information that lists different data. Click the field.
11. Then click **Next** button.

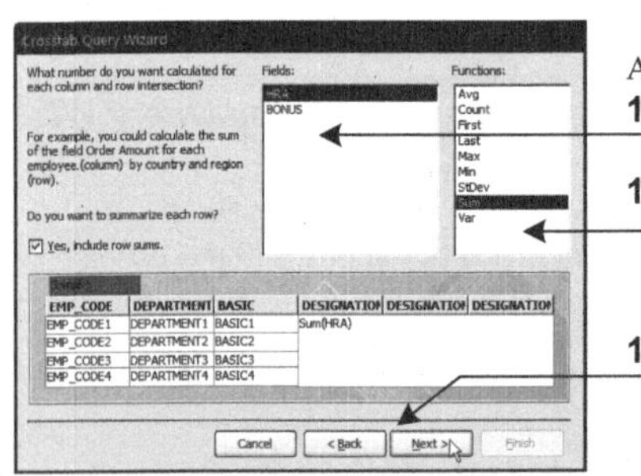

Another dialog box appears

12. Click a field that contains numerical data.
13. Then click mathematical function that you want to Access to calculate sum, average or count.
14. After that click on the **Next** button.

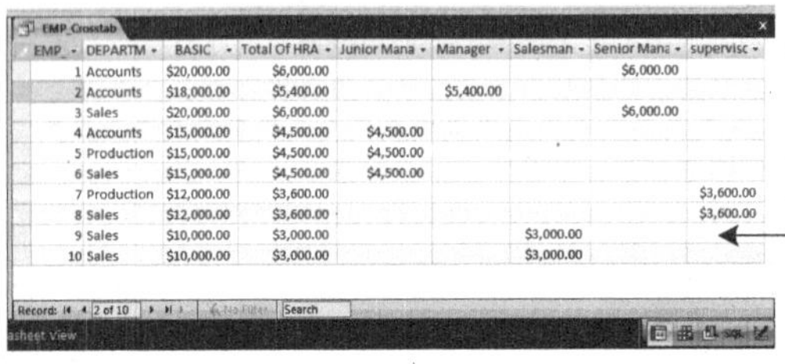

EMP_	DEPARTM	BASIC	Total Of HRA	Junior Mana	Manager	Salesman	Senior Mana	supervisc
1	Accounts	$20,000.00	$6,000.00				$6,000.00	
2	Accounts	$18,000.00	$5,400.00		$5,400.00			
3	Sales	$20,000.00	$6,000.00				$6,000.00	
4	Accounts	$15,000.00	$4,500.00	$4,500.00				
5	Production	$15,000.00	$4,500.00	$4,500.00				
6	Sales	$15,000.00	$4,500.00	$4,500.00				
7	Production	$12,000.00	$3,600.00					$3,600.00
8	Sales	$12,000.00	$3,600.00					$3,600.00
9	Sales	$10,000.00	$3,000.00			$3,000.00		
10	Sales	$10,000.00	$3,000.00			$3,000.00		

15. In the dialog box that appears, type a name for the Query.
16. Then click **Finish** button.
17. Access displays the result of the query in a **Datasheet View** as a separate tab.

Notes:

With the help of queries you can also find the duplicate data items in your database.

You cannot undo the results of a delete query. Therefore, you should back up your database before deleting a query.

Create Query to Finding Duplicate Items

Suppose, In a company, on the same day several employees had joined. But how can you find on the particular day who had joined. For this you could search database manually. It is very time consuming. But, with the help of Access 2010, you can create a query that finds the duplicate data items.

1. Click under the **Create** tab.
2. In the **Queries** group, click **Query Wizard**.
3. A New Query dialog box appears. In this dialog box, click **Find Duplicates Query Wizard.**
4. Then click **OK**.
5. In Find Duplicates Query Wizard dialog box, click on the table name.
6. Then click **Next** button.

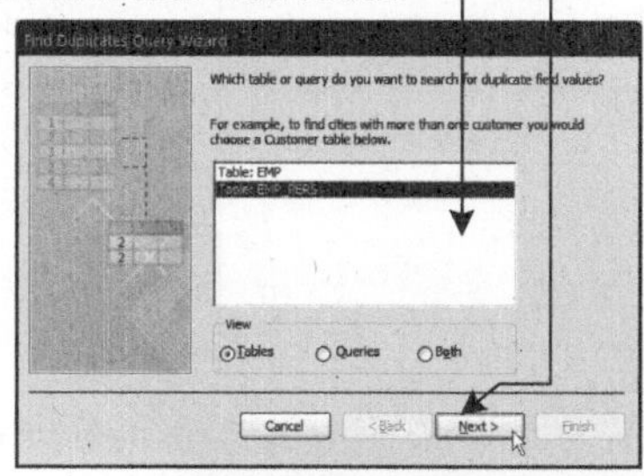

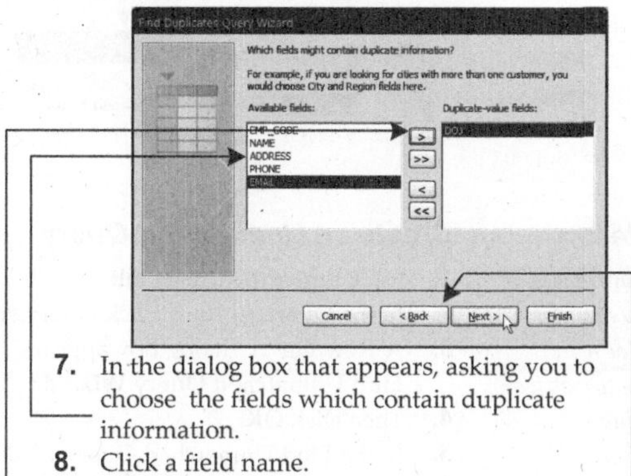

7. In the dialog box that appears, asking you to choose the fields which contain duplicate information.
8. Click a field name.
9. Then click > button
10. After that click **Next** button.

In Access 2010 new conditional formatting features, enabling you to achieve some of the same formatting styles as are available in Excel. For example, you can now add Data Bars to make a column of numbers more readable.

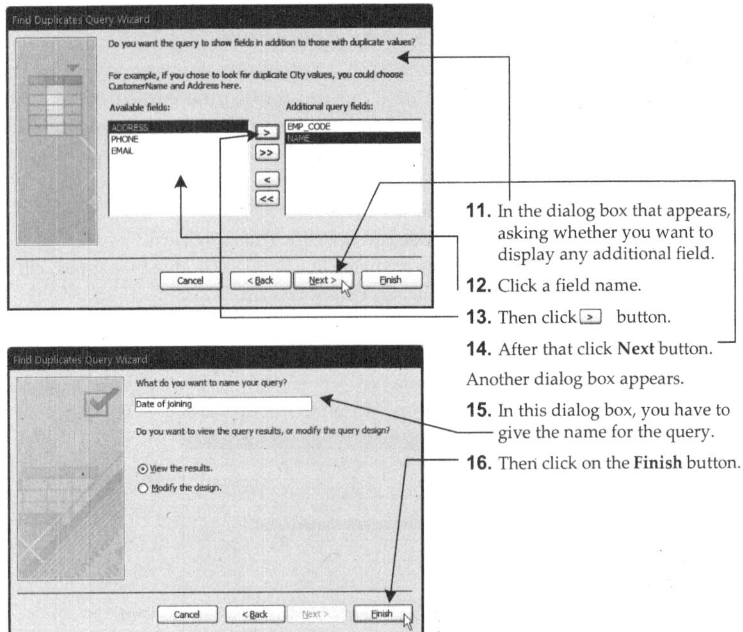

11. In the dialog box that appears, asking whether you want to display any additional field.
12. Click a field name.
13. Then click [>] button.
14. After that click **Next** button.

Another dialog box appears.

15. In this dialog box, you have to give the name for the query.
16. Then click on the **Finish** button.

Access displays the result of the query in a **Datasheet View** as a separate tab.

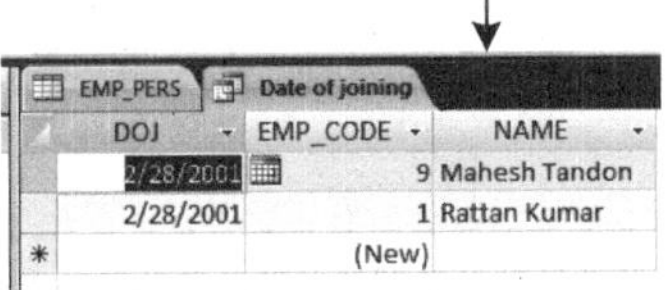

DOJ	EMP_CODE	NAME
2/28/2001	9	Mahesh Tandon
2/28/2001	1	Rattan Kumar
	(New)	

Create an Unmatched Query

Notes:

An unmatched query examines two (or more) tables to look for missing information.

1. Click under the **Create** tab.
2. In the **Queries** group, click **Query Wizard**.
3. A New Query dialog box appears. In this dialog box, click **Find Unmatched Query Wizard.**
4. Then click **OK**.
5. In the Find Unmatched Query Wizard dialog box, click the table that you want to search.
6. Then click **Next** button.
7. In the dialog box that appears, asking you to choose a table that contains at least one field that also appears in the table you choose earlier.
8. Click a second table and then click **Next** button.

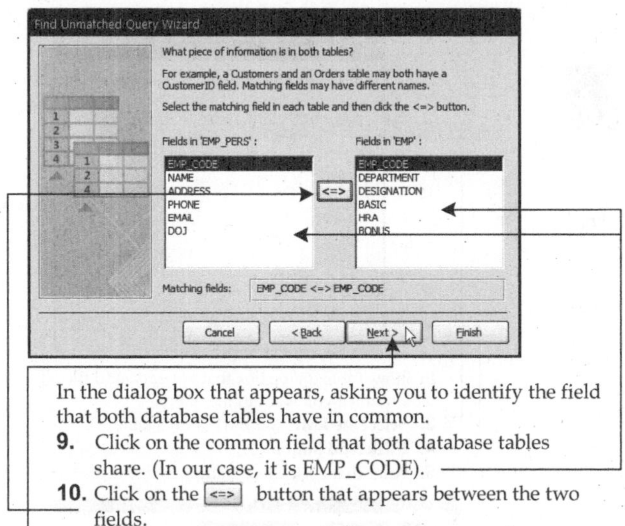

In the dialog box that appears, asking you to identify the field that both database tables have in common.

9. Click on the common field that both database tables share. (In our case, it is EMP_CODE).
10. Click on the [<=>] button that appears between the two fields.
11. Then click **Next** button.
12. Another dialog box appears that asks for the fields From the **Available Fields:** area. Select the fields which you want in your query.
13. Then click [>] button. The selected fields will move to **Selected Fields:** area.
14. Then click **Next** button.
15. Another dialog box appears. Here, you have to give the name for the query.
16. After giving name, click **Finish**.

Notes:

Criterians are restrictions you place on a query or an advanced filter to identify the specific records you want to work with.

Access displays the result of the query in a **Datasheet View** as a separate tab.

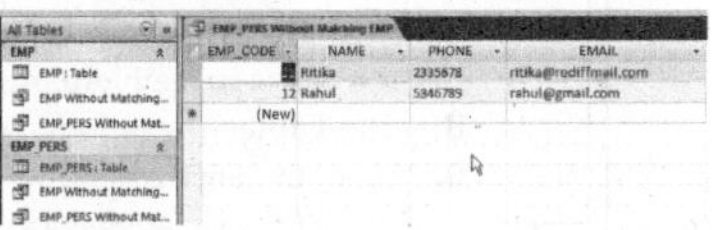

Creating Query using the Design View

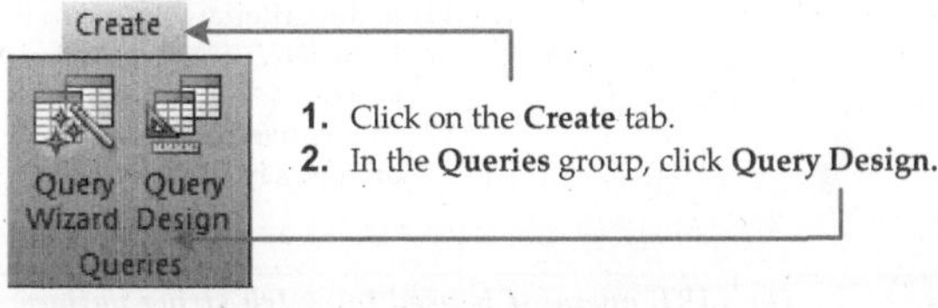

1. Click on the **Create** tab.
2. In the **Queries** group, click **Query Design**.

The criterion specifies a condition, based on field values, that expresses what you want to include in the query, such as "show only those records where the surname of Name field is Sharma".

Notes:

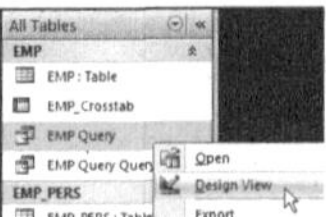

To open/modify an existing query do this:

1. In the ***Navigation Pane****, from the list of queries, right click the query which is to be modified.*

2. Then click ***Design View*** *option.*

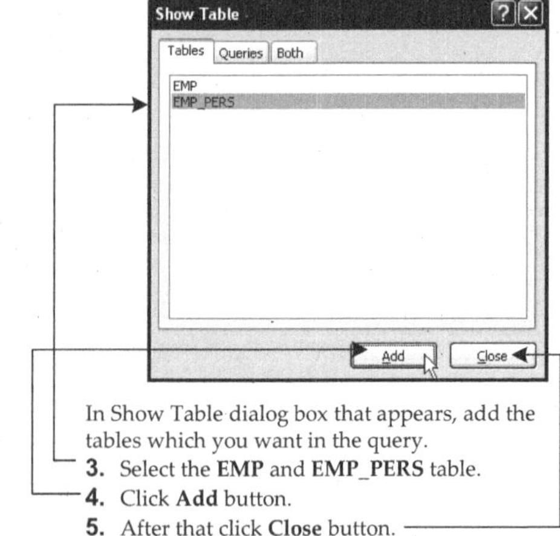

In Show Table dialog box that appears, add the tables which you want in the query.

3. Select the **EMP** and **EMP_PERS** table.
4. Click **Add** button.
5. After that click **Close** button.

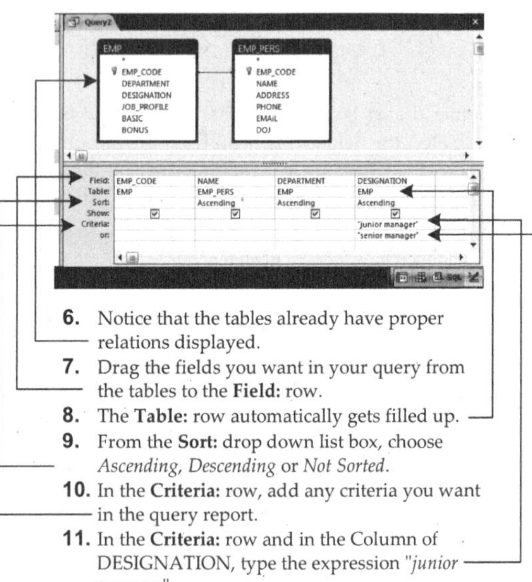

6. Notice that the tables already have proper relations displayed.
7. Drag the fields you want in your query from the tables to the **Field:** row.
8. The **Table:** row automatically gets filled up.
9. From the **Sort:** drop down list box, choose *Ascending, Descending* or *Not Sorted*.
10. In the **Criteria:** row, add any criteria you want in the query report.
11. In the **Criteria:** row and in the Column of DESIGNATION, type the expression "*junior manager*".
12. Alternative conditions can be entered in the **or:** row, say "*senior manager*".

The LIKE operator is used to match string pattern. Special characters '*' and '?' are used with LIKE operator to specify a pattern. * is for zero or more character but, ? is for single character.

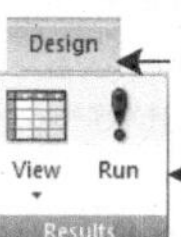

To view the Query Result:

1. Click the under the **Design Tab**.
2. Then in the **Results** group, click on the **Run** button.

You will see all the employees with the information you selected in a Datasheet View as a separate tab:

Query2

EMP_CODE	NAME	DEPARTMEN	DESIGNATIOI
4	Jogy	Accounts	Junior Manager
6	N.K.Sharma	Sales	Junior Manager
1	Rattan Kumar	Accounts	Senior Manager
3	Sharma Anand	Sales	Senior Manager
5	Sharmant	Production	Junior Manager
(New)			

Create a Form using the Form Tool

Notes:

Forms provide you with a "template" that you fill in whenever you enter a record. The form displays a blank box for each field in the table.

Controls are the objects that display data, perform certain actions and create special effects on the form. Text boxes, labels, list boxes, option buttons, push buttons and command buttons are examples of various controls.

When you want to include only selective fields in form, you can use the Form Wizard instead of Form tools.

You use Form tool in Access 2010 to create a form with a single mouse-click. When you use this tool, all the fields from the underlying data source are placed on the form.

1. In the **Navigation Pane**, click the table or query for which you want to make a form.
2. Click on the **Create** tab.
3. In the **Forms** group, click **Form**.

Create | Form | Form Design | Blank Form | Form Wizard | Navigation | More Forms | Forms

4. Access creates the form and displays it in **Layout view** along with the **Form Layout Tools** on the Ribbon.

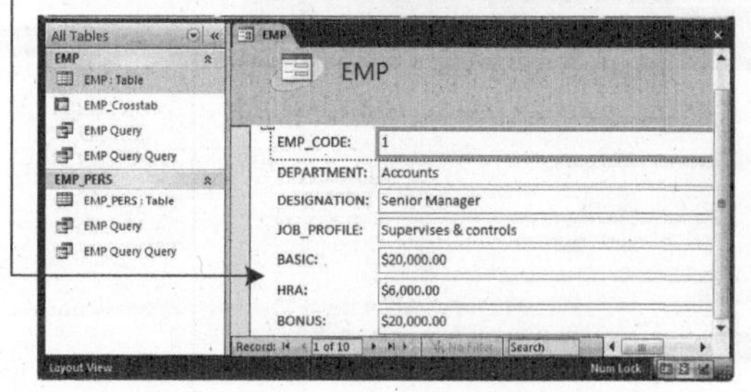

Create a Form using Form Wizard

1. Click under the **Create** tab.
2. In the **Forms** group, click **Form Wizard**.

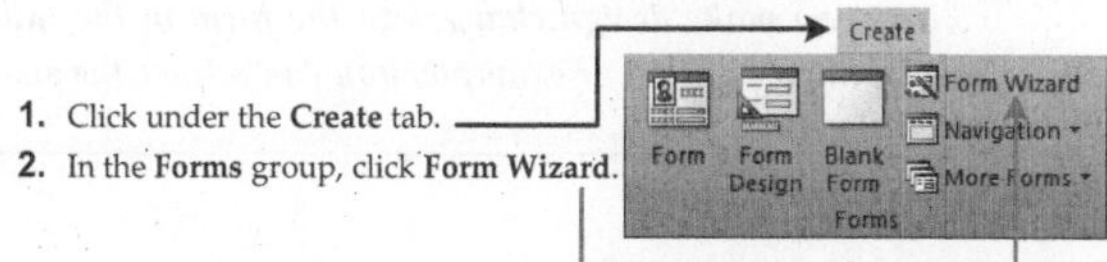

Notes:

With the help of Form Wizard, you can use fields from more than one table or query, provided you have specified the relationships among the tables and queries beforehand.

A Form Wizard dialog box appears.

3. In this dialog box, from the **Available Fields:** area, select the fields which you want in your form.
4. Then click [>] button.
5. After that click **Next** button.

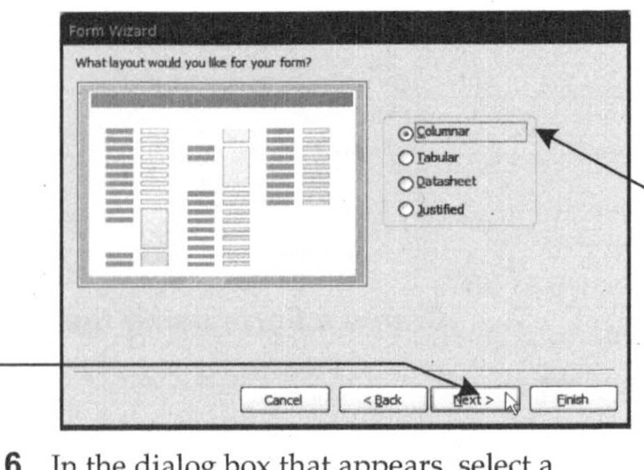

6. In the dialog box that appears, select a layout for the form. The various forms available are *Columnar, Tabular, Datasheet* and *Justified*.
7. Click **Next** button.

8. In the dialog box that appears provide a *title for the form.*
9. Then click **Finish** button.

The form will open in **form view**.

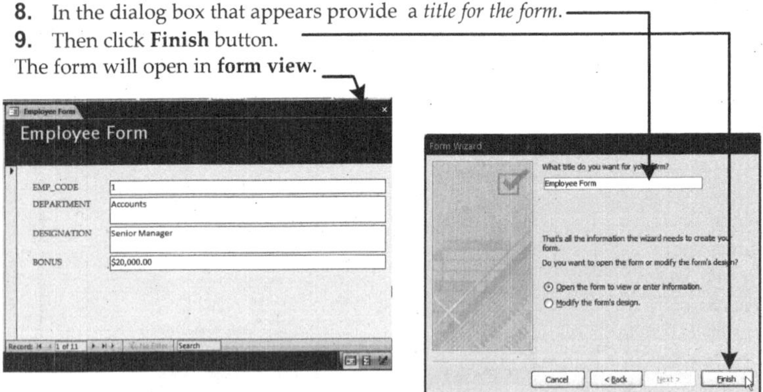

You can make design changes to the form in the layout view while it is displaying data. For example, you can adjust the size of the text boxes to fit the data.

Notes:

Form creation using Blank Form tool can be a very quick way to build a form, especially if you plan to put only a few fields on your form.

Split form feature gives you the benefits of both types of forms in a single form. For example, you can use the datasheet portion of the form to quickly locate a record and then use the form portion to view or edit the record.

Create a Form using Blank Form Tool

1. Click under the Create tab.
2. In the **Forms** group, click 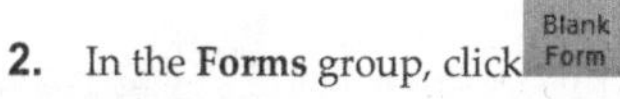.

Access opens a blank form in **Layout view** along with the **Field List pane**.

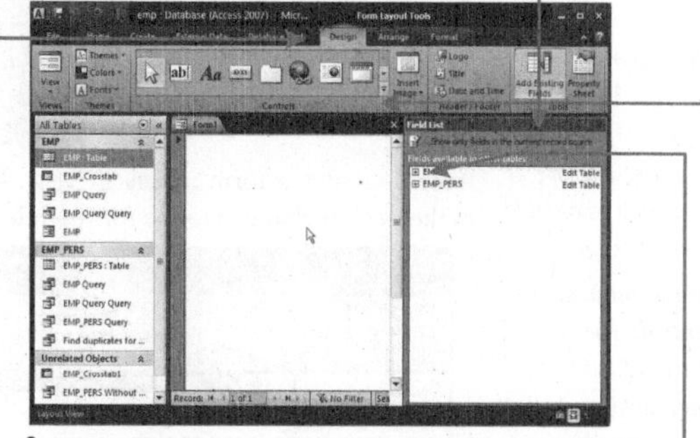

3. In the **Field List** pane, click the plus sign (+) next to the table that contains the fields that you want to include in the form.
4. To add a field to the form, double-click it.

If you want add tools in the form such as logo, title, page numbers, etc.

5. Click under the **Design** Tab.
6. In the **Controls** group, click the tool which you want.
7. After adding tool, the form will look like the following screen.

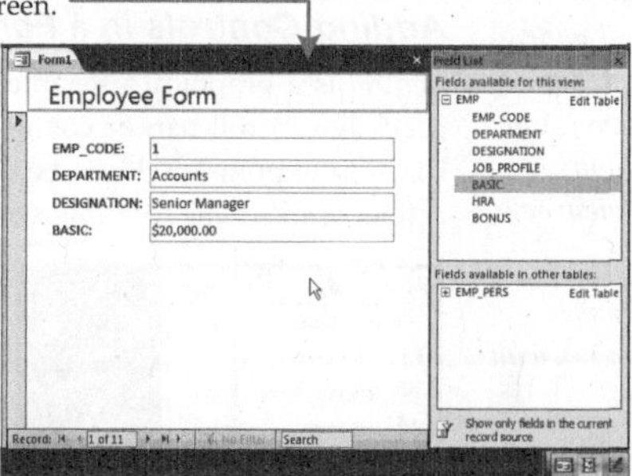

Create a Split Form using the Split Form Tool

Split form gives two views of the data at the same time i.e. *Form view* and *Datasheet view*. These views are connected to same data source and are synchronized with each other at all times.

Notes:

Controls can be of three types:

(a) ***Bound control:*** *It is a type of control whose source of data is a field in a table or query.*

(b) ***Unbound control:*** *This type of control does not have a source of data such as a field or expression.*

(c) ***Calculated control:*** *The source of data of calculated control is an expression, rather than a field.*

Some controls such as the ***bound control*** *is created when you add a field from the* ***Field List pane*** *to your form. But other controls can be created in* ***Design view*** *only.*

Most common views to work with forms are Form View *where you view or enter data and in* Design View*, you can add controls in a form, change properties and layout.*

1. In the **Navigation** Pane, click the table or query for which you want to make a form.

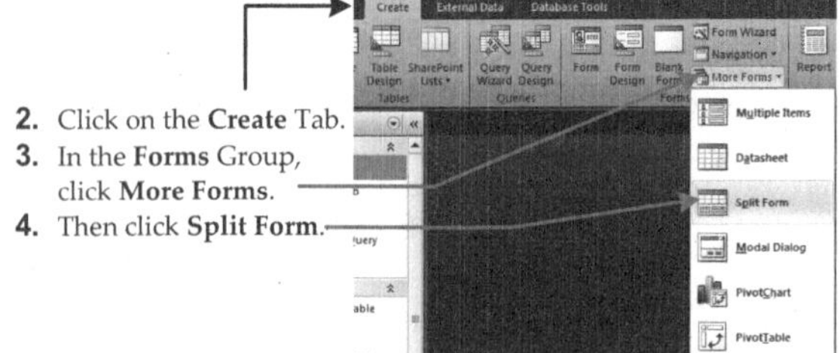

2. Click on the **Create** Tab.
3. In the **Forms** Group, click **More Forms**.
4. Then click **Split Form**.

Access creates a form in *Layout view*. In Layout view, you can make design changes to the form while it is displaying data.

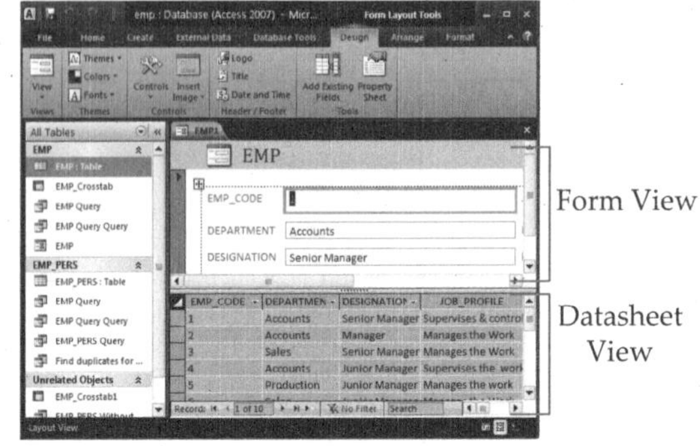

Adding Controls in a Form

Control is a graphical user interface object, such as a text box, check box, scroll bar, or command button that allows users to control the program. It can be used to display data, perform an action, or make the user interface easier to read.

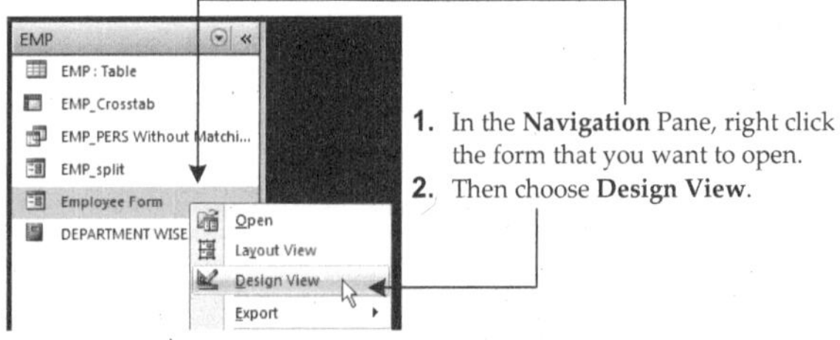

1. In the **Navigation** Pane, right click the form that you want to open.
2. Then choose **Design View**.

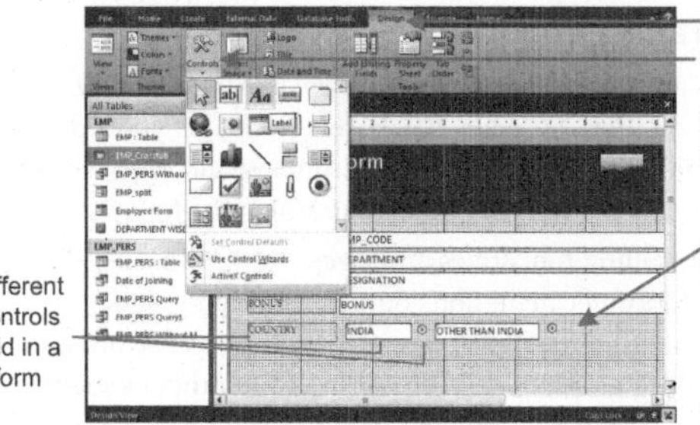

3. Click under the **Design** tab.
4. In the **Controls** group, click arrow next to **Controls**.
5. Then click on the desired tool.
6. Click in the form design grid where you want to position the upper-left corner of the control.
7. Then drag the mouse pointer in the form design grid to create a control of the size that you want.

A form after adding controls appears as seen in thisFigure.

Changing the View of a Form

1. In the **Navigation Pane**, click the form for which you want to change the view.
2. Now click under the **Home** tab.
3. In the **Views** group, click arrow next to **View**.
4. Then choose the desired view.

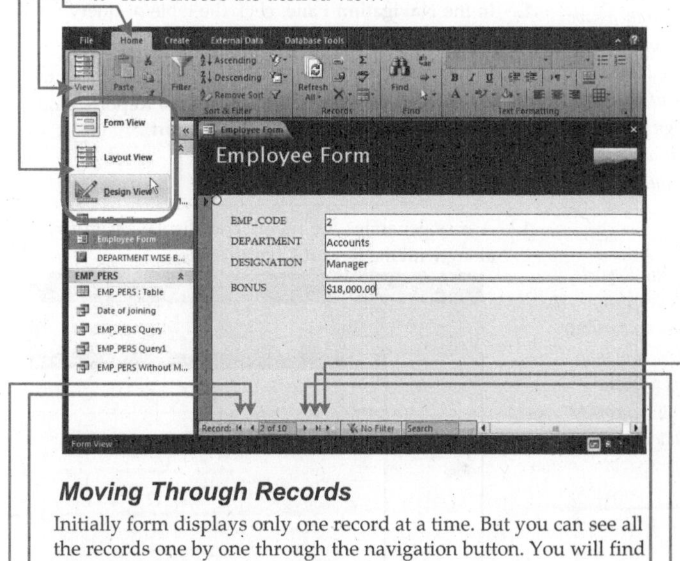

Moving Through Records

Initially form displays only one record at a time. But you can see all the records one by one through the navigation button. You will find navigation button at the bottom of your form view. There are five navigation buttons. These are:

(a) **First Record:** Displays the first record of the table.
(b) **Previous Record:** Displays the previous record of the table.
(c) **Next Record:** Displays the next record of the table.
(d) **Last Record:** Displays the last record of the table.
(e) **New (blank) Record:** Inserts new record at the end of the table.

Notes:

Reports let you define how you want your data to appear on the printed page.

The ***Report tool*** *may not create the final, polished product that you ultimately want. It is however, useful as a means to quickly look at the underlying data. You can then save the report and modify it in* ***Layout view*** *or* ***Design view*** *so that it will serves your purposes better.*

By using Report view, you can browse an accurate rendering of your report without having to print or display it in Print Preview.

Generating Reports

Reports are the most powerful and flexible way to view and print the information in your database. To make your data more presentable for others to read and understand, you would need to create reports. Reports are very useful in the following cases:

1. Controlling font styles and sizes.
2. Performing calculations on the underlying data.
3. Formatting data to fit forms such as purchase orders.
4. Adding graphics such as pictures and other elements.
5. Grouping and organizing data to form reports to read them easily.

Create a Report using Report Tool

The Report tool in Access 2010 provides the fastest way for you to create a report, because it generates a report immediately without prompting you for information.

1. In the **Navigation Pane**, click the table or query for which you want to make a report.

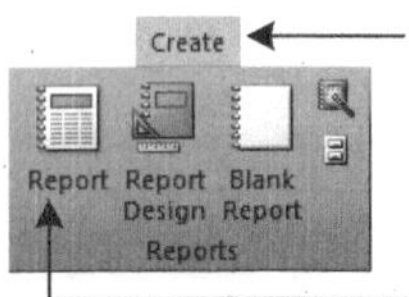

2. Click under the **Create** tab.
3. Then in the **Reports** group, click **Report**.
4. Access generates the report and displays it in *Layout view* along with the **Report Layout Tools**.

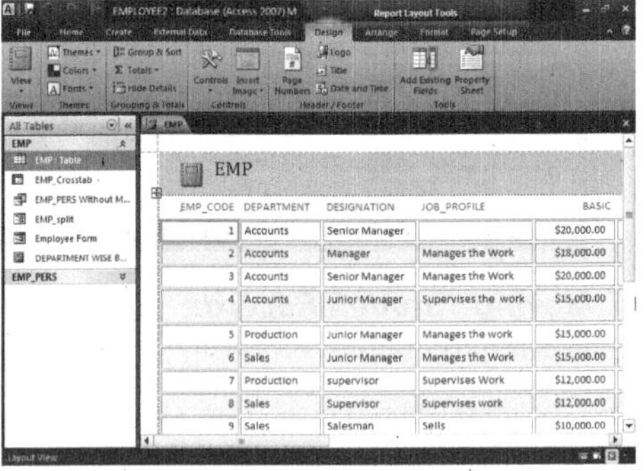

Creating a report using Report Wizard is the easiest way because it guides you step by step through arranging and selecting which data you want to print on a report.

Create a Report using Report Wizard

You can use the Report Wizard to be more selective about what fields appear on your report. You can also specify how the data is grouped and sorted, and you can use fields from more than one table or query, provided you have specified the relationships between the tables and queries beforehand.

1. Click under the Create tab.
2. In the **Reports** group, click button.

A Report Wizard dialog box appears.

3. In this dialog box, click in the **Tables/Queries** list box and choose the table or query name that contains the data you want in a report.

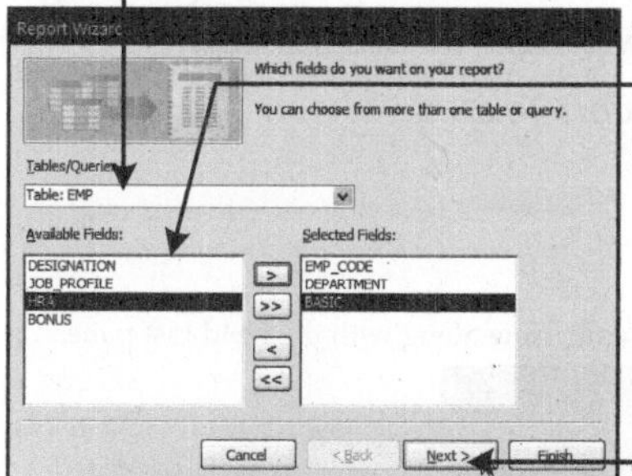

4. Then from the **Available Fields:** area, select the fields which you want in your report.
5. After that click > button.
   To select all the fields present in the **Available Fields:** area, click >> button.
   To remove a field from the **Selected Fields:** area click the < button. To remove all the fields, click the << button.
6. Click **Next** button.

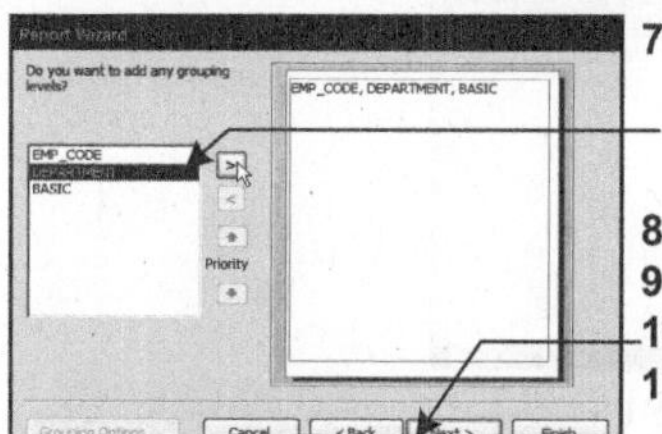

7. Another dialog box that appears, asking whether you want to group your data by a specific field, such as *EMP_CODE, DEPARTMENT.*
8. Click a field name displayed in the box.
9. Then click > button.
10. Click **Next** button.
11. In the dialog box that appears, choose a field for sorting your data in report. We have chosen BASIC field.
12. Click **Next** button.

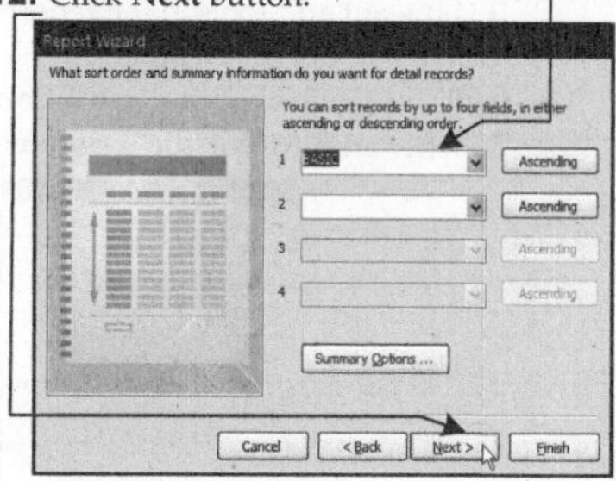

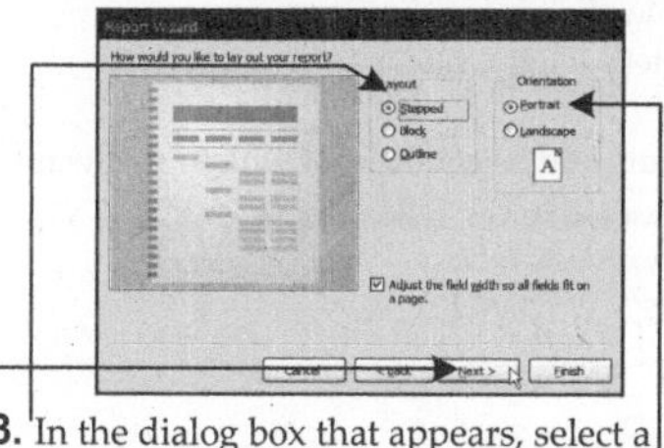

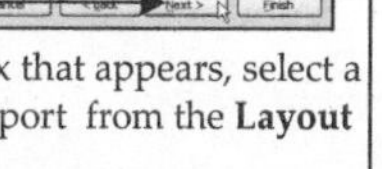

13. In the dialog box that appears, select a layout for the report from the **Layout group**.
14. Select orientation of the page from **Orientation group**.
15. Then click **Next** button.

Notes:

Blank Report tool can be a very quick way to build a report, especially if you plan to put only a few fields on the report.

16. In the dialog box that appears provide a title for the report.
17. Then click **Finish** button.

The report will open as shown in following Figure.

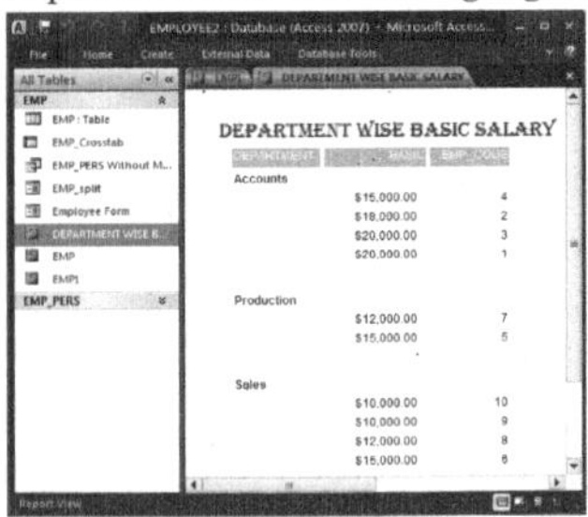

Create a Report using Blank Report Tool

1. Click under the Create tab.
2. In the **Reports** group, click Blank Report.
   Access 2010 opens a blank report in **Layout view** along with the Field List pane.

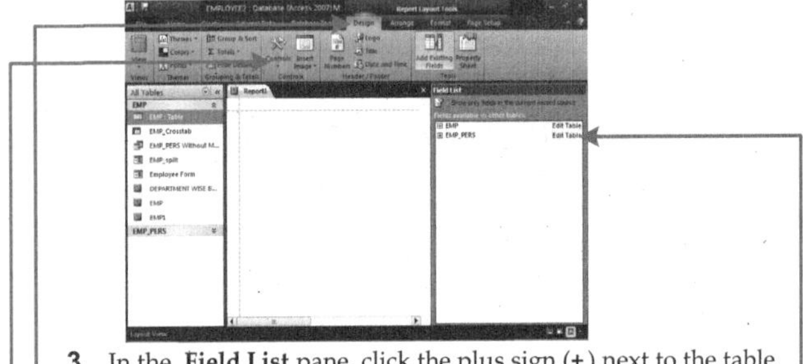

3. In the **Field List** pane, click the plus sign (+) next to the table that contains the fields that you want to include in the report.
4. To add a field to the report, double-click it.

If you want add tools in the report such as logo, title, page number, etc.

5. Click under the **Design** Tab.
6. In the **Controls**group, click **Controls** and select the tool which you want.
7. After adding tool, the report will look like the following screen.

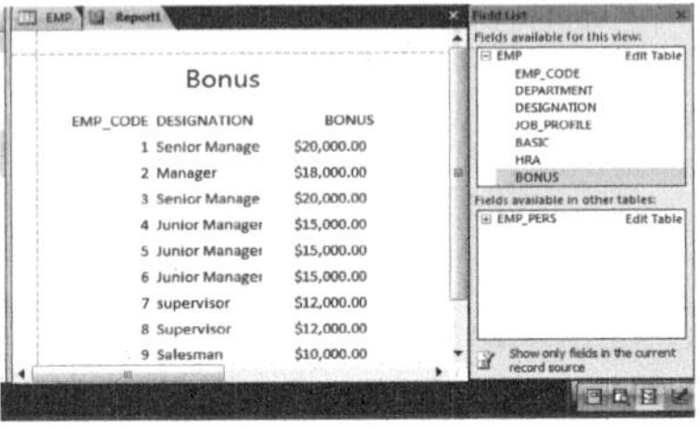

Sections of the Report

In Access 2010, the design of a report is divided into various sections. You can view a report in Design view to see its sections.

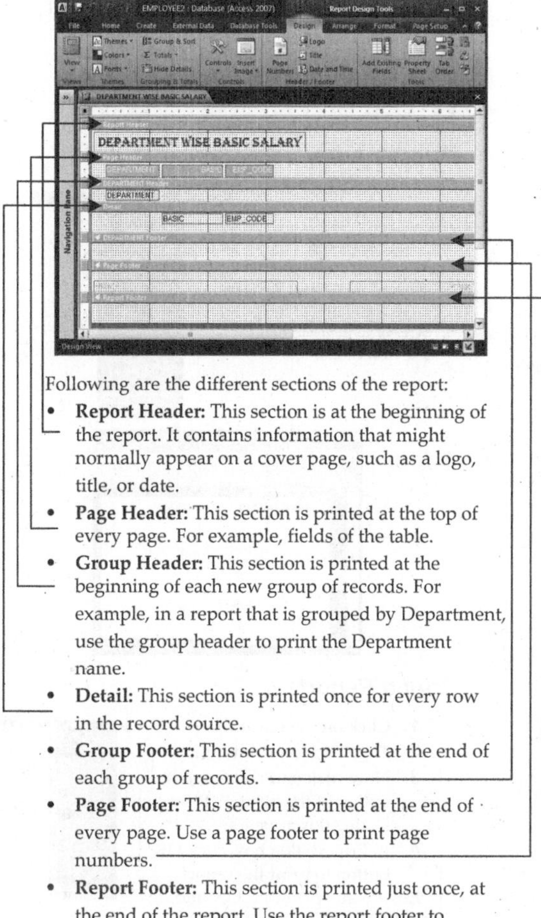

Following are the different sections of the report:

- **Report Header:** This section is at the beginning of the report. It contains information that might normally appear on a cover page, such as a logo, title, or date.
- **Page Header:** This section is printed at the top of every page. For example, fields of the table.
- **Group Header:** This section is printed at the beginning of each new group of records. For example, in a report that is grouped by Department, use the group header to print the Department name.
- **Detail:** This section is printed once for every row in the record source.
- **Group Footer:** This section is printed at the end of each group of records.
- **Page Footer:** This section is printed at the end of every page. Use a page footer to print page numbers.
- **Report Footer:** This section is printed just once, at the end of the report. Use the report footer to print report totals or other summary information for the entire report.

Notes:

Access 2010 has a better and more accessible way to group and sort reports.

Viewing a Report

1. In the **Navigation Pane**, click the downward arrow as show in this figure All Tables.
2. A pull down menu appears

Notes

Access 2010, layouts have been enhanced to allow for more flexible placement of controls on forms and reports.

*The new **Quick Create feature** automatically generates reports with professional looking designs along with headers and informative footers and totals.*

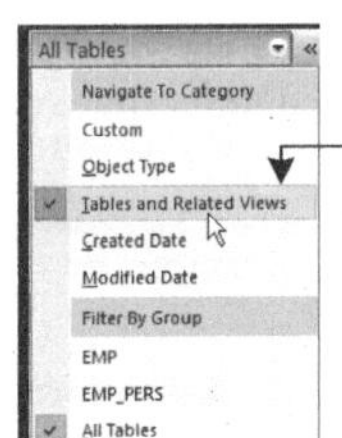

3. In this menu, click **Tables and Related Views**.
4. Access displays a list of all previously saved reports in the navigation pane.
5. Double click a report name which you want to view.

Print Preview a Report

1. Click on the **File** Tab.
2. Then click on **Print** option.
3. Now click on **Print Preview** from the option of the print.
4. Access switches to **Print Preview** mode.

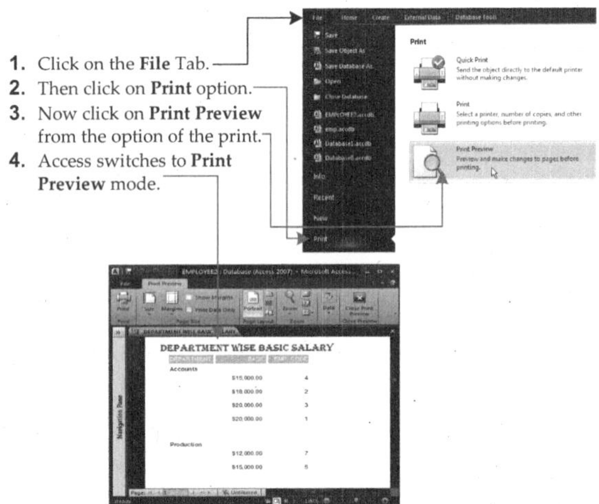

Print a Report

1. Click on the **File** Tab.
2. Then click on **Print** option.
3. Now click on **Print** from the option of the print. A Print Dialog box appears.
4. In Print dialog box, click **OK** button to print the report.

Ensure, the printer is ON and it is online.

Notes:

*For manipulating data in a report first of all you have to switch in **Layout view**. To switch to the **Layout view**, click **Layout view button** from the status bar.*

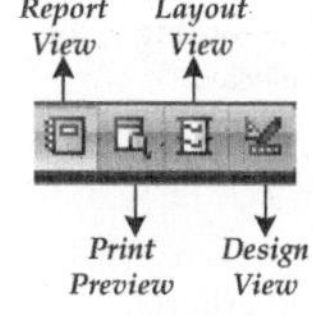

In Access 2010, you can export data to a PDF (Portable Document Format) or XPS (XML Paper Specification) file format for printing, posting, and e-mail distribution, provided that you first install and Publish it as PDF or XPS add-in.

Manipulating Data in a Report

After you create a report, you can manipulate the data displayed in that report i.e. sorting data in ascending or descending order or apply filter to display the data that meet the criteria.

Summing Records or Values (Add the Values Stored in Records)

To make report more useful, use summing facility. By summing records or adding up values stored in fields, Access 2010 can help you to interpret the data better and then display it in a report.

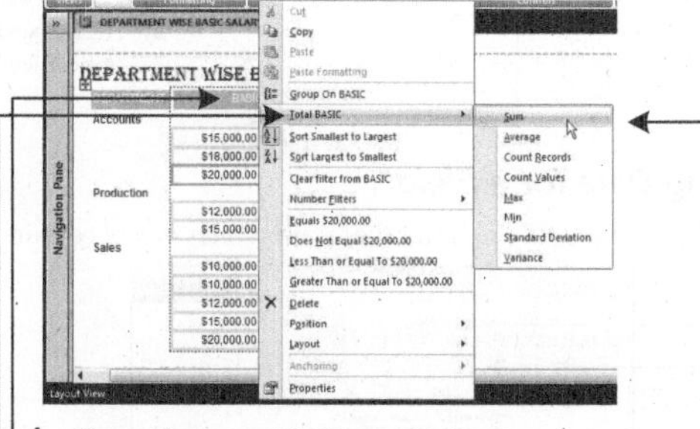

1. Open the report in **Layout view.**
2. Right click the column or field that you want to sum. Access displays pop-up menu.
3. The menu command displays the **TOTAL** command along with the field name you right-clicked, such as *TOTAL BASIC.*
4. Click **TOTAL BASIC.**
5. In sub menu, click on **Sum** command.
6. After sum up, report will look like as seen in the following Figure.

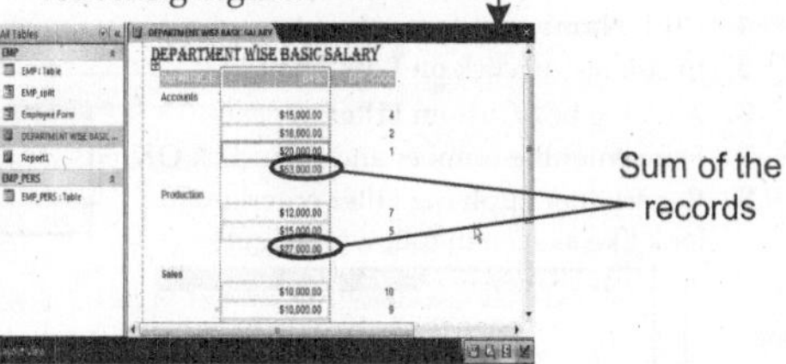

Exporting a form, report, or datasheet to a .pdf or .xps file lets you capture information in an easy-to-distribute form that retains all your formatting characteristics, but does not require others to install Access 2010 on their computers to print or review your output.

Notes:

Sorting a field rearranges the data in report according to your convenience.

Sorting Data in a Field

Access 2010 can sort data in each field in ascending or descending order.

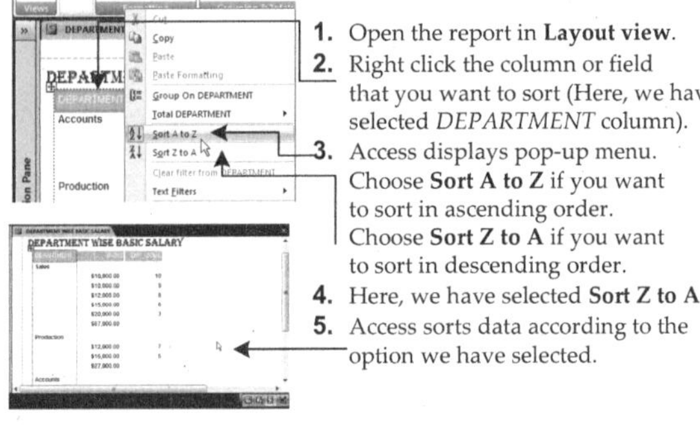

1. Open the report in **Layout view**.
2. Right click the column or field that you want to sort (Here, we have selected *DEPARTMENT* column).
3. Access displays pop-up menu. Choose **Sort A to Z** if you want to sort in ascending order. Choose **Sort Z to A** if you want to sort in descending order.
4. Here, we have selected **Sort Z to A**.
5. Access sorts data according to the option we have selected.

Filtering Data for a Field

Filtering means displaying only that data which meets certain desired criteria.

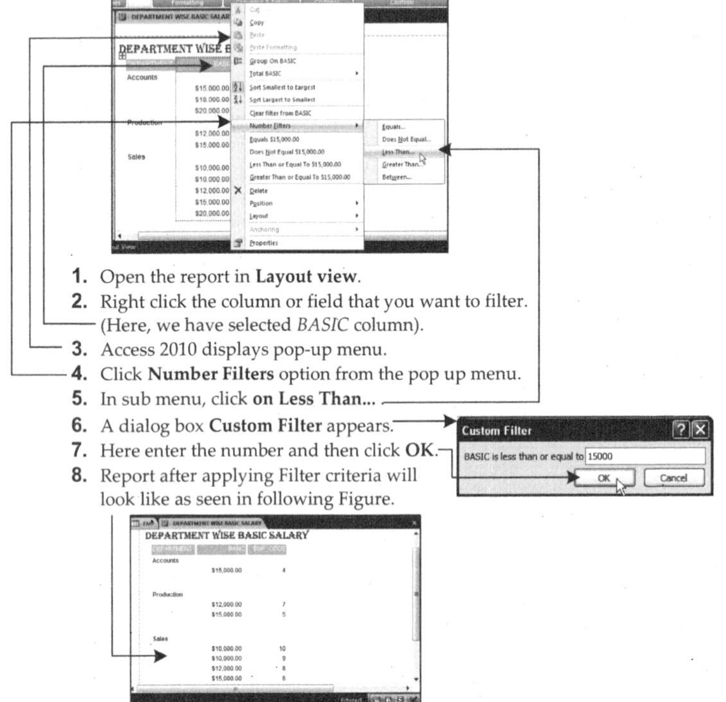

1. Open the report in **Layout view**.
2. Right click the column or field that you want to filter. (Here, we have selected *BASIC* column).
3. Access 2010 displays pop-up menu.
4. Click **Number Filters** option from the pop up menu.
5. In sub menu, click **on Less Than...**
6. A dialog box **Custom Filter** appears.
7. Here enter the number and then click **OK**.
8. Report after applying Filter criteria will look like as seen in following Figure.

Notes:

*In the **Design view**, you can modify the report such as move, resize, add or delete fields in the report.*

Editing a Report

After you created a report and if you want to modify it, then you must switch to the Design view of the report.

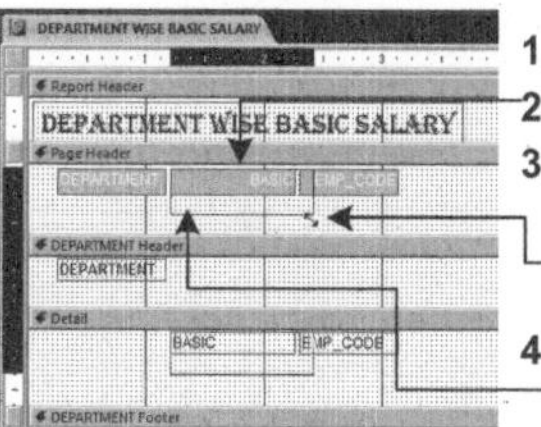

1. Open the report in **Design view**.
2. Click the field you want to resize.
3. Move the mouse pointer over the left or right edge of the field *until the mouse pointer turns into a two-way pointing arrow.*
4. Drag the mouse to resize and expand or shrink the field.

Deleting a Report

Eventually, you may find that you no longer need a report. So you want to delete it.

1. In the **Navigation Pane**, click the downward arrow. A pull down menu appears..
2. In this menu, click **Tables and Related Views**.
3. Access 2010 displays a list of all previously saved reports in the navigation pane.
4. Click the report you want to delete.

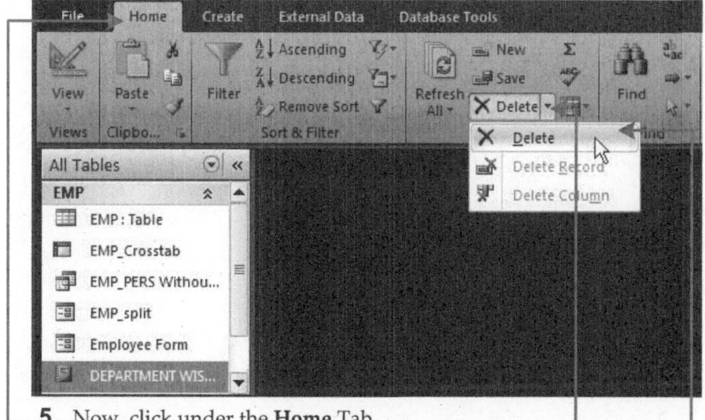

5. Now, click under the **Home** Tab.
6. In the **Records** group, Click arrow next to **Delete**.
7. Click **Delete**.
8. A dialog box appears, asking whether you want to delete report.
9. Click **Yes**.

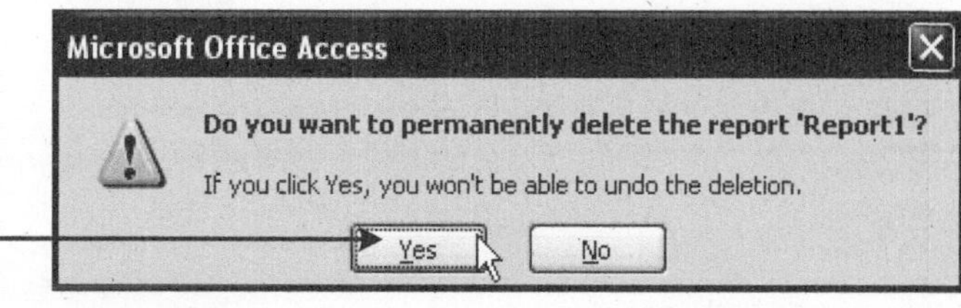

MS PowerPoint 2010

Getting Started

PowerPoint 2010 is a very popular presentation graphics software package. It has set new standards for the working of presentation graphics. PowerPoint 2010 helps you bringing *ideas* and *information* that you want to convey to your audience with no difficulty.

Notes:

To open any MS Office Package you need to use the same method as explained in the following steps.

Starting MS PowerPoint 2010

1. Click the **Start** button on the Taskbar.

2. Highlight **All Programs**, click **Microsoft Office**.

3. A sub menu appears, click **Microsoft Office PowerPoint 2010.**

*PowerPoint 2010 needs **Windows Vista** or **Windows 7** as operating system to run on an IBM PC. However, PowerPoint 2010 can also be used with **Windows XP** operating system, if **service pack 3** is installed on Windows XP.*

When you first start PowerPoint 2010, it displays a blank presentation showing a single slide.

Understanding the Screen Elements

The main elements of the PowerPoint 2010 window are given below:

Title bar: The *Title bar* is at the top of the screen. It shows the title PowerPoint and the name of presentation. If you have not yet saved any presentation then it displays the default name for the presentation which is *Presentation1*.

Ribbon: Ribbon is displayed just below the title bar. In Ribbon, commands are organized in logical groups, which are collected together under tabs.

Quick Access Toolbar: This toolbar is located by default at the top of PowerPoint 2010 window. By default, this toolbar displays the Save, Undo and Repeat buttons.

Minimize button: Shrinks the application window to a bar on the taskbar. You can click its button on the taskbar to reopen it.

Maximize button: A box at the right of a title bar that fills available space with the document or application.

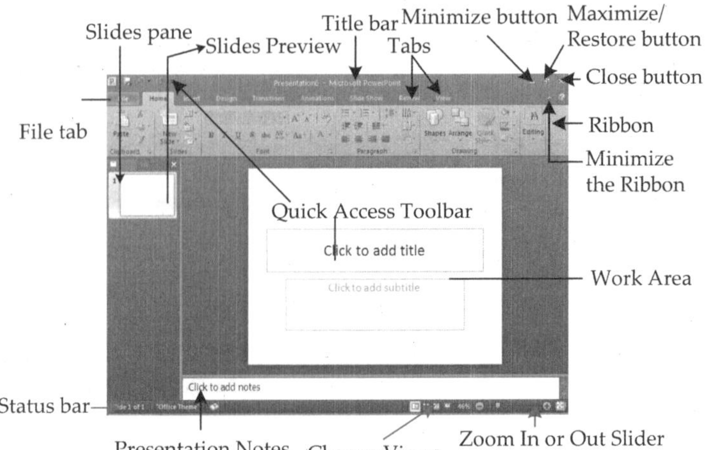

Presentations

You can make presentation in the form of slides, handouts or speaker's notes.

Restore button: A double box at the right of a title bar that restores an application or document into a sizable window.

Close button: A box at the right of a title bar (X) that closes the window or dialog box.

Work area: Where active PowerPoint slide(s) appear. It shows it in Normal view, but other views are available that make the work area appear differently.

Status bar: It gives the information about the presentation and provides shortcuts for changing the view and the zoom.

PowerPoint 2010 Interface

There is a new look for PowerPoint 2010. There is also a new user interface that replaces menus, toolbars, and most of the task panes from previous versions of PowerPoint. The new user interface is designed to help you to be more productive in PowerPoint; more easily find the right features for various tasks and also be more efficient.

Slides

Slides are individual "pages" of a presentation.

It may contain text, graphs, clipart, etc. You can even print slides for overhead projector transparencies.

Ribbon

The primary replacement for menus and toolbars in PowerPoint 2010 is the Ribbon. Designed for easy browsing, the Ribbon consists of tabs that are organized around specific scenarios or objects. The controls on each tab are further organized into several groups. The Ribbon can host richer content than menus and toolbars can, including buttons, galleries, and dialog box contents.

Notes:

Handouts

Handouts consist of printed versions of your slides—either two, three, or six slides per page.

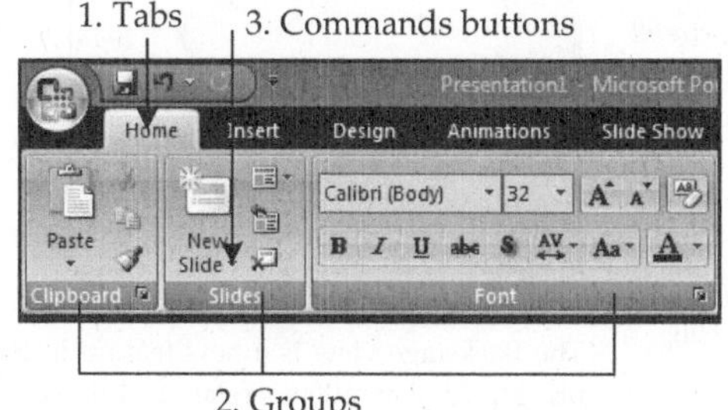

7. Tabs are designed to be task-oriented.
8. Groups within each tab break a task into subtasks.
9. Command buttons in each group carry out a command or display a menu of commands.

Contextual Tools

Contextual tools enable you to work with an object that you select on the page, such as table, picture, or drawing. When you click the object, the pertinent sets of contextual tab appears in color next to the standard tabs.

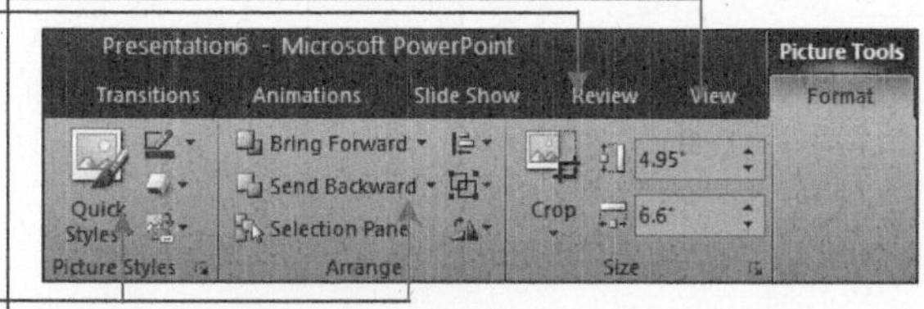

1. Select an object in your presentation..
2. The name of the applicable contextual tools appears in an accent color, and the contextual tabs appear next to the standard set of tabs.
3. The contextual tabs provide controls for working with the selected item.
4. A standard tab available on the Ribbon.

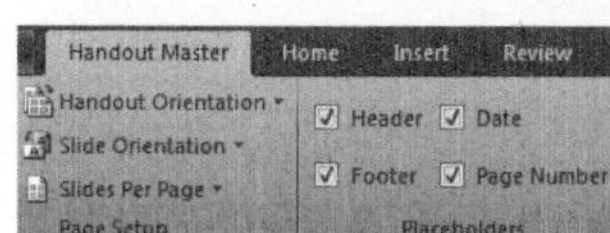

Program tabs replace the standard set of tabs when you switch to certain authoring modes or views, including *Slide Master, Handout Master, Notes Master,* and, in this example, *Handout Master.*

Menu Tabs

PowerPoint 2010 uses elements such as tabs, groups and commands that provide paths for accomplishing tasks. Following elements are more like the menus and toolbars that you may be familiar with from previous versions of PowerPoint.

Notes:

The new Microsoft Office Backstage view lets you quickly gain access to common tasks related to managing files, such as viewing document properties, setting permissions, opening, saving, printing and sharing your presentations.

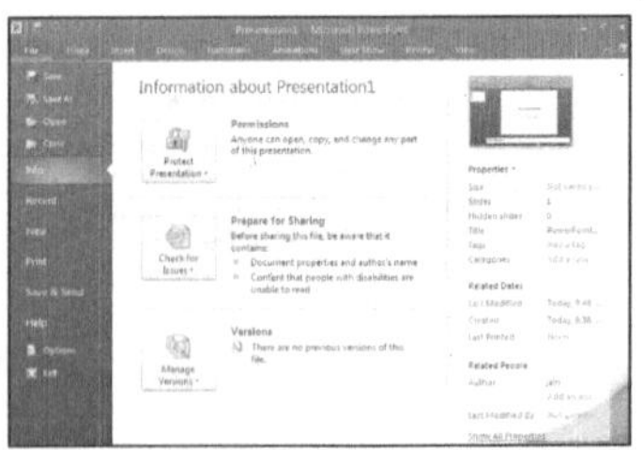

The Backstage view is a new feature in PowerPoint 2010 that brings together all the related options and capabilities in a single place.

Creating PowerPoint Template

Creating a presentation from one that already exists is usually simpler. The templates include complete presentations with all their details that you can change, as well as presentations with placeholders.

File → New

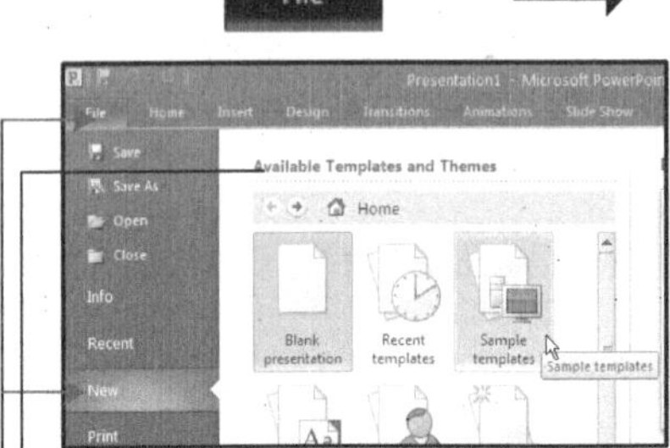

1. Click the **File** menu and choose **New**.

2. In the **Available Templates and Themes** click Samples templates.

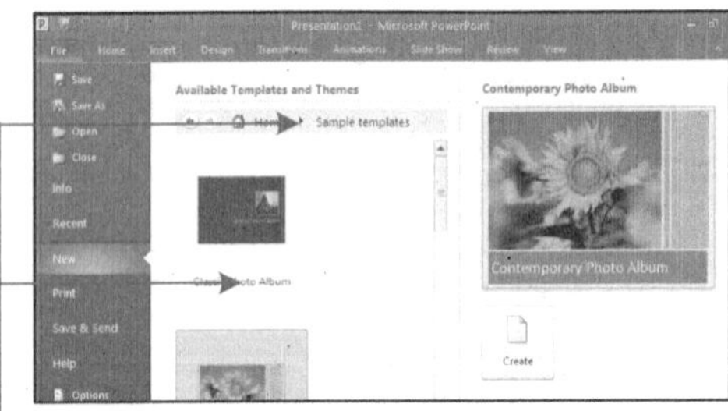

3. In the Sample templates, you can see a different types of templates, with all formatting, such as background, themes colors, font etc. Select the desired template you want to apply.

Notes:

The new design in Microsoft Office 2010 that includes the File tab replacing the Microsoft Office included in the 2007 Microsoft Office system release in the following programs: Word, Excel, PowerPoint, Access and Outlook. The Microsoft Office Button and the File tab are in the same general location but look different.

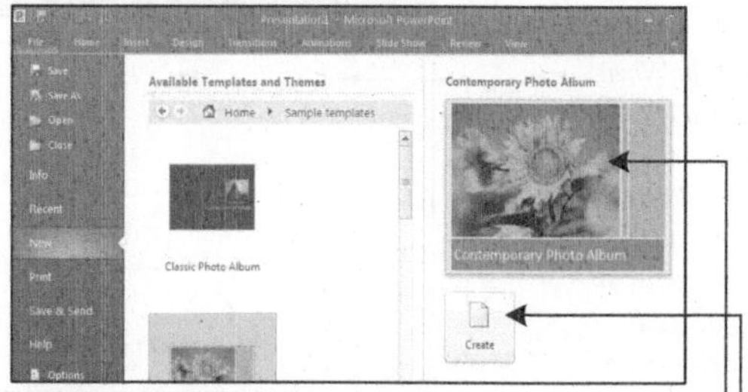

4. In the preview box, you see a sample presentation for which the template is designed.
5. Click **Create** button.

6. You can see the selected template as default presentation title name.
7. Now you can change or insert your own text and graphics with placeholders.

You can click the pushpin to the right of the file to keep the file permanently on the list.

Opening a Presentation

PowerPoint 2010 opens files in any of the several formats such as (.pptx, .pptm, .potx, .ppt, .pot, etc.)

1. Click **File** menu, and then click **Open** command. The **Open** dialog box appears. Or you can click from Quick Access Toolbar.

Presentations, templates and Slide show created in the PowerPoint 2010 file format (.pptx) are compatible with PowerPoint 2007.

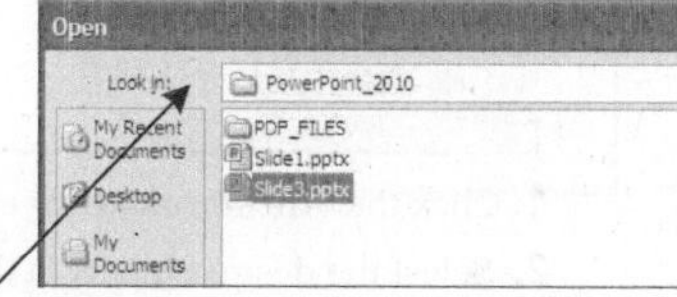

2. Choose the files and folders in the **Look in:** drop-down list.

Notes:

Home tab: *When you click it, this tab is active. Buttons related to working with document contents are organized in this tab. It has six groups: Clipboard, Slides, Font, Paragraph, Drawing and Editing. Only the button representing commands that can be performed on the currently selected document.*

Insert tab: *Click this button for related items you can insert. They are organized on this tab. It has five groups: Tables, Images, Links, Text, Illustrations, Media.*

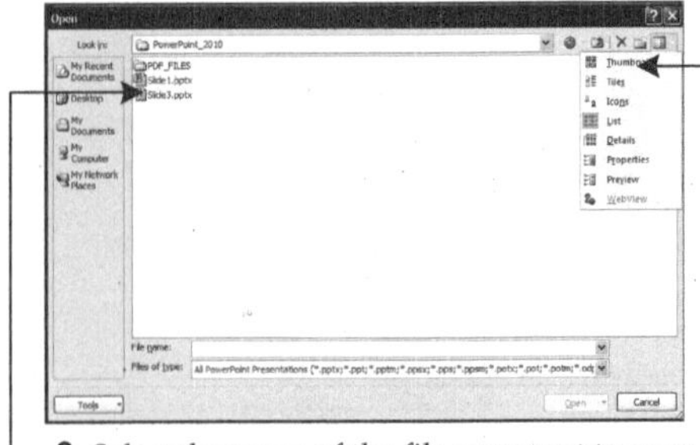

3. Select the name of the file you want to open.

4. Click the drop-down arrow next to the Views button to change the way the folder and file list is displayed.

a. **Thumbnails:** It displays icons as Thumbnails. When you click a folder name, a thick highlighted border appears.

b. **Tiles:** It displays icons in medium size.

c. **Icons:** It displays icons in smaller size.

d. **List:** Displays a list of commands.

e. **Details:** Displays the details of the size type, last modified, etc.

f. **Properties:** Displays the properties of the file.

g. **Preview:** Displays a preview of the file.

5. Click the **Open** button to open the file.

To open a recently accessed file

Many Office programs display the last few documents you opened in that program so that you can use to quickly access files. To use the **Open** dialog box to browse to the file to open it, after you save the file in its new location.

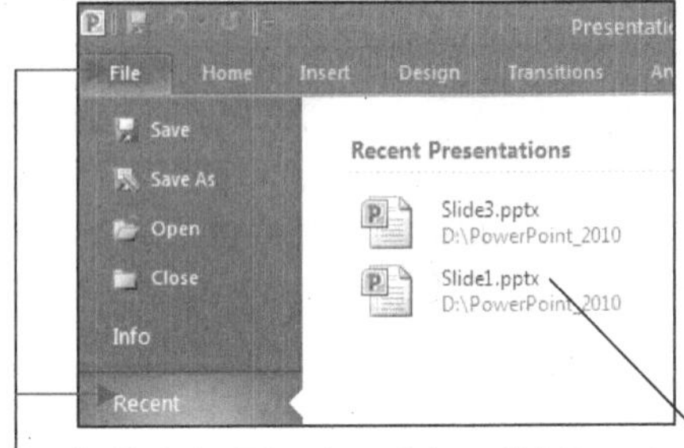

1. Click the **File** tab, and then click **Recent.**

2. Select the desired file from the list on the right of the menu.

Saving the Presentation

Notes:

***Design tab:** Click this tab which will show buttons that are related to items. You can give design to your slides. They are organized on this tab. It has three groups: Page Setup, Themes, and Background.*

When working on a presentation, it is very important that you save it at regular intervals so that in case there is system failure, you do not lose much of your work.

PowerPoint has two commands to save your file Save and Save As command.

The **Save** command is used to save the current presentation file.

The **Save As** command is used when you want to save an existing presentation under a new name or you are saving your presentation for the first time.

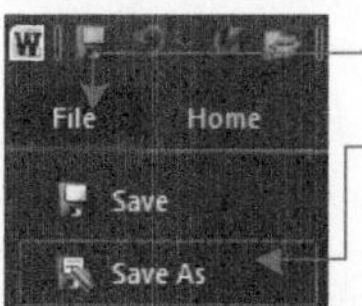

1. Click the **File** tab.
2. Then click **Save As.**

Or, Alternatively, choose the **Save** button on the **Quick Access** toolbar.

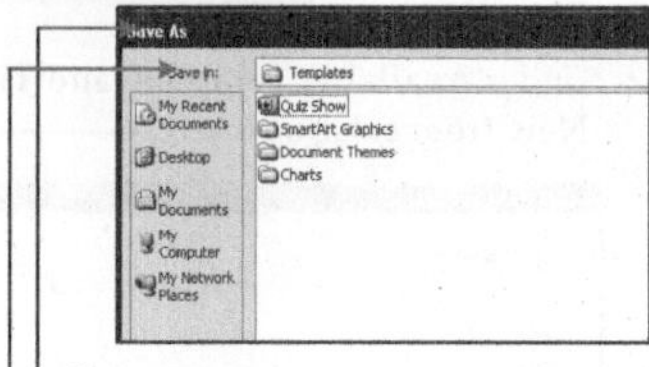

3. The **Save As** dialog box appears.
4. Choose the desired folder or drive you want to save in the **Save in:** drop-down list.

***Transitions tab:** Slide transitions are motion effects that occur in Slides, Show view when you move from one slide to the next during a presentation. You can control the speed, add sound and even customize the properties of transition effect.*

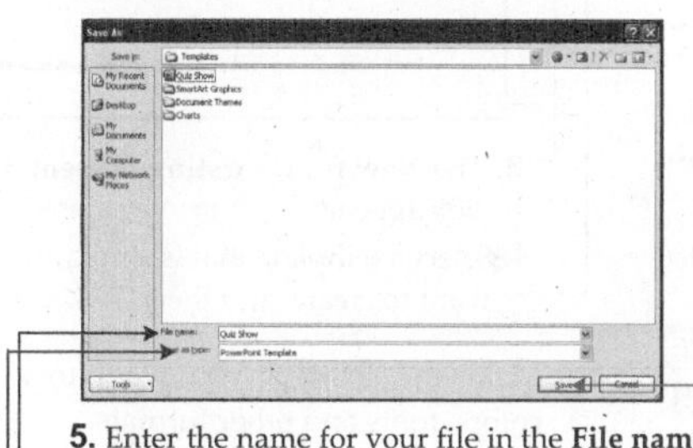

5. Enter the name for your file in the **File name:** drop-down list.
6. In the **Save as type:** list, click the file format that you want to save the file in. For example, if you select PowerPoint template, it adds the template to your list of available templates.
7. Click the **Save** button.

Notes:

Animations tab: *Click this tab which will show buttons that are related to items. You can give animations to your slides.*

The Save As option gives various file formats so that the presentation can be given without the presence of PowerPoint software package on your machine.

Slide Show: *Click this tab which will show buttons that are related to items. In this tab, you can view, take up the full computer screen, like an actual presentation. For example you can see how your graphics animated effects will look during the presentation. It has three groups: Start slide show, Set Up and Monitors.*

Creating a New Template based on an Existing Presentation

You can create a template in almost the same way as you create a presentation. If you have a template that already has most of the features you want, you will save time by creating a new presentation based on that existing template.

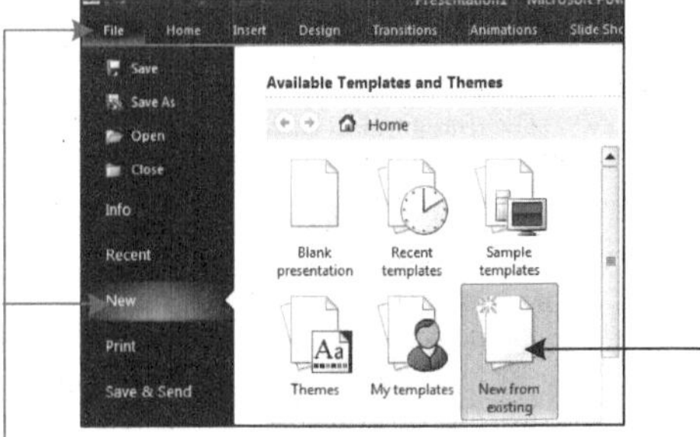

1. Click the **File** menu and choose **New**. The **New** Backstage view appears.
2. Under **Available Template and Themes** click **New from existing** icon.

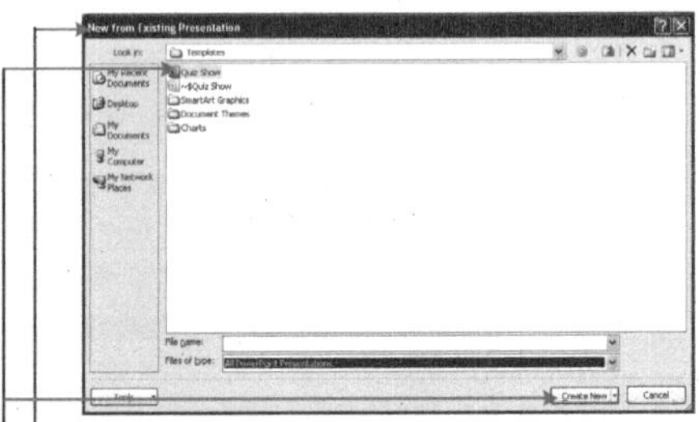

3. The **New from Existing Presentation** dialog box appears.
4. Select a template that is similar to the one that you want to create, and then Click **Create New**.
5. Make the changes you want to apply such as themes colors, fonts and other formats.
6. Click the **Save As** button to save the template.
7. The **Save As** dialog box appears. Give the new name to template file in the **File name:** drop-down list.
8. Select the PowerPoint Template in the Save as type: drop-down list, and then click **Save** button.

Notes:

Review tab: *Click this tab which will show buttons that are related to items. In this tab you can view and add comments to your presentation and you might prefer to check spelling all at once when you finish your document. It has four groups: Proofing, Language, and Comments and Compare.*

View tab: *Click this tab which will show buttons that are related to changing the view during presentation. It has six groups: Presentation views, window, macros, Show/Hide, Zoom, Color/Grayscale.*

Print and Previewing a Presentation

The simplest way to print a presentation is, click **File** menu and choose **Print**. Before you print a presentation, it is necessary to preview it to check the overall appearance of the presentation.

File → Print

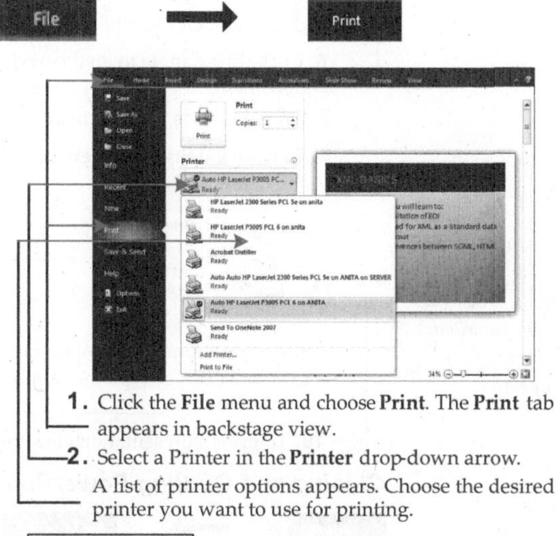

1. Click the **File** menu and choose **Print**. The **Print** tab appears in backstage view.
2. Select a Printer in the **Printer** drop-down arrow. A list of printer options appears. Choose the desired printer you want to use for printing.

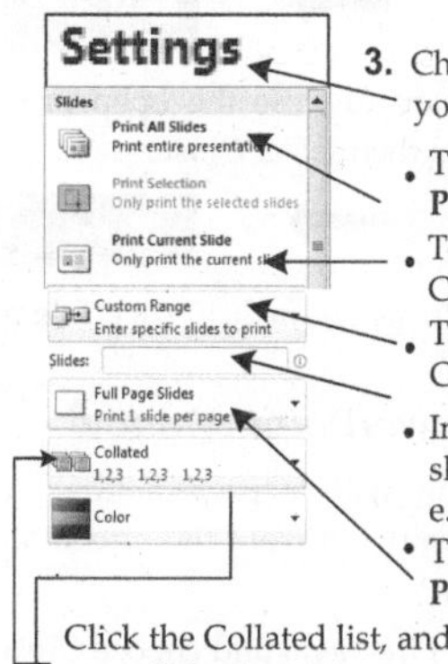

3. Choose one of the desired settings you want to print a presentation.
   - To Print entire presentation, select **Print All Slides**.
   - To print the current slide. Select Current Slide.
   - To print specific slides. Select Custom Range.
   - In the **Slides:** list box, enter specific slides number or slide ranges. For e.g. 3,5,7-11.
   - To click one side on full page, under **Print Layout**, click Full Page Slides.

   Click the Collated list, and then choose whether you want your slides to print

   Click the Color drop-down list and choose the desired options to select the either, Color, Grayscale or Pure Black and White.
4. To include or change headers and footers, click the Edit Header and Footer link, and then make your selections in the Header and Footer dialog box that appears.

Notes:

The keyboard shortcut to open a Print dialog box is by pressing Ctrl+Shift+F12 keys together.

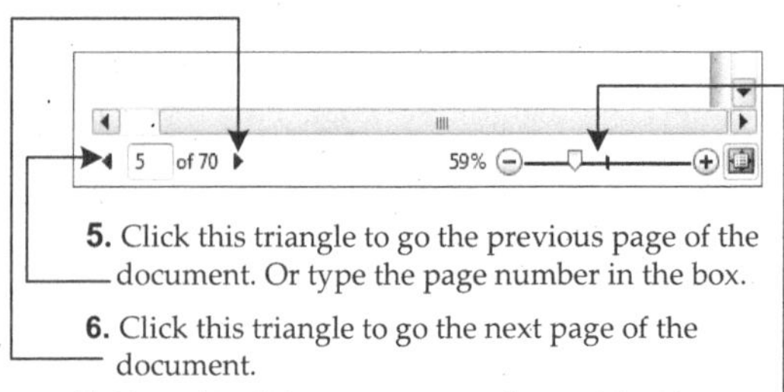

5. Click this triangle to go the previous page of the document. Or type the page number in the box.
6. Click this triangle to go the next page of the document.
7. Drag this slide to zoom in and out of the document
8. To close the **Print Preview** click the **Esc** key or click the **Home** tab.

*To change the properties for your printer, under the printer name, click **Printer Properties**.*

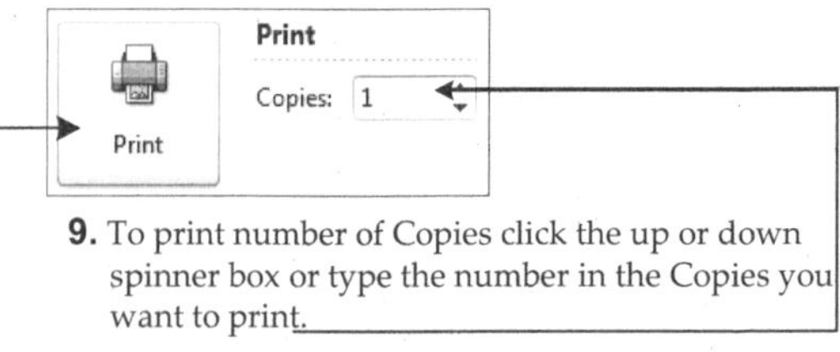

9. To print number of Copies click the up or down spinner box or type the number in the Copies you want to print.
10. To print a presentation click the Print icon.

Closing and Quitting PowerPoint

1. If you want to close the open presentation, choose File menu and then select **Close**.

1. To quit Presentation 2010 click **File** menu and choose **Exit** button.

*The new design in **Microsoft Office 2010** that includes the **File** tab replacing the **Microsoft Office Button** included in the 2010 Microsoft Office system release in the following programs: Word, Excel, PowerPoint, Access, and Outlook.*

Closing PowerPoint Window

After finishing with a presentation, you should close the window to remove it from the screen and to free computer's main memory.

1. Click the **File** menu and choose **Close**.

   Windows closes if no changes have been made to the presentation since the last save. However, if you made changes since the last time you saved the presentation, PowerPoint 2010 displays an Alert dialog box, asking whether you want to save changes you made to slide3.pptx?

Notes:

To close the active presentation window click the Control menu icon on the left side of the presentation's title bar.

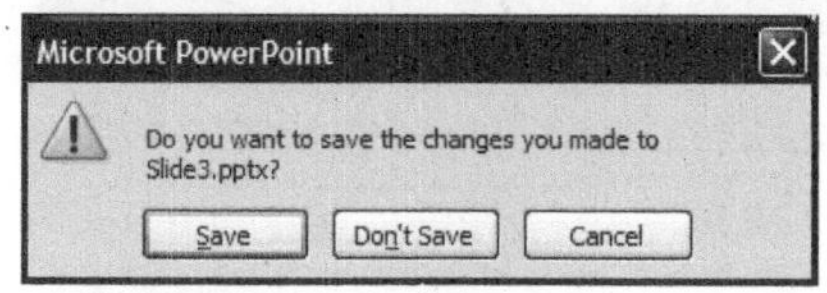

Getting Help in MS PowerPoint 2010

1. Click the MS PowerPoint 2010 Help button at the right corner of the window or press **F1** key.

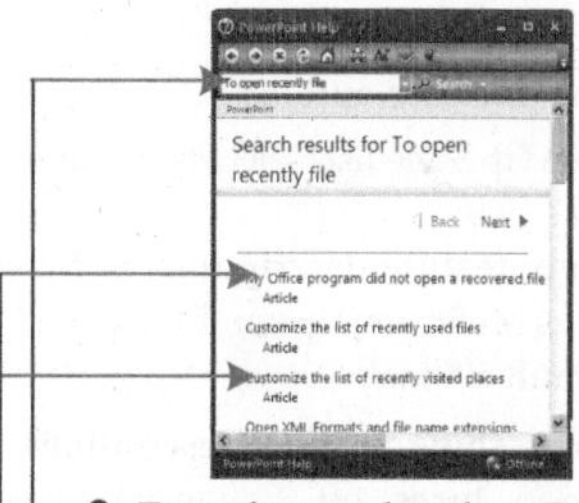

2. Type the word such as **Print and Preview** in the Type words to search for box and press Enter key.
3. The help window display a list of topics, i.e. searched for related topics. Choose the selected list topic you want.
4. The help window displays step-by-step explanations.
5. Click the **Close** button to close the **Help** window.

To resize the Help window, move the pointer over a corner of the Help window until you see the double-headed arrow and then drag the corner until the window is of the size that you want it to be.

To keep the Ribbon Minimize

1. To minimize the Ribbon, click Minimize the Ribbon. Minimize Ribbon button is in the upper-right corner of the program window.

Show or Hide ScreenTips

1. Click **File** menu and choose **Options**.
2. The **PowerPoint Options** dialog box appears.

*1. To **restore the Ribbon**, click **Expand the Ribbon** as shown below.*

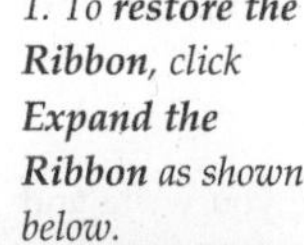

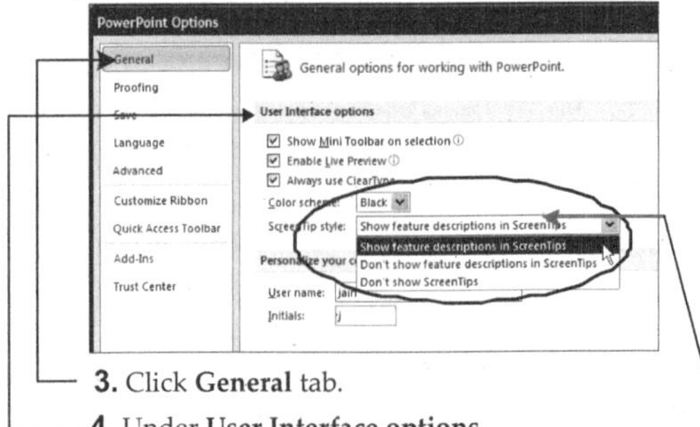

3. Click **General** tab.
4. Under **User Interface options**.
5. In the ScreenTip Style list, select the options that you want.

Notes:

ScreenTips are small windows that display descriptive text when you rest the pointer on a command or control.

- **Show feature descriptions in ScreenTips** — This option turns on ScreenTips and Enhanced ScreenTips. This is the default setting.
- **Don't show feature descriptions in ScreenTips** —This option turns off Enhanced ScreenTips. You still see ScreenTips.
- **Don't show ScreenTips**—This option turns off ScreenTips and Enhanced ScreenTips.

Displaying or Hiding Rulers

PowerPoint 2010 gives you the flexibility to hide or display ruler according to your working needs.

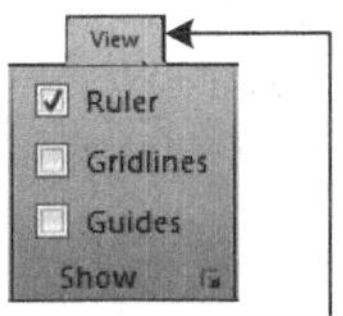

1. On the **View** tab, in the **Show** group, select the **Ruler** check box.

PowerPoint Views

PowerPoint offers four ways (*views*) to look at your presentation. Each view enables you to work on a different aspect of the presentation. The changes made in one view are also reflected in all other views.

To quickly minimize the Ribbon, double-click the name of the active tab. Double-click a tab again to restore the Ribbon.

Normal View

Normal view is the main editing view, where you write and design your presentation. The view has four working areas:

- Outline tab

Notes:

Enhanced ScreenTips are larger windows that display more descriptive text than a ScreenTip and can have a link to a Help topic. Enhanced ScreenTips are available in the following 2010-Office system programs: Access, Excel, PowerPoint, and Word. (see below icon)

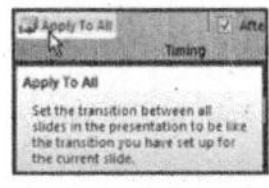

- Slides tab
- Slide pane
- Notes pane

These panes let you work on all aspects of your presentation in one place. You can adjust the size of different panes by dragging the pane borders.

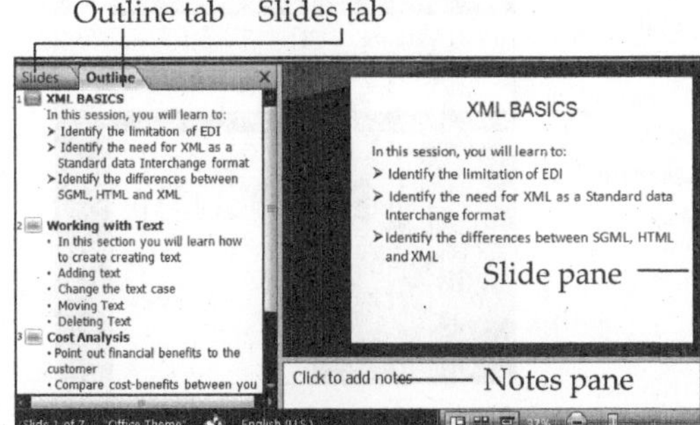

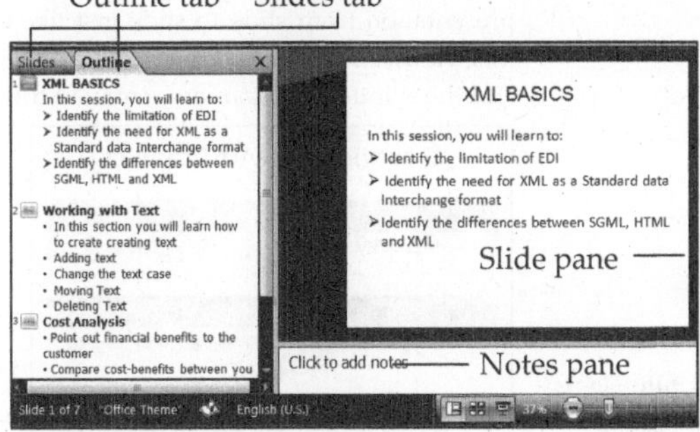

Slide Sorter View

__Notes pane:__ The notes pane lets you add speaker notes or information you want to share with the audience. If you want to have graphic in your notes, you must add the notes in notes page view.

The slide sorter view is a view of your slides in thumbnail form. In this view, you can see the design consistency and the flow of your presentation. If need be, you can easily reorder the slides, copy or delete the slides.

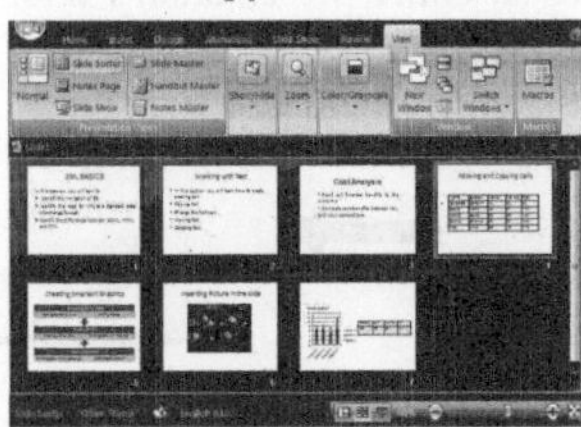

Notes:

Outline tab: *Use the outline tab to organize and develop the contents of your presentation. You can type all of the text of your presentation and rearrange bulleted points, paragraphs and slides.*

Slides tab: *This is a great place to view the slides in your presentation as thumbnail-sized images while you edit. The thumbnails make it easy for you to navigate through your presentation and to see the effect of any design changes.*

Notes Page View

This view helps you to prepare the speaker notes used while you are making the presentation to your audience. Notes pages view produces a smaller version of the slide on the top part of a page and leaves the lower part free for notes or key points.

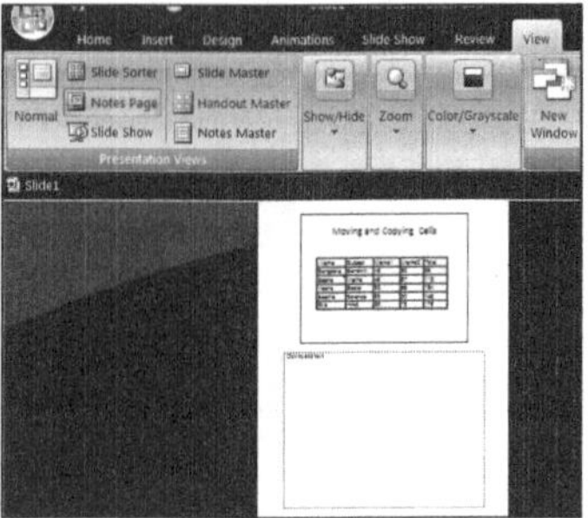

Slide Show View

This view of PowerPoint shows the progress of the presentation from slide to slide just like a real slide show. In this view, all *menus, toolbars, rulers,* the *status bar, scrollbars,* and the Windows *taskbar* are removed from the screen.

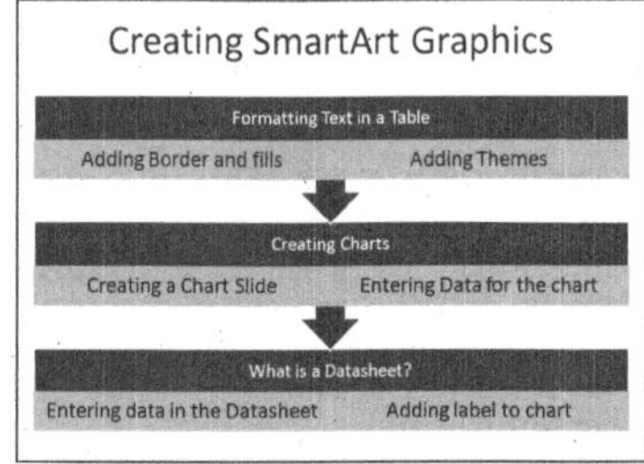

PowerPoint Layouts and Themes

A layout determines where text, graphics, charts and other elements appear on an individual slide. A theme determines the look of an entire presentation's colors, fonts, and overall format.

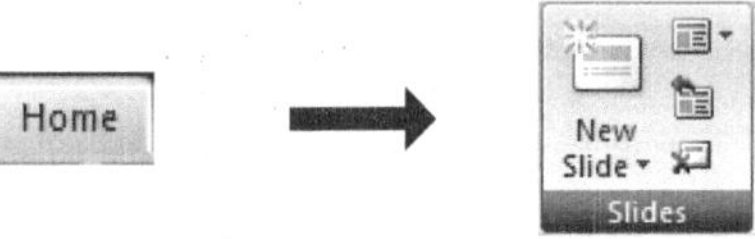

Notes:

Slide Pane:

The Slide pane displays a larger view of the current slide. In this view, you can add text and insert tables etc.

1. Click the **Home** tab, in the **Slides** group. Click the **New Slide** down pointing arrow.

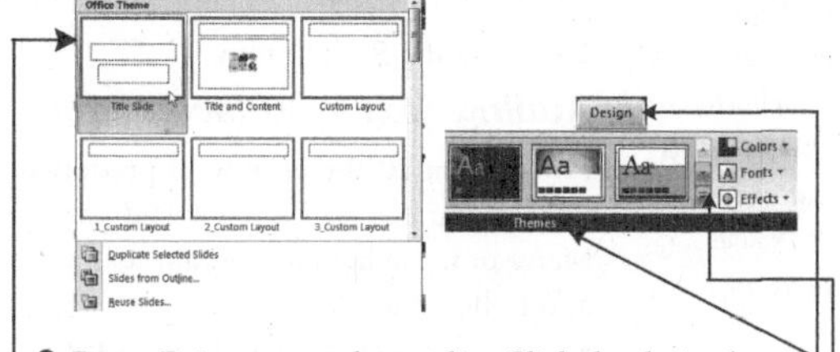

2. PowerPoint opens a layout list. Click the desired layout you want to apply.
3. When you click to select a layout, PowerPoint inserts a new slide at that location in your presentation with that layout.
4. Click the **Design** tab, in the **Themes** group.
5. Click the **More** button at the lower right corner in the **Themes** group.

A document theme is a set of formatting that include a set of theme colors, fonts and theme effects (including heading and body text fonts, lines and fill effects).

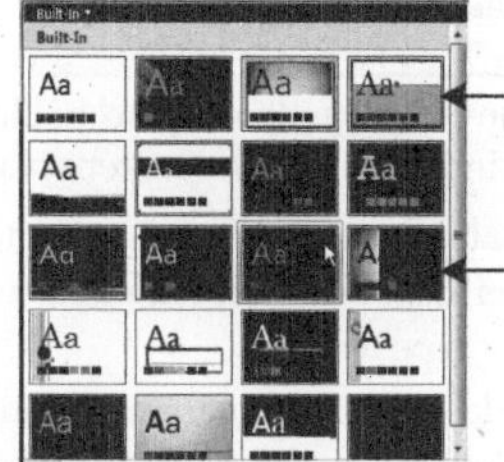

6. A list of Built-in themes options appears.
7. Select a desired style you want to apply in your Presentation.

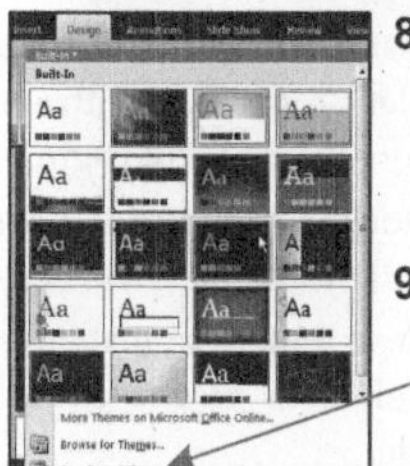

8. If you want to modify the theme, select from the Font, Colors, and Effect buttons to the right of the Themes group.
9. After you have modified a theme to your liking, click the down arrow next to the ribbon's themes and select Save Current Theme...

A theme is a set of unified design elements that provide a look for your document by using colors, fonts and graphics. You can use predefined themes that come with PowerPoint, or you can define your own.

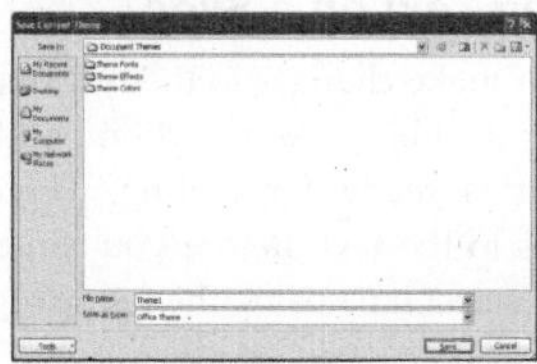

10. The **Save Current Theme** dialog box appears.

Notes:

*To display a blank PowerPoint presentation, click the New button on the Quick Access Toolbar or press **Ctrl + N** keys together.*

11. In the **Save in:** drop down list contains a default folder (Document Themes).
12. Give the name in the **File name:** drop down list.
13. Click the **Save** button.

Adding Text in a Placeholder

PowerPoint 2010 comes with predefined layouts you want to use, or you can add a blank slide and create a custom layout. Many of these layouts contain text placeholders for title, body and bulleted list.

1. Click the **Home** tab. In the **Slides** group click **New Slide** down pointing arrow. A list of layout slides appears.

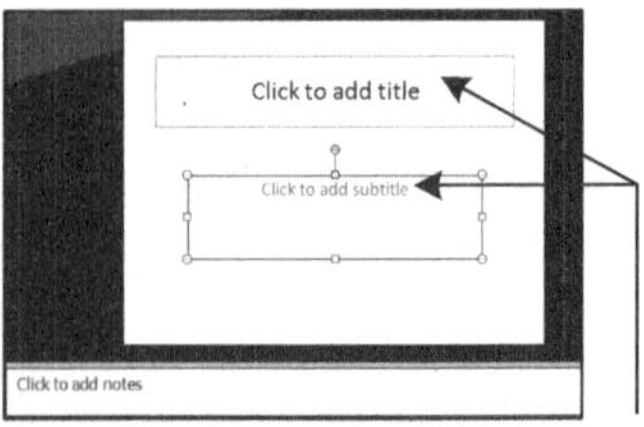

To enter text in a Presentation, there are two ways: Inserting a new slide with text placeholder or inserting text in an existing slide.

2. Click anywhere within a placeholder to select it. The border indicates that the current placeholder is selected.
3. The sample text disappears and an insertion point appears inside the placeholder, indicating that you can enter or type text.
4. In a title or subtitle placeholder, the insertion point may be centered.
5. In a bulleted-list placeholder, the sample text disappears and the bullet remains, with the insertion point positioned where the text will begin.
6. Type the text for the slide inside the selected placeholder and press Enter key.
7. When you finish entering text, deselect the object by clicking a blank area of the slide of the gray border around the slide.

Editing Text on a Slide

You might want to open more than one presentation to copy and paste from one to another.

You can make changes to the text in any text object simply by clicking the object. An insertion point appears, indicating that the text is ready for editing. Then you can start making changes to the text. Before you can change existing text, you have to select it by using the following techniques:

- Select an individual word by double clicking it. The word and the space following it are selected.

Notes:

Depending on your screen's resolution and the details in a presentation's slide, you might need to zoom in or out by dragging the Zoom slider in PowerPoint's lower-right corner.

- Alternatively, position the insertion point at the beginning of the text you want to select, hold down the **Shift** key, and either press an arrow key to select characters one at a time.

Copying Text

You can copy text that appears in one place to another place. Copying of text occurs with the assistance of the Windows Clipboard.

1. Select the text you want to copy.
2. In the **Home** tab, click **Copy** icon on the **Clipboard** group, move to the place in your presentation where you want to insert this text.
3. Click the **Paste** down pointing arrow and choose **Paste** command on the **Clipboard** group.

Moving Text

Moving text operation is similar to copying text operation except that text is moved i.e. it is deleted from the original location and copied to a new place.

Closing the Presentation: *When you finish giving or editing a presentation, close the presentation by clicking Office button and selecting **Close**.*

1. Select the text you want to move.
2. Click the **Cut** button on the **Home** tab.
3. Click the **Paste** button on the **Home** tab.

Deleting Text

You can delete characters, words, or all the text in a text box. using one of the methods:

- The **Del** key erases the character to the right of the cursor.
- The **Backspace** key erases the character to the left of the cursor.

Copy and Paste the multiple items

*To select all the text in a placeholder, click inside the placeholder and then click select and then **Select All** in the **Editing** group on the **Home** tab.*

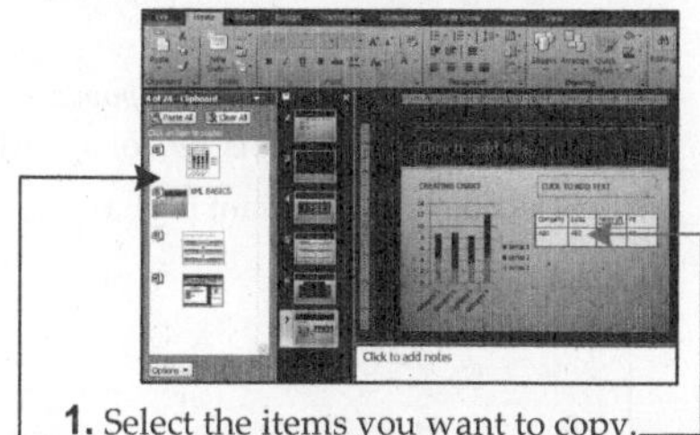

1. Select the items you want to copy.

2. It automatically send to the Clipboard dialog box.

3. To display the Clipboard toolbar, click the **Home** tab and choose **Clipboard Launcher** task pane appears.

Notes:

The keyboard shortcut key to copy text is Ctrl + C

4. If the text item you want to copy is in another program, switch to that program.
5. Select the text item you want to copy.
6. Repeat steps 3 to 5 until you have copied all the items (up to 12) you want to copy.
7. Click where you want the items to be pasted.
8. To paste all the items you copied, click Paste All on the Clipboard toolbar.
9. If you do not want to paste all of the items you copied, or if Paste All is not available, you can paste specific items.

The keyboard shortcut key to paste text is Ctrl + V.

Formatting Text

Formatting means applying characteristics and effects to text in order to enhance its appearance. The formatting you apply to the text in a presentation is very important because it affects the way your words are received by your audience.

Aligning Text in a Slide

Alignment is the way text is placed between the margins of a page or a text box on a slide.

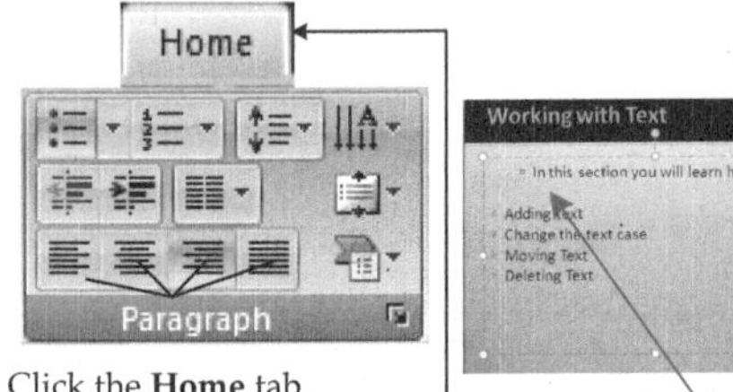

The keyboard shortcut key to cut text is Ctrl + X.

1. Click the **Home** tab.
2. Select the text that you want to align the text.
3. Click the desired alignment you want to apply in the **Paragraph** group.

Changing the Font Size, Style and Effects in Font dialog box

Font size is measured in *points,* which is a height measurement; each point is 1/72 of an inch.

1. Select the text you want to change.

If you delete text accidentally, you can undo your action by clicking the Undo button on the Quick Access toolbar.

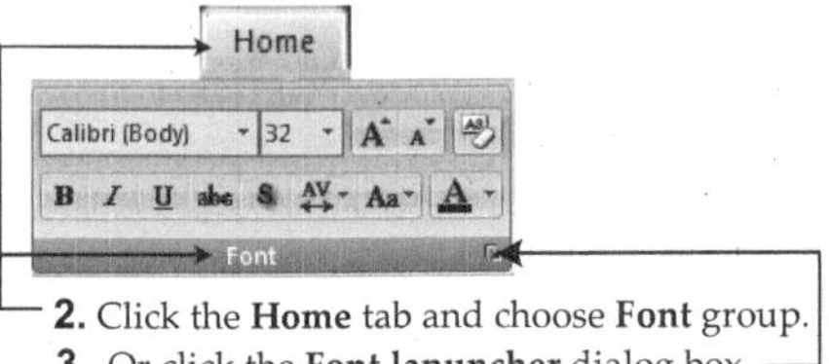

2. Click the **Home** tab and choose **Font** group.
3. Or click the **Font lanuncher** dialog box.

Notes:

*The shortcut key to decrease font size is **Ctrl + <.***

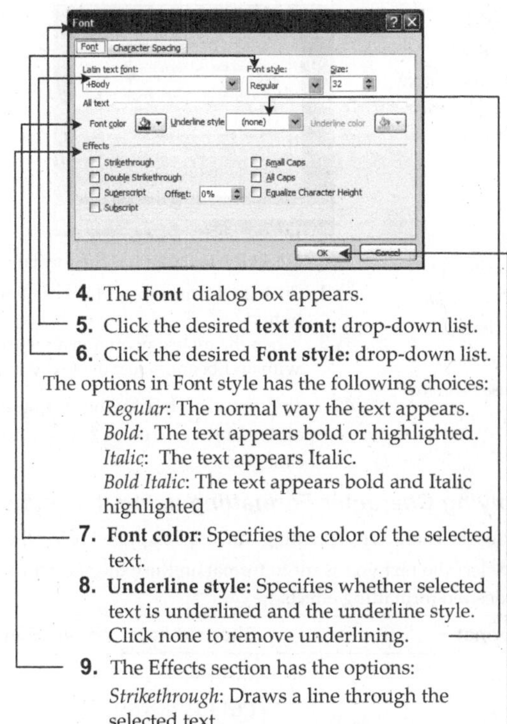

4. The **Font** dialog box appears.
5. Click the desired **text font:** drop-down list.
6. Click the desired **Font style:** drop-down list.

The options in Font style has the following choices:

Regular: The normal way the text appears.
Bold: The text appears bold or highlighted.
Italic: The text appears Italic.
Bold Italic: The text appears bold and Italic highlighted

7. **Font color:** Specifies the color of the selected text.
8. **Underline style:** Specifies whether selected text is underlined and the underline style. Click none to remove underlining.
9. The Effects section has the options:
   Strikethrough: Draws a line through the selected text.
   Superscript: The text appears raised like x^2y
   Subscript: The text appears lowered like H_2O
10. Click the desired options you want to check and then click OK button.

*The shortcut key to increase font size is **Ctrl + >.***

Right type and size of font creates good impression on your audience.

You can also align text in the Paragraph Launcher dialog box in the alignment section.

Copying Style Formatting

You can copy style formatting using one of the following two methods:

- Using Ribbon command
- Using the keyboard

You can also change the text color by clicking the Home tab of font group. Then click the Font color drop-down arrow. The font color palette appears. Move the mouse pointer over the color, you can see the effect changes in the text. Choose the desired color you want to apply the text.

Notes:

To resize a placeholder, drag one of its corner borders.

Move Placeholder

1. Click inside placeholder.

2. Drag with mouse to desired position.

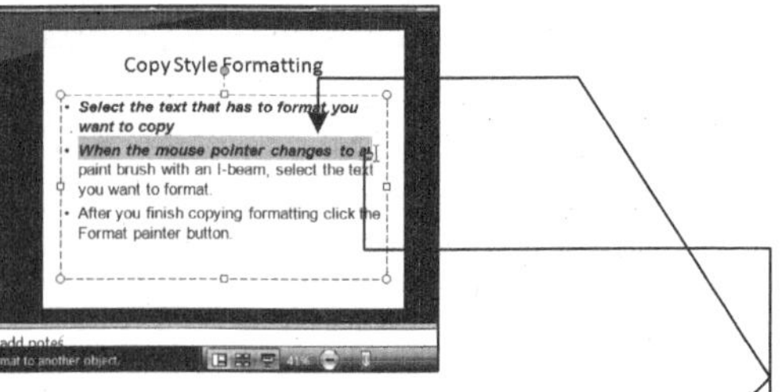

1. Select the text that has the format you want to copy.
2. Click the **Home** tab, and choose **Format painter** button.
3. When the mouse pointer changes to a paint brush with an I-beam, select the text you want to format.
4. After you finish copying formatting, click the **Format painter** button or press **Esc** key to restore the normal I-beam pointer.

Applying Character Formatting using the keyboard

Most of the character formatting can also be applied using the keyboard shortcut.

1. Select the text you want to format and use the shortcut key combinations for the desired formatting effects.

Format	Shortcut keys combination
Bold	**Ctrl + B**
Italic	**Ctrl + I**
Underline	**Ctrl + U**
Superscript	**Ctrl + Shift + +**
Subscript	**Ctrl + =**
Copy Formatting	**Ctrl + Shift + C**
Paste formatting	**Ctrl + Shift + V**
Remove formatting	**Ctrl + Spacebar**
Change case of letters	**Shift + F3**
Change the font	**Ctrl + Shift + F**
Change the font size	**Ctrl + Shift + P**
Increase the font size	**Ctrl + Shift + >**
Decrease the font size	**Ctrl + Shift + <**

Using the Change Case Command

PowerPoint provides the facilities to change capitalization of any text by using the **Change Case** command.

Notes:

Size Placeholder

1. Click inside placeholder.

2. Drag sizing handles to increase/decrease size.

1. Select the text for which you want to change capitalization.

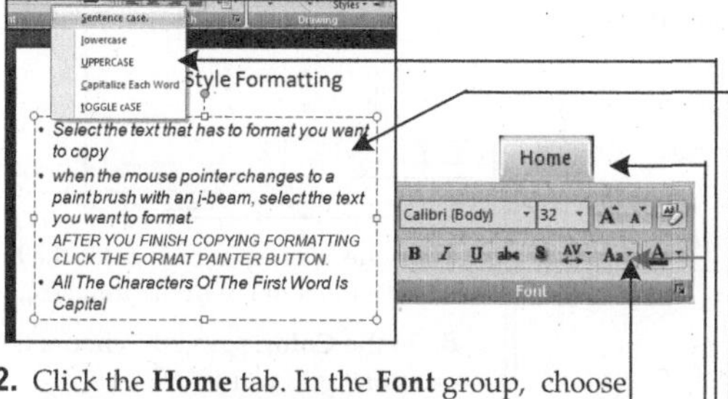

2. Click the **Home** tab. In the **Font** group, choose **Change Case** command icon. (i.e. Aa)
3. Click the down pointing arrow.
4. Select the desired option you want to apply to the text.
5. The different types of **Change case** command is applied in the text.

Bullets and Numbering

1. Select the text or paragraphs you want to add bullet.

Remove bullets and Numbering

1. Select the text you want to remove bullets and numbering.

2. In the Paragraph group of Home tab choose the bullets down arrow.

A list of bullet palette list appears, choose None. Or

3. You can press Backspace to remove bullet or numbering from an item in the list.

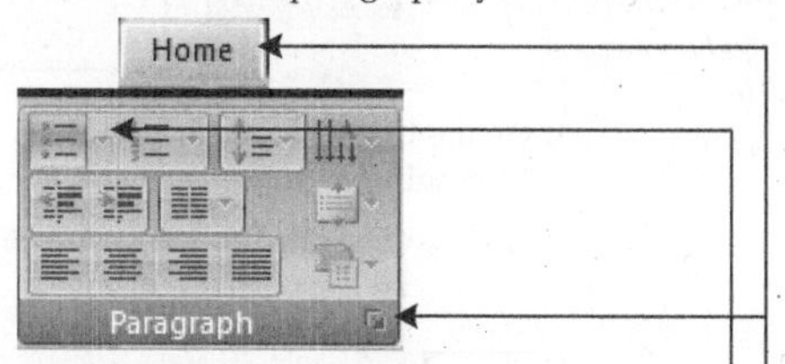

2. Click the **Home** tab, in the **Paragraph** group.
3. Click the down arrow to choose the **Bullets and Numbering** dialog box.

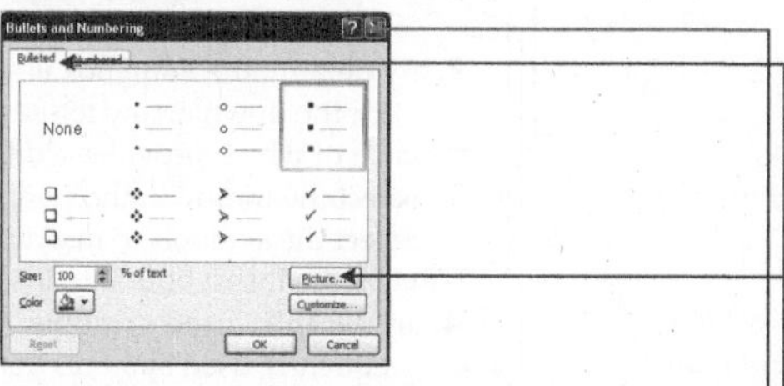

4. The **Bullets and Numbering** dialog box appears.
5. Click the **Bulleted** tab you want to modify.
6. You can select the **Picture...** button you can use the picture file to use as a bullet.

Notes:

Change Text Alignment

1. Select text or click in text paragraph.

2. Click desired alignment button in the Paragraph group.

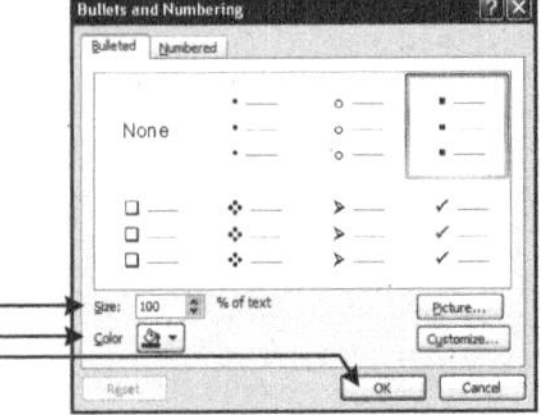

7. In the **Size:** spin box, enter the bullet size you want as a percentage of the font size.
8. In the **Color:** spin box, choose the color of the bullet you want.
9. Click OK button to accept the changes.

Adding Symbols

PowerPoint provides a full range of special symbol characters like the copyright or trademarks, registration symbol etc.

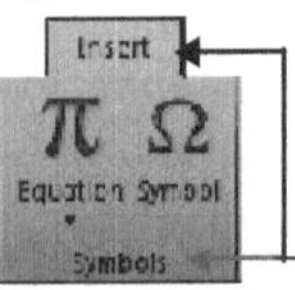

The Keyboard shortcut to apply bold formatting to selected text, press CTRL+B.

1. On the **Insert** tab. In the **Symbols** group, click **Symbol** icon.

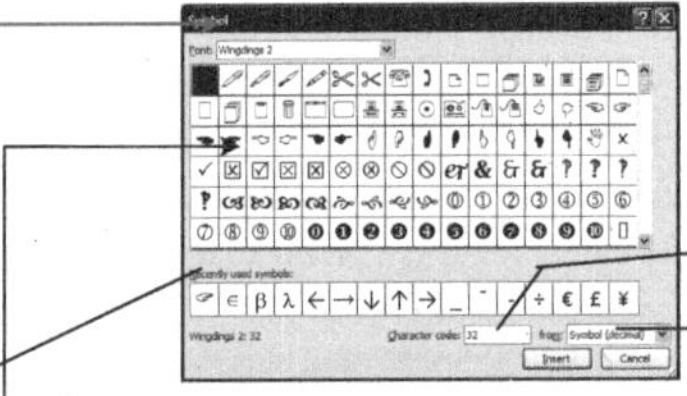

2. By default, the **Font:** box is set to normal text. Click the down arrow to see the choices for fonts, each of which provides a different set of symbols.
3. Select the font with the symbols you want to use. Select the symbols to insert by clicking it once. Or click the Insert button to insert the symbol.
4. In **Recently used symbols:** box, lists the most frequently used symbols that have been inserted.
5. **Character code:** list box, displays a unique code representing a symbol.
6. **from:** drop down list, specifies the character set on which the character code is based on.

The Keyboard shortcut to apply Italic formatting to selected text, press CTRL+I.

Notes:

*The **Keyboard shortcut** to apply Underline formatting to selected text, press **CTRL+U.***

7. After you selecting the desired symbol, the **Cancel** turned to **Close** button.

Formatting Paragraphs

A Paragraph can have the following characteristics:

Alignment, Tab and Indents, Line spacing and Space before and after the paragraph.

Alignment

You can change alignment for specific text with buttons in the Paragraph group in the Home tab.

Left alignment: aligns the text at the left margin and makes a zigzag right margin.

Right alignment: aligns the text to the right margin and makes a zigzag left margin.

Center alignment: centers text between the left and right margins on the center line. In this case both the margins are zigzag.

Justified: aligns the text at both the margins by increasing the spacing between the words.

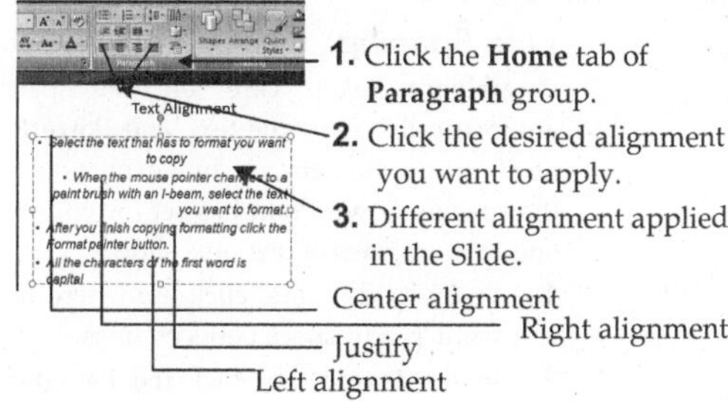

To remove all the tab stops

*1. In the **Paragraph** dialog box, click Tabs.*

*2. In the **Tabs** dialog box, Clear All. Or*

Tab settings

The function of a tab is to help you align text in your documents. The tab is a small marker that tells the text where you want to stop. PowerPoint gives you the option of choosing four different tab stops: left, right, center and decimal tabs.

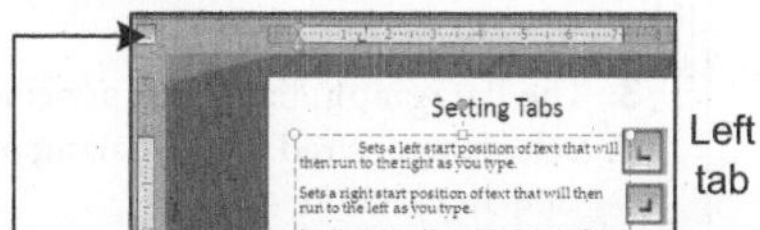

Notes:

To Clear a tab stop, drag the tab marker off the ruler.

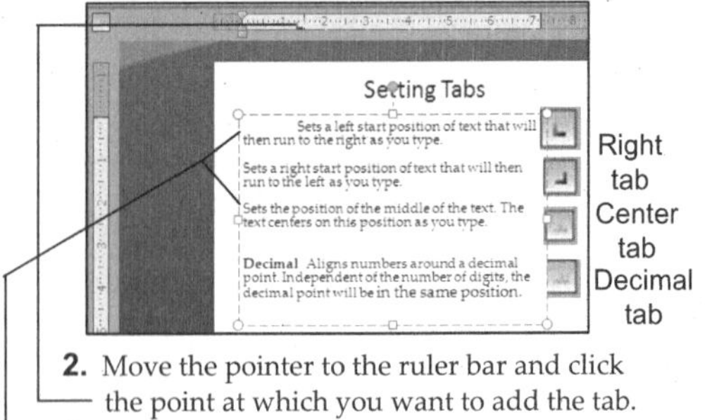

2. Move the pointer to the ruler bar and click the point at which you want to add the tab.
3. For example, to set different tabs appears in the slide.

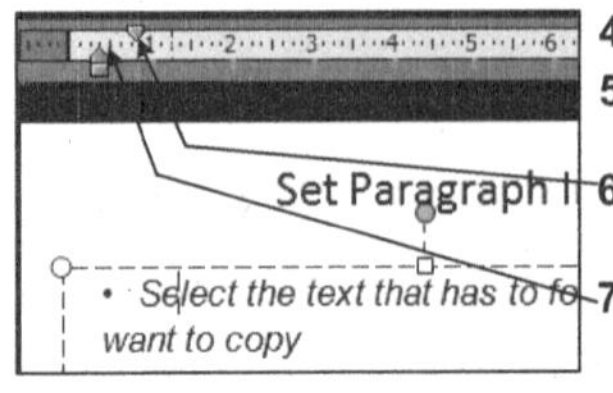

4. Select the text you want to set an indentation.
5. If the ruler is not displayed, click **View** tab and choose Ruler in the **Show/Hide** group.
6. To set the indent for the first line of a paragraph, drag the upper indent marker.
7. To set the left indent for other lines in a paragraph, drag the lower indent marker.

Notes:

Change Line Spacing

1. Click Line Spacing button.

2. Click desired spacing at drop-down list.

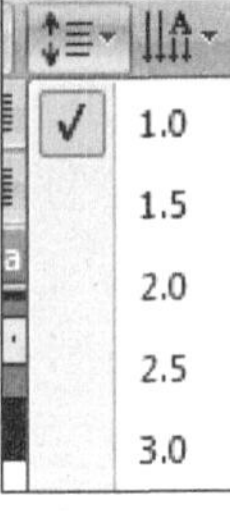

Line Spacing

PowerPoint takes care of the spacing of your text automatically. Type the text, and PowerPoint puts it where it needs to go. Sometimes, however, you may want to change the spacing PowerPoint has set for you. You might want to fit one or more lines of text on a slide.

1. In the Slide pane, click anywhere in the paragraph you want to add space between lines.
2. In the **Home** tab, click the **Paragraph Launcher** dialog box.

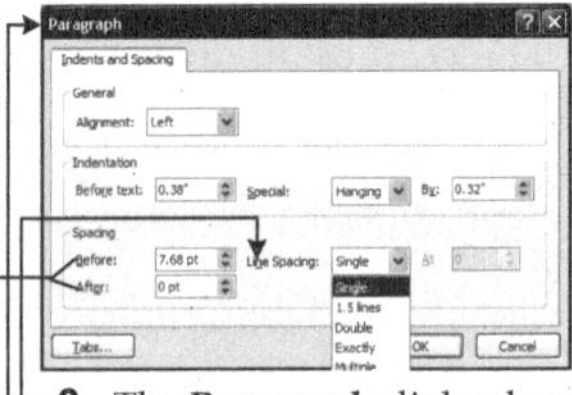

3. The **Paragraph** dialog box appears.
4. Select the desired **Line Spacing** options in the **Spacing** section.
5. In the spinner box, click up-arrow or down-arrow for adding space **Before** or **After** the paragraph.
6. After you make changes in the dialog box click OK button.

Notes:

The Shortcut key to open a Spelling dialog box is F7.

Using Spelling Checker

PowerPoint's spelling checker checks the spelling of the entire presentation all slides, outlines, notes pages, and handout pages. The spelling checker in PowerPoint compares all the words in your document with a dictionary file, in the way any MS Office application does.

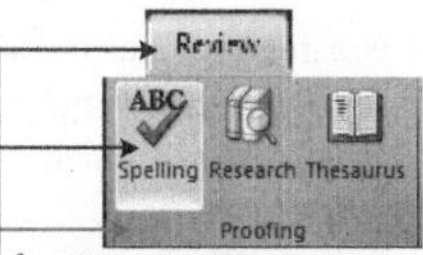

1. Click the **Review** tab. In the **Proofing** group, click **Spelling** icon.

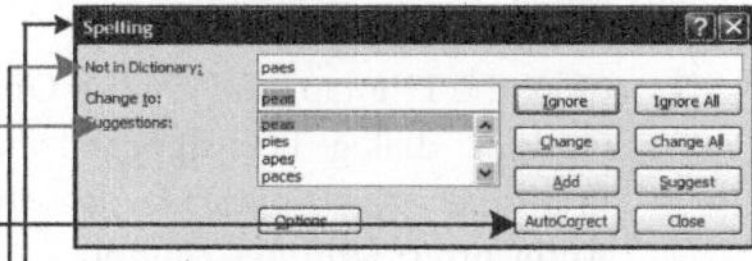

2. The **Spelling** dialog box appears.
3. The spelling checker highlights the first unrecognized word in the presentation file and displays the word in the **Not in Dictionary:** box.
4. Select the word from the **Suggestions:** list and click the AutoCorrect button to automatically correct the identical misspelling when you type it in the future.

Use Thesaurus

1. Click desired word.

2. Click Review tab.

3. Click Thesaurus button.

4. Position mouse pointer on desired replacement word in Thesaurus task pane, click down-pointing arrow at right of word, and then click Insert.

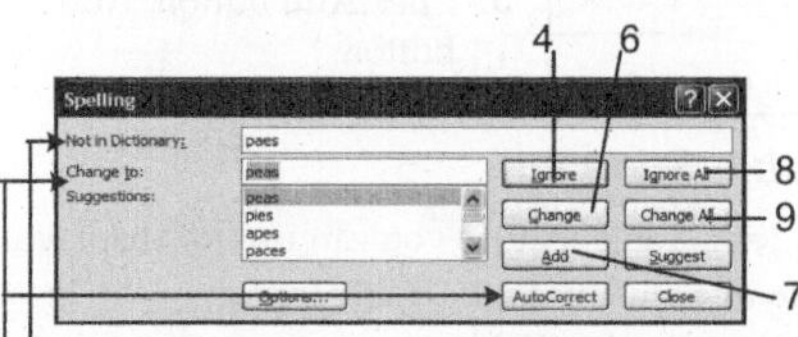

5. The spelling checker highlights the first unrecognized word in the presentation file and displays the word in the **Not in Dictionary:** box.
6. Click the **Ignore** button to leave the word as it is and go on to the next word.
7. Select the word from the **Suggestions:** list and click the AutoCorrect button to automatically correct the identical misspelling when you type it in the future.
8. Click the correctly spelled word in the **Suggestions:** list and click the **Change** button.
9. Click the **Add** button to add the word to the dictionary for future spell checks.

Notes:

Grammar checking is available only in Outlook 2010 and Word 2010.

10. Click the **Ignore** button to leave the word as it is and go on to the next word.
11. Click the correctly spelled word in the **Suggestions** list and click the **Change All** button to correct all identical misspellings throughout the document.
12. Click **Close** button after the spelling is completed.

Using AutoCorrect

AutoCorrect is a feature that automatically corrects common typing errors. The common typing errors involved in entering the word *the* or *When* (*teh, WHen* for example) are automatically corrected.

1. Click the **File** tab, and choose **Options**. The **PowerPoint Options** dialog box appears. In the left pane, click **Proofing** page options. In the right pane, click **AutoCorrect Options...** button.

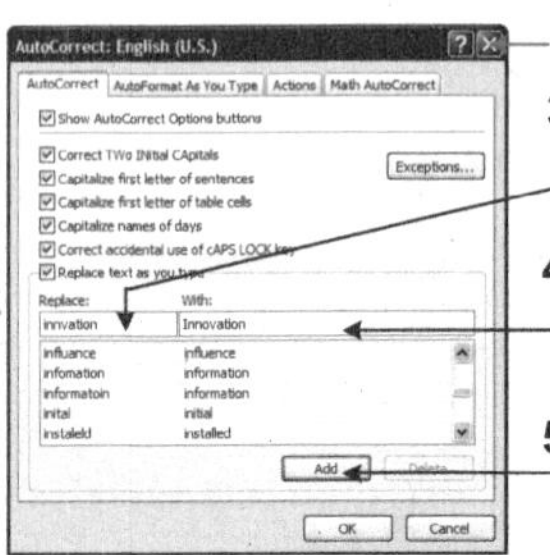

2. The **AutoCorrect** dialog box appears.
3. In the **Replace:** text box, enter the characters or words you want to type misspell. For example, type innovtion.
4. In the **With:** text box, type the correct spellings of the word. For example, type innovation.
5. Click **Add** button. And then click the OK button.

Inserting a Table Slide

PowerPoint includes a Table feature you can use for displaying columns and rows of data. Insert a table in a slide with the Table button in the Insert tab or with the Insert Table button in a Content placeholder.

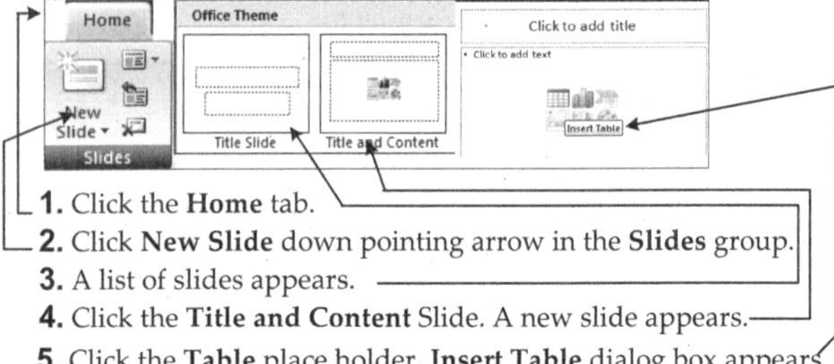

1. Click the **Home** tab.
2. Click **New Slide** down pointing arrow in the **Slides** group.
3. A list of slides appears.
4. Click the **Title and Content** Slide. A new slide appears.
5. Click the **Table** place holder. **Insert Table** dialog box appears.

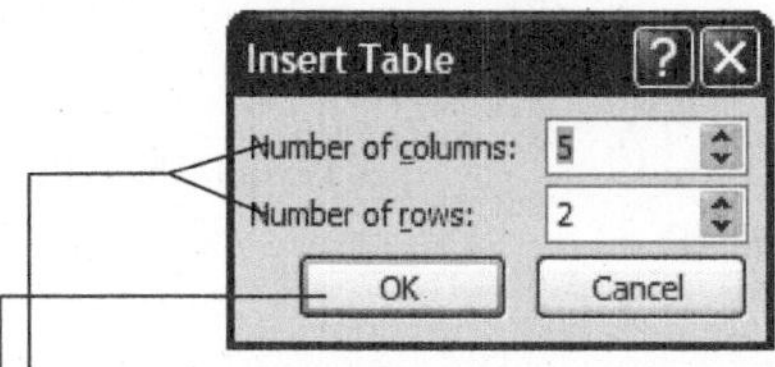

6. In the Insert Table dialog box, enter the number of columns and the number of rows you want to insert in the table. Or you can type the number of rows and columns.
7. After you specify the number of rows and columns, click OK to create the table.

Notes:

Selecting Columns and Rows

In Table Tools Contextual tab, click Layout tab. In Table group click Select drown pointing arrow and choose desired choice you want to select.

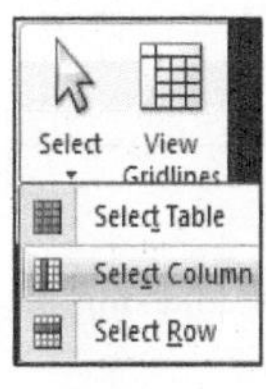

Entering Text in Table

When you create a new table, an empty table appears within a gray frame on the slide. When you insert a table, the insertion point flashes in the first cell in the upper left corner of the table. The text you type appears at the insertion point. After entering the text in the table and to exit the editing mode, click anywhere outside the table.

Editing a Table

Once you have created a table and entered text or numbers, you can modify its structure by adding, deleting, moving and copying cells, columns and rows. You can also change the width of columns, height of rows and merge or split cells to accommodate typed text in the cells.

Adding Columns and Rows

1. Click anywhere in the column next to where you want the new column to appear.
2. In **Table Tools** contextual tab, click **Layout** tab.

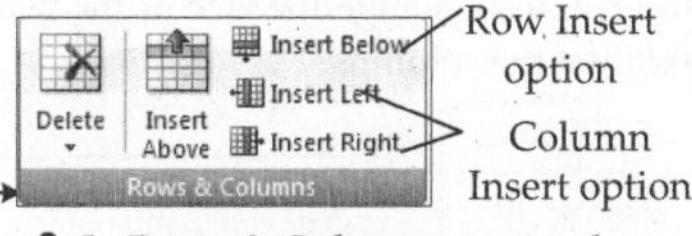

3. In **Rows & Columns** group choose Insert Columns to the Left or Right. A column is inserted to the left of the insertion point.

Hindi		Maths	Physics
45		56	35
68		35	45

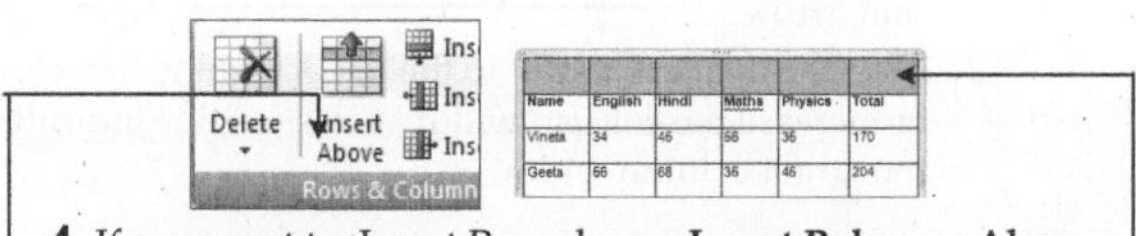

Name	English	Hindi	Maths	Physics	Total
Vineta	34	45	56	36	170
Geeta	56	68	35	45	204

4. If you want to Insert Row choose **Insert Below** or **Above.** **A Row** is inserted to the above of the insertion point.

Notes:

To insert column

Right click the mouse, choose Insert, a sub menu appears, choose Insert Columns to the Left or Right.

Deleting Columns and Rows

1. Select the columns/rows you want to delete.
2. In **Table Tools** contextual Tab, click **Layout** tab, in **Rows & Columns** group.

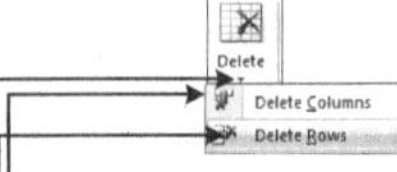

3. Click Delete down pointing arrow, a lists of option appears.
4. To Delete Columns choose **Delete Columns**. The column gets deleted.
5. To Delete Rows choose **Delete Rows**. The Row gets deleted.

Copying and Moving Cells

Once you select the contents of a cell, you can copy or move these to another location using drag and drop. Alternatively, use the **Cut**, **Copy** and **Paste** commands from the **Home** tab or from the shortcut menu that appears when you select a cell and click the right mouse button.

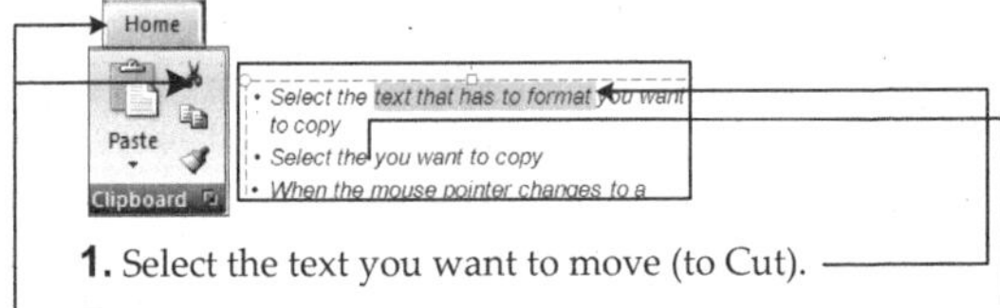

1. Select the text you want to move (to Cut).
2. Click **Home** tab and choose **Cut** option.
3. The selected text gets deleted.

To insert Row

Right click the mouse choose Insert, a sub menu appears, choose Insert Rows Above or Below.

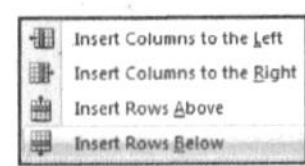

Changing Column Width

You can also change the size of the columns by adjusting the width of the columns.

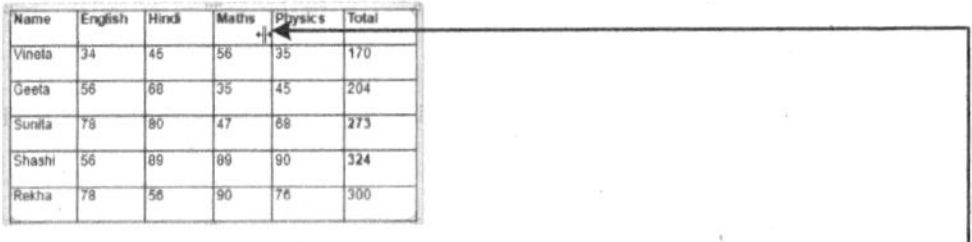

Name	English	Hindi	Maths	Physics	Total
Vinota	34	45	56	35	170
Geeta	56	68	35	45	204
Sunita	78	80	47	68	273
Shashi	56	89	89	90	324
Rekha	78	56	90	76	300

1. Position the pointer anywhere on the column's right border until the pointer changes to a double line and arrow.
2. Drag the column border to the left or right to decrease or increase the column width. A dashed line indicates the target column width.

Notes:

To move the selected text using drag and drop— Position the mouse pointer over the selected text, press and hold down the left mouse button and drag the text to the destination cell.

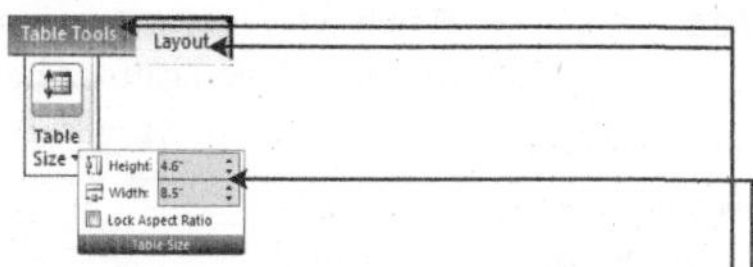

3. Release the mouse button. The column width is changed to the new size you specified by dragging.
   Or
4. In **Table Tools** contextual tab, click **Layout** tab. Click Table Size down arrow.
5. Select the **Column Width** up and down arrow, to set the width of the selected cells.

Changing Row Height

You can change the size of *rows* of a table by adjusting the height of the rows.

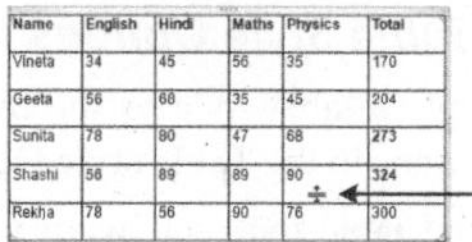

Name	English	Hindi	Maths	Physics	Total
Vineta	34	45	56	35	170
Geeta	56	68	35	45	204
Sunita	78	80	47	68	273
Shashi	56	89	89	90	324
Rekha	78	56	90	76	300

1. Position the pointer anywhere on the row's right border until the pointer changes to a double line and arrow.
2. Drag the column border to the left or right to decrease or increase the column width. A dashed line indicates the target column width.
3. Release the mouse button. The column width is changed to the new size you specified by dragging.

   Or

To copy the selected text using drag and drop— Position the mouse pointer over the selected text, press and hold the key, press and hold down the left mouse button and drag the text to the destination cell.

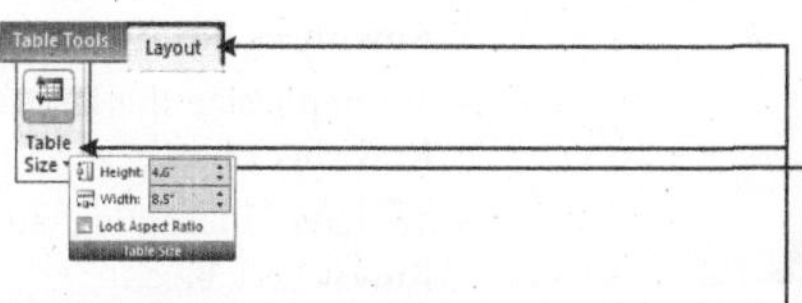

4. In **Table Tools** contextual tab, click **Layout** tab. Click **Table Size** down arrow.
5. Select the **Row Height** up and down arrow, to set the height of the selected cells.

Changing a Table Style

Any table that you add has a table style applied to it automatically. Thumbnails of table styles appear in the Quick styles gallery in the Table Styles group.

Notes:

When you delete the contents of a cell, you do not delete the cell. To delete the cell, you must merge the cell with another or delete the column or row.

When you place your mouse pointer over a Quick Style thumbnail, you can see how the Quick Style affects your table.

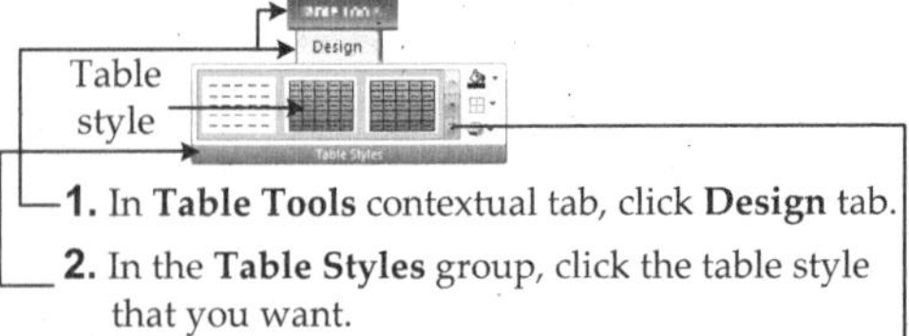

1. In **Table Tools** contextual tab, click **Design** tab.
2. In the **Table Styles** group, click the table style that you want.
3. Click the **More** button, a Style gallery opens.

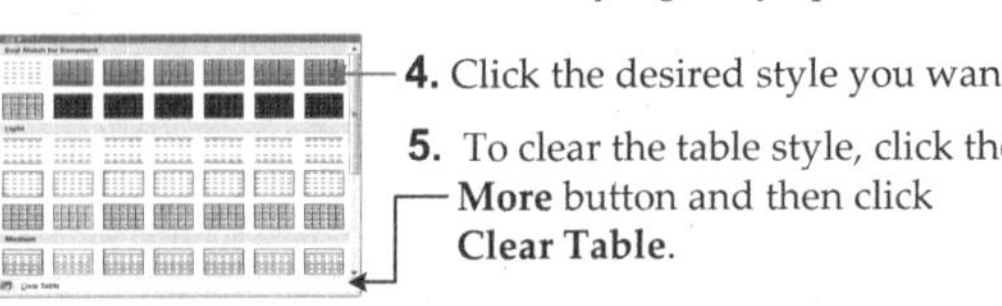

4. Click the desired style you want.
5. To clear the table style, click the **More** button and then click **Clear Table**.

Change Table Style Options

You can apply a table style to specific parts of your table by selection options in the **Table style Options** group.

1. Click the table that you want to change the table style option.

To add a row at the end of a table, click the last cell of the last row, and then press TAB.

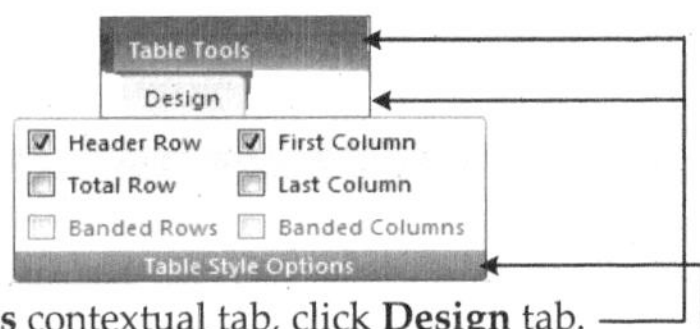

2. In **Table Tools** contextual tab, click **Design** tab.
3. In **Table Style Options** group, there are six options.
   - To emphasize the first row of the table, select the **Header Row** check box.
   - To emphasize the last row of the table, select the **Total Row** check box.
   - To have alternating striped rows, select the **Branded Rows** check box.
   - To emphasize the first column of the table, select the **First Column** check box.
   - To emphasize the last column of the table, select the **Last Column** check box.
   - To have alternating striped columns, select the **Branded Column** check box.
4. Select the desired options you want to apply in the table and click the options check box.

*To maintain the same ratio between the height and width of the table when you resize it, select the **Lock Aspect Ratio** check box.*

Notes:

To merge cells

1. Select the cells you want to merge.

*2. Click the **Layout** tab.*

*3. Click **Merge** down pointing arrow and choose **Merge cells** in the Merge group.*

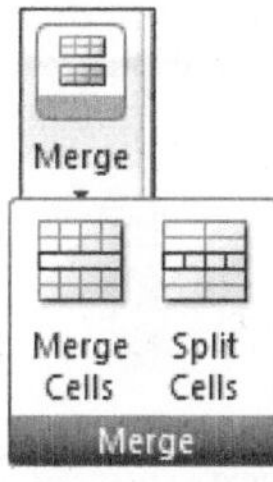

To Split cells

1. Select the cell that you want to split.

2. Click Split Cells options in Merge group.

3. The cell is split into two cells of equal width

Adding Border and Fills

PowerPoint establishes default borders around cells and the table itself, on the current presentation template. You can change borders separating cells, columns and rows or around the entire table.

1. Select the entire table, or the cells, columns, or rows around which you want to specify the border.

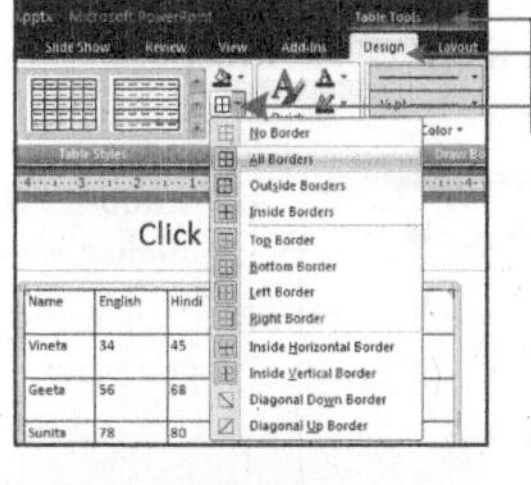

2. Under **Table Tools**, on the **Design** tab, click **Borders** down arrow. The actual name of this button changes depending on what was last selected.

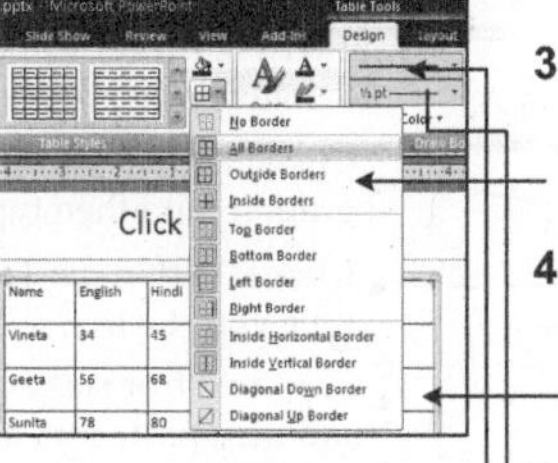

3. The borders drops down to show all the different border types. Click the border you want.
4. The selected portion of the table changes to reflect the new border type.
5. If you want to change the border line style, click down arrow and choose **Pen** Style in **Draw Borders** group.
6. Click the **Border Weight** and pen color in the **Draw Borders** group. Click the desired style you want to apply.

Creating a SmartArt Graphic

A SmartArt graphic is a visual representation of information that you can quickly and easily create, choosing from among many different layouts, to effectively communicate your message or ideas. When you create a SmartArt graphic, choose a type of SmartArt graphic, such as Process Hierarchy, Cycle or Relationship. It is similar to SmartArt graphic. Each type contains several different layouts. After you choose a layout, it is easy to change the layout for your SmartArt graphic.

To move a table and create a duplicate of it, press and hold Ctrl while you drag the table.

Notes:

You can use the ***Eraser*** *to delete borders between table cells. Under* ***Table Tools****, on the* ***Design*** *tab, in the* ***Draw Borders*** *group, click* ***Eraser****, or press and hold SHIFT while the pointer is a pencil ✎, and then click the borders that you want to delete.*

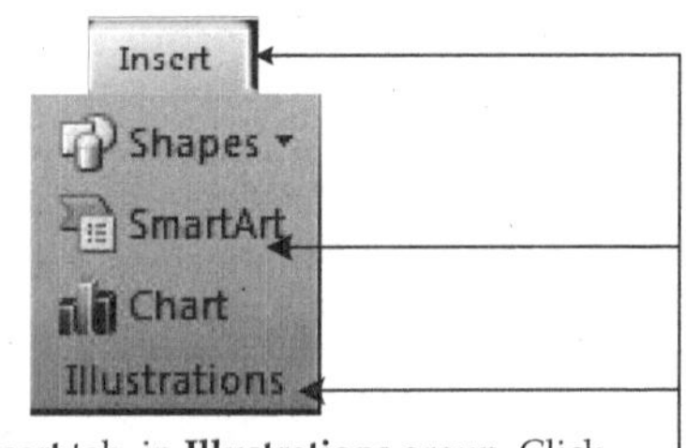

1. Click the **Insert** tab, in **Illustrations** group, Click **SmartArt** option.

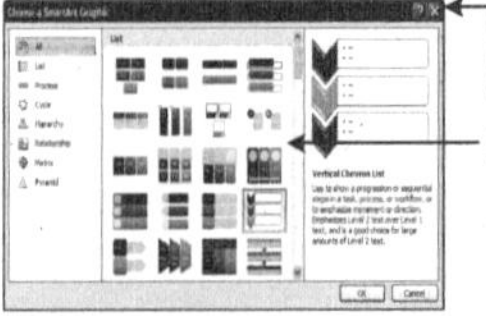

2. **Choose a SmartArt Graphic** dialog box appears.
3. Click the type of layouts that you want.

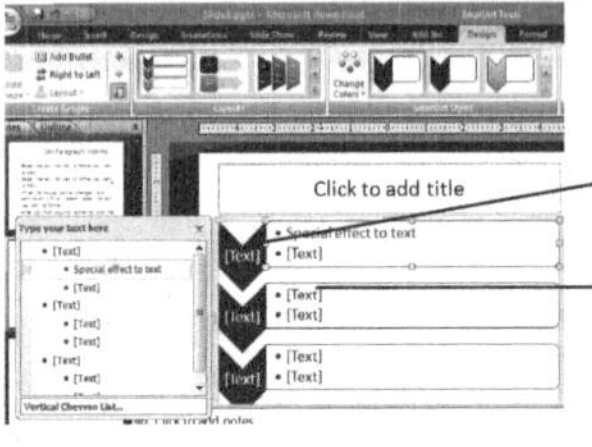

4. Enter your text by doing one of the following:
   - Click in a shape in your SmartArt graphic, and then type the text.
   - Click [Text] in the Text pane, and then type your text.
   - Copy text from other program, click [Text], and then paste into the Text pane.

Apply a SmartArt Style to a SmartArt graphic

A SmartArt Style is a combination of various effects, such as line style, bevel, or 3-D, etc. that you can apply to the shapes in your SmartArt graphic to create a unique and professionally designed look.

Notes:

You can use only Office PowerPoint 2010 to save your SmartArt graphic in a graphics file format such as .gif, .jpg and .png.

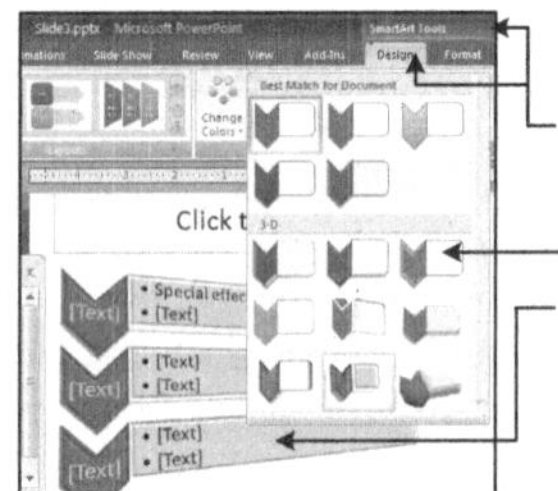

1. Click your SmartArt graphic.
2. Under **SmartArt Tools**, on the **Design** tab, in the SmartArt Styles group.
3. A list of SmartArt styles appear.
4. The selected styles applied in the slide.

Change the Colors of an Entire SmartArt Graphic

You can apply color variations that are derived from the theme colors to the shapes in your SmartArt graphic.

Notes:

If you want to create an organization chart, use the ***Organization Chart layout****. When you use this layout, additional functionality, such as the assistant shape and the hanging layouts, becomes available.*

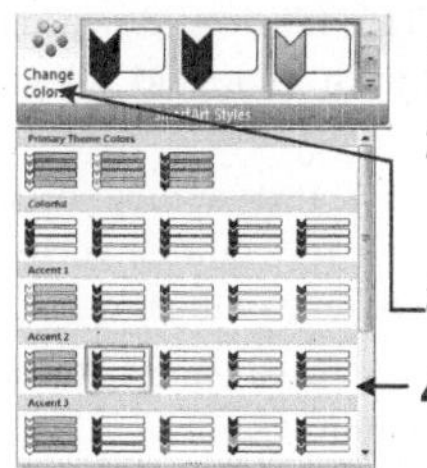

1. Click your SmartArt graphic.
2. Under **SmartArt Tools**, on the **Design** tab, in the **SmartArt Styles** group.
3. Click **Change Colors** down arrow.
4. A list of **Theme Colors** appears. Select the desired colors you want to apply.

Organization Chart

An *organization chart* is a graphical representation of the structure of an organization. By using a SmartArt graphic in PowerPoint 2010, you can create an organization chart and include it in your presentation.

To create an organization chart quickly and easily, you can type or paste text in the organization chart.

1. Click the **Insert** tab, in the **Illustrations** group, click **SmartArt** icon.
2. The **Choose a SmartArt Graphic** dialog box appears. Click **Hierarchy**, click an **Organization chart layout**, and then click OK.

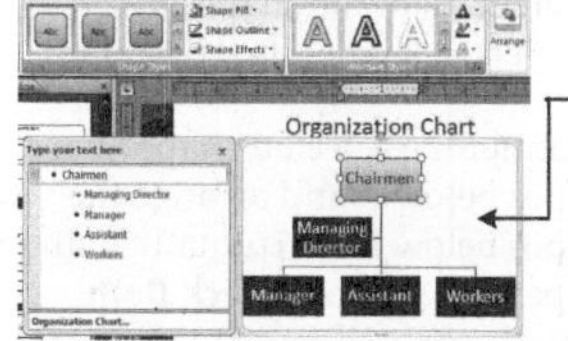

3. An Organization chart appears in the Slide.

Formatting the Organization Chart

Different components of an org chart which can be formatted are **Text Fill**, **Text outline** and **Text Effects**. While formatting the text, you can change fill, outline, effects of the text in the organization chart.

1. Select the text you want to format.

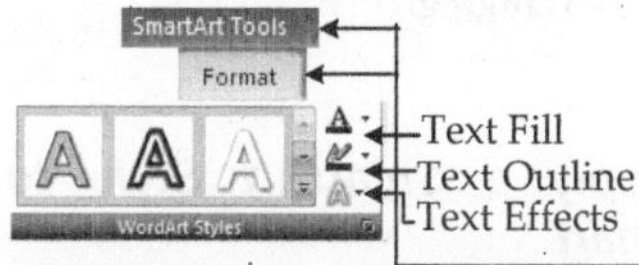

2. Under **SmartArt Tools** on **Format** tab, in **WordArt Styles** group.

Notes:

*The keyboard shortcut key to insert a new SmartArt graphic is **Alt + N + M** keys pressed together.*

Text Fill: Specify Text fill drop down menu and choose the desired text fill such as a solid color, gradient, picture or texture.

Text Outline: Specify text outline drop down menu and choose the desired text outline such as color, width and line style for the outline of the text.

Text Effects: Specify a visual effect to the text, such as shadow, reflection or 3-D rotation.

Changing the Hanging Layout of Organization Chart

A hanging layout affects the layout of all shapes below the selected shape.

1. Click the shape in the organization chart that you want to apply as hanging layout.
2. Under **SmartArt** Tools, on the **Design** tab, in the Create Graphic group, click **Organization Chart Layout** down arrow and then do one of the following options:

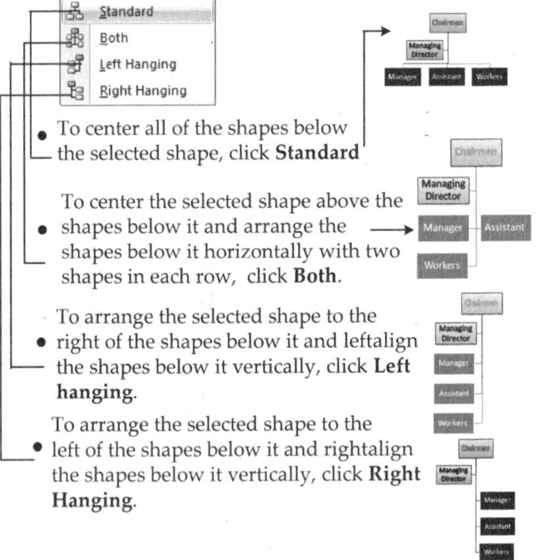

*The keyboard shortcut to switch between the Text pane and your SmartArt graphic is **Ctrl + Shift + F2** pressed together.*

Apply a SmartArt Style to an Organization Chart

A SmartArt Style is a combination of various effects, such as line style, bevel, or 3-D that you can apply to the shapes in your SmartArt graphic to create a unique and professionally designed look.

Notes:

Add a Picture fill to a Shape

*1. Click the shape in the **SmartArt** graphic that you want to add a picture fill to.*

*2. Under **SmartArt Tools**, on the **Format tab**, in the Shape Styles group, click the arrow next to **Shape Fill**.*

*3. Click **Picture**, locate the folder that contains the picture that you want to use, click the picture file, and then click **Insert**.*

Restore defaults layout and color:

*1. Click the **SmartArt graphic** to select it.*

*2. Under **SmartArt Tools**, on the **Design** tab, in the **Reset** group, click **Reset Graphic**.*

1. Click the SmartArt graphic whose SmartArt Style you want to change.

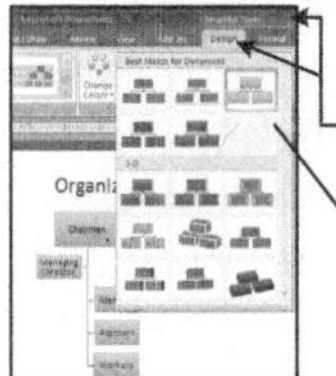

2. Under **SmartArt Tools**, on the **Design** tab, in the **SmartArt Styles** group, click the **SmartArt Style** that you want.
3. Click the **More** button to see the more Styles. Select the desired styles you want to apply.
4. When you place your pointer over a thumbnail, you can see how the SmartArt Style affects your SmartArt graphic.

Using Clip Art Gallery

Clip Art gallery is a collection of graphic files in PowerPoint that you can insert in presentations. It has built a gallery of clip art images into the Clip Art gallery.

1. Select the slide that contains a Clip Art slide.
2. Click the Clip Art icon in the slide. A clip art task pane appears.

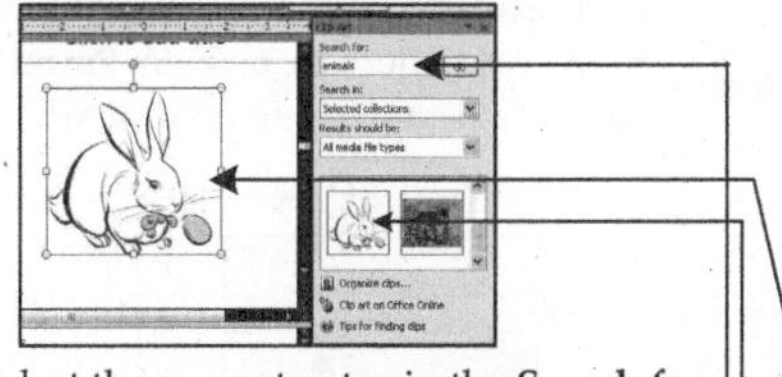

3. Select the current entry in the **Search for:** box or click in the box if there is no entry, type animals, and then click **Go**.
4. The task pane displays animals list.
5. Click the selected picture, once it appears at the center of the slide or select the picture, it appears a small arrow at the right of the side of the picture. Click the arrow and then Insert.
6. When you are finished using the **Clip Gallery**, click the **Close** button on the **Clip Gallery** title bar.

Insert a ScreenShot

You can quickly and easily add a screenshot to enhance the readability or capture information without leaving the program that you are working in.

Notes:

To create a perfect square or circle (or constrain the dimensions of other shapes), press and hold SHIFT while you drag.

1. Click the slide that you want to add the screenshot to.

2. Click the **Insert** tab in the **Images** group, choose Screenshot.

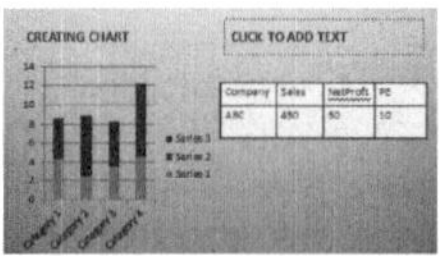

Do one of the following options:

- To add the whole window, click the thumbnail in the **Available Windows** gallery.
- To add part of the window, click Screen Clipping, and when the pointer becomes a cross, press and hold the left mouse button to select the area of your screen that you want to capture.

Add WordArt

WordArt is a gallery of text styles that you can add to your documents to create decorative effects, such as shadowed or mirrored (reflected) text. In PowerPoint 2010,. you can also convert existing text into WordArt.

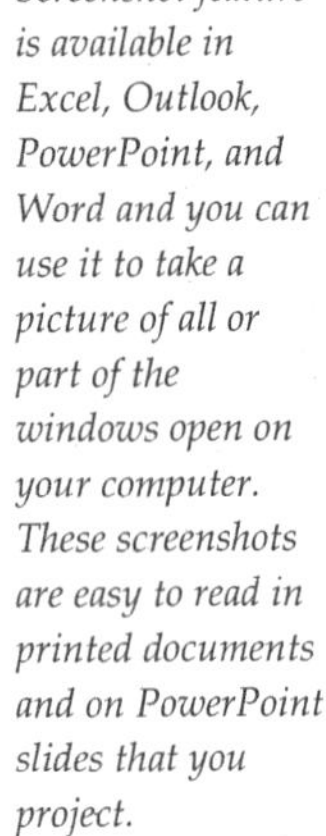

Screenshot feature is available in Excel, Outlook, PowerPoint, and Word and you can use it to take a picture of all or part of the windows open on your computer. These screenshots are easy to read in printed documents and on PowerPoint slides that you project.

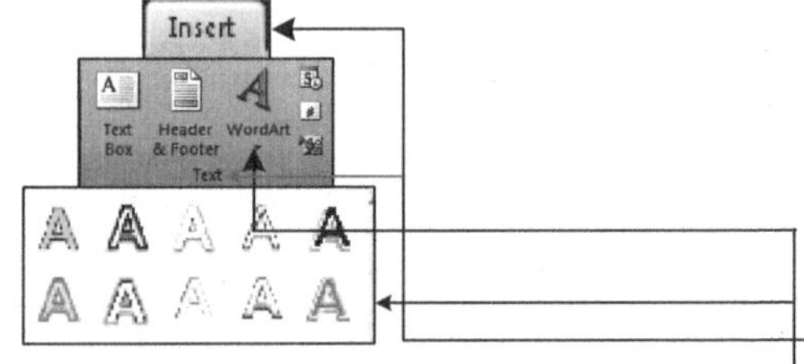

1. Select the slide on which you want to add a special effect.
2. Click the **Insert** tab, in the **Text** group.
3. Click **WordArt**, click down arrow and choose the WordArt style that you want.
4. Enter your text.

Drawing with Shapes

PowerPoint Shapes are familiar shapes that you are likely to use very often. These shapes are fully adjustable in size. Many shapes include additional adjusting handle, which allows you to adjust many characteristic features. A shape provides the following categories of tools: Lines, Block arrows, Rectangles, Stars and Banners, Basic shapes and Action buttons.

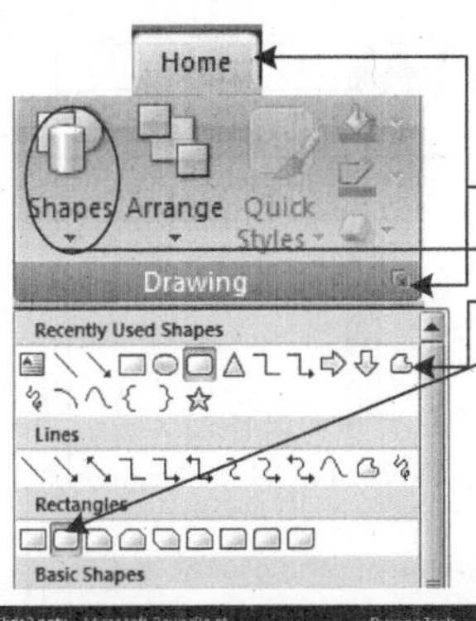

1. Click the **Home** tab, in the **Drawing** group.
2. Click **Shapes** down arrow.
3. A list of shapes gallery opens.
4. Click at **Rounded Rectangle** in the gallery.
5. After select the shape the mouse pointer changes to plus sign, drag the rounded rectangle. A rectangle appears. And you apply style to the shape.

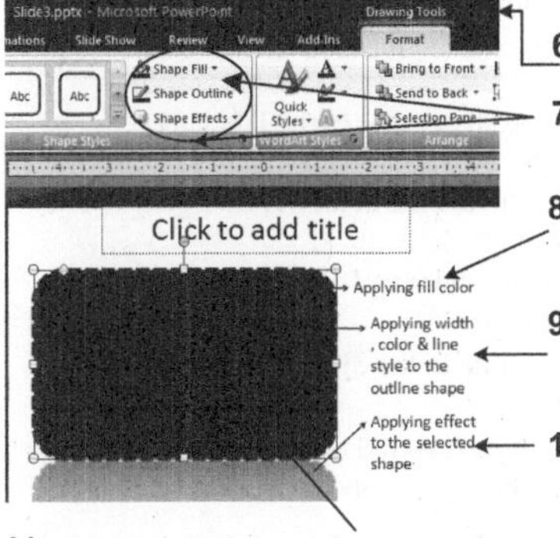

6. Select the shape and click **Drawing Tools**.
7. In **Shape Styles** group. You can add **fill, outline** and **effect** to the shape.
8. Applied shape fill color to the selected shape with a solid color, gradient, picture or texture.
9. Applied shape outline to specific color, width, and line style for the outline of the selected shape.
10. Applied shape effects to apply a visual effect to the selected shape such as shadow, reflection etc.
11. After applied the style to your shape appears as shown above.

Notes:

Flipping an Object

Flipping means to turn an object by 180°, either horizontally or vertically (leading to a lateral/vertical inversion respectively).

Rotating and Flipping Objects

You can change the position of shapes by rotating or reversing them. Reversing a shape is also referred to as creating a mirror image or flipping. You can rotate a single object or a group of objects around its own center.

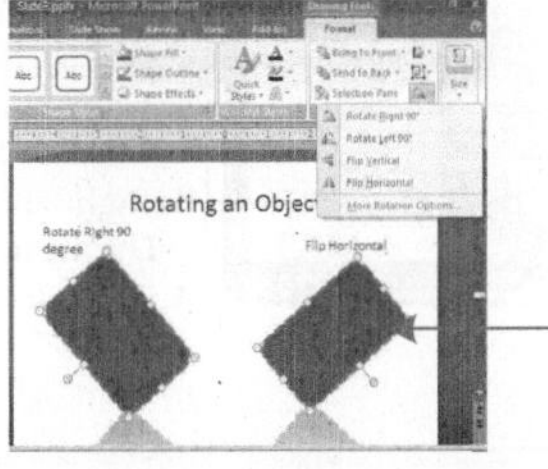

1. Select the drawing object, by clicking mouse pointer on it.

Notes:

To resize the shape, click it, and then drag its ***sizing*** ***handles****(sizing handle: One of the small circles or squares that appears at the corners and sides of a selected object. You drag these handles to change the size of the object.)*

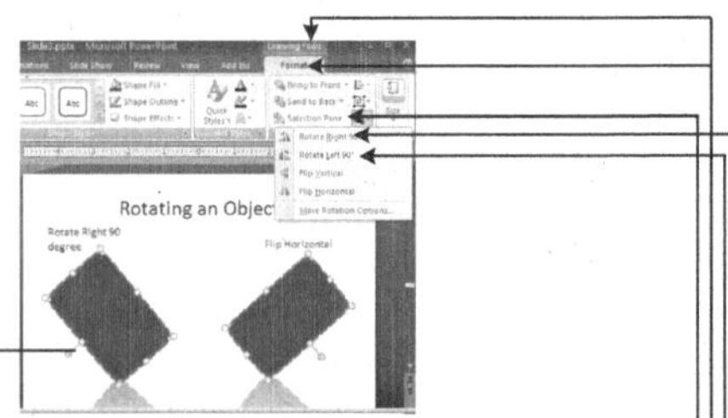

2. Under **Drawing Tools** in the **Format** tab of **Arrange** group.
3. Click **Selection Pane** down arrow and choose one of the following options:
   - To rotate the shape 90 degrees to the right, click Rotate Right 90°
   - To rotate the shape 90 degrees to the left, click Rotate Left 90° Or
   - **Flip Horizontal:** Mirrors the object left to right (lateral inversion)
   - **Flip Vertical:** Rotates the object 180 degrees top to bottom (vertical inversion)
4. Drag the rotation handle in the direction that you want to rotate the shape.
5. When the object is in the desired angle position, release the mouse button. The object appears in its new rotated position

Duplicating Slides

To add a slide that contains the content of an existing slide in a presentation, you can duplicate the slide. You can duplicate i.e. copy or delete selected slides in slide sorter view also.

Delete the ***WordArt***

1. Select the ***WordArt*** *that you want to remove, then press* ***Delete*** *key.*

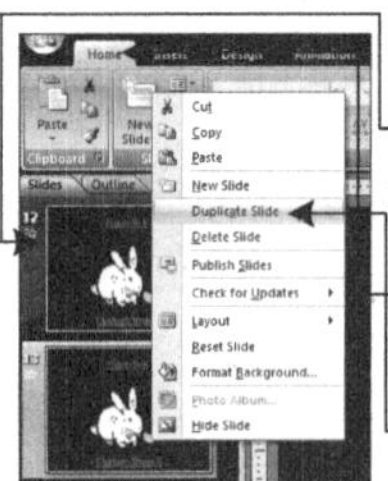

1. Select the slide or slides you want to duplicate.
2. Click the **Home** tab, in the **Slides** group, click **New Slide** down arrow and choose **Duplicate Selected Slides**. Or
3. Right-click the slide and choose **Duplicate slide**.
4. The selected slide gets duplicated.

To indent the new shape, press Tab from within the Text pane. To negative indent, press Shift +Tab.

Notes:

To select and delete multiple sequential slides, click the first slide that you want to delete, press and hold Shift key while you click the last side that you want to delete, right –click any selected slide, and then click Delete Slide.

Delete a Slide

To delete a slide from the presentation do the following:

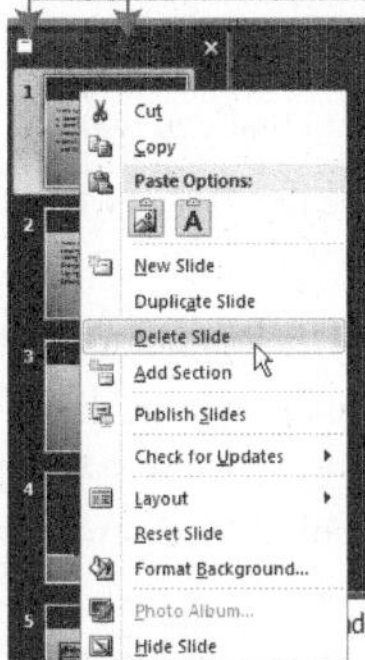

1. On the **View** tab, in the **Presentation Views** group, click **Normal**.
2. On the left pane that contains the Outline and Slides tabs, click the slides tab.
3. Right-click the slide and choose **Delete slide.**
4. After applying the command, the slide will get deleted.

Creating Charts in MS PowerPoint 2010

PowerPoint creates or modifies a chart using MS Graph. This a graphing program shared by all components like *Word, Excel, PowerPoint.* So if you know how to create graphics in one of the components, you can use the same technique in other components also.

Charts that you create will be embedded in PowerPoint 2010, and the chart data is stored in an Excel 2010 worksheet that is incorporated in the PowerPoint file.

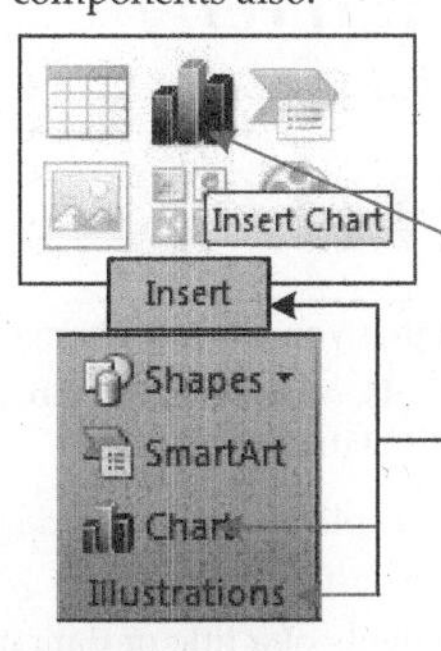

1. Click the **New Slide** in the **Slides** group. The new slide appears. The center of the slide contains *table, chart, Media Clips, SmartArt* etc. Or
2. Click the **Insert** tab, on the **llustrations** group, click the **Chart** icon.

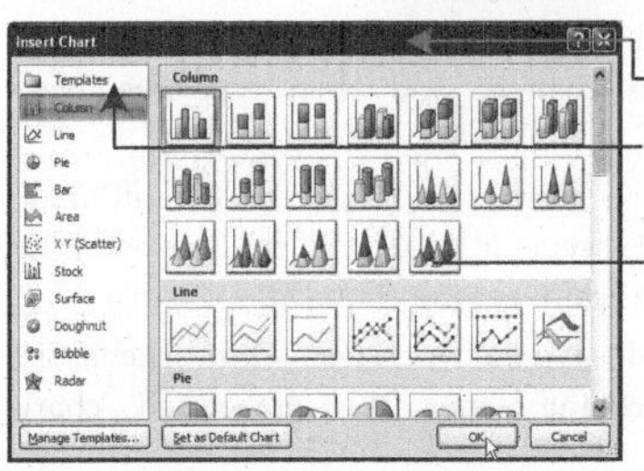

3. The **Insert Chart** dialog box appears.
4. Select the chart type under **Templates**.
5. For example, if you click the **Column** chart type, there are different types of columns in the column section. Select the desired chart type. Click OK.

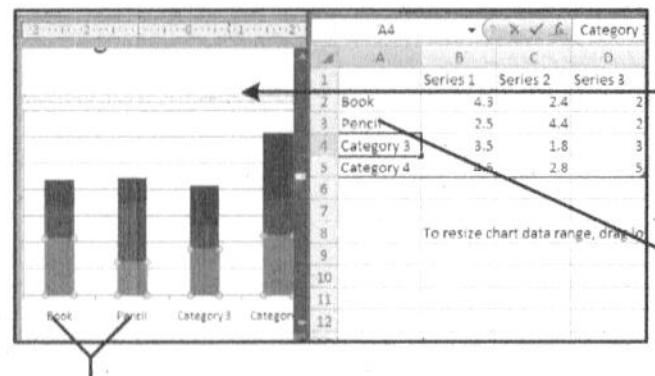

6. A sample chart appears in the Excel worksheet and the datasheet window containing the sample data for the chart appears.
7. In Excel to replace the sample data, click a cell on the worksheet, and then type the data that you want.
8. When you enter data in Excel you can see the data as well chart also simultaneously appearing in the PowerPoint.

Notes:

Edit axis or axis title

If a chart or axis title is not linked to a worksheet cell, do the following:

1. On a chart, click the chart or axis title to activate it, and then click it again to place the cursor in the text.

2. Type the new text

*3. Press **Enter**.*

*You can also right-click the title, and then click **Edit Text** on the shortcut menu.*

9. In Excel, click the **File** menu and then click Save **A**s.
10. In the Save As dialog box in the save **i**n: list, select the folder or drive that you want to save the worksheet.
11. In the File **n**ame: box, type a new name for the file.
12. Click Save.
13. In Excel, Click the File menu and then click **Close**.

Changing Data in an Existing Chart

If you create a chart for your presentation and then the data used in the chart changes, you can update the data so that the chart is accurate.

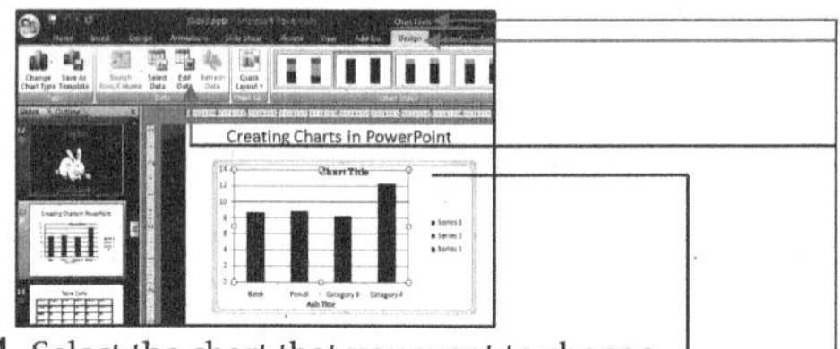

1. Select the chart that you want to change.
2. Under **Chart Tools**, on the **Design** tab, in the **Data group**, click **Edit Data**.
3. Excel opens in a split window and displays the worksheet that you want to edit.
4. To edit the contents of a title or data in a cell, in the Excel worksheet, click the cell that contains the title or the data that you want to change, and then type the new information.

   For example, if you want to change the default data (contain Category1), type it, you will see the chart in PowerPoint automatically getting changed.
5. If the chart is linked, save the worksheet. Or if the chart is embedded, PowerPoint saves the embedded chart automatically.

Notes:

*To add the background styles gallery to the Quick Access Toolbar, right-click a thumbnail, and then click **Add Gallery to Quick Access Toolbar**.*

6. After applying changes in Excel, click **File** menu and then click **Close**.

Adding Background Colour

You can not only add different colours and fill effects to the drawing objects, but also apply the same styles to the background of all the slides.

1. Click the slide or slides that you want to add a background style.

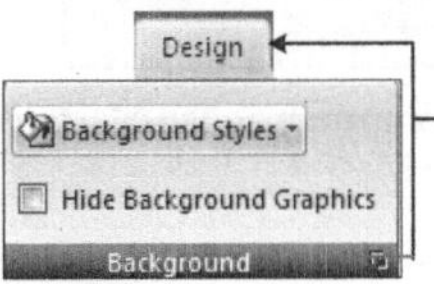

2. Click the **Design** tab, in the **Background** group, click the **Background Styles**.

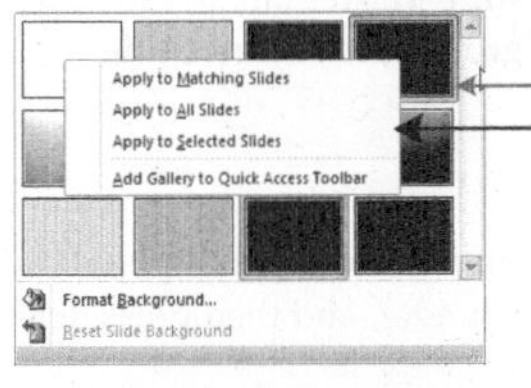

3. It displays a background gallery appears.

   Right click the background style that you want, and then do one of the following:

- To apply the background style to the Matching slides, click **Apply to Matching** slides.
- To apply the background style to the selected slides, click **Apply to Selected** slides.
- To apply the background style to all of the slides in your presentation, click **Apply to All** slides.

4. Click the desired option to apply the background style in presentation.

Notes:

PowerPoint Masters is a special slide that allows you to define all the formatting attributes and to add any common graphical object that will appear in your presentation.

PowerPoint Masters

PowerPoint Masters is an important concept. It is a concept for customizing presentation and giving it the design consistency.

PowerPoint 2007 has the following Masters:

1. Slide Master
2. Handout Master
3. Notes Master

Adding a Slide Master

A slide master is the top slide in a hierarchy of slides that stores information about the theme and slide layouts of a presentation, including the background, color, fonts, effects, placeholder sizes, and positioning.

Notes:

*The Shortcut keys to insert a new Slide Master is by pressing **Ctrl + M** keys together.*

The slide masters affect the look of your entire presentation, when you create and edit a slide master or corresponding layouts, you work in Slide Master view.

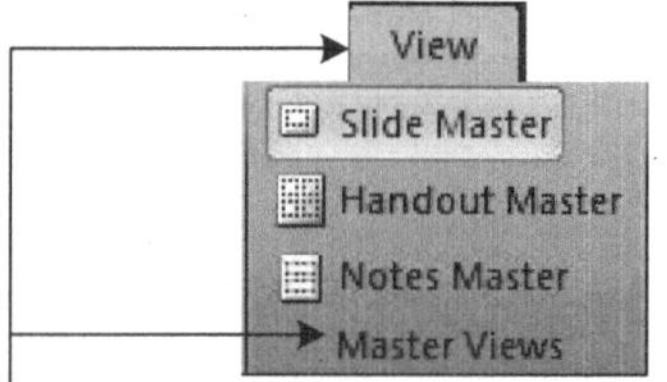

1. Click the **View** tab, in the **Master Views** groups, click **Slide Master**.

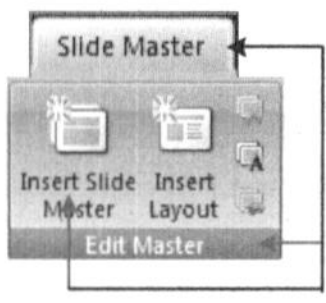

2. On the **Slide Master** tab, in the **Edit Master** group, click **Insert Slide Master**.

3. If you want to remove an unwanted, default placeholder, click the border of the placeholder, and then press delete.

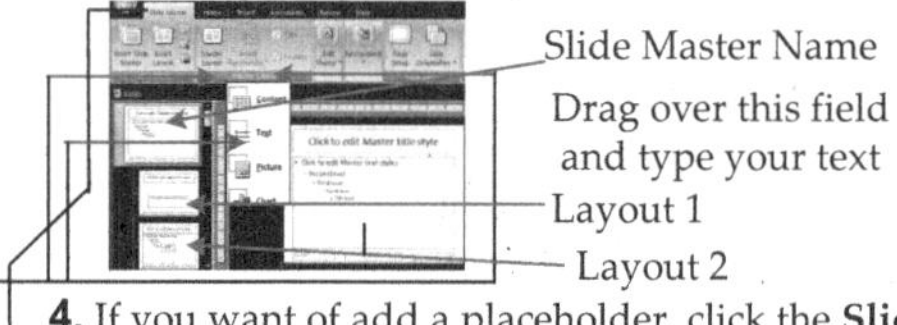

To resize a placeholder, drag one of its corner borders.

4. If you want of add a placeholder, click the **Slide Master** tab.
5. In the **Master Layout** group, click the arrow next to **Insert Placeholder**, and then click the type of placeholder you want.
6. Click the **File** menu and then click **Save As**.
7. In the **File name:** box, type a file name.
8. In the **Save as type:** list, click PowerPoint Templates, and then click **Save** button.

Using Notes Pages

Notes Pages act like a manuscript for your presentation. You would write the text you want to discuss during the course of a presentation, for each slide.

You can also type and format your notes as you work in Normal view, but to see how your notes pages will be printed and to see the full effect of any text formatting, such as font colors, switch to **Note page view**.

Notes:

Applying a Theme to a slide Master

*1. Click **View** tab, in the **Masters** groups, Click **Slide Master.***

*2. On the **Slide Master** tab, in the **Edit Theme** group, click the arrow below Themes, and then click a desired theme.*

Creating Notes

You would write the text you want to discuss during the course of a presentation, for each slide. You can also type and format your notes as you work in Normal view, but to see how your notes pages will be printed and to see the full effect of any text formatting, such as font colors, switch to **Note page view**.

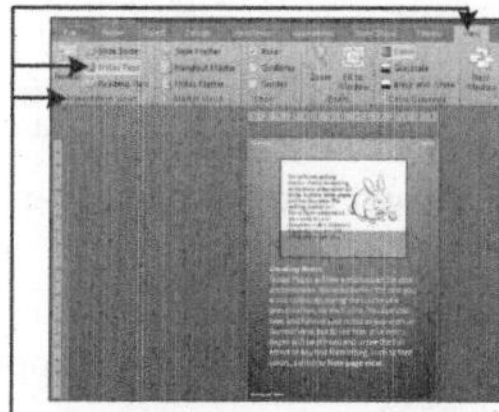

1. Click the **View** tab, in the **Presentation Views** click **Notes pages.**

In the **Notes Page View**, you see the entire Notes page as it will print. There is a picture of the slide at the top and a text place holder at the bottom. Click the place holder to begin entering the text for your Note.

Setting Date, Time and Page Numbers in Notes Pages

You can add date and time, headers, footers and page numbers to each of the Notes Pages also.

1. Click the **File** menu and choose **Print**. A **Print Preview** appears.

Notes Pages— These pages are like the script for your presentation. In this script, you have image of slides along with the words you want to speak for the specific slide.

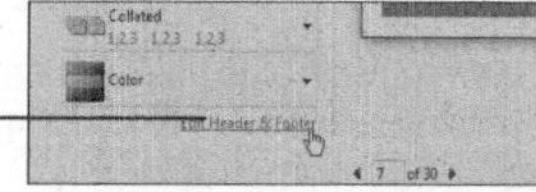

2. Click **Edit Header & Footer** option.

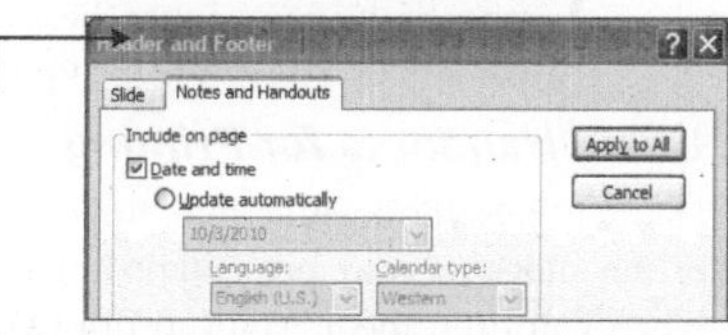

3. The **Header and Footer** dialog box appears. Now click the **Notes and Handouts** tab property sheet.

Notes:

Print the Notes Pages

1. Open the presentation for which you want to print notes.

2. Click the File tab, and then click Print

3. In the Print Preview ***view appears***

4. Under Setting *drop-down list and then choose* **Notes** ***pages.***

4. To specify the orientation, click the arrow under orientation and then click **Portrait** *or* ***Landscape.***

5. Click **Print**.

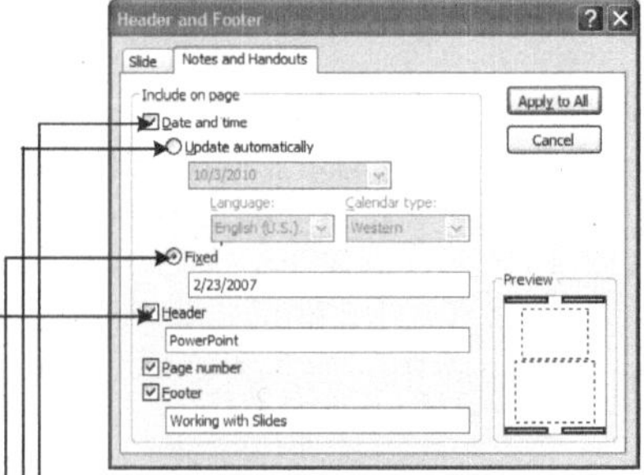

The **Header and Footer** dialog box offers the following options:

4. **Date and time:** If you select this option, the date and time appear in the upper right corner of the page.
5. **Update automatically:** select this option to print the actual date and time when printouts are made. Use the list box to select the format you would like the date and time to appear in.
6. **Fixed:** If you select this option, if you want to specify the specific date to be printed in text box.
7. **Header:** The header appears on the top left corner of the page. Enter the text for the header in the box below the option.

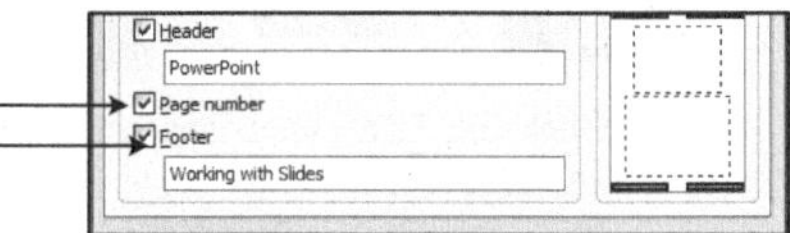

8. **Page Number:** The page numbers are shown as numerals only and appear in the lower-right corner of the page.
9. **Footer:** The footer appears in the lowerleft corner of the page. Enter the text for the footer in the box below the option.

Using Handouts for Printing

Handout lets you include two, three, six or nine small images of the slides in your presentation. You can select the format when you print them. You can print your entire presentation slides, outline, notes and audience handouts. You can also print specific slides, Full page slides, handouts, notes pages and outline pages.

Notes:

The header, footers, page numbers and the date on each handout will be printed if you have selected any of these items on your Notes Pages. The same is automatically applied to your Handouts.

1. Open the presentation you want to print.
2. Click the **File** tab and choose **Print**. The **Print Preview** view appears.

3. Click the **File** tab and choose **Print**. The **Print Preview** appears.
4. Under **Printer**, select the printer that you want to use.
5. Under **Settings**, do one of the following:

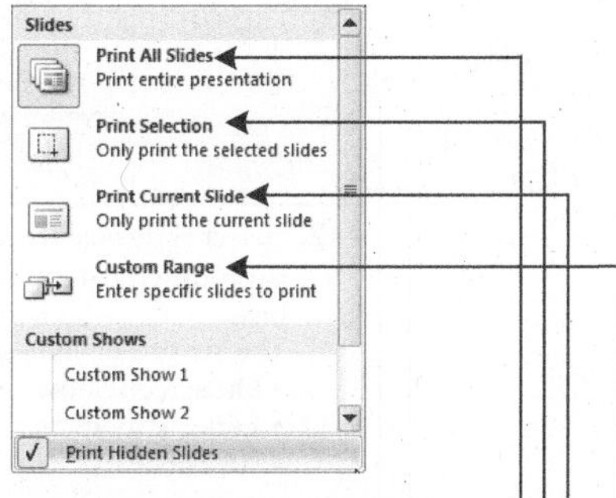

*The **Preview** box, located in the **Header and Footer** dialog box, displays the header and footer information in the location that the slide, handout, or notes page will display it.*

- To Print all slides, Click **Print All Slides**.
- To print one or more slides that you selected, click **Print Selection**.
- To print only the slide that is currently displayed, click **Current Slide**.
- To print specific slides by number, click **Custom Range of Slides,** and then enter a list of individual slides, a range or both. Use commans to separate the numbers and no spaces, for example, 1,5,7-11.

9. Select the options you want to apply.
10. After applying the option in the handouts section, click OK.

Set the Slide Size and Orientation for Printing

Notes:

The Handouts (3 Slides Per Page) format provides lines for the audience to take notes.

The page setup determines the size and orientation of the slides you created in PowerPoint 2010. In setting up the page you determine the orientation for the slides, the size of the slides, the starting number of the slides, the orientation for the notes, handouts and outline.

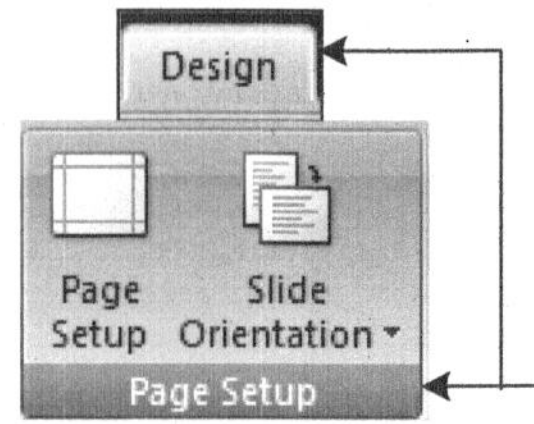

1. Click the **Design** tab, in the **Page Setup** group. Click **Page Setup**. The **Page Setup** dialog box appears.

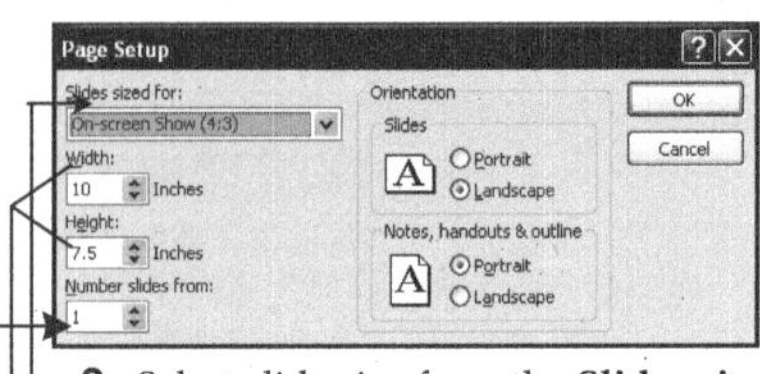

All slides in a presentation must be set to one type of orientation.

2. Select slide size from the **Slides sized for:** drop-down list in the **Page Setup** dialog box.
   The six preset slide sizes are:
   - On-screen Show
   - 35mm Slides
   - Letter Paper
   - Overhead Banner
   - A4 Paper
   - Custom
3. If you select custom option, then you specify the custom width and height in the **Width:** and **Height:** edit boxes.
4. To specify the starting number for the slides, enter the number you want to start the numbering of the slides in the **Number slides from:** edit box.

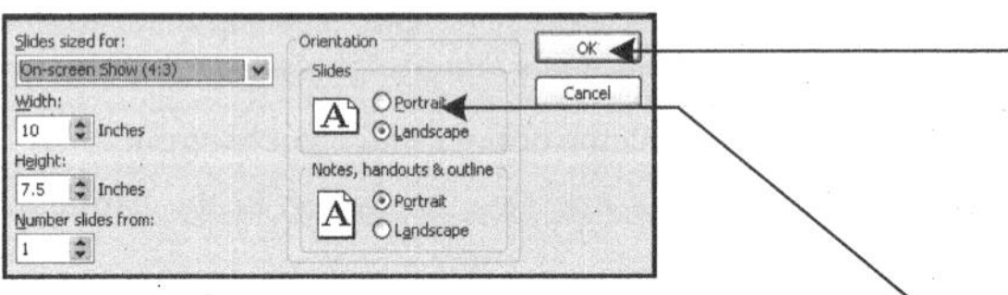

5. To set the orientation for the slide in the slides box, select between the **Portrait** and **Landscape** options.
6. Finally click OK.

Notes:

*Another way to select the slides to print is to switch to Slide Sorter or Outline view. For this, press and hold down the **Shift** key as you click each slide or slide icon. When you open the **Print** dialog box, click the Selection option in the **Print Range** section.*

*To select multiple sequential slides, click the first slide, and then hold down **Shift** key while you click the last slide that you want to select. To select non-sequential slides, hold down **Ctrl** key while you click each slide that you want to select.*

Overview of Layouts

You can use layouts to arrange objects and text on slide. A layout is one part of a slide master that defines positioning information for content that will appear on a slide. Layouts contain placeholders, such as titles and bulleted lists, and slide content such as SmartArt graphics tables, charts, shapes and clip art. While you can add text and object placeholder to a layout or slide master, you cannot add placeholders directly to a slide. PowerPoint 2010 includes five built-in, standard layouts. You can also create custom layouts that meet your specific needs.

Add a Layout

To add a layout, go to the Slide Master view, add a new layout, add text-specific and object-specific placeholders and then save the presentation as a template file.

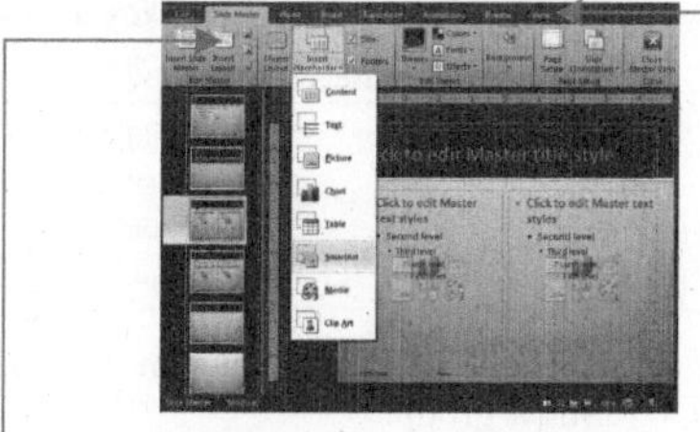

1. Click the **View** tab, in the **Master views**, click **Slide Master.**
2. In the pane that contains the slide master and layouts, click a location below the slide master where you want to add the new layout.
3. On the **Slide Master** tab, in the **Edit Master** group, click **Insert Layout**. A new layout slide is inserted.

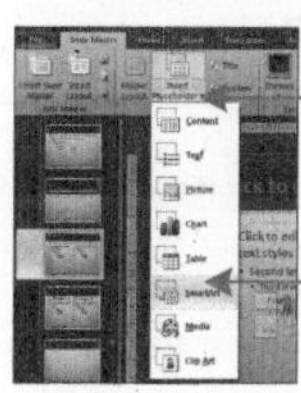

4. To add a placeholder, on the **Slide Master** tab, in the **Master Layout** group.
5. A list of Insert placeholder appears. Select the desired placeholder you want to apply.
6. The selected layout elements that you can include on a PowerPoint 2010 slide.
7. Click the **File** tab and then click **Save As.**
8. In the **File name:** box, type a file name.

Notes:

*To create a graceful ending to a slide show you can add a black slide at the end of presentation. Click **File** tab, click **Options**. **PowerPoint Options** dialog box appears. Click **Advanced Page**, under **Slide Show** click **End with black slide** check box. If you do not include the black slide option, then PowerPoint will reappear first slide after the last slide.*

To preview a custom show, click the name of the show in the Custom Shows dialog box, and then click Show.

9. In the **Save as type:** list, select PowerPoint Template and then click **Save** button.

Custom Shows

Use a basic custom show to give separate presentations to different groups in your organization. For example, if your presentation contains a total of five slides, you can create a custom show named "Custom 1" that includes just slides 1, 3 and 5. You can create a second custom show named "Custom 2" that includes slides 1, 2, 4 and 5. When you create a custom show from a presentation, you can always run the entire presentation in its original sequential order.

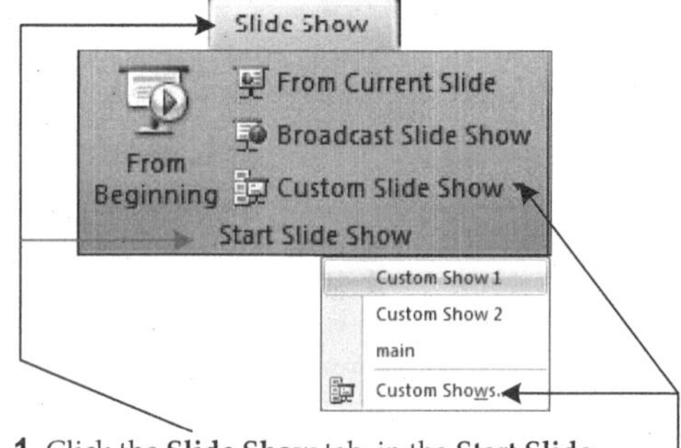

1. Click the **Slide Show** tab, in the **Start Slide Show** group.
2. Click the arrow next to **Custom Slide Show**, and then click **Custom Shows...** .

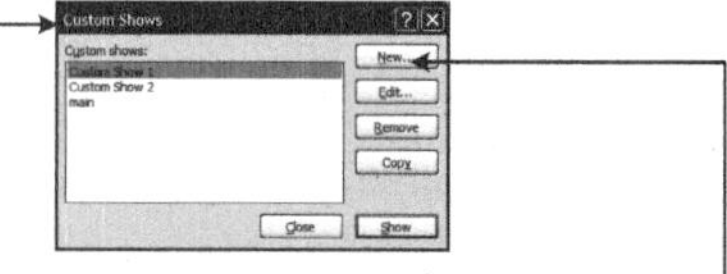

3. **Custom Shows** dialog box appears.
4. Click **New... button.**

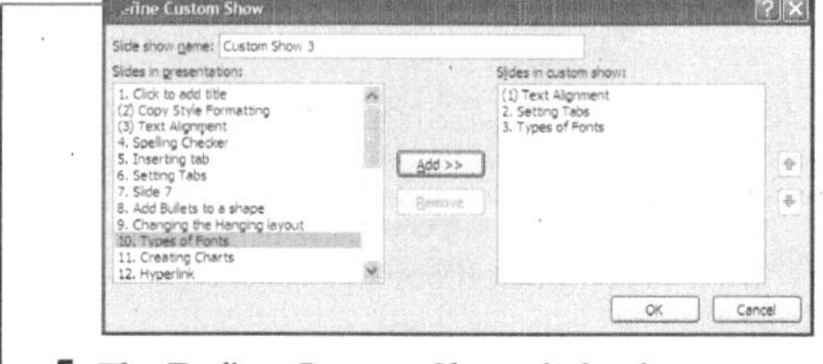

5. The **Define Custom Show** dialog box appears.

Notes:

Write on slides during a presentation

*1. In **Slide Show view**, right-click the slide that you want to write on, point to Pointer Options, and then click a pen or highlighter option.*

2. Hold down the left mouse button and drag to write or draw on your slides.

In Section A you will learn
Creating text
Adding text
Change the text case
Copying text

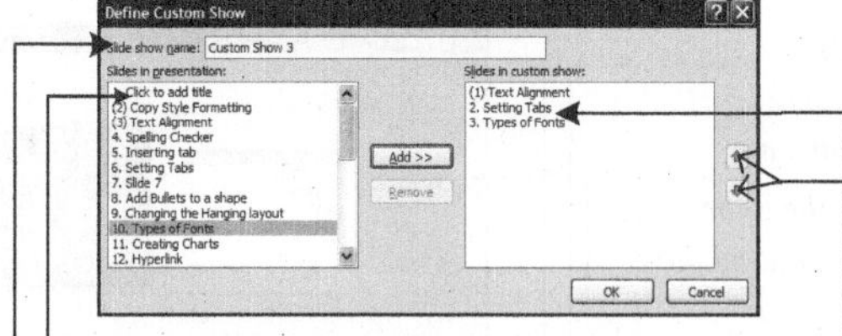

6. Under **Slides in presentation:** click the slides that you want to include in the custom show and then click **Add >>**
7. To change the order in which slides appear, under **Slides in custom show:** click a slide, and then click one of the arrow to move the slide **up** or **down** in the list.
8. Type a name in the **Slide show name:** box and then click OK. To create additional custom shows with any slides in your presentation, repeat steps 1 through 5.
9. To Preview a custom show, click the name of the show in the **Custom shows** dialog box, and then click Show button.

Hyperlinked Custom Shows

Use a hyperlinked custom show to organize content in a presentation. For example, create a **main** custom show about your company's new overall organization, you can then create a custom show for *department A* and name it as **custom show1** and then create a custom show for *department B* and name it as **custom show2** within the organization and link to these shows from the main presentation.

1. Repeat step from 1 to 5 as explained in Custom Show.
2. To create a hyperlink from the main show, select the text or object that you want to represent the hyperlink.

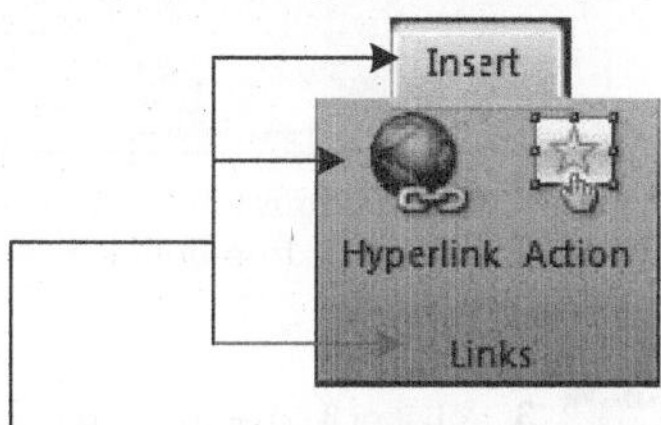

3. On the **Insert** tab, in the **Links** group, click **Hyperlink**.

✍ ***If you want to print your notes in color, select a color printer. Click the File tab, and then choose Print. The Print Preview view appears. Under Color drop-down list select Color options.***

Notes:

Remove a transition

*1. In the Pane that contains the Slides and Outline tab, select the **Slides** tab.*

2. On the Slides tab in Normal view, click the thumbnail of the slide that you want to remove the transition from.

*3. On the **Transitions tab** in the Ribbon, in the **Transition To This Slide** group, click **None**.*

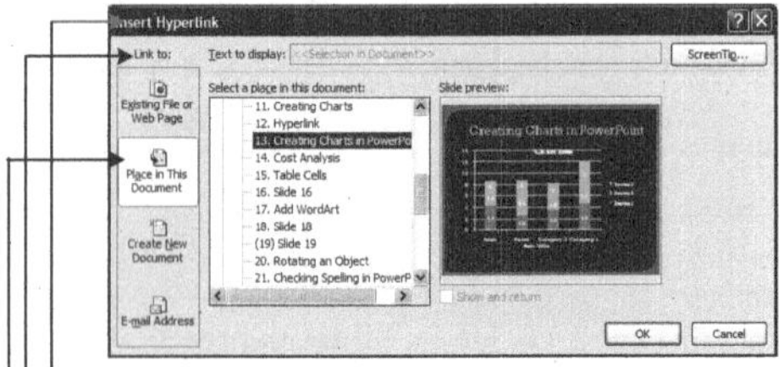

4. The **Insert Hyperlink** dialog box appears.
5. Under **Link to:** click **Place in This Document**.
6. Do one of the following:
   - To link to a custom show, in the **Select a place in this document:** list, select the custom show that you want to go through and then select the Show and return check box.
   - To link to a location in the current presentation, in the **Select a place in this document: list**, select the slide that you want to go to.
7. To **Preview** a custom show, click the name of the show (*main*) in the **Custom shows** dialog box and then click **Show** button.

Add Transitions between Slides

Slides transitions are the animation-like effects that occur in the slide show view, when you move from one slide to the next. You can control the speed of each slide transition effect. You can also add sound.

1. Select the slide(s) you want to add a transition effect.

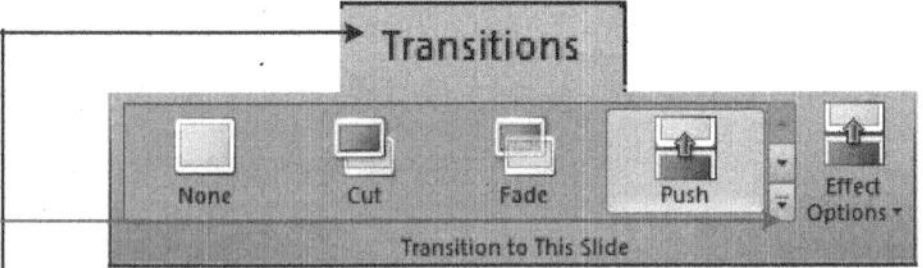

2. Click the **Transitions** tab. In the **Transition to This slide** group, click drop-down arrow and then click the **More** button.

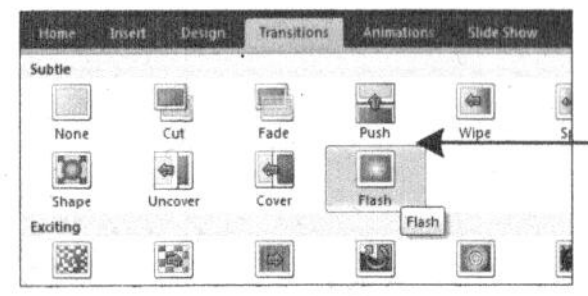

3. A list of Transitions Options appears. Select the desired effect applied during the slide show. For example here we select Flash under subtle.

Notes:

Change the transition to a slide

1. In the pane that contains tabs, select the Slides tab.

2. On the Slides tab in the normal view, click the thumbnail of the slide that has the transition that you want to change.

3. On the Transitions tab in the Ribbon, in the Transition To This Slide group, click a different slide transition effect for that slide.

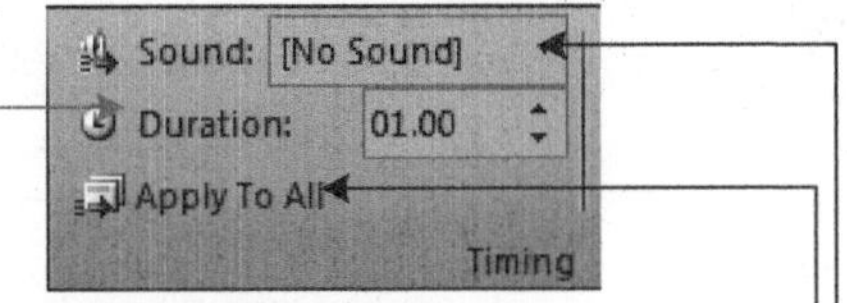

4. To set the duration of the transition between the previous slide and the current slide, click the **Duration:** box, type or select the speed that you want.

5. If you Apply to all slides, click **Apply to All** in the **Transition to This Slide** group.

6. Select the **Sound:** option to give sound transitions to your slide show from the Sound drop-down list in the **Timing** group.

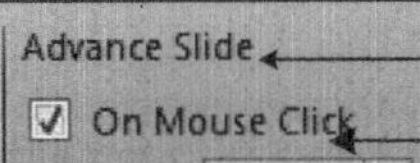

7. The Advance section has two options for transition:

- On mouse click check box if you want the transition to take place on clicking the mouse.

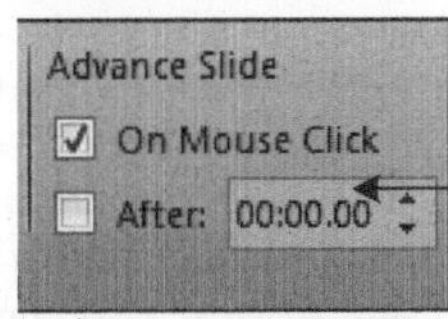

- To advance the slide at a specified time, click **After:** check box, enter the number of seconds that you want.

8. After applying all options, you can see the effect in the Slide show. Click the **Slide Show** tab, in the **Start Slide Show** group, click From Beginning icon. Click the next button (i.e.→) to go to the next slide.

Transitions are another way that you can add visual effects to your slides.

Animate Text and Objects

You can animate the text, pictures, shapes, tables, SmartArt graphics, and other objects in PowerPoint 2010 presentation to give them visual effects, including entrances, exits, changes in size or colour, and even movement.

The shortcut key to Insert Hyperlink press Ctrl + K keys together.

Notes:

Delete the sound effect

1. Click the slide that contains the sound that you want to delete.

*2. In Normal view, select the slide and then click the Transitions tab of Timing group Click **No Sound** in the Sound drop-down list.*

In the Set Up group Play Narrations if checked, plays back the narrations when the slide show displayed.

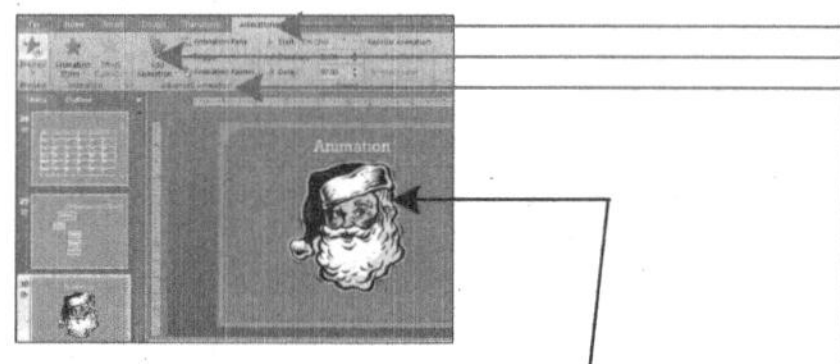

1. Select the object you want to animate.

2. Click **Animations** tab in the **Advanced Animation** group, click **Add Animation** drop-down arrow.

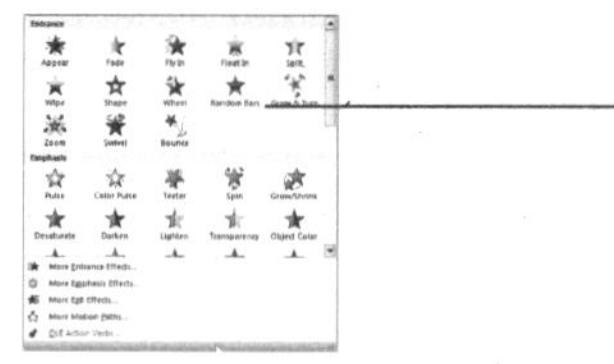

3. A list of animations options appears. Select the desired option you want to apply.

4. Click the **Preview** button in the **Preview** group. It will preview only the current slide only.

Running a Slide Show

When you develop a slide show in Slide Sorter view, you can get a preview of transition effects for all slides. But to see the transitions full-screen and to see animated or bulleted text slides, you must select the presentation as a slide show.

1. Click the **Slide Show** tab, on the **Slide Show From Beginning** icon or pressed **F5** keys.

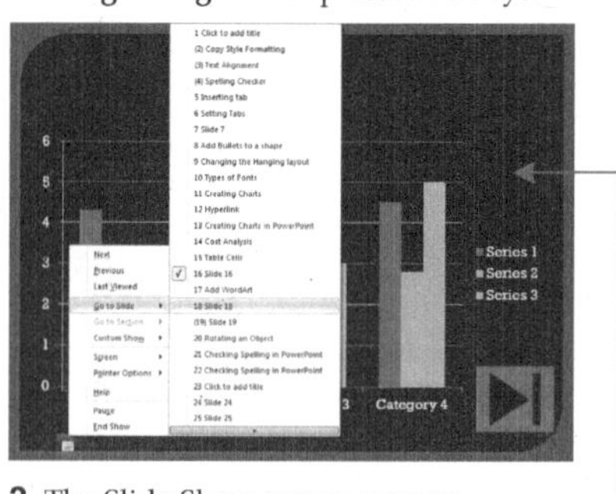

2. The Slide Show screen appears.

3. In the Slide show, you go to next slide, press **N** key or click the **Backspace** key to go the previous slide. Or

Notes:

Hide a slide

1. In the pane that contains the Outline and Slides tabs, click the Slides tab.

2. Right-click the slide that you want to hide, then click ***Hide Slide.***

3. The hidden slide icon ▧ *appears with the slide number inside, next to the slide that you have hidden.*

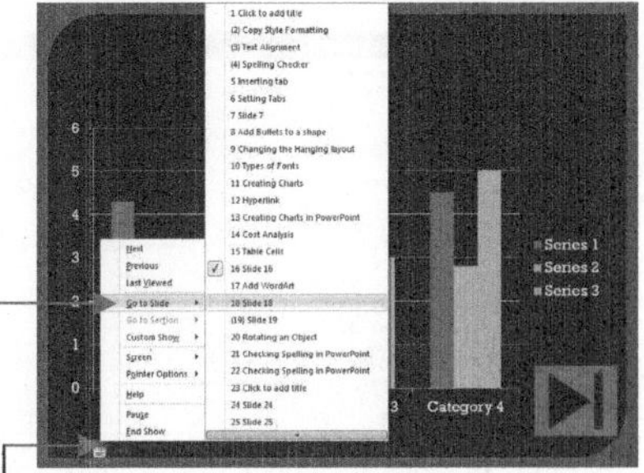

4. During the Slide show you can click the icon in the bottom of the screen.

5. A list of options appears. Click **Go to Slide** option. A sub menu appears, select the desired slide you want to go.

Set Up a Slide Show Option

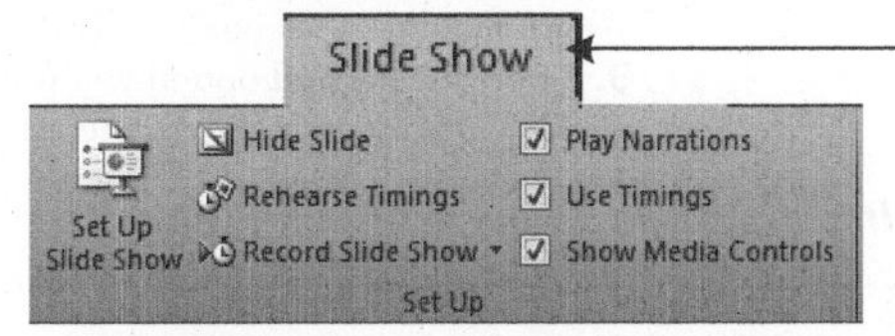

1. Click the **Slide Show** tab in the **Set Up** group, Choose **Set Up Slide Show** icon.

2. The **Set Up Show** dialog box appears.

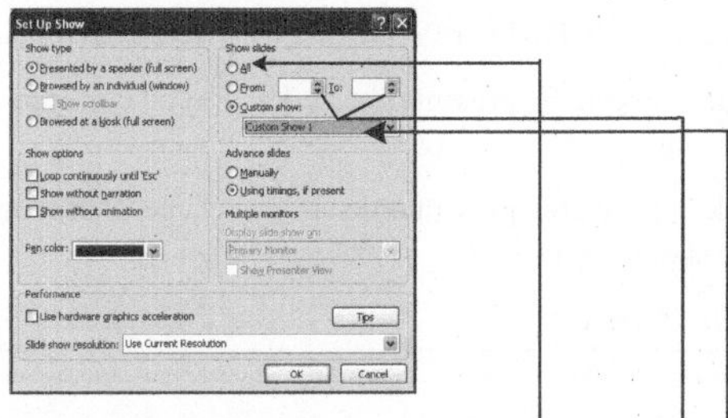

3. To Show all slides in your presentation, Click **All** in the Show slides section.

4. To show a specific group of slides from your presentation, enter a starting and ending slide in **From:** and **To:** edit boxes.

5. To start a custom slide presentation that derives from another presentation, click **Custom Show:** drop down list and then click the presentation that you want to view as a custom show.

Rehearse Timings: Displays the slide show in rehearsal mode, allowing you to set timings for each slide, a toolbar will be used.

Notes:

Record Slide Show: Record (with a microphone connected to the computer) narration, laser pointer usage, and create timing for playback later (more powerful version of Rehearse Timings) to go along with show for use when presenter is not available.

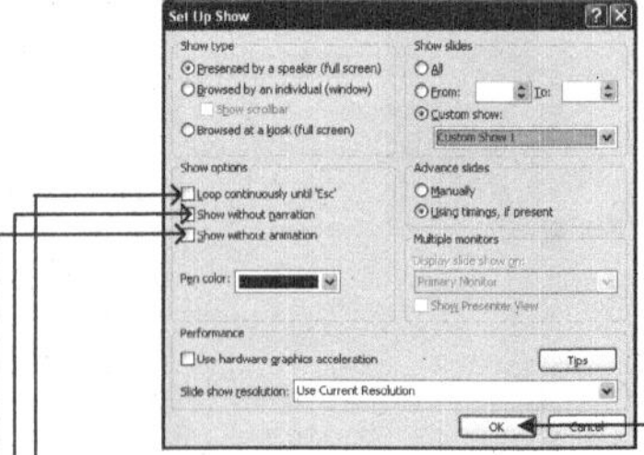

6. Click the check box, to play a sound file or animation continuously, select the **Loop continuously until press Esc** key.
7. To show a presentation without playing an embedded narration, select the show **without narration** check box.
8. To show a presentation without playing an embedded animation, select the Show without animation check box.
9. Select the desired option you want to set in the Set Up Show dialog box, then click OK button.

Controlling the Slide Show with a keyboard

Use timings if checked, uses the timings created previously when the slide show is displayed.

Press This	To Perform This Action
Spacebar, →, ↓, PgDn or N	Advance to next slide
Backspace ←, ↑, PgUp or P	Return to previous slide
Toggle between the presentation and a black slide	Type B or type a period (.).
Toggle between the presentation and a white slide	Type W or type a comma (,).
End the Slide show	Press Esc key or type a hyphen (-).

MS Outlook 2010

Getting Started

MS Outlook 2010 is an application package of MS Office. This is a powerful tool of *Personal Information Management* (PIM) program that helps a person in organizing his schedule, keep track of contacts and communicate with others. Many people have several appointments to keep and tasks to accomplish in a day. Outlook 2010 helps them by maintaining schedule and by organizing the information in a structured and readable manner. By having this facility, one can keep a track of meetings, e-mail messages, and notes with a particular contact. It consists of Outlook's Calendar, Contacts, Tasks and Notes. Contact information can be found via Find option, which can be accessed from the calendar, e-mail, and other Outlook components. PIMs gives an opportunity to individuals and workgroups to organize, find, view and share information in a convenient way.

Notes:

To open any MS Office Package you need to use the same method as explained in the following steps.

Starting MS Outlook 2010

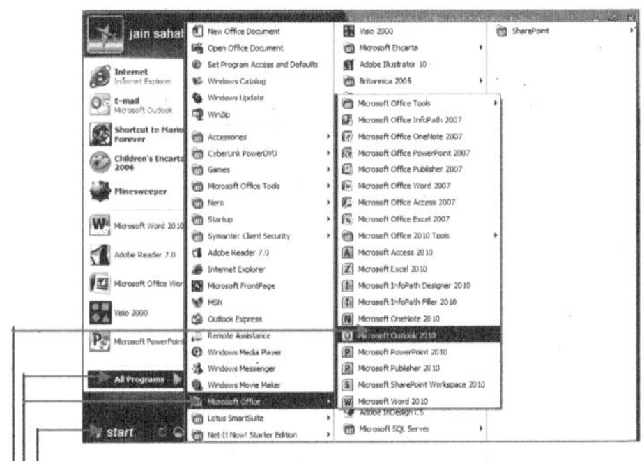

1. Click the **Start** button on the Taskbar.
2. Highlight **All Programs**, click **Microsoft Office**.
3. A sub menu appears, click **Microsoft Office Outlook 2010.**

Outlook 2010 needs ***Windows Vista*** *or* ***Windows 7*** *as operating system to run on an IBM PC. However, Outlook 2010 can also be used with* ***Windows XP*** *operating system, if* ***service pack 3*** *is installed on Windows XP.*

Outlook 2010 Window Screen

The Outlook 2010 opens in a default page. Top of the Outlook window has a title bar which contains Minimize, Maximize/Restore, and Close buttons. All the commands in Outlook 2010 are shown in the form of ribbon rather than Menus (as shown in earlier versions of Outook). Left pane of Outlook window contains *Personal Folder* and *Favorites Folders with All Mail Items, Calendar, Contacts* and *Tasks*. Right pane of Outlook window contains *Date Navigator, Appointments* and *Tasks list*. These are explained below.

Notes:

The Shortcut key to hide the ***Navigation Pane:*** *Press* ***Alt + F1*** *keys together.*

Use the tabs at the top of the view to select groups of commands. On the ***Home*** *tab are the commands for creating and working with Outlook items such as messages, calendar items or contacts.*

You can drag the edge of any window pane in Outlook to widen or shrink the columns of information.

Title Bar: Displays the name of the program you are currently using (Outlook) and the item you are currently working with.

Ribbon: The ribbon interface appears through Outlook 2010 and replaces many menus. Commands appear in groups within the ribbon to help make them easier to find and use. In Outlook 2010, the ribbon was available only on open Outlook items, such as e-mail messages or calendar items. The ribbon is now found everywhere in Outlook, including the main window.

Tabs: Use the tabs at the top of the view to select groups of commands.

Minimize button: Shrinks the application window to a bar on the taskbar. You can click its button on the taskbar to reopen it.

Maximize button: A box at the right of a title bar that fills available space with the document or application.

Restore button: A double box at the right of a title bar that restores an application or document into a sizable window.

Close button: A box at the right of a title bar (X) that closes the window or dialog box.

Help text box: As part of the user interface redesign in the Microsoft Office 2010 programs, the Type a question for help box was moved to the Help window for each Office program and renamed Type words to search for.

Close button: Click the close button in the Title bar to exit the Outlook program.

To-Do Bar: Keep tabs on your calendar, appointments, and tasks all in one place. The To-Do Bar can also be displayed in a minimized format.

Status bar: Displays messages and feedback.

Navigation Pane Buttons: Click a button to see the folders and tools for a certain category—i.e. *Mail, Calendar,* or *Contacts.*

Navigation Pane: It contains buttons and icons you can click to move among Outlook's folders and tools. The pane's contents change when you click a different Navigation Pane button—i.e. Mail, Calendar, or Contacts.

Mail folders: Displays all your mail folders, including the Inbox, Outbox, Junk E-mail, Drafts, and Sent Items folders.

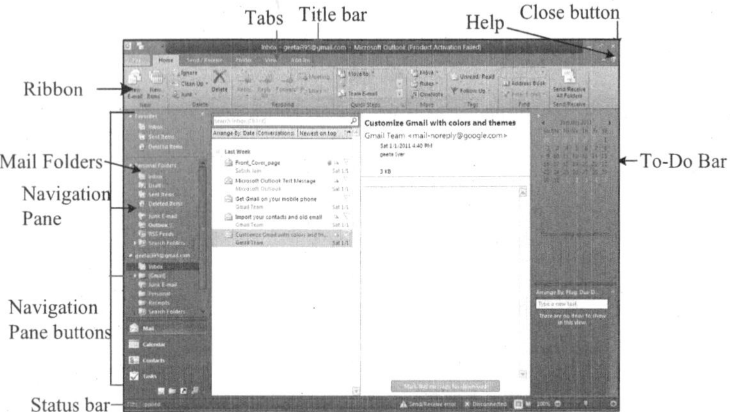

Notes:

Send/Receive: *Click the Send/Receive tab for commands related to checking for new Outlook items on the server or sending items.*

View: *On the View tab, you can change and customize how you view your folders.*

Scroll bars: Use the vertical scroll bars to view different parts of the panes.

Creating an E-mail Account

To send and receive e-mail messages with Office Outlook, you need to add your e-mail account information to it. Outlook 2010 supports Microsoft Exchange Server 2000, POP3, IMAP and HTTP e-mail servers. Your Internet service provider (ISP) or e-mail administrator can provide you with the configuration information that you need to manually set up your e-mail account in Outlook 2010.

Adding an E-mail Account in MS Outlook 2010

The Internet Connection Wizard makes short work of setting up your online mailbox by walking you through each step for every e-mail account you have set up.

Before you get going, make sure you know e-mail address along with the following information. [You may need to contact your ISP, (Internet Service Provider), to get it.]

First, information about the e-mail servers:

- The type of e-mail server you use: POP3 (most e-mail accounts), HTTP (such as Hotmail), or IMAP
- The name of the incoming e-mail server

For POP3 and IMAP servers, the name of the outgoing e-mail server (generally SMTP)

Second, information about your account:

- Your account name and password

Notes:

Folder: On the Folder tab are commands to create, move or share folders.

- Find out if your ISP requires you to use Secure Password Authentication (SPA) to access your e-mail account

Let us look at the steps which we need to follow for setting up an email account in Outlook 2010.

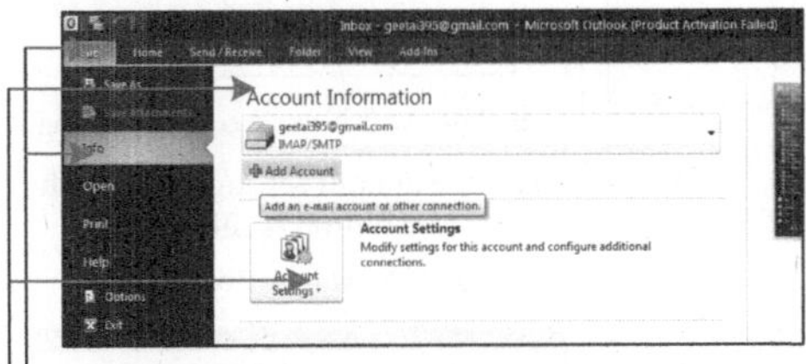

1. Click the **File** tab and choose Info tab.
2. Under **Account Information**, click **Add Account**. Or Account Settings drop-down arrow.

To minimize or expand the Navigation Pane in the window, click the Minimize Navigation Pane or Expand the Navigation Pane button at the top of the Navigation Pane.

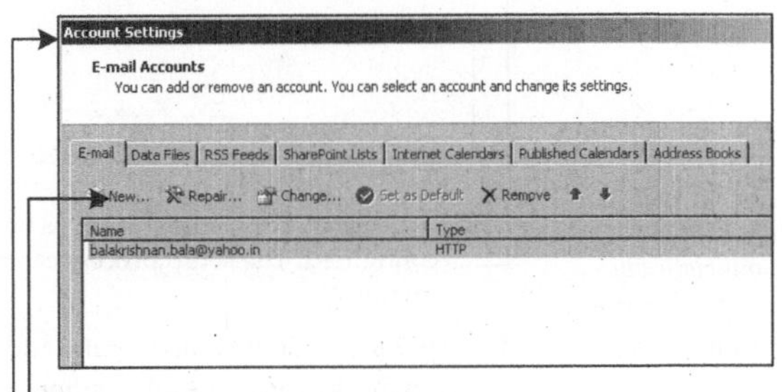

3. The **Account Settings** dialog box appears.
4. The **New...** option.

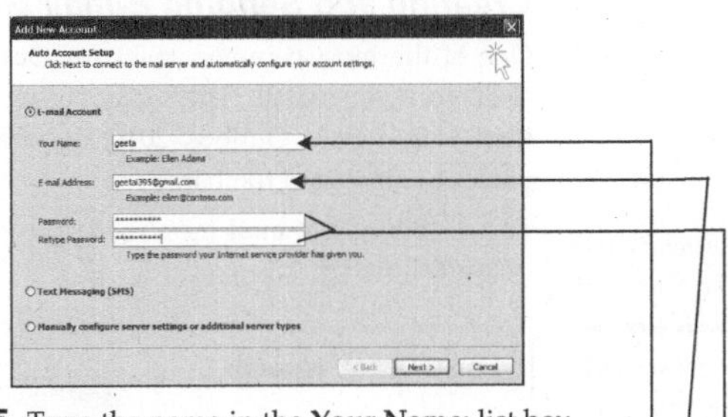

Display the To-Do Bar

*Select **View** menu and choose **To-Do Bar** and then select **Normal**.*

5. Type the name in the **Your Name:** list box.
6. Type E-mail Address in the **E-mail Address:** list box.
7. Type **Password:** and **Retype Password:** list box.
8. Click **Next >** button.

Notes:

To minimize the ***To-Do Bar****, click the Minimize the* ***To-Do Bar*** *button, which is located at the top of the* ***To-Do Bar****.*

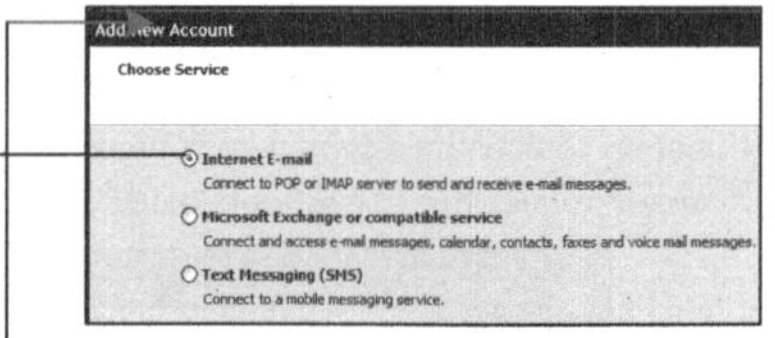

9. The **Add New Account** dialog box appears.
10. The default setting that has the Internet E-mail radio button is selected.
11. Click Next > button.

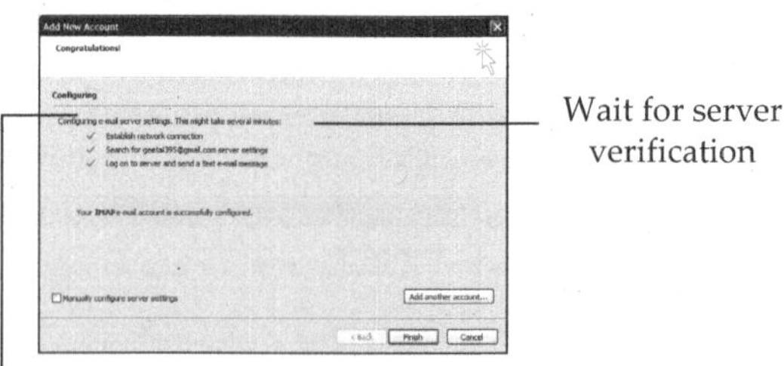

Wait for server verification

If your e-mail account cannot be automatically configured, you are prompted to configure it manually.

12. A progress indicator appears as your account is being configured. The setup process can take several minutes.
13. After the account is successfully added, you can add more accounts by clicking **Add another account...** .
14. To exit the **Add New Account** dialog box, click **Finish.**

Creating and Sending E-mail Messages

One of the most common tasks for Outlook users is sending and receiving e-mail. The mail message window, like other item windows in Outlook 2010, features the new Ribbon in place of menus and toolbars.

The shortcut key to open the New mail message is ***Ctrl + N*** *or* ***Ctrl + Shift + M*** *keys pressed together.*

To create a new e-mail message and type the e-mail address, do the following:

1. Click the **Home** tab in the **New** group, click **New E-mail** icon.

✎ ***If Outlook fails to set up the e-mail, there is one more thing it will try, so click Next if you get this message: An encrypted connection to your server is not available. Click Next to attempt using an unencrypted connection.***

Notes:

If Outlook is successful, three check marks will appear to the left of the Add New E-mail Account dialog box appears that displays text boxes for entering your server settings.

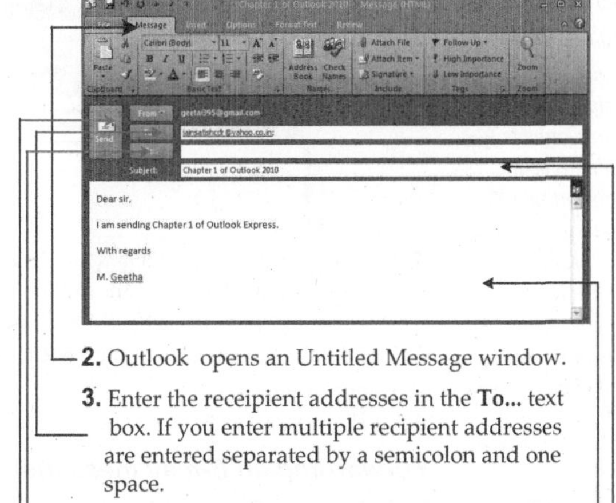

2. Outlook opens an Untitled Message window.
3. Enter the receipient addresses in the **To...** text box. If you enter multiple recipient addresses are entered separated by a semicolon and one space.
4. If you want to send a copy of the message to someone besides the recipient, enter the address in the **Cc...** text box.
5. The new message window's title bar appears. It displays Untitled - Message (Plain Text) until you enter text on the Subject line. The subject line then appears in the title bar of the message window.
6. Type the body of the message in the message window below the subject line.
7. Click **Send** icon to send the message.

To send and receive e-mail, you need to be connected to a mail server. You can think of the mail server as the post office. It is the computer with the network connection that receives your messages and directs your outgoing messages to other computers on a network. The computer is used to create your messages and read the messages you have received. This is known as the mail client.

Replying to an E-mail Message

Replying to an e-mail is like answering a letter—it acknowledges your receipt of the message and allows you to respond.

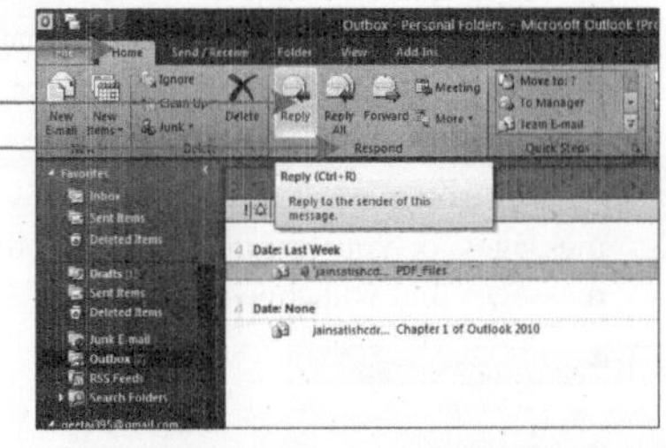

1. Click the **Home** tab, in the **Respond** group, click **Reply** or **Reply All** icon.

Notes:

If you send an e-mail to a recipient inside your Contacts folder, type the recipient name's first few letters and pressed ***Ctrl + K*** *keys together Outlook fills in the name and e-mail for you.*

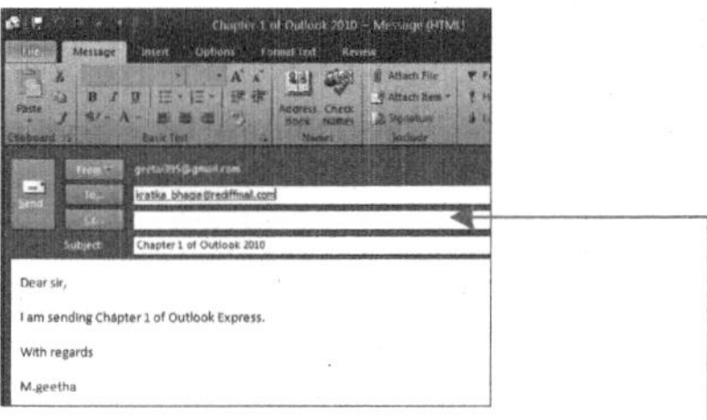

2. Outlook displays a message window with the recipient's e-mail address and subject line already typed in along with a copy of the original message.
3. To add a recipient, click in the **To**, **CC** or **Bcc** box.
4. Compose a message.
5. Click the **Send** icon.

Forwarding an E-mail message

Keeping your ***Inbox*** *folder sorted by date is important so that you will see new e-mail messages at the top of your Inbox.*

Sometimes you may receive a message, but rather than reply to it, you want to send it (forward it) to someone else. Forwarding a message essentially copies a message and sends it to someone else whom the original sender may not even know.

1. Click the **Home** tab in the **Respond** group. Click **Forward** icon or double-click the message that you want to forward.
2. A message window appears that contains your chosen message.
3. Click in the To... text box and type an e-mail address
4. Click in the message window and type any additional text you want to send along with the forwarded message.
5. Click the **Send** button.

Create and Add a Message Signature

You can create personalized signatures for your e-mail messages that include text, images, or even an image of your handwritten signature.

The Shortcut key to Reply a message is ***Ctrl + R*** *keys pressed together.*

Your signature can automatically be added to outgoing messages, or you can manually add the signature to only the messages that you choose.

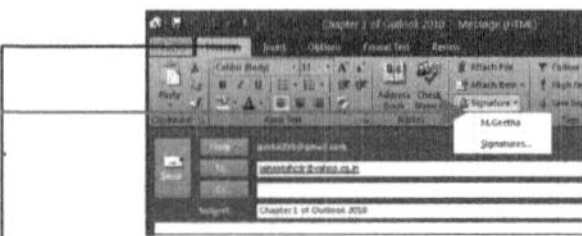

1. Open a new message. On the **Message** tab, in the **Include** group, click **Signature** drop-down arrow.

Notes:

*The Shortcut key to Forward a message is **Ctrl + F** keys together.*

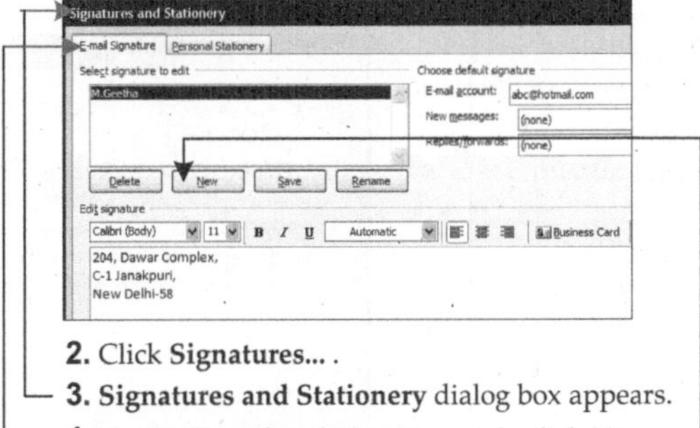

2. Click **Signatures...** .
3. **Signatures and Stationery** dialog box appears.
4. On the **E-mail and Signatures** tab, click **New.**

Mail messages can be forwarded to multiple recipients.

New Signature
Type a name for this signature:
M.Geetha
OK
Cancel

5. **New Signature** dialog box appears. Type a name for the signature, and then click OK.

*You must have at least one valid e-mail recipient in the **To**, **Cc**, or **Bcc** box.*

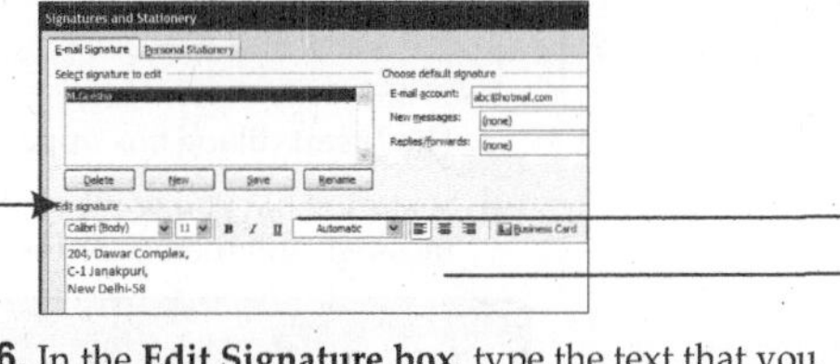

6. In the **Edit Signature box**, type the text that you want to include in the Signature.
7. To format the text, select the text, and then use the style and formatting buttons to select the options that you want.
8. To finish creating the signature, click OK.
9. The text message is added in the Signature option. When you to add a message, click the signature drop-down and then click the name you entered in the signature dialog box.

The signature that you just created or modified won't appear in the currently open message; it must be inserted into the message.

Attaching a file to a message

One of the most useful features of e-mail is the ability to attach one or more files to a message. You can attach pictures, documents, PDFs and more in Outlook 2010.

Attachments in the original e-mail are not forwarded with the new text message.

Notes:

If you want to forward two or more messages, select the first message, hold Ctrl keys and then select each additional message. Each message will be forwarded as attachments in a new message. Type the subject of the message in the ***Subject*** *box.*

1. To create a new e-mail message, type a subject and type an e-mail address.

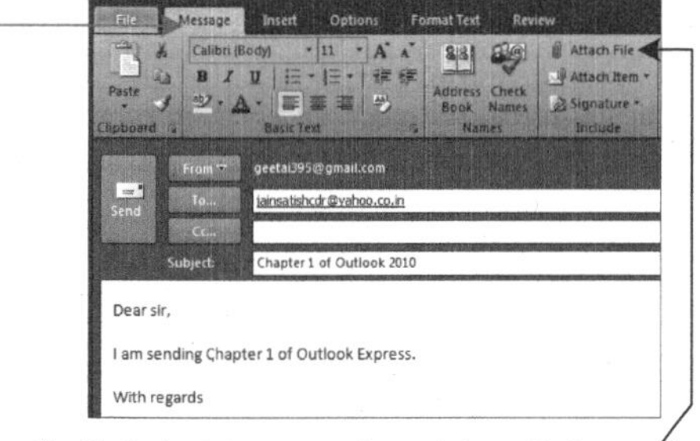

2. Click the **Message** tab, and then click **Attach File** icon.

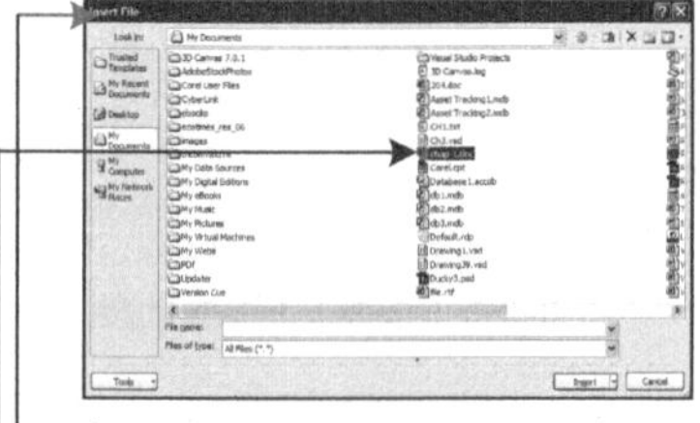

3. The **Insert** dilaog box appears.
4. Select the file you want to attach to your message and then click **Insert**.

You can forward only one message at a time.

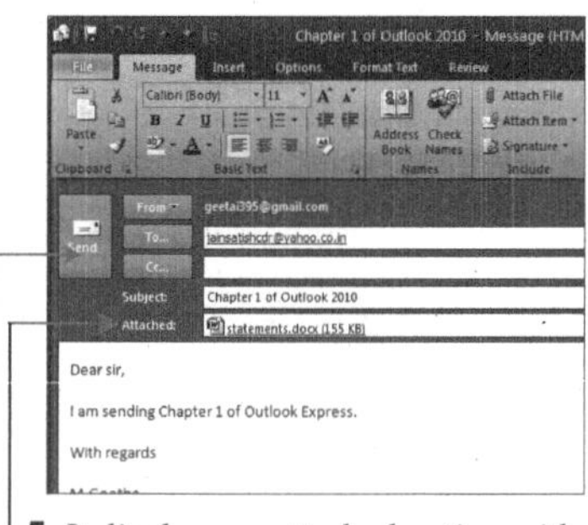

5. It displays an attached option with text box in the message window.
6. Select and right-click any file in the Attachment text box, a pop-up menu appears, choose **Remove** if you do not to attach a file to a message.
7. Click the **Send** icon.

If you hold down the ***Ctrl*** *or* ***Shift*** *key while clicking a file, you can select multiple files at once.*

Open and Save attachments

Attachments are files that can be included with an e-mail message. Messages that have attachments are identified by a paper clip icon in the message list. Depending on the format of the message that you receive, attachments appear in one of two locations in the message.

- If the message format is HTML or plain text, attachments will appear in the attachment box under the **Subject** line.
- If the message format is the less-common Rich Text Format (RTF), attachments will appear in the body of the message. Even though the file appears in the message body, it actually remains a separate attachment.

Open an attachment

You can open an attachment from the reading pane, or from an open message. To open an attachment from the message list, right-click the message that has the attachment, then click **View Attachments**, and then click the name of the attachment.

1. To open an attachment from the message list, right-click the message that has the attachment, then click **View Attachments** , and then click the name of the attachment.
2. You can preview attachments to HTML or plain text messages in the Reading Pane and in open messages. Click the attachment that you want to preview and it will show in place of the message body. To go back to the message, on the **Attachment Tools** tab, in the **Message** group, click **Show Message**.

Save an attachment

After opening and viewing an attachment, you may choose to save it to a disk drive.

To save an attachment do one of the following options:

1. **If the message is in HTML or plain text format** Click on the attachment in the Reading Pane or the open message. Then, on the **Attachments** tab, in the **Actions** group, click **Save As.** You can also right-click the attachment and then click **Save As.**
2. **If the message is in RTF format** In the Reading Pane or the open message, right-click the attachment and then click **Save As.**
3. Choose a folder location, and then click **Save.**

Notes:

Be careful when attaching files to messages. Many ISPs put a limit on the maximum size of an e-mail message, such as 25 MB. Try to keep any file attachments small if the recipient has a slow Internet connection, downloading a large file attachment can take a long time.

The format in which a message is composed is indicated in the title bar at the top of the message.

You can also attach files using the Insert tab of an open message, or drag files from folders on your computer and drop them on an open e-mail message.

Notes:

*The shortcut key to open the Contacts window is **Ctrl** + N keys pressed together.*

Deleting E-mail Messages

To delete an e-mail message from the message window or from the **Inbox** do the following options:

1. Click the e-mail in the **Inbox** folder you want to delete.
2. On the **Home** tab in the Delete group, click **Delete** icon.
3. Your message is deleted and sent to the **Deleted** Items folder.

Storing Contacts Information

The Contacts list contains information about people and organizations you interact with. The Contacts list lets you enter as much or as little information about your contacts as you want, such as their names, phone numbers, and addresses. You can then use the information in the Contacts list with the other Outlook tools.

1. Click the **Contacts** button in the **Navigation** pane.
2. Outlook displays a list of your current contacts. Or
3. Click the **Home** tab in the **New** group then click **New Contact**.
4. The **Contact** window appears.

Several of the fields in the Contact item window have buttons and list arrows next to them. The buttons display dialog boxes to assist you with the fields, while the arrows are used if a contact has more than one phone number, e-mail account, or address.

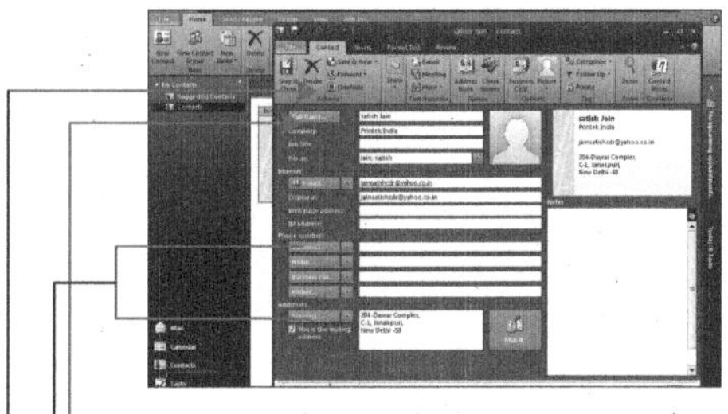

5. Click in the **Full Name** text box and type a person's name.
6. Type any additional information that you want to store about a person, such as additional e-mail addresses, telephone numbers.
7. Click **Save & Close** in the **Actions** group, to save your current contact information or click **Save & New** (to save your current contact information) and open a new Contact window to store another name.

To add a photo of your contact, click the photo icon, or on the Contact tab, in the Options group, click Picture and then click Add Picture.

Printing the Contacts List

Printing your Contacts list is no different from printing anything else in Outlook, except for a few unique options. For example, you can select a print style from card, booklet, memo, or phone directory formats, and also select the contacts you want printed.

1. Click the **Contacts** button in the **Navigation Pane**.
2. The Contacts list appears.

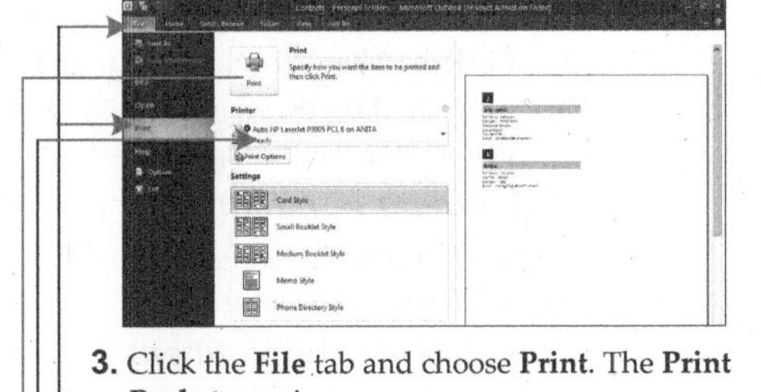

3. Click the **File** tab and choose **Print**. The **Print Backstage** view appears.
4. Select a Print Style from the Printer drop-down list.
5. Select the Contacts style from the **Settings** list, and then click **Print** icon.

Notes:

Delete a contact

You can also delete contacts if you no longer need them.

*1. Select a contact in the Contacts list and click the **Delete** icon on the Home tab of Delete group.*

*2. The contact is moved to the **Deleted Items** in the **Mailbox**.*

*To print only selected contacts, hold down the **Ctrl** key as you select contacts in the Contacts list, then select Only selected items in the Print range area of the Print dialog box.*

Using the Calendar

Calendar is one of the most-used tools in Outlook. The Calendar lets you keep track of appointments, such as a visit to the dentist and events, such as a vacation.

Viewing the Calendar

There are three main Calendar views in Outlook: *Day, Week* and *Month* view. We shall learn about each of these views, and how to navigate within them.

Display the Calendar

First, we need to display the Calendar.

1. Click the **Calendar** button in the **Navigation** pane.
2. The **Calendar** appears.

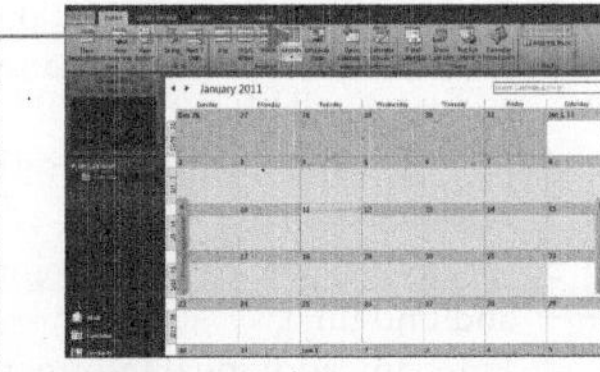

3. The Calendar opens in the month view.

Day view

Day view gives you an hour-by-hour breakdown of your daily schedule.

*1. Click the Day icon in the **Arrange** group of **Home** tab.*

Notes:

The shortcut key to open days in a ***Work week*** *is* ***Ctrl + Alt + 2*** *all keys pressed together. And to open entire* ***Week*** *is* ***Ctrl + Alt + 3*** *all keys pressed together.*

The shortcut key to open the Month is ***Ctrl +<Alt> + <4>*** *all keys pressed together.*

In Calendar, you can drag the appointment to a different date. You also can edit the subject by clicking the description text, pressing F2, and then typing your changes.

Week view

Week view has two display choices: *Work Week* and *Full Week*. Work Week view displays your schedule *Monday* through *Friday*, while Full Week view displays the full seven-day work week.

1. Click the **Week** icon in the **Arrange** group of **Home** tab.

Month View

Month view is the default view in the Calendar. Month view shows your schedule for the entire month.

1. Click the **Month** icon in the **Arrange** group of **Home** tab.
2. Click the **Month** drop-down list and choose the desired options you want to apply.

Scheduling Appointments and Events

Outlook's Calendar is great for keeping track of your appointments and events.

Schedule an appointment

An *appointment* is any scheduled activity that takes place within a one-day time period. When you schedule an appointment, the Calendar blocks off the specified time span—for example, from 10 a.m. to noon.

1. Click the **New Appointment** icon on the **Home** tab of **New** group.
2. An Untitled—Appointment window appears.

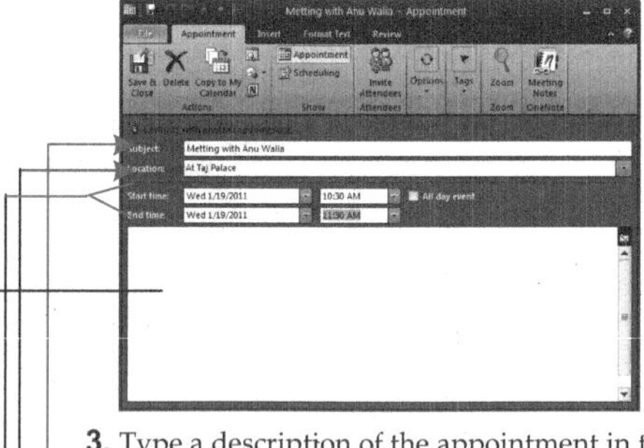

3. Type a description of the appointment in the Subject: field. After you entered the subject it will appear in the title bar.
4. Enter the appointment's location in the Location: field.
5. Specify the date of the appointment and its Start and End time.

Enter any additional information about the appointment, if desired.

Notes:

Double-click any blank area on the calendar grid to create a new appointment.

6. Click the **Save & Close** button in the **Actions** group. The **Appointment** window closes and the event appears in your calendar.

Working with Recurring Appointments

A *recurring* appointment is an appointment that occurs at regular intervals; for example, every Friday at 11 a.m.

1. Click the **New Appointment** icon on the **Home** tab of **New** group.
2. An Untitled—Appointment window appears.
3. Type a description of the appointment in the **Subject Field** (for example, Staff Meeting).
4. On the **Appointment** tab, in the **Options** group, click **Recurrence**.

In Day/Week/Month view, you can quickly create an event by double-clicking the darker shaded area beneath the date heading of the day of the event.

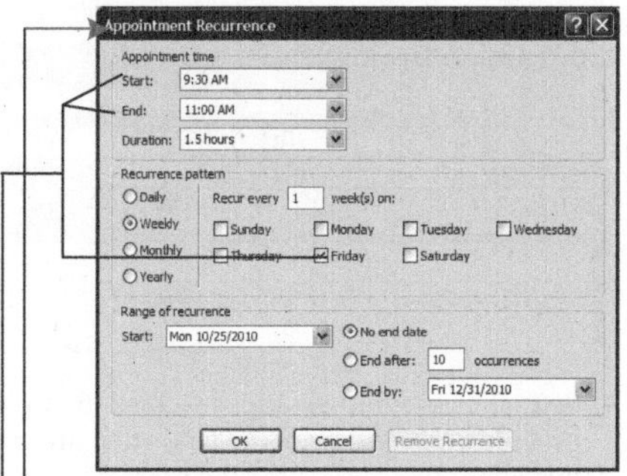

5. The **Appointment Recurrence** dialog box appears. Here you need to specify the time of the appointment, how often the appointment should recur (for example, every Friday), and the start and end date of the recurrence.
6. Make your specifications in the Appointment Recurrence dialog box, and click OK.
7. Click the **Save & Close** button in the **Actions** group.

*To create a new task from any folder in Outlook, press **Ctrl + Shift + K**.*

Creating a Task

Recording your tasks makes them easier to remember and manage. Outlook tasks provide a good way to organize what you need to get done.

To turn on or off the To-Do Bar, on the View tab, in the Layout group, click To-Do Bar and click Normal, Minimized, or Off. This changes the To-Do Bar only in the current view, not in all views.

Notes:

To turn on or off the Daily Task List, in Calendar, on the View tab, in the Layout group, click Daily Task List and select Normal, Minimized, or Off.

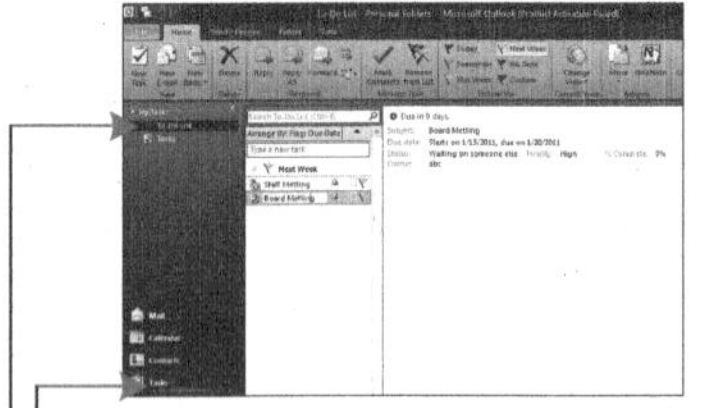

1. Click the **Tasks** button in the **Navigation** Pane.
2. The **To-Do** List appears in Tasks.
3. Click the **New Task** icon in the **Home** tab of **New** group.

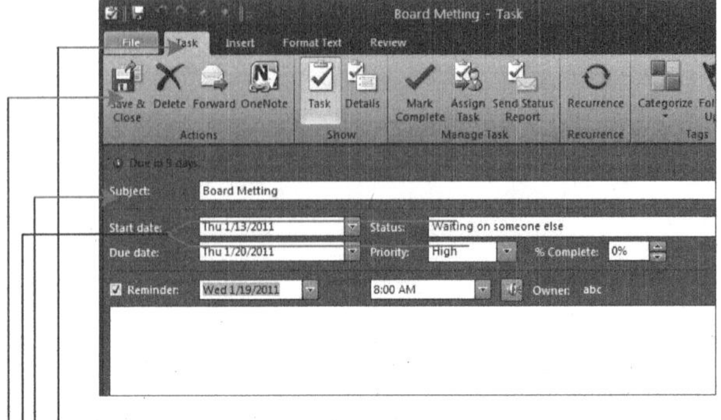

4. A **Task** item window appears. Task Item Window Fields provide an overview of the fields that are available in this window.
5. Enter a subject and other information about the task.
6. You can add detail about the task in the text area.

   Enter task details in the text area.
7. Click the **Save & Close** button in the **Actions** group on the Ribbon.

Index

Computer Introduction

Introduction to Internet

MS Word 2010

MS Excel 2010

MS Access 2010

MS PowerPoint 2010

MS Outlook 2010